DYING AND THE VIRTUES

Dying and the Virtues

Matthew Levering

WILLIAM B. EERDMANS PUBLISHING COMPANY
GRAND RAPIDS, MICHIGAN

Wm. B. Eerdmans Publishing Co.
2140 Oak Industrial Drive NE, Grand Rapids, Michigan 49505
www.eerdmans.com

27 26 25 24 23 22 21 20 19   2 3 4 5 6 7 8 9 10

ISBN 978-0-8028-7548-8

Library of Congress Cataloging-in-Publication Data

Names: Levering, Matthew, 1971– author.
Title: Dying and the virtues / Matthew Levering.
Description: Grand Rapids, Michigan : William B. Eerdmans Publishing Company,
    [2018] | Includes bibliographical references and index.
Identifiers: LCCN 2017029708 | ISBN 9780802875488 (hardcover : alk. paper)
Subjects: LCSH: Virtues. | Death—Religious aspects—Christianity.
Classification: LCC BV4630 .L48 2018 | DDC 236/.1—dc23
    LC record available at https://lccn.loc.gov/2017029708

To Andrew Hofer, OP

Contents

Acknowledgments

A number of wonderful people, friends in Christ, made the writing of this book possible. It began with an invitation from Tom McCall and Geoffrey Fulkerson of the Henry Center at Trinity Evangelical Divinity School. I presented early versions of chapters 4 and 5. A shortened version of chapter 5 has appeared as "The Dying of Macrina and Death with Dignity," *Trinity Journal* 38 (2017): 29–52. Thanks to George Kalantzis, my co-organizer for the March 2016 "On Christian Dying" conference at Wheaton College, I presented an early version of chapter 1 and received valuable feedback, especially from John Sikorski and Todd Billings. A version of this paper will appear in *Christian Dying*, edited by George Kalantzis and Matthew Levering (Eugene, OR: Cascade Books, 2018). Thanks to Carlos Casanova, I traveled to Santiago, Chile, to deliver an early version of chapter 7 to the III Congreso Internacional de Filosofía Tomista at the Universidad Santo Tomás. This was a wonderful opportunity to meet distinguished Chilean, Argentinian, Spanish, and Polish Thomistic scholars and doctoral students. A version of this paper will appear in the conference volume edited by Carlos Casanova.

Thanks to Matthew Umbarger, I gave three lectures as part of the August 2016 CIT/NSP Summer Symposium at Newman University in Wichita, Kansas. I presented versions of what became chapters 1, 3, and 5, and received helpful responses in an atmosphere of warm collegial friendship. Thanks to Chad Raith, I presented an early version of chapter 4 to a September 2016 conference titled "Engaging the Book of Acts, Engaging One Another: Catholics, Orthodox, and Evangelicals," sponsored by the Paradosis Center at John Brown University. A version of my paper will appear in the conference volume that Chad is editing (Washington, DC: Catholic University of America Press, 2018). In November 2016, Philip Porter and Thomas Pfau invited me to deliver "The Unbearability of Annihilation: Job's Challenge to His Creator" to the Thomistic Institute at Duke University Divinity School, where I received more valuable corrections. Thanks to Michael Dauphinais and Roger Nutt, I gave a Theology Graduate Programs Master Seminar at Ave Maria University in January 2017, at which I delivered a version of chapter 7. Lastly, at a March 2017 conference titled "Imagining the Eschatological State," which George Kalantzis and I coorganized at Wheaton College, superb papers by Rita George-Tvrtkovic and Cyril O'Regan prompted last-minute corrections to chapter 9. I am particularly grateful to Rita for her generous help in assembling secondary literature related to chapter 9.

Five of the nine chapters, then, received extensive corrections during the writing process from audiences of scholars and students. Fortunately for me, the other chapters—and indeed the whole manuscript—benefited from three generous friends who were willing to read drafts of the manuscript. Alex Pierce, who was once my student and is now a dear friend (and who this fall will enter the PhD program in patristics at the University of Notre Dame), read the entire manuscript at a late stage and made a large number of crucial emendations. Father Andrew Hofer, OP, likewise read the manuscript with care and insight and caught some major errors. At the final stage of the project, Todd Billings read the whole manuscript with an encouraging eye, and he too gave me an important correction.

At Eerdmans, Michael Thomson supported this manuscript when it was only an idea. Michael, whose friendship over the past few years has been a delight, read the manuscript at an early stage and made important corrections especially in chapter 8. Jenny Hoffman and Gary Lee, the copyeditor for Eerdmans, did a fantastic job with the manuscript in the production stage.

Let me thank the rector and the academic dean at Mundelein Seminary, Fr. John Kartje and Fr. Thomas Baima, respectively, for making my job much easier than it would be without their presence. My gratitude extends also to Jim and Molly Perry, who generously endowed the chair that I hold at the seminary. My superb research assistant and dear friend David Augustine (now a PhD candidate in systematics at Catholic University of America) helped with chapter 1, and he also graciously did the bibliography for this book. I owe special thanks also to Mary Bertram, whose excellence is legendary at the seminary, and to Kim O'Neill, who generously helped me with printing over the past year. To my children and my wife Joy, what would I do without you? Joy, you are "beautiful and lovely" (Gen. 29:17 Revised Standard Version [hereafter RSV]). May God reward your faith, your profound love, your care for others, and your hard work.

I dedicate this book to a man who befriended me and my family a decade ago, when in July or August 2006 he carried an air conditioner up the stairs of a rental house in South Bend, thereby making our life bearable in the hottest house that I have ever lived in! He has been a wise and serene counselor, generous and encouraging. Dear God, bless your servant Andrew Hofer, and make his life in service to your kingdom "exceedingly fruitful" (Gen. 17:6). Enable him, together with his many friends, to journey "through the valley of the shadow of death" (Ps. 23:4) to the place whose "lamp is the Lamb" (Rev. 21:23).

Introduction

The meaning of dying—and thus the question of what comes after death—is obviously a crucial one for Christians.[1] The theologian William Greenway claims that "death is an utter disaster" *only* for "those who can ultimately affirm only self-interest" and who therefore cannot abide the annihilation of their own ego. But even he admits that "the question of life after death" can arise with equal urgency out of selfless love for "those innumerable creatures—including humans—who have known only lives of loneliness, despair, abuse, pain, suffering, and death," and who deserve a better life. Although Greenway's affirmation that an afterlife should be hoped for is tempered by his strong fear of "fomenting a heightened spirit of self-interest," the bitter fate of so many of his fellow creatures in this life presses him, quite rightly, to hope for an afterlife.[2]

Greenway's connection of fear of personal annihilation with self-centered egoism is understandable but mistaken. After all, personal annihilation cuts off any future possibility of selfless communion with God and others, and humans who have experienced such interpersonal communion cannot avoid desiring its continuance. Thus, as Anthony Thiselton points out, for much of the Old Testament "the worst feature of death was possible separation from God, after a life of communion with him."[3] Especially now that we have experienced the joy of knowing and loving Jesus Christ, annihilation would be a dreadful fate, cutting us off from divine friendship. The apostle Paul remarks along these lines, "If for this life only we have hoped in Christ, we are of all people most to be pitied" (1 Cor. 15:19). We would be "most to be pitied" because our intense experience of communion with God in Christ would end in literally nothing.

1

As Paul knows from personal encounter with the risen Lord, however, "in fact Christ has been raised from the dead" (1 Cor. 15:20). Therefore, Paul looks forward confidently to the final conquest of death through the new creation of the whole cosmos in Christ, who through the Spirit will establish God's people in everlasting communion with the Father. Well aware that he is using imagery to describe realities too glorious for description, Paul tells the Corinthians that "the trumpet will sound, and the dead will be raised imperishable, and we will be changed.... When this perishable body puts on imperishability, and this mortal body puts on immortality, then the saying that is written will be fulfilled: 'Death has been swallowed up in victory.' 'Where, O death, is your victory? Where, O death, is your sting?'" (1 Cor 15:52, 54–55).

Is dying, then, a "disaster" for Christians, or is it simply a passageway to the Lord? In an existentially realistic manner, the Orthodox theologian Georges Florovsky argues that indeed "death is a catastrophe for man" because "death strikes at personality."[4] Dumitru Staniloae adds that death is not an arbitrary divine punishment of the first humans, but pertains to the "consequences of our alienation from the source of life."[5] As such, death is rightly fearful even for Christians. Death, as we experience it in this fallen existence, "is a low business" that, on the surface of things at least, "lacks sense and comfort" and "suffocates life's meaning and breaks life's covenants."[6] Even for Christians, therefore, the awareness that one is facing death has, as Thomas Aquinas says, a tendency to "stun the human mind."[7]

Balthasar's Three Paths

If dying leads to the fullness of life in and through Christ and his Holy Spirit, how can Christians truly fear dying without (absurdly) fearing union with Christ?[8] The Catholic theologian Hans Urs von Balthasar offers a set of perceptive answers to this question, in which he shows that dying is best viewed from a diversity of angles. Consider first his *Life out of Death: Meditations on the Paschal Mystery.* The opening page describes well the devastating personal impact of dying, despite its being accepted as a normal event by others: "Dying is the most ordinary thing ... and yet in an individual case it is the most incomprehensible thing because it crushes the little bit of meaning that has been arduously gathered in a lifetime and disperses it to the four winds."[9] In this crushing and dispersing of a lifetime's "little bit of meaning," he sees a contradiction: how is it that there can be "meaning" if all we see around this little bit of meaning is "an infinite sea of meaninglessness"?[10] Yet, as he points out, we are certain that there *is* meaning in the fragment or part (a person's life), even if we cannot see how there is meaning in the whole. The heart of the contradiction is this: the existence of real meaning in the part implies that the whole too must have meaning (or else there could be no meaning in the part), and yet the whole looks like "an infinite sea of meaninglessness." Balthasar asks how it is that we yearn "to create something permanent, something above time, to make a definitive statement that would be the expression of his personal uniqueness," despite the fact that we know well that "everything earthly is drawn on the sand of transitoriness," destined sooner or later for absolute oblivion.[11] For example, a young couple desires "to love each other definitively," forever, and yet "one of the two will die before the other," seemingly putting a definitive end to that love, as the couple well knows.[12]

We find a second approach to dying in Balthasar's *You Have Words of Eternal Life: Scripture Meditations*, which he wrote shortly before his death. In his eighty-fourth meditation, entitled "Even If He Dies He Will Live," his first sentence is startling: "It is nearly incomprehensible how lightly the New Testament deals with physical death."[13] For the New Testament, physical death belongs to a process that starts already at baptism, when, according to Paul, the baptized person dies with Christ and enters into "a new hidden and resurrected life."[14] Balthasar takes the title of this meditation from John 11:25, where Jesus says, "he who believes in me, though he die, yet shall he live" (RSV). Here, as Balthasar says, physical dying is almost nothing, since for the believer, filled with charity, it is simply an entrance into eternal life: "everyone who lives and believes in me will never die" (John 11:26). Faith and eucharistic communion in Christ mean that we "will live forever" (John 6:58), so that we do not need to worry about dying.[15]

A third approach appears in Balthasar's *Moment of Christian Witness*. He begins with "God's willingness to die for the world he loves, for mankind and for me as an individual."[16] What God reveals in Christ's crucifixion gives us two options. Either we are nothing other "than a fugitive figure without hope, all of whose illusions are rendered worthless by death"; or we are much more than this, but "solely by virtue of Christ's death, which opens up . . . the possibility of fulfillment in God."[17] On this view it is Christ's dying, and it alone, that truly enables us to flourish. Balthasar puts it vividly: "I blossom on the grave of God who died for me. I sink my roots deep into the nourishing soil of his flesh and blood."[18]

Balthasar, then, offers the following three paths: dying is a devastation and a contradiction, since it seemingly obliterates the meaning that we are sure is there and for which we so urgently strive; dying is basically nothing, since in Christ we have already died and have already begun to share in his resurrected life; and dying is our response to God's dying for us in Christ, whose death is the source of our true life.

All these paths or perspectives are true for Christians. Dying is both a devastating threat to be feared and, in Christ, a passage to the fullness of life whose mode is self-surrendering love. It follows that, in the words of Terence Nichols, "If we want to die well, to die into God . . . we need to start working on our relationship with God (and with others) while we are young and healthy, rather than waiting until death is knocking at the door."[19] In the actual process of dying, many people report encountering "a heavy burden," "a fog of uncertainty," and "terror."[20] Todd Billings remarks from personal experience that those who are suffering from a mortal illness sometimes "feel too weary and weak to trust that the new creation is coming"; and even for a faith-filled Christian, dying can "*appear* to be absurd: an abrupt and seemingly arbitrary end to a life with so many strands, so many joys from God's good creation, so many stories longing for completion."[21] Billings therefore directs attention to the importance of Paul's teaching in Colossians 3:3 that "you have died, and your life is hidden with Christ in God."[22] Likewise, through his image of blossoming "on the grave of God who died for me," Balthasar highlights the reality that, through faith and the sacraments, we now share in Christ's dying in such a way as already to share in his resurrected life.

The Virtues of Dying

What would it look like for a dying person to have a "life . . . hid with Christ in God" and to "blossom" on Christ's grave? My answer involves what I call the "virtues of dying."[23] These virtues are not a form of works righteousness, as though on our deathbed we should expect to congratulate ourselves on our perfect embodiment of all the needed virtues. Nor are they an individualistic project of personal growth, unconnected with the community of the church.[24] Rather, these virtues, given by God, inscribe a Godward and utterly God-dependent mode of living in Christ, as members of his body. As we will see, these virtues exhibit that "it is only the cross of Christ that makes ultimate sense of human death," without which dying would be merely "the great wrecking ball that destroys everything."[25] Particular theologians highlight particular virtues of dying. Thus Balthasar emphasizes self-surrender in love, and Billings emphasizes gratitude, repentance, faith, hope, trust, "our new identity in union with [Christ]," and the need to "*seek out*" those who are suffering.[26]

Citing Jesus's parable of the talents (Matt. 25), Balthasar points out that "in Christ's Church, one possesses only in order to give and is enriched that way."[27] Again, however, dying can be an utterly agonizing dispossession. It can seem (as a dying man tearfully told Henri Nouwen) that "I have no future anymore."[28] As Kerry Walters observes, "How can my consciousness, my sense of self, my *me*, just vanish as if I never was? The non-being with which death threatens us is unimaginable and dreadful."[29] The dying Thérèse of Lisieux urged, "Oh! how necessary it is to pray for the agonizing! If you only knew!"[30] Although true virtues, bestowed by the Holy Spirit, do not take away the radical physical and mental anguish of dying, such virtues do provide an interior path through mortal suffering, in union with Christ and his suffering body the church.[31]

Underscoring the significance of dying, the Orthodox philosopher Nicholas Berdyaev comments that "a system of ethics which does not make death its central problem has no value and is lacking in depth and earnestness."[32] Similarly, Socrates observed that "true philosophers make dying their profession, and . . . to them of all men death is least alarming."[33] Even if this is an exaggeration, as Samuel Johnson insists it is in his novel *Rasselas*,[34] it remains the case that virtue ethics takes shape around the human journey that culminates in dying, and that the virtues are not worth much if they cannot nourish our dying. In a book on the art of dying, the virtue ethicist Christopher Vogt focuses "on three virtues that are essential for a contemporary development of the Christian art of dying well: patience, compassion, and hope."[35] Among the many virtues of dying, I will explore the following nine: love, hope, faith, penitence, gratitude, solidarity, humility, surrender, and courage.[36]

As Vogt points out, "Virtues are not qualities that can be switched on instantly by sheer force of will. This implies that if you wish to be patient and hopeful at the hour of your death, you should have endeavored to become patient and hopeful during the more active stages of your life."[37] At the same time, if we find ourselves unprepared on our deathbed, we can and should beg God to give us through his Holy Spirit the love, hope, faith, penitence, gratitude, solidarity, humility, self-surrender, and courage that we need for enduring this trial. These virtues are not a checklist, as though persons who do not exhibit these virtues on their deathbed are thereby outside God's salvific will. Drawing upon William Perkins, Vogt rightly remarks that "a person's manner of death should not be regarded as indicative of his or her prospects for salvation," not least given that under the manifold forms of suffering and bodily corruption that dying can involve, we can easily lose the full command of reason.[38]

In the present book I examine nine virtues of dying, but I explore these virtues by taking up numerous other topics. These topics are carefully chosen to display some of the most important sources for Christian understanding of death: the book of Job, Ezekiel 20, the dying of Jesus Christ, the dying of the first martyr (Stephen), Hebrews 11, Gregory of Nyssa's account of the dying of his sister Macrina, the tradition of *ars moriendi* (Robert Bellarmine, Francis de Sales, Jean-Pierre de Caussade), the consolations of philosophy (Josef Pieper), the divine mercy (Faustina Kowalska), the sacrament of anointing of the sick, liberation theology's emphasis on solidarity with those who are suffering, biblical eschatology, and contemporary medical perspectives—in addition to the fear of annihilation expressed so frequently in elite culture today, and to the New Age spirituality that is popular in less intellectual circles. My book is therefore a work on the border of virtue ethics and other theological, exegetical, and cultural domains, as required by the effort to retrieve and engage Christian resources on dying. Balthasar notes that those "who 'follow the Lamb wherever he goes' (Rev 14:4) are both those who follow him from life into death and those who follow him from death into life . . . under the law of living and dying for others (for all)."[39] We need to be among those who follow Jesus in this way, because the life of the Lamb—of possessing in order to give away—is the only true and meaningful mode of living, just as it is the only true and meaningful mode of dying.

I contend throughout the book that dying involves something far more radical than what Jay Rosenberg supposes that believers in life after death want, namely, "an 'afterlife' of light and music where, at the end of that long dark tunnel, they would be reunited with those beloved departed."[40] In dying we are stripped of almost all that we thought belonged firmly to us; but when the virtues of dying enable us to freely give all this away, we gain not "light and music" but the fruition of our earthly communion with the self-surrendering God—not a continuation or reunion of earthly life, but a new creation utterly translucent to the unfathomably glorious love that is the triune God. To put this perspective in the simple terms offered by Jaroslav Pelikan: "The core of Christian faith is pessimism about life and optimism about God, and therefore hope for life in God."[41]

The Plan of the Work

In each of the chapters I engage a specific virtue of dying and at the same time, as noted above, address a particular topic. Although the book's conversation partners are diverse, the chapters have a systematic coherence. I begin by addressing the threat of annihilation (ch. 1).[42] I argue that when Job, in his mortal suffering, insists that only a cruel God could will to annihilate a rational creature who loves him, God responds by manifesting himself to Job (and to us) as the wise, powerful, and caring Giver of life. The book of Job testifies that God cares about the enduring communion of love between himself and us.

Yet annihilation can remain a real threat haunting our intellect and imagination.[43] In his letter *To the Elderly*, Pope John Paul II remarks that death "forces men and women to ask themselves fundamental questions about the meaning of life itself. What is on the other side of the shadowy wall of death? Does death represent the definitive end of human life or does something lie beyond it?"[44] When we confront such questions we need not only to experience the personal presence of God (as does Job at the end of the book of Job), but also to have our mind informed by philosophical reasoning about the spiritual dimension of the human person and to have our imagination informed by the vivid biblical teaching about the life to come.[45] This task is the burden of chapter 2, which focuses upon the formation of our intellect and imagination in hope, fully trusting in divine providence to accomplish that for which we hope.

On the basis of the work done in the first two chapters to move past our natural fear of annihilation, in the third chapter I ask a further existential question: Does Jesus really fulfill the desires of dying persons, and, indeed, what precisely *are* the desires of dying persons? To get a sense of the latter, I examine two popular books about caring for the dying, one authored by a medical doctor and the other by a hospice volunteer. I argue that faith in Jesus, which unites us with his body, does indeed supremely fulfill the desires—above all for life, reconciliation, and communion—that dying persons have.

The next two chapters address the process of dying. During their final days, dying persons often look back upon their lives and evaluate them; and dying persons also look forward and ask what kind of future they have. I devote chapter 4 to the task of looking back in repentance. In my view, penitence must be the first attitude with which we look back upon our lives, since God knows all the wounds we have caused and Christ commands us to "repent" (Mark 1:15). Then in chapter 5 I focus on the task of looking back upon our life with gratitude. In all things, gratitude to God for all his gifts—preeminently for the gift of knowing the love of Christ, during the course of our lives and in the life to come—should be our principal motivation and existential stance. Of course, in each of these two chapters, *both* penitence and gratitude appear, since the two virtues are ultimately inseparable for the Christian.

Existentially, then, the first five chapters form a whole with respect to the process of Christian dying: addressing dying persons' natural fear of annihilation or everlasting loss of interpersonal communion (chs. 1 and 2); addressing dying persons' unfulfilled desires (ch. 3); and addressing dying persons' process of looking back upon their life and looking toward their future (chs. 4 and 5). In the sixth and seventh chapters I continue this movement by addressing dying persons' inevitable questions about what good can come from their suffering and dying, and about why they have to suffer and die even after Christ has conquered death. In chapter 6 I explore the Christian call to solidarity with those who suffer, and I argue that the divine mercy flows through union with the transformative and life-giving power of Christ's suffering in love. Another name for this reality is the "redemptive suffering" of the Christian who is enabled to suffer with Christ. In chapter 7 I address the question of why God's path of salvation is one of suffering. Can a God who wills to save his people through an "eschatological tribulation," endured by Christ and by his followers, be anything but a masochist? I argue that at the bottom of this path of suffering is our need for redemption from sin and, especially, from pride. When we gain humility, we are again able to love as we were created to do.[46]

Having addressed these existential questions about the meaning of suffering in God's plan of salvation, I turn in the final two chapters to the last days of the dying person's life. In chapter 8 I ask whether dying persons should receive the sacrament of anointing of the sick in their final days. To some Catholic liturgical scholars, it seems that this practice obscures the sacrament's healing purpose. I argue that what primarily needs to be healed is the remnants of the rebellion that we all suffer from when we want our own way rather than God's. The sacrament of anointing of the sick heals us from these rebellious remnants and strengthens us to surrender our lives to God. In chapter 9 I ask whether the dying Christian can expect to find a familiar country on the other side of death. Arguing that indeed the life to come is marked by radical transformation, I suggest that embracing this transformation requires courage on the part of the dying person.

In this book, therefore, I undertake a theological journey through various stages of Christian dying, beginning with the natural fear of annihilation and the pain of unfulfilled desires, then turning to the dying person's looking back upon his or her life and forward to the future, next addressing the dying person's questions about whether suffering and dying are meaningful, and finally engaging the dying person's final struggle to surrender his or her life to God and to say goodbye to the present life. Each of these stages, as I will make clear, is ecclesially contextualized: we neither live nor die as isolated individuals. "If one member suffers, all suffer together with it; if one member is honored, all rejoice together with it. Now you are the body of Christ and individually members of it" (1 Cor. 12:26–27).

What Dying Is Not and What It Is

Let me attend briefly to three thinkers who have cautioned against certain paths that misconstrue dying, and who thereby can help us to appreciate more fully the Christian virtues of dying that undergird my book.

First is the Catholic theologian Romano Guardini, who cautions against failing to appreciate the tragic character of the death of human persons. Responding to Rainer Maria Rilke's influential *Duino Elegies*, Guardini notes that Rilke deprives "Death of its real seriousness" by trying to posit death, in itself, as a good for human beings.[47] The argument that death in itself is good for humans does not face the fact that we are *compelled* to die and that the separation of body and soul (let alone annihilation) cannot in itself be a good for a human person, who is a rational animal oriented toward interpersonal communion.[48] Guardini says in response to Rilke that "nobody can call Death the 'friendly inspiration of the Earth' if he knows the meaning of the word 'person'—any more than he can believe that the climax of love is attained when both the subject and the object have been excluded."[49] A romantic view of death celebrates it as "a Dionysian absorption into the Universe," but this claim only depersonalizes and disincarnates human love.[50]

Second is the Orthodox theologian Alexander Schmemann, who

cautions against viewing death as a happy flight of the soul from this world. The Neoplatonic approach to death assumes that our spirit gladly rids itself of the chains of matter, so that we find release from the misery of this world in the ethereal joys of the afterlife. Schmemann argues that this idealist conception of immortality led, in modernity, to the rejection of all religion as pie-in-the-sky fantasy, unworthy of credence on the part of serious people. As Schmemann asks rhetorically, "can it really be that God created the world and life and all of its beauty, all of its possibilities, only in order that man would reject them and forego all these glorious possibilities in the name of some unknown and only vaguely promised *other* world?"[51] Obviously, the answer must be no, and indeed God calls us to share in a renewed creation at whose center is Christ. An appreciation of the risen Christ enables us to realize that, as Schmemann says, "Christianity is not concerned about coming to terms with death [e.g., as an allegedly good escape from material bonds], but rather with the victory over it."[52]

Third is the Anglican theologian Ephraim Radner, who cautions against construing our dying (or any moment of our living) as an event isolated from the entirety of the body of Christ and thus from the entirety of time. Radner compares the lack of "socially experienced mortality" in modern society to the situation of a clock that is "aimed only at ordering the *now*, coordinating present moments in their multiplied and discrete details."[53] Christians today tend to see our lives and deaths as involving only ourselves or only people whom we know or who are now alive. We thereby distort what living and dying really involve, since we excise the real context of our living and dying, which is the church as "a gathering, a communion, a historical reach that does not simply develop but grows without ever changing in some sense."[54] Our earthly time indeed is "Christ's time," because it is the time of his body.[55] Therefore, our dying can only be rightly appraised by recognizing that it has "an intrinsic connection with the vast gathering of human beings who represent the movement from the First to the Second Adam."[56]

These exemplary Christian teachers instruct us that in the process of dying, we should not imagine ourselves to be separated from our bodies, from the material creation, or from Christ's body, the church. In conception and birth, we receive embodied existence, participation in the material cosmos, and a share in the history of the church. Admittedly, dying seems to shuttle us back into nothingness—not the nothingness from which we came but a crueler nothingness that forever will conceal the fact that we, whose unique consciousness once existed, are now absent. Dying seems to be an antibirth, the devastating and absolute negation of all for which birth hopes.

Fortunately, as Vigen Guroian observes, "God, not nothingness, is the beginning, ground, and 'end point' of all persons. . . . We come from God and are bound to return to God. But even if unrepentance obstructs our way back to God, our fate is not nothingness."[57] In itself, then, dying does not cut us off from Christ's body, and dying is not the last word for the cosmos either: God has promised that the general resurrection and the new creation will bring his creation to a glorious fulfillment. Though dying is most certainly not good in itself, therefore, it can be accepted and even, in Christ, embraced. Vogt rightly remarks that "it is necessary for Christians to come to see their own dying as a venue where the possibility exists to find deepened self-understanding and to bear witness to God."[58] To see our dying in this way, he says, we must see that dying, like living, belongs to discipleship to Christ.

What then does discipleship involve? When Paul proclaims us to be "heirs of God, and joint heirs with Christ," he counsels that we will only be such if, by the grace of the Spirit, we recognize ourselves to be "children" (Rom. 8:16–17). Jesus likewise teaches that we must "change and become like children" in order to "enter the kingdom of heaven" (Matt. 18:3), and the first virtue he names in this regard is humility.[59] Indebted to this instruction, Henri Nouwen insists that "becoming a child—entering a second childhood—is essential to dying a good death."[60] The dependence of children can instruct us in what Alasdair MacIntyre calls "virtues of acknowledged dependence," since even seemingly self-sufficient adults, who privilege the "virtues of independent rational agency," are dependent upon others "for the achievement of [their] common good" and upon "some particular others to achieve most of [their] individual goods."[61] The virtues that pertain to dependence are the ones that I highlight in this book.

Nouwen suggests that discipleship means our coming to accept that our "deepest being" is "a dependent being" and that "all human dependencies are embedded in a divine dependence [i.e., dependence upon God] and that that divine dependence makes dying part of a greater and much vaster way of living."[62] Since God loves us and is the Giver of life, freely embracing our dependence upon God in the process of dying leads not to humiliating slavery and death, but to true freedom and life. Nouwen observes that we must "come to the deep inner knowledge—a knowledge more of the heart than of the mind—that we are born out of love and will die into love, that every part of our being is deeply rooted in love and that this love is our true Father and Mother."[63] The virtues of dying enable us to embrace our dependence upon divine love. But receiving these virtues requires that we seek them: as Warren Smith points out, "Participation in the divine virtues is voluntary."[64] As we prepare for dying, then, let us above all heed the words of the Lord Jesus: "Ask, and it will be given you; search, and you will find; knock, and the door will be opened for you. For everyone who asks receives, and everyone who searches finds, and for everyone who knocks, the door will be opened" (Matt. 7:7–8).

CHAPTER 1

LOVE

Job's Challenge to His Creator

Joseph Ratzinger has argued that "man's longing for survival" arises from "the experience of love," in which "love wills eternity for the beloved and therefore for itself."[1] Love makes us yearn for everlasting communion with the beloved. But as we are dying, can we be sure of God's enduring love for us?[2] Across the chasm of death, does love lead to everlasting divine-human "networks of relationship and love," or is love something that we experience now, but that God will take away from us forever, so that human love is ultimately destroyed by death?[3]

Inquiring into the endurance and power of love (divine and human), I focus in this chapter on the book of Job. The Jewish biblical scholar and theologian Jon Levenson suggests that the central question of the book of Job is whether Job can indeed "rely on God's much-acclaimed faithfulness to rescue from Sheol—not at the end of days, to be sure, but in his own time of lethal torment."[4] According to Levenson, the book of Job is about whether God will show his real care for Job by rescuing him from mortal suffering. Levenson notes that Job's friend Bildad thinks that Sheol is solely "the place of those who do not know God" (Job 18:21), not the place of God's servants. On this view, for Bildad and most importantly for the author(s) of the book of Job, Job's vision of "hopelessness and gloom" cannot be the "universal human destiny," because "Sheol" names only a terrible *earthly* fate, namely an early and miserable death (70). If so, then the tension of the book of Job consists in whether God will show his love for Job by sparing him from going down to "Sheol" in this earthly sense.

Levenson accepts the later Second Temple and rabbinic doctrine of the resurrection of the dead, and his *Resurrection and the Restoration of Israel* offers a subtle and valuable defense of that doctrine. According to Levenson, however, "in the Hebrew Bible, death is malign only to the extent that it expresses punishment or otherwise communicates a negative judgment on the life that is ending" (72). Levenson therefore holds that to die at the end of a long and praiseworthy life is not a problem for the Hebrew Bible, and neither is it a problem for the book of Job, which concludes happily with Job recovering from his mortal illness and living 140 more years. The final verse of the book of Job is that "Job died, old and full of days" (Job 42:17). Levenson concludes that Job died "fulfilled" and facing "no future terrors or miseries whatsoever" (73).[5]

It would seem, however, that in the face of impending death, Job actually faces *nothing* whatsoever, let alone "future terrors and miseries." If no personal existence awaits humans after their death, as in Levenson's view the book of Job holds, then surely death simply annihilates Job once and for all. But Levenson argues that to think along those lines is to miss the way in which personal identity was constructed in this period of ancient Israel's history. Since personal identity was linked tightly with one's extended family, the survival of the family sufficed to enable the person to face everlasting death with equanimity. In Job's case, in his final years he obtained an entirely new family that overcame the deaths of his seven sons and three daughters. Levenson explains the difference between our perspective on death and that of the book of Job (and of ancient Israel generally): "To us, the shadow of death always overcasts to an appreciable degree the felicity that the books of Ruth and Job predicate of Naomi and Job at the end of their travail. We look in vain for some acknowledgment that the newfound or recovered felicity is not absolute, since death is. The authors of these books thought otherwise" (119).[6] On this view, death remains a threat for the book of Job, but it is a threat only insofar as it raises the possibility that the family (not the person) will come to an end.

Levenson admits that the evidence of the Psalms shows that individual Israelites did indeed experience existential terror in the face of death, but he contends that in Genesis and throughout the Hebrew Bible, "the great enemy" is "death in the twin forms of barrenness and loss of children," not the death of the individual person (120).[7] I recognize that the book of Job ends on a happy note by having Job die in old age with a prosperous family surrounding him. Nonetheless, I think that the book of Job actually confronts head-on, with real terror and agony, the problem of personal death understood as annihilation.[8] My contention is that Job challenges God precisely on the grounds that it would be unloving and unjust for God to annihilate (or to permit to be annihilated) a human being such as Job, who obeys God and who yearns for an ongoing relationship with God. At stake in the book of Job is whether God truly loves Job, and whether Job's love for God (and neighbor) ultimately means anything at all.[9]

Thus I do not think that Job's main concern is either the sudden death of his "seven sons and three daughters" (Job 1:2), leaving him temporarily without heirs, or even simply the fact that he suffers terribly. It is *mortal* suffering and its seeming consequence—annihilation—that most bother Job. Admittedly, he remains able to appreciate that at least death brings suffering to an end: "There the wicked cease from troubling, and there the weary are at rest. There the prisoners are at ease together; they do not hear the voice of the taskmaster. The small and the great are there, and the slaves are free from their masters" (Job 3:17–19; cf. 7:1–4, 15–16). But this is not much comfort. Rather than complaining about his lack of heirs, furthermore, Job hardly speaks about his relatives except to notice that they do not honor him now that he is incapacitated and about to die. I grant that the book of Job raises the question of why the just suffer, and I value interpretations of the book of Job that focus on this question.[10] But I consider that the book of Job's central concern has to do with mortal suffering and God's love. Specifically, if God is a loving creator, then Job's impending annihilation is unjust and unbearable.[11]

As we will see, Job repeatedly returns to the question of whether God intends to annihilate him. Indeed, the perseverance of Job in pressing this challenge to God, and in this sense the "endurance of Job" (James 5:11), can stand as a parallel to Jacob's stubborn wrestling with the mysterious stranger as Jacob prepares to enter the promised land. Jacob refuses to let the mysterious stranger go until he blesses Jacob, and from this stranger— whom Jacob deems to be God—Jacob receives the gift of his new name, Israel: "You shall no longer be called Jacob, but Israel, for you have striven with God and with humans, and have prevailed" (Gen. 32:28). Likewise, Job wrestles with God until God makes clear that God can be trusted not to abandon Job everlastingly.

Job's challenge to God over what happens to us when we die accords with Job's status as a non-Israelite from "the land of Uz" (Job 1:1), since, as Levenson shows, the question of or yearning for a personal afterlife simply does not arise in the Torah. At the same time, however, Job is a representative of Israel at its best, since Satan's prediction that Job will curse God when Job's temporal goods are gone (see 1:9–11; 2:10) turns out to be completely erroneous. Like the people of Israel at their best, what

Job truly wants is not temporal goods but rather the everlasting good of communion with God in love, and Job cannot put a brave face upon his mortal suffering without assuring himself of this love. At the end of the story, God concludes that Job has "spoken of me what is right" (42:7). Job is right that if God only loved his human lovers for a short time and then obliterated them, then God's goodness and real love for us would be radically thrown into question, and the basis of our love for God would be undermined. In the book of Job, then, we find the deepest problem that confronts dying persons: in the midst of the terror and darkness of mortal suffering, can and should we love our Creator God?[12]

God speaks at the end of the book of Job to make clear that God is the wise and generous Giver of life, possessed of the power to restore Job's standing. In response, Job confesses, "I have uttered what I did not understand, things too wonderful for me"; and Job repents before God "in dust and ashes" (Job 42:3, 6).[13] Thus, although God permits Job to face with terrifying immediacy his vulnerability to annihilation, God makes himself experientially present as the supremely powerful Giver of life in the midst of Job's mortality.[14] Pope Benedict XVI observes in his encyclical *Spe Salvi* that "the human being needs unconditional love."[15] In the book of Job, the conditions of divine and human love are tested, and we discover love's power even in the darkness of dying.

God and Job's Suffering

The Book of Job as a Parable

If read as historical reportage, the first two chapters of Job would be misread. The opening phrase, "There was once a man in the land of Uz," already indicates the parabolic, rather than historical, character of this text.[16] In the second sentence of the book of Job, we learn that Job has "seven sons and three daughters" (1:2), and these symbolic numbers are echoed in the next sentence's observation that Job also had "seven thousand sheep" and "three thousand camels" (1:3). The parabolic character of the story similarly informs the description of the heavenly court. Job 1:6 states, "One day the heavenly beings came to present themselves before the LORD, and Satan also came among them." In God's dialogue with Satan, God and Satan are like two powerful men arguing about whether a slave can perform with the grace that his master attributes to him.[17] Their dialogue is important for setting the scene for the testing that Job undergoes, but it should not be taken, of course, as a literal description of God's attitude toward Job. Job is a "blameless and upright" man "who feared God and turned away from evil" (1:1). Since Job also has a large family and significant wealth, the obvious question is whether Job performs pious actions toward God out of love of his own earthly prosperity, rather than out of love for God. Many people have done precisely this, as the storyteller well knows. The dramatic tension of the parable, therefore, is whether when Job loses every earthly thing, he will still love God. Since God's providential power is unquestioned by the storyteller, Job can lose his earthly goods only if God permits it to happen. In the story, God does not directly cause the evil that befalls Job, but he permits it.

Beginning in Job 1:13, four disasters are reported to Job in quick succession: the killing of all of Job's oxen and asses, and some of his servants, by Sabean marauders; the killing of all of Job's sheep, and some of his servants, by lightning; the killing of all of Job's camels, and some of his servants, by Chaldean marauders; and the killing of all of Job's sons and daughters by a great wind that blew down the house in which they were eating. In each of these four devastating events, exactly one servant escapes to tell the tale to Job. The afflictions next shift to Job's own person. Job comes down with a case of "loathsome sores from the sole of his foot to the crown of his head" (2:7) and goes to sit "among the ashes" (2:8). His wife tells him, "Curse God, and die" (2:9), and his three friends simply weep and lament at the sight of him.

Having lost everything, Job, who is "blameless and upright" (1:1), makes clear that he never loved God simply because of the blessings he has enjoyed. In his crucible, he remarks with real love of God, "Naked I came from my mother's womb, and naked shall I return there; the LORD gave, and the LORD has taken away; blessed be the name of the LORD" (1:21); and "Shall we receive the good at the hand of God, and not receive the bad?" (2:10).[18] The narrator approves Job's righteousness in both instances: "In all this Job did not sin or charge God with wrongdoing" (1:22); and, "In all this Job did not sin with his lips" (2:10).

Job's Insistence upon His Innocence

In chapter 3, however, Job—whose physical decline is so grave that his friends at first "did not recognize him" and could only sit with him in stunned silence for seven days (2:12–13)—suddenly pours forth an impassioned curse against the day of his birth. His friend Eliphaz the Temanite reprimands him for not seeing the earthly goodness of divine providence: "Think now, who that was innocent ever perished? Or where were the upright cut off? As I have seen, those who plow iniquity and sow trouble reap the same. By the breath of God they perish, and by the blast of his anger they are consumed" (4:7–9). Eliphaz goes on to point out that Job, in his claim that he is righteous before God, is being sinfully presumptuous. Eliphaz claims to have heard a voice in a dream that said: "Can mortal man be righteous before God? Can a man be pure before his Maker?" (4:17). The point is that Job is being reproved and chastened by God for his sins. Eliphaz urges Job to respond sensibly: "Behold, happy is the man whom God reproves; therefore despise not the chastening of the Almighty. For he wounds, but he binds up; he smites, but his hands heal" (5:17–18). If Job repents, Eliphaz says, Job will have many descendants and a long life.

Job refuses to listen to Eliphaz's rebuke, again claiming his own righteousness before God.[19] Bildad the Shuhite therefore takes his turn at reasoning with Job. He points out to Job that if, indeed, "you are pure and upright, surely then he [God] will rouse himself for you and restore to you your rightful place" (8:6). The key point is that God does not "pervert justice" (8:3). Bildad then argues that if Job is charging God with iniquity in bringing Job low, Job is in the wrong, since "the hope of the godless shall perish" (8:13), and "God will not reject a blameless person, nor take the hand of evildoers" (8:20). If Job is indeed innocent, Job has nothing to fear, and certainly nothing to slanderously blame God about; God "will yet fill your mouth with laughter, and your lips with shouts of joy" (8:21).

Zophar the Naamathite next takes a turn at answering Job. Zophar accuses Job of babbling proud nonsense and of mocking God. It is not surprising, Zophar says, that Job claims to be "clean in God's sight" (11:4), since the wicked often persuade themselves that they are pure. Zophar concludes that since God sees far more deeply than Job can see, Job can be sure that "God exacts of you less than your guilt deserves" (11:6). Zophar urges Job to repent immediately: "If you direct your heart rightly, you will stretch out your hands toward him. If iniquity is in your hand, put it far away, and do not let wickedness reside in your tents. Surely then you will lift up your face without blemish; you will be secure, and will not fear" (11:13–15). Job responds forcefully against Zophar, accusing him and the other two friends of being "worthless physicians" who "whitewash with lies" (13:4).

Eliphaz, however, does not allow things to stop there. He condemns Job in stark terms. He tells Job that "you are doing away with the fear of God, and hindering meditation before God" (15:4). He warns that Job has forgotten that all humans are sinners. Job's presumptuous insistence upon his own innocence in the face of the calamities that have befallen him shows, Eliphaz says, that Job's mouth has been carried away by "iniquity" and that Job's spirit has turned "against God" (15:5, 13). When Job responds once more, this time in a more despairing vein (although without giving in to his friends), Bildad chimes in against Job by insisting that calamities come justly to the wicked. Again Job bemoans his fate, only to have Zophar repeat and amplify Bildad's description of the calamities that befall the wicked, and that have now befallen Job. Job replies with exasperation. After noting that the wicked often enjoy long and prosperous lives, he asks his three friends: "How then will you comfort me with empty nothings? There is nothing left of your answers but falsehood" (21:34).

Eliphaz now turns upon Job with strong condemnations suited to the sorry state in which Job finds himself: "Is not your wickedness great? There is no end to your iniquities" (22:5). Eliphaz lists a large number of extremely grave sins that he attributes to Job, and then at the end of his discourse he once again urges Job to repent: "Agree with God, and be at peace; in this way good will come to you. . . . For God abases the proud, but he saves the lowly" (22:21, 29). But Job merely repeats his innocence and accuses the all-powerful God of not caring about the just while sustaining the life and prosperity of the wicked. When Bildad again urges Job to recall that all humans are sinners before God, Job responds by repeating his lamentations at even greater length: "[God] has cast me into the mire, and I have become like dust and ashes" (30:19). The section concludes, "So these three men ceased to answer Job, because he was righteous in his own eyes" (32:1).

At this stage, Elihu the Buzite, a man younger than both Job and Job's three friends, intervenes. Elihu "was angry at Job because he justified himself rather than God" (32:2). Disgusted with the inability of Job's friends to persuade Job, Elihu asks why Job complains that God will not hear him. God speaks in various ways, says Elihu. One way that God works to "keep [people] from pride" (33:17) is to allow disease to afflict us; but the person who prays to God, and who finds an angel or mediator to intercede for him or her, can recover from a mortal disease. Elihu deems that when Job complains that God does not hear him, it is because Job has not cried out in repentance to God but instead has continued to rely upon his own righteousness and has not adequately reckoned with the fact that "God is great, and we do not know him" (36:26).

Love at the Heart of Job's Lament

Is Job proud? What is the fundamental basis of his lament? Since God eventually intervenes and condemns Job's friends, I think that we can take Job's innocence for granted, as the story's way of bracketing the fact that suffering and death are a punishment of human sin. Having removed this justification for suffering and death, the book of Job can probe the deeper issue, namely whether annihilation is fitting or just for a rational creature who loves God and who has been made by and for divine love.

In this section, I will trace the centrality of dying-as-annihilation for the parable of Job by means of a chapter-by-chapter analysis of Job's lament. Consider first Job's cursing of the day of his birth and also of the night of his conception. He urges that complete darkness and oblivion swallow up that day and night, and he wishes that he had never known anything. He asks, "Why did I not die at birth, come forth from the womb and expire?" (3:11). Had he died at birth, then without ever regretting anything, he could have simply been dead. Job complains that "the thing that I fear comes upon me, and what I dread befalls me" (3:25). His situation is not solely or even primarily one of physical suffering; it is one of mental agony caused by approaching death. He states, "My days are swifter than a weaver's shuttle, and come to their end without hope. Remember that my life is a breath; my eye will never again see good" (7:6–7). This apprehension of annihilation stands at the center of his complaint to God.

Against the notion that he selfishly or egotistically wants to exist, he describes his coming death in terms of the sudden ending of all interpersonal communion: "The eye that beholds me will see me no more; while your eyes are upon me, I shall be gone" (7:8). His death will affect more than himself alone; those who love him will never again be able to interact with him. They will see only his corpse, because he will never again know or interact with anyone. The descent to "Sheol" constitutes a permanent ending. This belief drives Job to deep anguish and complaint. If this is what life is, then life must be rejected. A God who creates humans to be annihilated does not really care about what humans do in their lives and should not punish humans. Job challenges God, "If I sin, what do I do to you, you watcher of humanity?" (7:20). Soon, says Job, "I shall lie in the earth; you will seek me, but I shall not be" (7:21). Doomed to move quickly from life to a state of everlasting nonexistence, Job does not believe that God truly loves him.[20]

Job grants that God exists and that no one can contend against God. In his power, God has made everything to be as it is, and no one can stop God when God "snatches away" life (9:12). Job knows that God's power is such that no argument with God can be won by a creature. Even though God "destroys both the blameless and the wicked" (9:22)—as Job says, "if it is not he, who then is it?" (9:24)—Job admits that "though I am blameless, he [God] would prove me perverse" (9:20). God's power is such that no creature can argue successfully against him, and yet the fact that all humans go quickly into everlasting death means that goodness and wickedness in life are "all one" in the end (9:22). Job himself can do nothing but move swiftly toward annihilation: "My days are swifter than a runner; they flee away, they see no good. They go by like skiffs of reed, like an eagle swooping on the prey" (9:25-26). It is clear that he is not merely complaining here about suffering. Job's accusation centers upon his fast-approaching annihilation: "Your hands fashioned and made me; and now you turn and destroy me. Remember that you fashioned me like clay; and will you turn me to dust again?" (10:8-9).

Not only is the Creator destroying forever the man Job—the Creator's own creature—but also, as Job points out, the Creator had previously shown him great love. Making and preserving Job was no easy thing. Job states, "You clothed me with skin and flesh, and knit me together with bones and sinews. You have granted me life and steadfast love; and your care has preserved my spirit" (10:11-12). But now God is hunting Job so as to obliterate him. This action makes no sense, since it would seem that the creation of a human being, to whom God shows "steadfast love," should lead not to death as annihilation but to an enduring mutual relationship of love. Job again cries out that if this is what life is—to be destroyed by the God who has loved one into existence and whom one has loved—then "would that I had died before any eye had seen me" (10:18). He again tells God, who has seemingly betrayed him, to leave him alone while he lives out his brief remaining days. Job speaks of his remaining days of life as being "before I go, never to return, to the land of gloom and deep darkness, the land of gloom and chaos, where light is like darkness" (10:21-22). This is the land (Sheol) where human consciousness turns dark and goes off forever, never again to be restored.

As he continues with his complaint, Job adds that he can hardly believe that matters have come to such a grim conclusion. After all, he previously enjoyed a loving relationship with the one who is now working to annihilate him: "I, who called upon God and he answered me" (12:4). Job is well aware that every living thing is in the hand of God, and that God wills a finite lifespan for everything on earth. God does not allow any human or any nation to endure for long, since human strength and pride are as nothing in comparison with God's strength. Job knows all this, and yet he makes clear to God that it is unjust that he (and all humans) should merely waste "away like a rotten thing, like a garment that is moth-eaten" (13:28).

Job 14 makes an especially important contribution to understanding Job's complaint against the injustice of annihilation.[21] Here Job first compares human existence to that of a flower that quickly withers and a shadow that is soon gone. He then points out that God, having determined to give humans such a short existence, should not punish humans on earth for their sins, since humans will soon enter into nonexistence anyway. In this situation, says Job, human life is more pitiful than that of a tree. A tree can have "hope" to live again, since even if its roots grow old and its stump dies, nonetheless its shoots can come forth again from the ground. By contrast, "mortals die, and are laid low; humans expire, and where are they?" (14:10). A dead human is like a dried-up river: the same river will never flow again. Job paints a portrait of terrifying annihilation: "mortals lie down and do not rise again; until the heavens are no more, they will not awake or be roused out of their sleep" (14:12). The imagery does not portend a day on which the dead man will awake, since the implication is that the heavens will always exist.

Job then puts the matter into interpersonal terms that are deeply moving. He tells God that he would be glad if God would place him in Sheol, if only this were not an everlasting annihilation. He wishes that God would "appoint me a set time, and remember me!" (14:13).[22] He wants to be remembered (and thus truly loved) by the God who created him; he wants to be restored to the interpersonal relationship with God that he has only just begun to enjoy: "If mortals die, will they live again? All the days of my service I would wait [in Sheol] until my release should come. You would call, and I would answer you; you would long for the work of your hands" (14:14-15). This is a depiction of a God who loves the person whom he has created. Job would respond with joy and love to the God who calls him in love. The yearning of Job for ongoing mutual love would be met by the Creator's own yearning, rather than being suppressed through everlasting annihilation.

Such a God would mercifully not allow death to be the destruction of the human person. Humans would not know and love for a fleeting period only to be everlastingly destroyed. Again, Job does not doubt that God exists. It is God's goodness that Job challenges. Job compares the way God treats humans to the way that running water washes away soil. In time, each mountain "falls and crumbles away" (14:18), and in this way, says Job, "you [God] destroy the hope of mortals" (14:19). God destroys us as though he did not love us. Job uses the image of sending away a friend forever: "You prevail forever against them, and they pass away; you change their countenance, and send them away" (14:20). Our countenance turns to stone, and we no longer know anything. Since dying persons will be cut off from interpersonal communion, Job suggests that the dying become totally self-focused; now "they feel only the pain of their own bodies, and mourn only for themselves" (14:22).[23] What kind of God would treat his beloved in this way, or allow his beloved to come to such a state?

After a pause for a response by one of Job's friends, Job continues his attack upon the injustice of death as annihilation. Job complains that God has worn him out and shriveled him up. Worse, Job observes, God "has torn me in his wrath, and hated me; he has gnashed his teeth at me" (16:9). God has shown himself to be not a loving Creator or a faithful God, but an enemy who desires the destruction of a human being who loves God. Job had been in good health, but now God attacks and breaks Job. Describing this attack vividly (and building upon the poignancy of Job 14), Job states that God "slashes open my kidneys, and shows no mercy; he pours out my gall on the ground. He bursts upon me again and again; he rushes at me like a warrior" (16:13–14). Although Job is innocent and he weeps piteously, God does not care. Job argues that God should have a law preventing God from killing humans, just as God has a law that a human must not kill a human.

Given this portrait of a vicious and hateful Creator, Job expresses deep despair about his coming death. He has nothing to look forward to. He complains about the humiliation of his situation, about the "mockers" (17:2) who lord it over a dying man. He emphasizes that there is literally nothing to hope for in Sheol: "My days are past, my plans are broken off, the desires of my heart. . . . If I look for Sheol as my house, if I spread my couch in darkness, if I say to the Pit, 'You are my father,' and to the worm, 'My mother,' or 'my sister,' where then is my hope? Who will see my hope? Will it go down to the bars of Sheol? Shall we descend together into the dust?" (17:11, 13–16). The answer is that the Pit (another term for Sheol or the grave) and the worm, total darkness, obliterate all hope.

God created Job to have hope, and God once seemed to love Job, but now God is going to mercilessly and everlastingly crush Job's hope. The injustice of this situation is the fundamental complaint of Job. Having created humans for interpersonal communion, for hope and love, how can God justly annihilate them? Such a God is a brutal hunter. Job states that God has "closed his net around me. Even when I cry out, 'Violence!' I am not answered. I call aloud, but there is no justice. He has walled up my way so that I cannot pass, and he has set darkness upon my paths" (19:6-8). Job's words nicely portray the existential standing of a human being confronting his or her own death (understood as annihilation).[24] The future is "walled up"; the path is utterly dark. God the hunter has trapped Job, has given him no escape, and will soon kill him, despite Job's desire for interpersonal communion and love. By leading Job into annihilation, God has acted as though Job were a mere animal, as though Job was not a unique and unrepeatable person reaching out in love for God. The glory of Job was Job's ability to give free worship to God, to seek for and love God. Now God crushes Job as though Job were an enemy or a mere animal. As Job puts it, "He [God] has stripped my glory from me, and taken the crown from my head. He breaks me down on every side, and I am gone, he has uprooted my hope like a tree" (19:9-10). God has created a glorious creature, able to know and love and plan and hope, but death utterly destroys that creature as though the human being were a mere animal.[25]

Job next responds to Zophar, who had proclaimed that God ensures that the wicked suffer during their earthly lives for their sins. In response, Job insists that many thrive who make clear that they have no interest in God or God's ways. Here Job returns to his concern regarding annihilation: both the wicked and the good "lie down alike in the dust, and the worms cover them" (21:26), so that all are obliterated and end up in the same state. Job knows that he himself has obeyed God and has lived righteously: "My foot has held fast to his steps; I have kept his way and have not turned aside. I have not departed from the commandment of his lips; I have treasured in my bosom the words of his mouth" (23:11-12). Despite Job's obedience to God's law, God will annihilate Job. It is God, therefore, who terrifies Job. Job complains that "the Almighty has terrified me; if only I could vanish in darkness, and thick darkness would cover my face!" (23:16-17). According to Job, God treats both the poor and the wealthy in the same way that we treat "heads of grain" (24:24). Heads of grain serve us, we consume them without thinking twice about it, and they never exist again.

Again, Job is not concerned about questions of whether God exists or whether God is all-powerful. He has no doubts on such matters. It is precisely because God is so powerful that Job challenges him. Having created Job, God appears to unjustly will to annihilate him. Job states that God "has taken away my right" (27:2). There is no hope for "the godless . . . when God takes away their lives" (27:8). Even one who wishes to "take delight in the Almighty" (27:10), as Job does, loses existence forever at the moment of death. It seems that God does not care about those who wish to delight in him; God coldly destroys them. In this way, what once was a beautiful relationship with God in love has now been turned to nothing. Job cries to God but God makes no answer. God is tossing Job "about in the roar of the storm" (30:22) in preparation for bringing Job "to death" (30:23).[26] Although Job obeyed God and God once gave Job his favor, now God is like a faithless friend who brutally turns upon Job. Job details all the ways in which he has obeyed God by avoiding lust, falsehood, adultery, vengeance, reviling, hypocrisy, and greed, and by caring for justice, for the land, for the poor, for sojourners and strangers, and for widows and orphans. Yet God has now abandoned him to everlasting death, and Job insists that this is a profound injustice. Does not God owe a far better destiny to a person who has enjoyed the loving "friendship of God" (29:4)?[27] Thus the book of Job confronts the unbearable darkness of death for a person made for love, and challenges God to defend his love.

God's Defense against Job's Charge

Toward the end of the book of Job, God answers Job "out of the whirlwind" (38:1), a "whirlwind" that signifies the vastness of the divine life. God's fundamental answer to Job is to present himself as the wise Giver of existence and life, and to remind Job that he lacks knowledge about the origin, sustenance, and future of God's creation. Since Job knows nothing about the origin and sustenance of life, Job can know nothing about what happens after death. Along these lines, God begins by posing a series of rhetorical questions to Job, the first of which has to do with the moment of creation: "Where were you when I laid the foundation of the earth?" (38:4). God is the one who wisely ordered the earth so that it could sustain life, by giving bounds to the sea, which would otherwise have swallowed everything in chaos. God then asks what Job knows about death: "Have the gates of death been revealed to you, or have you seen the gates of deep darkness?" (38:17). Job knows nothing about the governance of the universe, of the snow and rain or of the courses of the stars. Job cannot sustain the life and strength of animals, nor does he understand how the variety of wild animals and birds came to be. In describing all these natural things, God emphasizes that the wisdom that sustains nonrational things comes from him. He asks, for example, "Who has put wisdom in the clouds, or given understanding to the mists? Who can number the clouds by wisdom?" (38:36–37 RSV).[28] Likewise, he asks, "Is it by your wisdom that the hawk soars, and spreads its wings toward the south?" (39:26). God also lays emphasis on his power, which is obviously greater than even immensely powerful created things. God describes "Behemoth" and "Leviathan," two creatures—perhaps the hippopotamus and the crocodile—whose physical power far overshadows human power.

When God first established the universe, he tells Job, "the morning stars sang together and all the heavenly beings shouted for joy" (38:7). One can see why they would do so; creation is so magnificent, and it elicits wonder and love for its Creator. God observes that he alone is the giver of such a good thing, and so all creatures belong to God: "Who has given to me, that I should repay him? Whatever is under the whole heaven is mine" (41:11 RSV). God alone has the wisdom and power to understand the existence, energy, and life that we find in the cosmos. In reply to God, as noted above, Job admits that "no purpose of yours can be thwarted" and that "I have uttered what I did not understand, things too wonderful for me, which I did not know" (42:2–3).

Why, however, does Job conclude that God has made a sufficient answer to the charge of unjustly annihilating humans? I have suggested above that God's response to Job indicates that God, as the all-powerful Giver of life, can be counted upon to order things in such a way that brings forth the joy of those who love him.[29] Proclaiming his power to create and sustain all things, God implies that he should be trusted to sustain Job's life after death rather than annihilating Job; but Job will have to take this on trust or faith. This amount of hope seems to be enough for Job, especially since God has personally responded to his entreaties. God does not unveil the mystery of human death, but God gives Job enough hope to reassure him that death does not negate love.

The final narrative portion of the book of Job seems to promise, symbolically, even more. Job, who previously was on the very point of death, now recovers and has his earthly goods restored twofold. God "blessed the latter days of Job more than his beginning" (42:12). One might interpret this as the Lord making up for "all the evil that the LORD had brought upon him" (42:11), and it certainly is not less than that. But in the context of the parable, it is a sign that God is always a God of love, blessing, and life. The moral is not the mere fact that no matter how sick one is, God can restore one's health and fortunes. Job has already deconstructed that temporal hope by pointing out that one will simply die later—as indeed Job does, "old and full of days," in the last line of the book (42:17). Rather the moral is in the pattern of movement from tribulation and death to blessing and life. Knowing the God of love, we can anticipate that death will not be the last word for us, and that our communion with God in love will continue because God truly loves us. The injustice of flowering into consciousness and communion only to face everlasting death and nothingness stretching out endlessly consists in the fact that humans, while mortal, are created for a communion of love with the infinite God. The book of Job suggests that God ensures that annihilation is not what happens to his human creatures.

Conclusion

Humans face death in such a way that it feels like an annihilation, like standing on the brink of oblivion and then stepping into everlasting darkness and nothingness from which there will never be an escape. Job's complaints, therefore, are deeply moving: "Even when I cry out, 'Violence!' I am not answered; I call aloud, but there is no justice. He has walled up my way so that I cannot pass, and he has set darkness upon my paths. He has stripped my glory from me, and taken the crown from my head" (19:7–9). As Job says, dying seems to be nothing less than God killing Job, God stripping Job of all the love that God had shown for Job, without the slightest care for Job's loving obedience to God. In dying, Job seemingly can look forward to no future: he is trapped within a rapid and humiliating descent to nothingness. Job says that God "has uprooted my hope like a tree" (19:10), and Job wishes that he could be even a mere tree, since at least "there is hope for a tree, if it is cut down, that it will sprout again" (14:7). Job fantasizes about a God who truly loves him, a God who might place Job for a time in the darkness of death, but who would then revive him by calling him to return to relationship with God: "You would call, and I would answer you; you would long for the work of your hands" (14:15). Can God truly be good and loving if God turns his back forever upon a rational creature who loves him? Assailed by mortal suffering, Job presses the issues of whether God truly loves us and whether God is lovable.

Certainly no theological speech can exhaust the mystery of God's actions or make pain and mortal suffering fully intelligible in this life. But in the book of Job, neither God nor Job remains silent, although the final resolution is one of awe-filled love rather than of words. The foolishness of Job's friends consists largely in their inability to apprehend that death-as-annihilation is not a just situation for humans who, through God's gracious gifts, have come to know and love God. Job's friends continually bring up the context of sin and argue that God consistently punishes sinners and rewards the just during their earthly lives. Obviously, they are wrong. But Job's deeper point is that it cannot be just or loving for God to draw his human creatures into a relationship of love with God, only to abandon and annihilate those who love him. God firmly approves of Job's words.

Katherine Sonderegger aptly says about God, "To be Omnipotent, for the True God, is to burn with Blessing. From Him, pours out Generation and Gift, Life Itself; and behold, It is Good, and altogether Very Good."[30] Job's struggle with God requires us—along with Job's friends, well rebuked by God—to speak firmly and decisively against the surd of everlasting death for those who love God. We must hear the word of the God who creates wisely and who gives life powerfully; we must learn that even if death looks like annihilation, we are not wise enough to know what death is unless God reveals it to us. If death simply annihilates humans who love God, then, with Job, we would have to insist that no amount of blessings in this life could comfort us in the face of such a terrible prospect.[31] Fortunately, God confirms that Job is right to protest against such a prospect, and God makes himself present to Job as the wise giver and powerful sustainer of life.

In the encounter with God that is mortal suffering, therefore, we must love ever more urgently, and—in the space of silence before eternity that dying opens up—seek to receive what God has willed from creation to give us: his divine love. As he does to Job, the all-loving God will respond.

CHAPTER 2

HOPE

Meditatio Mortis

In a book written shortly before his death, Terence Nichols observed what for many might seem obvious: "People fear death because they have no positive vision of afterlife."[1] This lack of intellectual and imaginative foundation for envisioning an afterlife impedes the blossoming of Christian hope. As Nichols points out, "A consequence of the uncertainty about afterlife is that people don't think about death and therefore don't prepare for it. It's easier to deny it—why dwell on what you can't change? So people typically don't think about death until it's too late. They don't prepare to meet death; rather, it runs into them like a truck."[2] As the foremost reason for uncertainty about an afterlife, Nichols names philosophical materialism, the view that matter is all that is. If there is no God and no spiritual soul, humans will never think or love again after death. Instead, from the perspective of philosophical materialism, all that awaits us is everlasting nothingness, eternal absence of interpersonal communion.

Along these lines, David Rieff recounts the hopeless dying of his famous mother, the American writer and philosophical materialist Susan Sontag. He describes "her desperate panic on learning she was once again in cancerland and that this time the odds against her were worse than they had ever been."[3] As an acclaimed writer, Sontag had long felt special, set apart for a truly important labor. When her cancer returned after a long remission, Sontag struggled desperately against it. She refused to hear that she was dying, even in the midst of agonizing treatments; she dreamt and spoke continually "of what she could do when she got out of the hospital and once more took up the reins of her life. The future was everything. Living was everything. Getting back to work was everything" (104–5). She insisted that she would make a completely fresh start, and would write in a new way and do the things that she had always wanted to do, rather than wasting her time doing things that she had previously done out of mere duty. As Rieff says, she concentrated her limited energy in undertaking a "revolt against death," and she died "unreconciled to her own extinction" (109, 127).[4]

Sontag, of course, did not believe in God or in life after death. Seeking to beat her essentially unbeatable disease, her sole hope consisted in medical and scientific data and in the treatment plans of her physicians, since hope based in any other source—for example, in her friends' assurances—"actually deepened her sense of hurtling toward extinction" (133). Rieff concludes that the problem was that Sontag hoped too much; her force of will and repeated success at remaking her life prevented her from despairing utterly, and so she reached out for some impossible medical hope to the very end. But he also concludes, at the same time, that the reason for her desperate clutching to medical hope was that she "could not get enough of being alive. She reveled in *being*. . . . No one I have ever known loved life so unambivalently" (143). Nothing, not even the longest life, could have "made her any more reconciled to extinction" (143). As Rieff remarks, "She thought the world a charnel house . . . and couldn't get enough of it. She thought herself unhappy . . . and wanted to live, unhappy, for as long as she possibly could" (147). She could not give up on the idea of having a future, even though she held apodictically and despairingly (as does Rieff) that death is annihilation. Rieff credits her with "an almost childlike sense of wonder" that impelled her toward more and more life, since her zest for discovery never diminished (149).

Toward the end of the book, Rieff confesses that he too is "crippled by the fear of extinction" (150). For himself, he hopes for an eventual sudden death by a massive heart attack, so that he will simply go from living to everlasting annihilation without having to stare directly into the abyss. His mother was in mental agony because she had no future, no real next step; she could not use the moments of her dying to connect more deeply with others, because she felt so acutely the despair and loneliness of entering into everlasting nothingness. Weeping and panicked as she neared her death, she told the nurse she was dying, with the implication that the whole thing was horrific, incomprehensible, and absurd. Her son describes her final moments as "watching a human being end" (165). He identifies himself and his mother with the perspective of Marguerite Dumas: "I cannot reconcile myself to being nothing" (167).[5]

Rieff is aware that some people, at least if we can trust their own testimony, seem to be able to reconcile themselves to their own annihilation, comforted by the fact that the cycle of life, with all its beauty, will continue at least for some time to come, despite their own nothingness. By contrast, Rieff observes that Sontag could not "love a world without herself, much as the moralist in her would have despised herself for not doing so. Because she could not free herself from her hope about life . . . she never really had a chance of freeing herself from her terrible fear of extinction, of not being" (168). Thus her irrepressible hope paradoxically increased her ultimate despair. When deprived of any hope for avoiding imminent death, she was left with nothing but "despair and panic and meaninglessness" (169). Rieff therefore deems "hope" to be a "poisoned chalice," because in the end there can be no hope for ongoing personal existence, terrifying as everlasting annihilation may be (169). Reflecting upon her embalmed corpse rotting in a Parisian graveyard alongside the corpses of many other famous writers, he concludes that "unless you believe in spirits or the Christian fairy tale of resurrection," those who have died simply "no longer exist" and never will exist again (172).

More recently, the eminent doctor and writer Oliver Sacks—who wrote a laudatory back-cover blurb for Rieff's book—has written about his own diagnosis with terminal cancer and his thoughts on his quickly approaching death.[6] On the one hand, he says that he feels "intensely alive," and "I want and hope in the time that remains to deepen my friendships, to say farewell to those I love, to write more, to travel if I have the strength, to achieve new levels of understanding and insight."[7] He sees himself as a person devoted to passionate growth in interpersonal communion. But on the other hand, he notes that his way of dealing with death is to focus on "the physical sciences, a world where there is no life, but also no death"— on "metals and minerals, little emblems of eternity."[8] Even after the heat death of the universe, presumably, some of the elements in the periodic table will still exist. In the book's final section, after recalling his childhood as a member of an Orthodox Jewish family, he considers the possibility of a secular meaning of the Sabbath, namely the possibility of conceiving of death as a permanent rest from a well-lived and fruitful life.[9] His book abruptly breaks off here. Although he was tremendously grateful for his life, he could not square the contrasting impulses of his intense desire for ever-deepening interpersonal communion and, at the same time, his retreat to nonliving minerals of the periodic table as a way of dealing with the prospect of the everlasting annihilation of his relationships.

The examples of Sontag and Sacks suggest how deeply the expectation of annihilation has become ensconced in contemporary culture, especially among the educated elite. Ian Brown plays to this elite in his recent *Sixty* (a diary of his sixty-first year), which records the daily terror of sliding ever closer to annihilation, with so many hopes and dreams unfulfilled.[10] Likewise, Steven Luper's *Philosophy of Death* simply assumes as a given that "death entails annihilation, the end of our existence."[11] The philosopher and scientist Raymond Tallis insists that "those whom we call 'the dead' neither enjoy their peace nor endure their loss"; they are simply "cancelled" and undergo irrevocable "extinction," even though he holds out some very slight hope that consciousness (forever inexplicable by science, in his view) makes possible an unimaginable "continuation in being despite utter transformation."[12]

In his *Very Brief History of Eternity*, the Yale scholar Carlos Eire confirms the current dominance in elite culture of the assumption that death annihilates the human person, but he takes a quite different approach nonetheless. After describing the evanescent lifespan of each human being and the coming heat death or cosmic annihilation of the universe, he reflects that "thinking and feeling that one *must* exist is part and parcel of human experience. Conceiving of *not being* and of *nothingness* is as difficult and as impossible as looking at our own faces without a mirror."[13] Proposing that this fact contains an important lesson, he makes a twofold argument. First, he suggests that our persistent desire for permanent and enduring communion has significance and should not be simply dismissed, especially by those who care about the history of "lived beliefs."[14] Second, he argues (again with a focus on "lived belief") that the Protestant Reformers' rejection of prayers for "the poor souls in purgatory" and prayers to "the saints in heaven" led to a new situation in which "death and the afterlife stopped being a communal experience," with the result that "*this* life and *this* world . . . became the sole focus of religion" and so a "significant first step" was taken "toward the elevation of this world as the ultimate reality and towards the extinction of the soul."[15]

I agree with Eire that our desire for ongoing interpersonal communion and for transcendence of the short span of our mortal existence has something to teach us about dying, and that the loss of religious and imaginative connections with the realm of the dead has had a reductive impact upon what we dare to hope for. With the philosopher Carol Zaleski, I affirm that "the persistence of the eschatological imagination" is not irrational.[16] On this basis, the present chapter pursues a twofold path for renewing the virtue of hope in the face of death. First, after briefly sketching some biblical background regarding despair and fear of death, I examine Josef Pieper's philosophy of death, immortality, and the spiritual soul in light of our desire for ongoing interpersonal communion. Second, I explore the meditations upon the final judgment, hell, and heaven offered in the seventeenth century by Robert Bellarmine and Francis de Sales.[17] These resources need retrieval in a time of much despair in the face of dying, because, as John Swinton and Richard Payne point out, "To a great extent, one can only imagine what one has been taught to imagine."[18] As a final step, I set forth Jean-Pierre de Caussade's spirituality of abandonment to divine providence as a path for approaching our dying in "hope for what we do not see" (Rom 8:25).

Josef Pieper on Death and Dying

The Existence of God and the Goodness of Creation

According to the Epistle to the Hebrews, persons who have true faith are self-consciously "strangers and foreigners on the earth" who "desire a better country, that is, a heavenly one" (Heb. 11:13, 16). The same epistle speaks of death at crucial points. Notably, it presents the divine Son as becoming human so "that through death he might destroy the one who has the power of death, that is, the devil, and free those who all their lives were held in slavery by the fear of death" (Heb. 2:14–15). The Wisdom of Solomon—composed not too long before the Epistle to the Hebrews[19]— conveys the characteristic elements of such slavery to the fear of death. It presents those who have no hope as saying to themselves: "Short and sorrowful is our life, and there is no remedy when a life comes to its end. . . . For we were born by mere chance, and hereafter we shall be as though we had never been, for the breath in our nostrils is smoke, and reason is a spark kindled by the beating of our hearts" (Wisd. of Sol. 2:1–2).[20] In response to their logic, Wisdom of Solomon insists that "the souls of the righteous are in the hand of God" and that it is only "in the eyes of the foolish" that righteous humans seem to have been destroyed by death (3:1–2).[21]

Josef Pieper devoted much of his philosophical work to defending the Wisdom of Solomon's view that "the souls of the righteous are in the hand of God." In *In Defense of Philosophy*, Pieper argues that asking truly philosophical questions is rare and comes about only when we face such things as our own dying. Faced with death, we stand up and pay attention; mere platitudes do not suffice anymore. Pieper credits "the confrontation with death" with providing the necessary "shock" that serves to initiate the process of true philosophy in human thought, by forcing us to face "the question as to the meaning of the world and of existence."[22] In this regard, Pieper's description of the philosophical attitude is significant. He states that "the true philosopher . . . approaches his unfathomable object unselfishly and with an open mind."[23] Importantly, however, the true philosopher must "acknowledge, before any consideration of specifics and without regard to usefulness, that reality *is good in itself*—all things, the world, 'being' as such, yes, all that exists, and existence itself."[24]

But how can we acknowledge the goodness of "all that exists" before we are assured, presumably through a philosophical quest, that the processes of the universe are not a massive annihilating force, a devouring monster? Pieper is aware of this circularity. In *Hope and History*, he recalls an earlier lecture in which he argued that "it is not worth talking seriously of hope if there is no hope for martyrs."[25] Pieper goes on to say that if death is annihilation, then indeed there is no real hope for anyone or for human history.[26] He recognizes that if we have no hope facing death, then we will not be able to love reality's goodness and we will not be able to philosophize, with the result that our philosophical quest—as distinct from mere writing about philosophical questions—will immediately be brought to a halt by despair and horror.

In answer to this problem, Pieper makes clear that philosophy is not *simply* openness to questions of meaning. Philosophy also demands from the outset a view of reality that permits true philosophical questioning to proceed. As Pieper says, "the explicit denial of the world as creation carries with it vast consequences."[27] He argues that the precondition of philosophy is the rejection—requiring a kind of faith and hope—of "the nihilistic dogma that the world as such is absurd."[28] The philosopher who opens himself or herself to the world in joyful wonder must trust that it is good and that our yearning for communion is not ultimately absurd. For Pieper, this means that the philosopher, in order to philosophize, must be committed at least implicitly to the claim that "the world, as creation, is willed by God, which means that it is created *in love* and is therefore, by its very existence, good."[29]

Has the philosophical quest, then, been shown by Pieper to be a vicious circle, which assumes the reality of God and meaning for which it allegedly quests? The answer is no, because at the outset of the philosophical quest, one has to assume that the truth of things is *knowable*. This philosophical assumption, Pieper notes, leads to God. Pieper's reasoning is as follows: if there is no Mind behind the things that exist, we could not rightly assume that things are actually intelligible to mind. Without a creative Mind, from where could intelligible order, which is so evident in things, come? Pieper concludes that it is "impossible to deny categorically, on the one hand, the rootedness of all things in the thought of an inventive and creative Mind, and on the other hand to take for granted, and to explain as if nothing had happened, the empirically manifested fact of the knowability of these very same things."[30] The philosophical quest, then, presumes at least implicitly the existence of God, and it does so on philosophical grounds: namely, a commitment to the knowability of things that allows persons to ask philosophical questions with existential seriousness, rather than despairing at the outset. Already, then, authentic philosophy greatly strengthens the foundations of hope.

Death and the Act of Dying

In *Death and Immortality*, Pieper explores the act of dying as a human action and not solely as a bodily event.[31] As Ephraim Radner comments with regard to the act of dying: either "we freely abandon ourselves into the incomprehensible meaning of God's 'hands' . . . or we freely withhold ourselves from that which will take us anyway."[32] Inquiring into dying as a human act, Pieper first specifies that death is not merely the separation of body and soul as if they were two distinct entities from the outset. Instead, death ruptures a real unity: the person, and not just his or her body, dies.[33] Rather than liberating the spiritual soul from its bodily cage, death wounds the soul, which loses its natural perfection of unity with the body. Death therefore constitutes a real destruction of the dying person's nature, not merely a destruction of the dying person's body. Rather than being a deliverance, death is an evil for the person; it is antinatural and an outrage against one's human dignity.[34]

In this light, Pieper supports the biblical view that death is a punishment, a view found also in ancient philosophy. Its status as punishment allows human death to be not only bad but also good, since "punishment 'makes good again' and restores to order something which had been wrong."[35] For Christians, actively accepting death as a punishment involves repenting of our sins and acknowledging the sovereignty of God. In this way we can embrace our dying and freely choose it as a good. We thereby transform our dying into an event that has positive value for us, without denying the destructiveness of death.[36] Put simply, in the act of dying, we choose either to refuse God or to find our fulfillment in God.[37]

Pieper is aware of the objection that many dying persons are unconscious or hardly conscious. But he takes encouragement from the testimony of many to "the fierce energy with which a man . . . seeks to make ultimate order within the space of his interior existence, and the concern, overshadowing all else, to put himself into the fitting state of mind for this last step."[38] Pieper also notes the experience that dying people have had of seeing their entire life pass before their eyes in a fraction of an instant. In arguing for the reality of this final decision, Pieper makes clear that he is not proposing that we can prepare ourselves for it by devoting our lives to thinking about death. All we can do is to practice offering ourselves to God with the recognition (possible in the *fullest* way only when we are truly dying) that in reality "one possesses only what one lets go of."[39]

The Immortality of the Soul

In light of this understanding of active dying, Pieper reflects upon the philosophical doctrine of the immortality of the soul.[40] He first takes note of the raptures about the immortality of the soul expressed by German Enlightenment thinkers such as Moses Mendelssohn, Gotthold Lessing, Christophe August Tiedge, Immanuel Kant, and Johann Gottlieb Fichte. Digging deeper, he shows that Mendelssohn's broadly influential *Phädon, or On the Immortality of the Soul* (1767) distorted Plato's account of the soul in the *Phaedo*, both by ignoring the role of Platonic myth, and by ignoring Plato's conception of a final judgment (rather than "a mere continued existence").[41] Moreover, Plato's *Phaedrus* takes a quite different approach than does the *Phaedo*, since the *Phaedrus* emphasizes the unity of soul and body and makes clear that immortality, far from consisting in an extended life of the mind along the lines of what we enjoy now, cannot be conceived.

Pieper argues in favor of the immaterial constitution of the soul, on the grounds of the human ability to apprehend universal truth, which, "however it makes use of the physical senses, is essentially a process independent of all material concatenations."[42] This independence can be seen in the difference between physiological mechanisms and the freedom of conscious knowing, a freedom that is required for "truth" to exist, as distinct from the determinate product of physiological mechanisms, which may or may not coincide with real states of affairs. The belief that we have a immaterial soul means that there can be hope for our bodily resurrection, whereas if we were simply material stuff, death would obliterate us and "resurrection" could mean no more than the production of a *replica* of us, a replica that would have no real unity with our prior existence.

Pieper would agree with Zaleski that "it is not a matter of arriving at a philosophic faith in immortality by reasoned steps, and then complicating this faith by adding to it the rather more extravagant claim that there will be a resurrection."[43] The unity of body and soul precludes this procedure. Christian philosophers need not deny or bracket their Christian faith and its entailments, and they can show that the intellectual powers of human beings require an immaterial soul without thereby producing a "philosophic faith" or a hope grounded in philosophy alone. The point is simply that, as Zaleski observes, it is not "improper for Christians to maintain that by the natural light of reason and experience one may find grounds to hope for life beyond death."[44] In the face of dying, we need not choose either reductive materialism or a blind leap of faith.

The Eschatological Imagination

Notwithstanding the consolations of philosophy, we also need to be able to *imagine* life after death in order to live and die with a strong Christian hope. Here I heed Robert Jay Lifton's observation: "We live on images. As human beings we know our bodies and minds only through what we can imagine."[45] Although Lifton exaggerates—since the imagination is not the only portal of knowledge—it remains the case that when we lack the ability to imagine our bodies in a state other than our earthly one, our belief in life after death almost inevitably becomes what John Henry Newman describes as "notional" rather than "real."[46] Zaleski comments that "if we do not permit ourselves to form images of personal and collective existence after death, then we have no way of testing who we are or of sounding our deepest ideals."[47] Fortunately, for the Christian, the basis for this task of imaginative hope is the New Testament itself.

When Jesus Christ in the Gospels depicts life after death, he does so through a variety of images of rejoicing with God and the blessed (heaven) and despairing with the demons and the damned (hell). Certainly, none of these images can give us an adequate conception of what eternal life will be like. Regarding the new creation and the life of the blessed, Aidan Nichols rightly says that "faith cannot imagine this new world."[48] More sharply, however, Nichols's fellow British Dominican, Herbert McCabe, warns against all eschatological images: "Pictures of hell seem to have been largely projections of vindictive or sadistic fantasies. And pictures of heaven are just unspeakably boring. . . . We need to give up on the pictures."[49]

I disagree. The images revealed by Christ serve the purpose of concretizing believers' hope in the world to come.[50] My examples in what follows come from Robert Bellarmine's *The Art of Dying Well* (1619) and Francis de Sales's *Introduction to the Devout Life* (first edition 1609, final edition 1619).[51] Both Bellarmine and de Sales highlight the biblical images of eternal life, and they ground our hope in dying (and in living) upon the kingdom of Christ, which is already inaugurated in our earthly communion with Christ.[52] I aim to show that Zaleski is right that "imaginatively rich conceptions of the future life may coexist with a genuinely sacrificial willingness to face death."[53] With God's kingdom in view, we can surrender ourselves to God's care and live in hope rather than in "slavery" to the "fear of death" (Heb. 2:15).

Robert Bellarmine: Dying Well

In the first chapter of *The Art of Dying Well*, Bellarmine remarks that the fundamental aspect of this art is to *live* well. Living well requires loving God rather than loving the world through lust, greed, and arrogance. Drawing upon 1 Corinthians 7:29–31, where Paul urges the Corinthians to live in remembrance of the fact that "the present form of this world is passing away" (1 Cor. 7:31), Bellarmine calls upon Christians to live as Paul requires. Bellarmine encourages us to be "dead to world and live only for God," in such a way that dying should not worry us, just as it did not worry Paul.[54] He grants that "the goods of this world, wealth, honors, and pleasures, are not completely forbidden to Christians," by contrast to "the immoderate love of things of this world which is called by John the Apostle 'the lust of the flesh, the lust of the eyes, and the pride of life' (1 Jn 2:16)" (244). He insists, however, that living well should mean that our *desire* for worldly wealth, honors, and pleasures will lessen significantly, because our priority will consist in loving God and neighbor. Those who are not sufficiently detached from worldly things will love mammon over God and will desperately hold on to what we must in fact let go.

Bellarmine also warns against the temptation to cling now "to our sins, deceived by the empty hope that much of our life still lies ahead and that we will do serious penance in plenty of time" (248). He adds that even the desire to do good works on earth must not be allowed to take the place of desiring to meet Christ. While he cautions first and foremost against the "lust of the flesh" as an impediment to our desiring to meet Christ, he observes that "all concerns of this life, even the best and most necessary, should not so occupy our minds that they impede the primary consideration of meeting Christ, when he calls us by death" (250). Like Paul, we must prefer to "be away from the body and at home with the Lord," although "whether we are at home or away, we make it our aim to please him" (2 Cor. 5:8–9).

Bellarmine's purpose is to exhort us to live in the world in a God-centered and selfless way rather than in a self-centered and selfish way. As an example of the latter, he points out that "the error" of many wealthy persons is that they "think the wealth they possess is absolutely and unconditionally theirs," whereas in fact they "are masters of their possessions in comparison with other men, but in comparison with God they are not masters, but administrators, or stewards, or overseers" (254). With a great deal of care, Bellarmine works to show the biblical grounds for viewing ourselves as mere stewards of the goods that we have been given or have obtained for ourselves. He urges that what is at stake is nothing less than our eternal destiny. In light of Jesus's parable of Lazarus and the rich man, he observes that practices such as "lavishly clothing the body with clothes of exorbitant price, the vast daily expenditure on banquets, and the numerous servants and dogs, along with the merciless treatment of the poor man full of sores, is a sufficient cause for the rich man to be buried in hell and tortured by eternal flames" (257).[55] He goes on to insist that "wealth beyond our needs is not ours, but belongs to the poor" (260).

For Bellarmine, reflection on life after death should lead us to reassess how we should live now. We must begin to live now as we hope to live after death. With regard to the gospel's testimony to eternal life with God, Bellarmine recognizes that unfortunately "the crowd . . . believes in or values only what it sees" (261).[56] This state of affairs, in which we approach death empirically and conclude that upon the death of our body our "spirit will dissolve like empty air" (Wisd. of Sol. 2:3), continually plagues fallen humans, as we have already seen. Against such despair, Bellarmine directs our attention to divine revelation as conveyed by Scripture.

In the Gospels, Jesus Christ teaches us to value God above all and

39

value worldly goods as nothing by comparison. When we live in this grace-filled way, God will reward us, as Christ makes clear in Matthew 25 and elsewhere. Among the biblically attested fruits of charitable almsgiving, Bellarmine lists freeing the giver "from eternal death," meriting "eternal life," "destroying sins in both their guilt and their punishment," increasing joyful trust in God, forming "a disposition for the grace of justification" (see Acts 10:4), gaining the prayers of those whom one benefits, and even sometimes increasing our temporal goods.[57] Bellarmine here emphasizes the glory of receiving eternal life (heaven) and the pain of entering eternal death (hell). In his view, the divine revelation of hell as a possibility for us after death—a possibility that may become an actuality if we have lived selfishly—should be enough to persuade us to give alms now out of love of God and neighbor. He comments pithily that "if one should wish to argue that what is superfluous need not be given to the poor in strict justice, he still cannot deny that it should be done out of charity. However, it matters little whether one goes to hell from a lack of justice or from a lack of charity" (279).

When death draws near, that is, when we are no longer "in the prime of life" or when we have a serious disease, Bellarmine advises meditating in hope upon death (321).[58] Although death separates body and soul, neither body nor soul is without hope, since the soul is not "snuffed out" (as both true philosophy and Scripture teach) and since the body awaits the resurrection of the flesh (322).[59] The reason that we should meditate on death is that it is the decisive entrance into the life to come, which will be either a life of eternal communion with God or a life (if such it can be called) of everlasting alienation from God.[60] As Pieper emphasizes, dying therefore has great importance, rather than being merely life's final collapse. But since we do not know the hour of our death and our death may come unexpectedly, we need to prepare now by living well. For Bellarmine, living well involves giving gifts to "the poor of Jesus Christ," along with manifesting a desire for forgiveness and a focus on our eternal goal (330).[61] Here he cites Sirach 7:36, "In all you do, remember the end of your life, and then you will never sin" (324). Sirach 7 contains instruction to fear and love God, to give to the poor, and to care for those who are in mourning and who are sick.

Since divine revelation has given us some knowledge about what is to come after death, Bellarmine speaks about what is to come after death in vivid images. His account of hell's "darkness, tight confinement, and need" and imprisonment "in the deepest part of the earth" may be overly concrete, but these images mirror the concreteness of Christ's warnings about hell—warnings that each of us must hear as directed toward ourselves rather than toward our neighbor (331).[62] In Bellarmine's hands, as in Jesus's, these concrete images aim to lead us to change our lives. In this vein, Bellarmine warns about those who spend their wealth on themselves rather than on others: "In hell rich men will remember the abundant delights of their life on earth, whether in food or drink or in expensive clothes, or in hunting or fowling, in gardens and vineyards, in theaters and various games. But this memory will only increase their pain as they see themselves in hell lying naked, despised, wretchedly stripped of their goods and fortunes" (332).[63] To avoid this situation, rich men need to follow Christ here and now by faith and charitable almsgiving.

Next Bellarmine treats heaven, again emphasizing its concreteness, "the place, the time, and the manner" (334). He envisions heaven as the crowning place in the new creation of our present cosmos: "The place of the heavenly paradise is high above all the mountains of the earth, above all the elements, above all the stars" (334).[64] He speaks about its spaciousness, the ability of the blessed to "move from place to place in a moment," its pure air and lack of disease, its peace (335). Most importantly, he speaks about heavenly "honor, power, riches, and pleasures," and he argues that their counterparts in our earthly lives are mere shadows of the heavenly reality (336). The point is that those who are spending their lives sinning against God, themselves, and their neighbors in pursuit of honor, power, riches, and pleasures—and many are indeed doing so—should be pursuing the heavenly realities of such things rather than the mere fleeting shadows of such things in earthly life. As he puts it: "What, I ask, would a miser in this world not give in order to possess all riches? What would the lover of pleasure not give in order to attain all the pleasures he desires? What would an ambitious man not give to receive all the honors and dignities that he seeks?" (337).[65]

Rather than being a miser, a lover of pleasure, and ambitious in the worldly sense—rather than harming ourselves and others by our greed, lust, and hunger for power—we should use the same energy to seek the heavenly realities of true riches, pleasures, and honor by now loving God and neighbor. Like the biblical images of hell, then, the biblical images of heaven should stir up our desire to live charitably for others in the present life. The images of heaven and hell help us to know something of our destination after death, and thereby to resist with more than philosophical knowledge the hopeless notion that "hereafter we shall be as though we had never been" (Wisd. of Sol. 2:2).

Francis de Sales: Learning to Hope

In Francis de Sales's classic *Introduction to the Devout Life,* he speaks directly to Christians who have not "quitted the world" but rather "are living in towns, at court, in their own households, and whose calling obliges them to a social life."[66] Much like Ignatius of Loyola, de Sales devises a set of meditations or paths of contemplation that believers may profitably follow. De Sales's First Meditation begins with creation. He urges us to consider that God created us out of nothing because of his goodness. In humility, we should place ourselves in the presence of this glorious God, absent whom we would not exist and who has given us the ability to be united to him eternally. This meditation upon our radical contingency and upon God's loving creative and salvific action sets the stage for consideration of the realities of human life in the meditations that follow.

In his Fifth Meditation, then, de Sales turns to the mystery of death. He asks us to grasp fully that on the day of our death, which will likely come unexpectedly, "the world is at an end as far as you are concerned" (25). By appreciating that human history will continue without him or her, the dying person has the opportunity to discover what the truly lasting realities are and what the incomparably lesser passing shadows are. De Sales encourages us to place ourselves in the position of the dying person, and to reflect upon whether we are cleaving to things that are coming quickly to an end. If we *are* cleaving to passing things, we must realize that cleaving to passing things is irrational, given that we are mortal. De Sales exhorts us to embrace the detachment that consists in cleaving to God above the things of this world.[67]

In the Sixth Meditation, de Sales then places us imaginatively at the scene of the final judgment, in which all the things we have done will be made manifest for all to see, and in which the sheep will be separated from the goats. Having made clear to us that we cannot hide anything from God and that even our neighbors will come to know all that we have done and all that we truly are, de Sales shows that we will ultimately have nothing of value if we do not love. The only thing that will separate the sheep from the goats is that the sheep rejoice in divine love, whereas the goats repel it.

On this basis, grounded in the divine mercy and love manifested by creation ex nihilo and by Christ, the Seventh Meditation confronts us with the possibility of hell. De Sales urges us to think of how our senses, with which we now pleasurably practice carnal vices, will in hell be overwhelmed by utmost misery. The turning of our carnal vices into torments should strike home, since we already experience a foretaste of this in the present life.[68] De Sales compares hell to being sick or having the irritation of an insect bite everlastingly; we will never be comfortable again. In light of such concrete sense images, he points out that our greatest misery in hell will be the loss of that for which we were created and that which fulfills our deepest yearnings, namely intimate sharing in the infinite goodness of God. He calls us to conceive of "the privation and pain of loss of God's Glory" (29). If we think about it, we truly cannot bear to lose God.

De Sales's Eighth Meditation focuses on heaven. He develops superb images drawn from the beauty of creation to describe the glory of our heavenly country. Thus he invites us to imagine "a lovely calm night," with the sky filled with stars, and also to imagine "the utmost beauty of a glorious summer's day" (30). As the new creation, heaven will have such beauty and far, far more. We can easily conceive of the wonder and awe we feel under a starry night and of the joy and strength we feel on a beautiful summer day, and so these images calm our fear of undergoing the change from this life to the next. De Sales similarly invites us to consider the "beauty and perfection of the countless inhabitants of that blessed country," inhabitants who will float in an atmosphere of love, and who will sing God's praises while God generously pours forth blessings (31). We will be plunged deeply and fully in the Spirit of God. Just as we now breathe in air so as to sustain our life, we will be sustained most perfectly in eternal life by God himself, who will be intimately and utterly present to us. Hope for the beauty and blessedness of heaven should push us to undertake acts of self-giving love in the present life, through which we are configured to Christ's love and perfected as adopted children in the Son.

De Sales concludes these meditations on the last things by means of a Ninth Meditation on the choice between heaven and hell that we are now making, whether we know it or not. He suggests that we should imagine ourselves to be now literally choosing between the goods of heaven and the torments of hell. Which will we choose? Jesus himself is lovingly and mercifully begging us to share in his love now and forever, as are the saints. They are experiencing everlasting happiness, joy, and peace; why do we not choose to join them? Here de Sales is pressing us with the best kind of peer pressure. We must simply follow the path to which Jesus and the saints direct us. De Sales portrays the saints as stirring up our hope and courage: "Press on boldly, dear friend. . . . Whoso will ponder well the path by which we came hither, will discover that we attained to these present delights by sweeter joys than any this world can give" (33). These joys are found in faith-filled works of love, as shown by de Sales's insistence that we imitate the saints by laying down our lives for others out of imitation of Christ. For de Sales, this need not mean that we must do anything especially unusual or obviously heroic. He has in mind simple things that normal people do, such as "husbands and wives living in all tender love and mutual cherishing," committed to Christ's "holy laws and ordinances" (34–35).

But has de Sales merely replaced fear of annihilation with fear of hell, given that we can reject the mercy of Christ? Here de Sales counsels us to remember "the Infinite Mercy of His [God's] Heavenly Goodness" (37). When we come to know Christ, we will realize that he is constantly seeking our "best happiness," and we will understand how great is the foundation of our hope (81). De Sales proclaims in this regard that "God moves us, entering our hearts by His Fatherly love and care, and awakening, exciting, urging, and attracting them to goodness, to Heavenly Love, to good resolutions, in short, to whatever tends to our eternal welfare" (73). The only way that we can go to hell is if we refuse all of God's love and care and literally insist upon hell as what we want. There is no reason to abandon hope simply because hell is a possibility, since hope is rooted in the strength of the God who loves us powerfully.

Jean-Pierre de Caussade: God Wants Only True Life for Us

As de Sales perceives, breaking free from the despairing temptation expressed in Wisdom of Solomon 2:1–5 ultimately requires not only philosophical reasoning and the illumination of the afterlife by divine revelation, but also a willingness to hope and trust in God's loving care. Jean-Pierre de Caussade, a Jesuit who lived a century after de Sales and was deeply influenced by de Sales's writings, therefore urges us to make "the most direct and wholehearted surrender to God's will."[69] In this way can we experience God's active love in the full; otherwise we will always be at least slightly distrustful and turned away from what God is really doing in our life. For de Caussade, the great treasure of the gospel is available to every person who is willing to "submit to God's will in all that they have to do or suffer" (24, 26).[70] This submission opens the door to a true experience of God, freed of the barriers that we set up against him.

When this counsel is applied to dying, it means that we must accept our illness—even while seeking appropriate medical care—and be at peace with the idea that God may have appointed this time for us to die. As Allen Verhey puts it, then, we must be "cured of [our] conceit of independence."[71] We need to be spiritually detached from our own earthly plans and from the earthly goods that God grants us to enjoy, since God does not will that these earthly goods should be enjoyed by us forever. De Caussade instructs us to learn to "believe with firm faith and resolute confidence that what it [God's will] assigns for each moment is best," rather than "seeking for other things or try[ing] to fathom the links between events and God's designs" (28).[72] This does not mean that we should avoid medicine that improves our health, since medicine obviously belongs to God's overall plan. It means simply that we not rebel against God in despair when we discover that a particular earthly condition—in this case, mortal illness—is now ours.

From this perspective, we must realize that even though death is a punishment and not good in itself, "all things owe their nature, their reality and their strength to the will of God, which adapts them so they benefit our souls" (28). Even such a miserable thing as dying can be to our benefit, and indeed will be to our benefit if we recognize our situation and embrace God's will for us in hope, whether his will turns out to be further earthly life or the full dregs of the cup of dying. De Caussade shows that holiness does not involve accepting what seems good to us while rebelling against what seems detrimental to us (30). We may certainly experience and express a natural sorrow at having to suffer and depart from our friends, but our rational will should be focused upon trust-filled acts of hope, love, mercy, and repentance until death comes.[73]

The basic insight here comes from Paul: "For I am convinced that neither death, nor life, nor angels, nor rulers, nor things present, nor things to come, nor powers, nor height, nor depth, nor anything else in all creation, will be able to separate us from the love of God in Christ Jesus our Lord" (Rom. 8:38–39). Undeniably, we will be separated from God if we end up alienated forever from God in hell. De Caussade makes clear, however, that we can only be separated if we refuse to accept what God bountifully wishes to give us. Again, this does not mean accepting evils that can be avoided; de Caussade emphasizes that we must not "in any way" seek out trouble for ourselves, and we should avoid suffering and should heal the suffering of others when we can (26). But de Caussade's path does mean accepting troubles, such as illness and dying, when they come our way, rather than rising up against God for taking away all the finite goods that we treasure on earth.[74]

We must allow ourselves obediently to be separated from the finite goods that we value so much, without despairing. Like Job, we must place our hope solely in God and say: "Naked I came from my mother's womb, and naked shall I return there; the LORD gave, and the LORD has taken away; blessed be the name of the LORD" (Job 1:21). Pope Emeritus Benedict, strongly affirming his trust that "the loving God cannot forsake me," was asked by an interviewer what he would say when he meets the Lord after death.[75] His response, which we must imitate, was to place his hope in God's mercy in Christ: "I will plead with him to show leniency towards my wretchedness."[76]

Conclusion

In this chapter I have investigated resources for dying in hope: philosophical recognition that God exists and that we possess a spiritual soul that serves to bridge death and bodily resurrection; divine revelation's provision for imaginative anticipation of everlasting life in Christ; and an absolute reliance upon God's love for us. Katy Butler points out that for the teachers of the *ars moriendi*, dying was not expected to be a merely passive or serene process. Rather, strong hope is necessary because the dying person can suffer the temptation to despair. Since this is so, the deathbed is not merely a place of bodily corruption and humiliation—though it is that—but also and primarily a "battleground . . . for control of the soul," a "spiritual ordeal," and thus a place where the dying person is fighting against common "temptations to sin: wavering faith, despair, impatience, regret for past misdeeds, reluctance to say good-bye, and . . . fear of death and hell."[77] Pressed by such temptations due to the rending apart of earthly bodily life, the dying person needs hope.

In hope, Christians do not despair of being united to God forever as his adoptive children, because we trust not in our own power but in God's.[78] At the same time, such hope can be severely weakened by our contemporary materialist philosophical culture, in which educated people generally assume that we are nothing but bodies and that death destroys all that we are. As noted above, Pieper takes this contemporary situation to be an opportunity, in the sense that the encounter with death—either the death of a loved one or our own approaching death—can provide the salutary shock needed to get true philosophical questioning started in contemporary persons. Pieper shows the path by which philosophical reasoning leads us to recognize the reality of spiritual realities, God and the soul. This path strengthens hope when we are faced with potential despair due to the threat of dying. Bellarmine and de Sales help us to see that imagining the eschatological state can strengthen us, in hope, to choose to live for God in our dying. Their images about heavenly life are simple, intensely personal images that accessibly express the fulfillment of our yearning for perfect communion with God and for a peace-filled, serene, and perfected creation, in which God "will wipe away every tear from their eyes. Death will be no more; mourning and crying and pain will be no more" (Rev. 21:4). In turn, the concrete images of hell show the misery of cleaving to the things of this world rather than receiving them with gratitude as sheer gift.[79]

When we refuse to receive the things of this world as God's gift, we inevitably end up—in the words of Paul Griffiths—attempting to "expropriate" or "dominate" them, "to usurp the place of the Lord" with regard to them.[80] Since only God can be God, and since no matter what we do the things of the world really are passing away and ultimately out of our control, our attempts at domination succeed only in leading us to despair. When our minds are unable to think beyond the empirical, so that spiritual fulfillment after death seems impossible or deeply implausible, we inevitably follow the despairing path sketched by sinners in the Wisdom of Solomon: "Come, therefore, let us enjoy the good things that exist, and make use of the creation to the full as in youth. Let us take our fill of costly wine and perfumes, and let no flower of spring pass us by. . . . Let our might be our law of right, for what is weak proves itself to be useless" (2:6–7, 11).

Hope avoids this despairing path. Drawing upon the *Crafte and Knowledge for to Dye Well* (1490), Verhey notes, "The pain and suffering of the deathbed are especially dreadful to those who are not ready to die, or who die against their will."[81] When one supposes that death means annihilation and one understands what this truly means, it is impossible *not* to die against one's will. A dying person can want his or her suffering to end, but, as Augustine shows, a dying person cannot truly want to have literally no future, everlasting nonexistence, eternal separation and isolation.[82] Since annihilation causes a great loss due to its everlasting lack of interpersonal communion, fear of annihilation is not egotistical. Such fear simply means that one wishes for interpersonal communion to continue rather than to be broken off forever.[83] Since this is so, our "great hope can only be God, who encompasses the whole of reality and who can bestow upon us what we, by ourselves, cannot attain."[84] Thus, as Pope Benedict XVI says, "God is the

47

foundation of hope: not any god, but the God who has a human face and who has loved us to the end, each one of us and humanity in its entirety."[85]

Mother Teresa wrote to a dying person, "Keep the joy of loving Jesus in your heart and look forward to meeting Him face to face."[86] As we know from personal experience, however, "the mind that is set on the flesh is hostile to God" (Rom. 8:7). It follows that our hope is fragile, and we need help from both wings—faith and reason—in lifting our minds to God. By lifting our minds to spiritual realities, philosophical reasoning can strengthen our faith and assist us to "hope for what we do not see" (Rom. 8:25). When our minds are lifted to God in Christ as the one "who has loved us to the end" and who will not abandon us, we can truly hope in his power to unite us to himself—not merely as individuals but in union with his whole people, by the power of his Holy Spirit. Strengthened in hope, we can "be patient in suffering" (Rom. 12:12) and can reach the triune God, with his saints in Christ's body, through the arduous path of dying.

CHAPTER 3

FAITH

Jesus and What Dying Persons Want

The Second Vatican Council's Pastoral Constitution on the Church in the Modern World, *Gaudium et Spes*, teaches that "the dignity of man rests above all on the fact that he is called to communion with God" (§19), so that "without hope of eternal life his dignity is deeply wounded" (§21).[1] Yet death puts the whole human person in doubt; it compels us to confront the possibility of "the utter ruin and total loss" of our personality (§18). In this context of anxiety and profound yearning, says *Gaudium et Spes*, the gospel proclaims that "God has created man in view of a blessed destiny that lies beyond the limits of his sad state on earth" (§18). *Gaudium et Spes* concludes with regard to death: "It is therefore through Christ, and in Christ, that light is thrown on the riddle of suffering and death which, apart from his Gospel, overwhelms us" (§22). On this view, only faith in Christ makes death bearable, since Christ is "the focal point of the desires of history and civilization" and "the fulfilment of all aspirations" (§45).

Is it really true, however, that only faith in Christ fulfills "all aspirations" and answers our fears and hopes about death? For *Gaudium et Spes*, Christ answers our *fears* because, by his resurrection, he shows us that death is not the end of our personal and communal existence. Christ answers our *hopes* and fulfills our *aspirations* because we yearn for the deepest possible communion with God and one another. We do not want everlasting existence of the kind we have now, marked by toil, suffering, and boredom. We want the beatitude that is found only in God. Christ invites us into a real sharing in the divine life, not an extrinsic sharing in an aloof God, but a real adoption through which we are united to the Father in the Son by the Holy Spirit. Moreover, we will share in God's beatitude not as creatures

49

stripped of our bodies or denuded of the created order that surrounds us, but rather as resurrected and glorified humans in a new creation in which everything is governed by love and by the immediate presence of God.

In this chapter I ask whether *Gaudium et Spes* is correct that faith in Christ gives dying persons what they want. Or do dying persons have hopes and aspirations that faith in Christ does not address or cannot fulfill? Moreover, do dying persons need faith in *Christ*, or does belief in a "higher power" suffice to meet the desires of dying persons? Obviously, dying persons do not desire to experience what Raymond Tallis calls the "nightmare . . . of entering the judgement" of a *merciless* deity who knows our innermost hearts.[2] But the question is whether *Gaudium et Spes* is right that only faith in Christ, who is filled with mercy and calls us to become adoptive children of God, fulfills all the true desires of dying persons.

In what follows, I first seek to ascertain what dying persons want, according to authors who have talked at length with many dying persons. I focus on Kathleen Dowling Singh's *Grace in Dying*, which arises from her experience as a longtime hospice volunteer with an interest in New Age spirituality, and David Kuhl's *What Dying People Want*, which conveys his extensive research as a medical doctor with an expertise in palliative care for the dying. Advocating a spirituality that many Christians find very attractive (and whose parallels in Neoplatonic thought she recognizes), Singh argues that most dying people eventually realize their need to embrace dying as a welcome release of the spirit from the chains of the body.[3] In her view, dying consists in the passage of the ego back to the One: dying should not be feared, since in fact earthly existence involves us in an illusory project of self-identity, an estrangement from the all-encompassing One. Kuhl's book, by contrast, hones in upon the process of reviewing one's life and upon achieving a sense of completion and peace prior to dying, largely through reconciliation with others. For Kuhl, dying is something to be feared, and yet dying people can use the dying process as an opportunity for bringing closure and peace to their lives. Both Singh and Kuhl encourage dying persons to have recourse to a divine being during their final days, but they do not identify this divine being as Christ, nor do they advocate faith in Christ. Singh argues that many names for the divine being are equivalent: "Holy Spirit, Ground of Being, Unity, Source, Mind, Love, Light, Noumenon, *ohr ain zof*, Tao, Dharmadhatu, Sunyata, Brahman, the Void, Allah, the One."[4] Kuhl urges his readers to take an interest in "God, Buddha, Allah, Shiva, Brahman, Vishnu, or any higher power."[5]

After surveying these two books, I compare the desires that they attribute to dying persons with what the New Testament tells us about Christ's redemption of persons doomed to die. I find that faith in Christ does indeed fulfill the desires that Singh and Kuhl ascribe to dying persons, with one exception: Singh and Kuhl do not portray dying persons as aspiring to reconciliation with God. Instead, Singh and Kuhl suggest that dying persons today conceive of God (when they believe in a God) as a fount of love who does not judge and therefore does not need to be reconciled with. Carol Zaleski similarly points out that "those who flock to buy books on near-death experience want to hear that they will not be robbed of the satisfaction of continued personal existence; they do not want to hear that they will be held accountable for sins."[6] In the New Testament, by contrast, the relationship of people to God always possesses dramatic overtones; faith in Christ involves repentance and conversion. If contemporary dying persons *do not want* to repent and be reconciled to God on their deathbeds, then this would be an aspiration that faith in Christ cannot fulfill. Dying persons who seek to avoid the drama of reconciliation with God would be better served by a "generic spirituality" than by faith in Christ.[7]

Since communion with the living God requires self-giving love, we must in fact turn to God in repentance and love, even and especially on our deathbeds. Either some dying persons no longer recognize this true need, or Singh and Kuhl have minimized it in their deathbed reporting. Just as reconciliation with our relatives and friends requires work, so does reconciliation with God, which belongs to our perseverance in faith. Faith in Christ fulfills all the hopes and desires of dying persons, but always within the dramatic struggle depicted by Paul when he exhorts us "to withstand on that evil day" by "[taking] the shield of faith, with which you will be able to quench all the flaming arrows of the evil one" (Eph. 6:13, 16). My argument, therefore, will be that faith in Christ does indeed fulfill all the desires of dying persons, once the need for reconciliation with God is appreciated.

Singh and Kuhl: The Desires of Dying Persons

Kathleen Dowling Singh: Death as a Remerging with Our Essential Nature

In *The Grace in Dying*, Kathleen Dowling Singh argues both that dying will not harm us by negating our being, and that the process of dying can help us by transforming us spiritually. Through this spiritual transformation,

Singh holds, we become attuned to "realms beyond this one of bodies and words" and find ourselves "forever connected" in the Spirit with our loved ones.[8] She explains that the process of dying involves a "natural enlightenment" and a "coming home to our true self," because in dying "we gradually open to deeper levels of our being" and "we re-merge with the Ground of Being from which we once emerged" (2).[9] On the basis of her experience as a hospice worker, she argues that there is "an apparently universal process of transformation inherent in death itself," which she calls our "deathright" that draws us deeply into the most profound "dimensions of Spirit" (2).[10] Singh's preference when describing these higher spiritual dimensions is to name them as "the Clear Light or the Ground of Being" (6).

In what Singh calls the Nearing Death Experience,[11] dying persons gradually relax or let go of attachment to the struggles of the world, and with positive energy (rather than negative despair) turn inward toward the center of being. As we are dying, she says, our experience takes on a "liminal" or "threshold" quality. In this sacred interiority, in which the dying person is opened to love, the dying person rests between the earthly world and other "dimensions of being beyond our normal consciousness, experience, and identity" (9). Consciousness and identity take on a "transpersonal" rather than merely "personal" character. The spirit prepares to leave the body with a rush of energy. Singh emphasizes the overcoming of separation: "Nearing death, people begin to manifest the *quality of merging*. There is an end of separation, a cessation of duality. This suggests that in finally coming face-to-face with the Source of All Being, we recognize that we are looking in a mirror" (11).[12]

Death, Singh emphasizes, is no tragedy. There is anguish, certainly, but the Nearing Death Experience exhibits far more "grace and warmth and Spirit" (14). In light of the Hindu practice of disciplining the self for renunciation, she argues that the moments when we are near to dying draw us into this transformative discipline. We enjoy nothing less than "a natural and conscious remerging with the Ground of Being from which we have all once unconsciously emerged. A transformation occurs from the point of terror at the contemplation of the loss of our separate, personal self to a merging into the deep, nurturing, ineffable experience of Unity" (15). This happens not because we consciously desire transcendence prior to our experience of dying; rather, it simply happens. Dying becomes not only bearable but also deeply positive for those who are near to it. We enter into "Unity Consciousness," transcending our egoistic limits, and we realize our "identity with the Ground of Being" (16). In the process of dying, normal persons attain what the great saints and mystics of all religions find through prayer and meditative practices, namely a "psychospiritual transformation" or overcoming of the separatedness of the ego that enables the human person "to realize Spirit" (18).

What, in Singh's view, is the "Ground of Being" or "Spirit"? It is "our Original and Essential Nature" (21). It is our origin and our home; it is what we mean by "God" (see 22). Singh argues that all religious language, all naming of "God," has the same Ground of Being in view: "We speak in equal measure and cadence of Holy Spirit, Ground of Being, Unity, Source, Mind, Love, Light, Noumenon, *ohr ain zof*, Tao, Dharmadhatu, Sunyata, Brahman, the Void, Allah, the One" (22). None of these names, of course, captures the inexpressible reality of the Ground of Being, but the Ground of Being is knowable empirically by all who skillfully practice prayer. The Ground of Being itself is "undifferentiated," and out of the Ground of Being emerge "patterns of excitation, events, and beings" (23). Dying helps us to return to identity with that from which we have emerged. Although we came forth from the Ground of Being unconsciously, we return consciously. In this return, we relinquish our concentration upon the ego and expand beyond our "personal mind, body, and emotions," so that we rise above "thoughts of an 'I'" (25). We discover the illusory character of our carefully constructed "I" as a separate field of private consciousness, and we discover the inadequacy of mind-body dualism (41).

For Singh, terminal illness breaks down the walls of the self that we have constructed. We experience this event first as painful; indeed, in the face of death, we cower in anguish, because "we have forgotten that *the task at mid-life is to know ourselves to be the consciousness that is using our body as a vehicle of Spirit's experience-in-form*"; and when we discover that we are truly dying, we lack a way to distinguish the "vehicle" (our dying body) from "the consciousness" (54). At first, we assume that the loss of our "separate sense of sense" will mean annihilation (57). Singh well describes the incredible terror and rage experienced by people who believe they are facing annihilation. The agony is especially severe in those who are compelled to die in young or middle age, and who therefore feel that they were owed more life. To get past this stage, we must surrender our ego, and the dying process assists with that.

The main point, says Singh, is to discover that Consciousness is not fundamentally divided, but rather is One and Whole. When we have come through disillusionment (due to the futility of the ego's identity project) and despair (due to awareness of our emptiness), we will surrender our ego and thereby begin the transformative return to the Ground of Being. The stultifying pressures of all sorts of tensions are released, and we become more deeply mindful of the radiance of Reality and find that consciousness consists in free-flowing love. All dualisms begin to dissolve as we appreciate that Consciousness is one and undying. We realize that we are utterly one with God, since all Consciousness (Spirit) is one. The result is that "our sense of identity envelops the All" (85). We realize that death leads us not into annihilation, but into the joyful state of becoming, once more, the conscious All.

Singh describes this transformative movement as one of "grace," overcoming the "fault in our nature" that consists in "believing self to be separate from the Ground of Being" (89). This fault in our nature leads us inexorably into many miseries and tragedies, until finally the illusion of the self is cracked and grace leads us to return to the Ground of Being. Terminal illness, with its extraordinary anguish and loss, forces us to let go and thereby, generally to our surprise, to discover anew our essential nature. Rather than clinging to a hoped-for earthly future, we are forced to live entirely in the present and thereby mindfully to encounter Presence. Far from being a surd, then, dying consists in a return to sanity, a return to health from the dualisms that would otherwise continue to consume us.

Although Singh appreciates the value of the dying person's reviewing his or her life for the purposes of "psychological closure" with the goal of moving "beyond the mental ego," she cautions that the ego can get stuck here and refuse to surrender itself (89). We must move beyond "life review" to the stage of "life resolution," which she defines as "a stance of the being where accounts are not balanced but deleted, where problems are not solved, but dissolved" (165).[13] We must bid a definitive goodbye to the "identity project," so that our constructed boundaries of self do not prevent us from making our journey of self-surrender and return to the Center.

Singh holds that part of good dying is the release of guilt. She describes a certain kind of remorse as part of the process of "life resolution." Remorse helps to dissolve any bitterness, shame, and anger at ourselves that we might feel. Singh reports working on a dying man's energy field (without touching him), focusing on his loins because they were the locus of many of his misdeeds. Without him doing anything, her exertions upon his energy field were able to help dissipate his "regrets, self-recriminations, and feelings of guilt" (201).

Singh admits that the dying process involves some emotional pain, since it involves letting go of the ego, which we often do only at the stage of despair. In surrendering ourselves, we encounter the turbulent power of the Ground of Being. At first it may be disturbing, but as we near death, says Singh, "consciousness begins, a bit, to transcend the separate self. During this particular phase of transformation, the transpersonal realms are experienced with less turbulence, with increasing calm" (206). Dying itself, then, becomes a joyful fulfillment of our worldly journey from self-enclosed ego to transpersonal Ground. We become our "Essential and Original Nature"; we become identical with the Absolute. Singh observes, invoking Christian Scripture, "The self is at deep and great peace in its integration with the Ground of Being. This is the peace which, literally, passeth understanding" (211).[14] Love, the Ground of Being, pours into us and pours through us. All dualisms dissolve, and we attain to Unity Consciousness. For Singh, therefore, "death is not an outrage," nor is death "humanity's implacable enemy" (169; *pace* 1 Cor. 15:26, "The last enemy to be destroyed is death," and Rev. 20:14, "Then Death and Hades were thrown into the lake of fire").[15]

David Kuhl: What Dying People Want

In *What Dying People Want*, David Kuhl focuses on the specific things that dying persons talk about and seem to want. He considers that "dying, like living, presents opportunity for personal growth and development," although he also states, "People generally die as they have lived."[16] He begins his book with the moment in which the doctor gives the patient a terminal diagnosis. He then explores "death anxiety," which involves the fear of how one's death will affect one's loved ones, the fear of annihilation, and the fear of possible sufferings during the dying process and after death (purgatory or hell). The fear of annihilation, he observes, is particularly strong; he terms it "a universal anxiety" in the sense that "it is an emotion without boundaries, like floating in a limitless ocean, no horizon in sight" (20). He discusses the situation of those whose suffering is so strong that they wish to commit suicide, and he argues that the ongoing effort to improve palliative care provides a better answer for dying persons than does euthanasia.[17]

In response to the fears expressed by dying persons, Kuhl states that a positive first step can be to undertake a "life review," in which one looks back over one's life and also asks oneself what activities are the most important during the remaining time of one's life (31–32).[18] He devotes a chapter to the palliative control of physical pain, which needs to be taken care of so that the dying person can address emotional issues.[19] He describes a situation in which a woman, freed of physical pain by opioids, confesses to her daughter that she (the mother) felt as though she had been a bad mother. The daughter is then able to assure her that the opposite was the case. In another chapter, Kuhl explores the power of touch to remove pain, and he also discusses the value of weekly group sessions for those facing the same illness. He recommends holding a family meeting to evaluate treatment options and as a venue for the dying person to express what he or she wishes to do in the next weeks or months. Such a meeting can also provide an opportunity for talking about the journey toward death.

In his chapter on the "life review," Kuhl draws upon the work of gerontologists who have worked on autobiography for older adults. The "life review" takes its structure from the "major branching points" that one identifies in one's life, beginning with one's family of origin and continuing through the major transition events of one's life (142). He advises discussing such things as family, money and career, health and body image, experiences of other people's deaths (including potential guilt feelings), and one's own ideas about dying. He devotes sections of the life review to one's aspirations and goals, and to one's understanding of the meaning of life and of "spirituality" or religious experience.[20] Further sections include one's loves and hates, sexual identity, sex roles, and sexual experiences.

In setting forth what a life review should include, Kuhl alternates between telling bits and pieces of one woman's story and listing the questions that one might ask oneself in each section of the life review. He describes the result of the "life review" for the woman whose story he has been telling: "For Florence, her life review resulted in the acknowledgment of her deep-seated grief over the death of her daughter, her husband, and the loss of relationships with her surviving children" (156). In addition to this grief, he notes that Florence's life review recalled her experience of "some kind of higher power" in reconnecting with her mother before her mother's death, and her pride in her career (156). Before she died, Florence asked Kuhl to arrange a way that she and her three children could meet and talk about the past, but Florence died before the meeting could be arranged.

During the process of conducting a life review, Kuhl cautions, "unexpected emotions will likely be aroused—despair, hopelessness, anger, rage, sadness" (161). He thinks therefore that when one is doing one's life review, it is good to have present a trusted family member or friend with whom one can share everything and who will listen patiently. Kuhl observes that the dying persons who told him their stories, and who thereby reviewed their lives, said that they felt better after doing so. In Kuhl's opinion, a life review enables the dying person to process emotions and past hurts in such a way as to open the dying person to reconciliation and intimacy in the present, prior to dying.

After the chapter on the life review, Kuhl's next chapter is on truth telling, and it begins with a confession he received from a dying man named Ron, who confessed to Kuhl (many years after the events) that he had watched his fellow gang members while they stole and raped. Kuhl remarks that "the dominant feature of Ron's story was an overwhelming sense of having lived a duplicitous life. . . . For three decades, Ron's secrets held him hostage, isolating him from others" (171). Likewise, when a dying woman named Frieda did her life review with Kuhl, she confessed great guilt over a number of past misdeeds, although she refused to specify what those misdeeds were. Kuhl reflects upon how the diagnosis of terminal illness leads people to confront guilt, and he describes a process of recognition, remorse, recompense, and release. He emphasizes that a crucial part of one's life review must be exposing areas where one still feels guilt, confessing what one has done, and undertaking the process of recompense in order to attain release. Otherwise, the person will die in unresolved emotional distress (see 179).[21] Emotionally, we need to experience forgiveness, to be forgiven and to forgive ourselves.[22]

Kuhl defines forgiveness as making whole what would otherwise remain broken. Forgiveness does not mean condoning bad behavior. Rather, the process of forgiveness begins by acknowledging how hurtful the behavior was. We have to acknowledge our emotional suffering and be truthful about what really happened. We must release our real feelings. Only then can we express remorse truthfully. As Kuhl notes, "The process of self-forgiveness is similar to that of forgiving another person" (184). We must acknowledge the truth about what we have done and take responsibility for our actions. Once we have done that, we can have a chance of forgiving ourselves for what we have done. Although we usually cannot undo what has been done, we can offer some kind of recompense to the one(s) we have harmed. Kuhl explains, "When remorse is genuine—whether real or symbolic—you will experience release" (187).

Kuhl adds that it is especially important that the dying person be able to talk honestly and openly to his or her family members prior to dying, and that careful listening be practiced both by the family members and by the dying person.[23] Alienation from family members especially weighs upon dying persons. Furthermore, as Kuhl observes, family and friends often do not wish to admit that their relative or friend is dying; in front of the dying person, they refuse to speak about that person as dying. This dishonesty makes it impossible for the dying person to reach closure in his or her relationships with family and friends. Without such conversations, the dying person comes to feel deeply isolated in what he or she is going through, and the dying person yearns for conversations that reflect the reality that his or her life is ending.

In addition to the need for confession, forgiveness, and honest conversation, another topic that flows from "life review" is loving and being loved. Dying persons suffer not only emotional pain from guilt, but also emotional pain from loneliness. Kuhl observes, "People who know they have a terminal illness speak of a desire to be in a relationship" (203). This desire includes the desire to mend broken relationships.[24] It also involves the desire to belong fully to a group or family. Kuhl identifies our psychological needs as including "the sense of self and the relationship to others" and our spiritual needs as including "the awareness of and connection to a source of power or strength bigger than oneself" (204).[25]

In dying, we can remove the masks, whether personal or professional, that obscured the true core of our being. Kuhl argues that "to understand one's truth and accept it is to die healed—not cured, but healed" (232). In this context, Kuhl also explores shame and its debilitating form, which he calls "toxic shame," a feeling of worthlessness (237). In dying, we have a choice between despair (dying with deep psychological wounds) and integrity (acknowledging and overcoming the wounds). Those who choose the latter path turn the process of dying into a positive event in their lives.

The final chapter of Kuhl's book has to do with spiritual beliefs. Kuhl explains that in the dying process, as people explored their interior life more deeply, some of them encountered "a stranger within them waiting to be introduced, recognized, and acknowledged as essential to their well-being and wholeness," such that they "felt united with a higher power" (254–55). For some of the dying persons Kuhl interviewed, the slogan "Let go and let God," popularized by Alcoholics Anonymous, well described their dying. Kuhl describes one dying woman who came to have deeper insight into herself and "ultimately to trust in a higher power for her own sense of fulfillment and for the well-being of her daughters" (259). Kuhl encourages his readers to ask themselves how they would define "spirituality" and what it might mean to meet "God."

For one of Kuhl's interviewees, "forgiving himself and others was a key element of spirituality, as was addressing the issue of God"—namely by prayer (262).[26] Assured that God exists and that God loves him, this particular dying person lost his fear of death and was able to appreciate the world as a beautiful gift. Kuhl also finds some agnostics turning, as their process of dying progresses, toward God. Other interviewees who are atheists speak of the importance of a moral code. Summarizing the journey of spiritual discovery that some of his interviewees underwent—and connecting this journey with the dying person's "life review"—Kuhl states: "Because the higher power offers forgiveness and love without judgment, the individual is also able to forgive herself and others for all transgressions. In the strength of this higher power, one experiences healing and a deep connection with self and others" (270).[27] Some dying persons feel a unity with nature and a connection to the higher power, so that they are "filled with joy, a sense of purpose, and all fear of death vanishes" (270). Kuhl notes that for his oldest sister, who was dying during the time he completed his book, "faith was a tremendous source of strength" in the latter stages of the dying process (277). He therefore encourages his readers to ask questions about the meaning of life, life after death, reincarnation, and the significance of "God, Buddha, Allah, Shiva, Brahman, Vishnu, or any higher power" (271).

Evaluation: Jesus's Fulfillment of the Desires of Dying Persons

Although I disagree with her theology (and anthropology), Singh shows how much humans desire existence, communion, and unity. We want a living union with our Creator, a union that also brings about the union of humans with one another. Similarly, Kuhl's emphasis on our need for confession of guilt, for being forgiven and forgiving others, and for being loved and loving others is of great value in understanding human dying. As Kuhl underscores, we wish to belong fully to a family or a people and to possess an attitude of trust that God loves us.

In all of these ways, faith in Jesus Christ does fulfill our deepest hopes. Christ shows that God cares for us, not only individually but as Christ's body and people. In Christ, who reconciles us with God and one another, we find forgiveness and love. Christ's resurrection from the dead shows us that the grave does not annihilate us. The communion with the Trinity that Christ promises his followers shows us that we are destined to be one family as adopted children of God, enjoying an inexhaustibly glorious communion. The entire New Testament powerfully attests to the reality of Christ's resurrection.[28]

Kuhl's emphasis on repentance, recompense, forgiveness, and love accord notably with Jesus's teaching and actions. Jesus's parables call repeatedly for repentance as the first act of the disciple, alongside faith. In the parable of the prodigal son, for example, the father has never stopped loving his prodigal son, but the son, having wrecked his life by separating himself from his father, says to himself with great repentance: "I will get up and go to my father, and I will say to him, 'Father, I have sinned against heaven and before you; I am no longer worthy to be called your son; treat me like one of your hired hands" (Luke 15:18–19). Since sin wounds relationships and produces a debt in the order of justice, Jesus offers "recompense" for sin, a recompense whose purpose is to establish our everlasting communion with our merciful and loving God. As Jesus approaches his death, he states that he "came not to be served but to serve, and to give his life a ransom for many" (Mark 10:45). This "ransom" pays the recompense for all sins. With particular clarity, Ephesians emphasizes the unity of recompense, mercy, and love in Christ's death on the cross, by which God reconciles his entire family to himself (see Eph. 1:7; 2:4–5; 3:14–15).

In dying, we desire union with each other and with God. Singh's insistence that the boundaries of the individual self must be utterly overcome is an exaggeration, but one whose foundation in our need for interpersonal communion cannot be denied. Jesus fulfills our desire for radical communion. Explaining the mystical body of Christ into which we are drawn, Paul tells the Corinthian congregation that "you are the body of Christ and individually members of it," so that "if one member suffers, all suffer together with it; if one member is honored, all rejoice together with it" (1 Cor. 12:26–27). Similarly, in the Gospel of John, Jesus proclaims that he will share with his disciples the unity that he has with his Father (see John 17:22–23). Of course, the unity that Jesus proclaims does not require (even in the Trinity itself!) the destruction of distinctive personhood. The unity of the church retains the individuality of the members who belong to one loving family.

Furthermore, Jesus makes us his friends. He says, "I do not call you servants any longer. . . but I have called you friends, because I have made known to you everything that I have heard from my Father" (John 15:15). In addition to being Jesus's friends, we are Jesus's family, adopted children in the Son. Paul proclaims that we "have received a spirit of adoption.

When we cry, 'Abba! Father!' it is that very Spirit bearing witness with our spirit that we are children of God, and if children, then heirs, heirs of God and joint heirs with Christ—if, in fact, we suffer with him so that we may also be glorified with him" (Rom. 8:15–17). The church is nothing less than "the household of God" (1 Tim. 3:15), in which God's children are gathered in Christ and through the Spirit. In fulfilling our desire for intimate union with God and each other, Jesus fulfills what is perhaps the deepest desire of dying persons.

Yet Jesus states repeatedly that we can reject our deepest desire. We often refuse "to acknowledge God" (Rom. 1:28). We become "filled with every kind of wickedness, evil, covetousness, malice," and we show ourselves to be "gossips, slanderers, God-haters, insolent, haughty, boastful, inventors of evil, rebellious toward parents, foolish, faithless, heartless, ruthless" (Rom. 1:29–31). We slavishly approve of others who act in such ways, because of the power and wealth that such persons obtain, which we prefer to divine approval. In this light, Paul warns urgently: "Be reconciled to God" (2 Cor. 5:20).

The dying process, therefore, involves high stakes that require not merely belief in a "higher power" (as Kuhl puts it) but faith—whether explicit or implicit—in the Redeemer who comes to "be lifted up, that whoever believes in him may have eternal life" (John 3:14–15).[29] As Jesus says in the Gospel of John, "I am the resurrection and the life. Those who believe in me, even though they die, will live" (11:25).

Conclusion

Depicting human history as "combat" and a "battlefield," in which the victor is the one who does good even at the cost of suffering and death, *Gaudium et Spes* states somberly: "The whole of man's history has been the story of dour combat with the powers of evil, stretching, so our Lord tells us, from the very dawn of history until the last day. Finding himself in the midst of the battlefield man has to struggle to do what is right, and it is at great cost to himself, and aided by God's grace, that he succeeds" (§37). In this battle, our great enemies are not other persons but rather "pride and inordinate self-love," and these internal enemies "must be purified and perfected by the cross and resurrection of Christ" (§37). *Gaudium et Spes* urges, therefore, that to become truly "free," we must "put aside love of self" and turn to Christ (§38). In dying, we can "put aside love of self" without fear, not only because of Christ's cross and resurrection, but also because we can already see God's inaugurated kingdom in the grace-filled lives of holy men and women who touch and inspire us by their actions of self-giving love.

Insofar as dying persons wish to avoid this "battlefield," Jesus Christ is not and cannot be "the fulfilment of all aspirations" (*Gaudium et Spes* §45). But the aspiration to remain mired in our own selfish self-love is not a good one, and so it is fitting that Christ does not fulfill it. When Singh is confronted with a dying man's "regrets, self-recriminations, and feelings of guilt," she seeks to replace these "negative" energies with "positive" ones, so that "what is inessential"—namely evil actions—"begins to evaporate, disappearing like dew in the morning."[30] Such evaporation, however, requires a change of will, and thus requires personal repentance. More cogently, therefore, Kuhl recognizes the deep need for repentance, remorse, and recompense for our bad actions. He recognizes that reconciliation, which dying persons (like other living persons) deeply need, must include taking responsibility for our actions and admitting the pain that we have caused others. Kuhl, however, still puts the matter quite blandly, as though God asks nothing of us: "Because the higher power offers forgiveness and love without judgment, the individual is also able to forgive herself and others for all transgressions."[31] The living God revealed in Jesus Christ redeems us from sin, but he also requires us to repent of sin and to "fight the good fight of the faith" so as to "take hold of the eternal life, to which you were called and for which you made the good confession" (1 Tim. 6:12).

I find, then, that faith in Christ does indeed fulfill dying persons' deepest yearnings for life, reconciliation, and interpersonal communion, once the dramatic character of this fulfillment—the need to embrace Christ's judgment against sin so as to receive his wondrous mercy—is recognized. N. T. Wright aptly describes the power of faith: "Faith in Jesus as the resurrection means that we share the resurrection not only in the future but here and now, under cover of the secrecy of faith. The death we die in repentance is a sharing of Jesus's death, and the life we live in faith (not yet, of course, in sight) is life with him in heaven."[32] Confident in faith that God loves us and that God is merciful, we can openly confess our sins and ask forgiveness, knowing that Christ has reconciled us. Mother Teresa is reported to have said: "It is very simple. The dying need tender loving, nothing more."[33] If such "tender loving" did not give dying persons life, reconciliation, and interpersonal communion, then it would not be enough. But the tender loving that Mother Teresa offers, and that she knows dying persons need, derives from and bears witness to faith in the crucified and risen Christ. She urges that "we must cleave to Jesus. Our whole life must simply be woven into Jesus."[34] Dying persons, who need interior reconciliation with "the God of love, compassion, and mercy," find all their aspirations fulfilled in Jesus Christ, whom they meet in faith.[35]

CHAPTER 4

PENITENCE

The Stoning of Stephen

Thomas Aquinas defines the virtue of *poenitentia*—a virtue that is sometimes translated "penance" but that I term "penitence" in this chapter—as "sorrow for past sins."[1] He explains more fully that *poenitentia* "is a special virtue not merely because it sorrows for evil done (since charity would suffice for that), but also because the penitent grieves for the sin he has committed, inasmuch as it is an offense against God, and purposes to amend."[2] To describe what he has in mind, Aquinas cites Psalm 51:17, "The sacrifice acceptable to God is a broken spirit; a broken and contrite heart, O God, you will not despise."[3] We find the same thing in 2 Corinthians 7:10, "For godly grief produces a repentance that leads to salvation and brings no regret." Aquinas distinguishes the virtuous habit of *poenitentia* from specific acts of penance that express sorrow for sins and that seek to make amends in Christ. The first act of the virtue of *poenitentia* is the act of repentance, in which we undergo a change of heart.[4]

In the present chapter I explore the virtuous penitence of dying persons by focusing on Stephen's speech in Acts 7, a speech that precipitates his martyrdom. Christopher Vogt has shown that "the parallels between the description of Jesus' death in Luke's gospel and the account of the deaths of early Christian martyrs in Acts indicate that the author had in mind a connection between Jesus' death and the way a Christian should approach dying."[5] In this chapter, I propose that the way in which Stephen looks backward to Israel's past and forward to life with Christ sheds light in particular on the communal dimension of penitent dying. As the first martyr, Stephen in his speech teaches us that in dying as Christians, we do not die as isolated individuals; rather our dying belongs to the history of

God's people, whose head is Christ. The history of Israel and of the church is *our* history, and our dying has an intergenerational, communal context rather than being merely a lonely and private struggle.[6] As Karen Scheib remarks, "Because our life in God is lived out through the body of Christ, our living and dying is not a solitary journey but occurs in the company of all the faithful, both living and dead."[7]

When in the dying process we remember our history, however, we find it to be gravely distorted by sin. Our primary task, therefore, must be repentance. Stephen's speech suggests that to look forward in a hope grounded in union with the crucified and risen Jesus, we must repent of the sinful aspects of our history and embrace Jesus as the one who has redeemed our history.[8] Amy Plantinga Pauw rightly observes that Christians "need to acknowledge God's judgment and seek God's forgiveness in our dying as well as in our living."[9] By witnessing to Christ's giving up his life for us and to our need for Christ, Stephen shows us what it means to die as a Christian.

Yet, since Stephen's penitent confession of Israel's sins can seem to be merely an anti-Jewish polemic—indeed, many have heard it precisely in that fashion—I begin by contextualizing his speech in its Jewish setting in two ways.[10] First, I compare it with God's words in Ezekiel 20, where God looks back upon Israel's history in a strongly negative fashion and then looks forward in hope to his own redemptive work. I propose that Stephen's rhetoric echoes that of Ezekiel 20. Second, I point out that while Stephen looks back upon Israel's history negatively, Hebrews 11 looks back to the same history positively.

Given the two ways that Israel's history can be remembered,[11] I suggest that our history, namely the (communal and personal) past that we look back upon when we are dying, should be remembered with gratitude marked by deep repentance for sin. While in the present chapter I emphasize penitence, my next chapter—which examines the dying of the great fourth-century Christian, Macrina—emphasizes gratitude. In both chapters, I underscore that Christians die not merely as isolated individuals but as repentant and grateful members of "a royal priesthood, a holy nation, God's own people" (1 Pet. 2:9).

Ezekiel 20 as a Context for Stephen's History of Israel

Ezekiel 20 derives from the tumultuous period in which some Israelites had already been exiled to Babylon and others soon would be.[12] Elders of

Israel come to Ezekiel to inquire of God as to what will happen and what should be done. God responds that they do not deserve any response other than condemnation. Through the prophet Ezekiel, God recalls all the times that the people of Israel have sinned and he has had mercy on them. The emphasis of this historical remembering is to condemn the people and explain to them why they no longer will be spared.

In the background to this history is death, not only that of individuals but that of the people of Israel. This death is spiritual, without thereby lacking a physical dimension, since Ezekiel sees the two as connected. In Ezekiel 18, God tells the people through Ezekiel that "if the wicked turn away from all their sins that they have committed and keep all my statutes and do what is lawful and right, they shall surely live; they shall not die" (18:21).[13] Repentance and embracing the Torah is the path of life; one's sinful past need not be the final word. God emphasizes in this regard that he is never pleased by the death of a wicked person; God wishes instead that the wicked person would repent: "Have I any pleasure in the death of the wicked, says the Lord GOD, and not rather that they should turn from their ways and live?" (18:23).[14] In speaking about the wicked individual, God is speaking about the whole people. God urges Israel to repent of its sins and turn to God before it is too late. As God asks, "Why will you die, O house of Israel? For I have no pleasure in the death of anyone, says the Lord GOD. Turn, then, and live" (Ezek. 18:31–32).

Two chapters later, it becomes clear that Israel—the whole people—is going to die. Looking back on its past, dying Israel must accept that it deserves death, because it has repeatedly sinned. The history of our sins is never pretty, and Israel's is no prettier than a reader of the biblical narratives to this point would expect.[15] Even though God has chosen and blessed Israel, Israel did not respond as it should have. In dying, Israel now has to face this fact.

God begins the history not with Abraham, but with the chosen people in Egypt. As God recalls, "On the day when I chose Israel, I swore to the offspring of the house of Jacob—making myself known to them in the land of Egypt" (Ezek. 20:5).[16] God swore to Israel that he would rescue them from slavery in Egypt and bring them into the land he had appointed, "a land flowing with milk and honey, the most glorious of all lands" (20:6). When God made this promise, he asked simply that Israel worship him rather than worshiping the false gods of Egypt. But the people rebelled against God and remained attached to their Egyptian idolatry.[17] Therefore, even when the people were still in Egypt, God thought to obliterate them in his wrath. But because of what God owed to his name, he chose not to obliterate them; and, as he had promised, "in the sight of the nations" he brought "them out of the land of Egypt" (20:9).

Having freed them from Egyptian slavery and brought them to the wilderness (Mount Sinai), God gave them the law and the Sabbath, so that they would be able to flourish and to be sanctified by the living God. But they rejected the commandments of the law and neglected the Sabbath. Again God thought to obliterate them then and there, but again God "acted for the sake of my name, so that it should not be profaned in the sight of the nations" (Ezek. 20:14).[18] In sparing them, however, God ensured that the generation that rejected the law and Sabbath and continued in idolatry would not attain to "the most glorious of all lands" (20:15).

Ezekiel's history so far has not been positive in its presentation of the people of Israel. But it becomes much worse, and goes so far as to seem (as Stephen's accusers say about Stephen's own speech) to "speak blasphemous words against Moses and God" (Acts 6:11). Having twice thought to obliterate the people he had chosen from out of all nations, God spoke to the children of the exodus generation, and he commanded these children to remember that "I the LORD am your God" (Ezek. 20:19) and to obey the law, observe the Sabbath, and not commit idolatry. But still the people did not worship God, rejecting him despite his efforts to be their God. Again God thought to obliterate them, and again he spared them for the sake of his name. But, while this new generation was still in the wilderness, he willed to punish them in two ways. First, he promised to "scatter them among the nations and disperse them through the countries" (Ezek. 20:23): because of their disobedience, exile would be their destiny. Second, he "gave them statutes that were not good and ordinances by which they could not live," and he even made them offer their firstborn in horrific human sacrifice to him (20:25–26).[19]

These punishments seem even worse than obliterating the people of Israel, because if God literally means what he says, then God deliberately caused his beloved people to commit the most terrible sins. This would imply that God causes evildoing, and therefore that God is not infinitely good, innocent, and worthy of worship (see James 1:13). It is therefore worth pointing out that earlier in the book of Ezekiel, God strongly condemns the Israelites precisely for the sin of sacrificing their firstborn children: "You took your sons and your daughters, whom you had borne to me, and these you sacrificed to them [idols] to be devoured" (Ezek. 16:20). As God asks in this context, "As if your harlotries were not enough! You slaughtered my children and delivered them up as an offering to them [idols]?" (16:20–21). Given that Ezekiel 16:21 (like 20:31) condemns in the strongest possible terms the ritual sacrifice of children, I consider that God did not literally make Israel offer "all their firstborn" (20:26), just as in 16:3 God condemns idolatrous Israel by *metaphorically* asserting that "your father was an Amorite, and your mother a Hittite."[20]

Ezekiel's scathing recounting of Israel's history continues by observing that Israel, having settled in the promised land, proceeded to offer sacrifices in all the idols' shrines—"any high hill or any leafy tree" (20:28). Here God again condemns the Israelites for sacrificing their own children as did idolatrous nations. God states, "Will you defile yourselves after the manner of your ancestors and go astray after their detestable things [idols]? When you offer your gifts and make your children pass through the fire, you defile yourselves with all your idols to this day" (20:30–31). The point is that Israel has no standing to judge God for abandoning Israel; it is solely God, innocent of any evil, who has been abandoned and who can stand as judge: "And shall I be consulted by you, O house of Israel? As I live, says the Lord GOD, I will not be consulted by you" (20:31).

The purpose of God punishing Israel through the destruction of Jerusalem and exile, then, is to make clear to Israel that God is precisely not an idol of the kind that they have been worshiping, the kind that commands people to offer children in sacrifice. The prophetic judgment contained in Ezekiel 20's highly negative narrative of the history of Israel concludes with God insisting that Israel's efforts to deny God and to worship idols will not succeed. As God says, Israel wants to "be like the nations, like the tribes of the countries, and worship wood and stone" (20:32). But God promises that Israel will never succeed in definitively making itself into a mere idolatrous nation among all the other idolatrous nations. God promises that the purpose of his deadly and destructive wrath is Israel's salvation. The end result of the deadly punishment that God inflicts will be that "I [God] will be king over you" (20:33) and that Israel will worship the living God. God will judge Israel in order to purge and purify it, not in order to destroy it (cf. 20:34–38).[21]

Indeed, God states that for his name's sake, he will accomplish the fulfillment of all he has covenantally bound himself to be and do for his people Israel. This unmerited consummation will include the restoration of Jerusalem, perfect worship, the return of all exiles, and Israel's repentance. Ezekiel depicts this consummation: "For on my holy mountain, the mountain height of Israel, says the Lord GOD, there all the house of Israel, all of them, shall serve me in the land; there I will accept them, and there I will require your contributions and the choicest of your gifts, with all your sacred things. As a pleasing odor I will accept you, when I bring you out from the peoples" (Ezek 20:40–41). This promise befits the God who says, "Why will you die, O house of Israel? For I have no pleasure in the death of anyone. . . . Turn, then, and live" (18:31–32). After Israel does inded die by undergoing the judgment that God will administer "with a mighty hand and an outstretched arm, and with wrath poured out" (20:33), Israel will be restored and far more than restored, with the result that Israel will finally "know that I [God] am the LORD" (20:44).

No wonder that God later leads Ezekiel in prophetic vision to a valley of dry bones, where God speaks to Ezekiel: "Prophesy to these bones, and say to them: O dry bones, hear the word of the LORD. Thus says the Lord GOD to these bones: I will cause breath to enter you, and you shall live" (37:4–5). Indeed, the prophet witnesses their restoration to life: "I prophesied as he commanded me, and the breath came into them, and they lived, and stood on their feet, a vast multitude" (37:10).[22]

Thus Ezekiel's prophetic remembering of Israel's sins, sins that distort Israel by enchaining it to a false god who is the embodiment of all the evil that God is not, shows that the seeming death of the people will lead, due to God's faithfulness, to the superabundant fulfillment of God's good promises. Through Ezekiel, God shows that his condemnation of Israel is total. There is nothing in Israel's covenantal history that God (in Ezek. 20) identifies as good. Yet God loves his people and without doubt he "will be king" (20:33) over his people. Israel's dying is not the final word. God's love and royal power will be the final word, and will change Israel's death into perfect life for "all the house of Israel" (20:40).

Further Context: Grateful Remembering in Hebrews 11

Ezekiel 20 remembers Israel's history as perceived in light of Israel's failures and God's righteous punishment. It is a chapter of deeply repentant remembering. Israel's history, however, can also be represented in the opposite way, as found in Hebrews 11. In this section, I will survey Hebrews 11 for what it teaches about looking back at our (communal) past in gratitude for what God has accomplished in our lives (broadly understood). Although Acts 7, like Ezekiel 20, strongly emphasizes repentance, I wish to make clear that this emphasis is not at odds with remembering one's past with gratitude, as does Hebrews 11.

Hebrews 11 is best known for its opening verse: "Now faith is the assurance of things hoped for, the conviction of things not seen" (11:1). The context of this passage needs attention. The author of Hebrews recalls to his congregation that after their conversion to Christ, they "endured a hard struggle with sufferings, sometimes being publicly exposed to abuse and affliction, and sometimes being partners with those so treated" (10:32–33).[23] They were able to endure this "hard struggle" due to their confidence in Christ and in the "great reward" (10:35) promised to those who have faith in him. Although in danger of death, they looked forward to eternal life. The lesson inculcated by the author of Hebrews is that in face of deadly danger, "you need endurance, so that when you have done the will of God, you may receive what is promised" (10:36).

A central part of the lesson conveyed by Hebrews 11 consists in that the great Israelite heroes "died in faith, without having received the promises" (11:13).[24] Presumably, Christians should have even stronger faith than did the Israelites, since we have received what was promised, namely the Messiah who conquered sin and death by his Pasch. Christian faith, however, is the same faith in God's promises as that possessed by the Israelites. Therefore, remembering how the great figures of Israel (as well as those who preceded Israel) faced suffering and death should be helpful to dying Christians.

The first representative model of faith named by Hebrews 11 is Abel.[25] Abel exemplifies righteous worship: he offered a pleasing sacrifice to God, and "through this he [Abel] received approval as righteous, God himself giving approval to his gifts; he died, but through his faith he still speaks" (11:4). In faith, Abel knew that holiness in God's sight was worth dying for; and Christ proves him right, since the reward of faith becomes fully manifest in the risen Christ. The next hero of faith is Enoch, who avoided death altogether due to his faith and to the fact that he pleased God. Next is Noah, who trusted in God to prepare for "events as yet unseen" (11:7); he too became "an heir to the righteousness that is in accordance with faith" (11:7). The pattern of risking one's life out of trust in God's promise continues in Abraham, who braved great dangers because "he looked forward to the city that has foundations, whose architect and builder is God" (11:10). In the context of Hebrews, this "city" or land is eternal life, established for us by Jesus's dying: "Let us then go to him [Jesus] outside the camp and bear the abuse he endured. For here we have no lasting city, but we are looking for the city that is to come" (13:13–14).

Sarah too appears as a hero of faith, because she trusted God that she would conceive the son promised by God. Abraham ended up having a huge number of descendants despite being "as good as dead" (11:12) at the time of Isaac's conception. When they died, their death was not like that of those who lack faith, "but from a distance they saw and greeted them [the promises]. They confessed that they were strangers and foreigners on the earth" (11:13).[26] The mark of the faithful people of Israel is that "they are seeking a homeland" (11:14)—they do not act as though earthly life and comfort were the goal, but instead "they desire a better country, that is, a heavenly one" (11:16). It is precisely for this reason that they are able to overcome fear of death and live in faith and trust; and the result is that "God is not ashamed to be called their God; indeed, he has prepared a city for them" (11:16).

Isaac has a role among the heroes of faith, although his role derives from Abraham's, since Isaac's pivotal moment comes when God tests Abraham to see whether Abraham trusts God's promises enough to offer up to God the son of the covenant. Hebrews makes clear that God is testing Abraham rather than actually desiring child sacrifice. Hebrews also suggests that Abraham's willingness to relinquish his son shows Abraham's faith in the resurrection of the dead. Isaac thereby becomes a symbol of the resurrection to come, since God returned Isaac to Abraham. Isaac, Jacob, and Joseph are also portrayed by Hebrews as heroes of faith because, in dying, they looked forward in faith to "blessings for the future" (11:20) and trusted in God's promises.

According to Hebrews' recounting of Israel's history, the next hero of faith is Moses, as we would expect. Hebrews presents Moses as great because his faith leads him to spurn earthly goods and instead to seek divine reward. Thus Moses chose "rather to share ill-treatment with the people of God than to enjoy the fleeting pleasures of sin. He considered abuse suffered for the Christ to be greater wealth than the treasures of Egypt, for he was looking ahead to the reward" (11:25–26).[27] Risking death, he despised the privileges of Pharaoh's court and opposed Pharaoh to his face. He celebrated the first Passover with its sprinkling of sacrificial blood, so as to preserve the people from the deadly plague. In so doing, he exhibited faith in the Christ who was to come—since it is Christ's blood that conquers death and gives eternal life.

The whole people of Israel, and not solely their representatives, receive praise for their faith during the exodus from Egypt (quite a contrast to Ezek. 20!). Hebrews 11 observes that it was by faith that the people managed to cross the Red Sea on dry land, and likewise the victory over Jericho took place by the power of faith rather than military might. Rahab, though a prostitute and not an Israelite, earns a place among the heroes of faith due to the assistance she gave to the Israelite spies. Hebrews goes on to emphasize that faith enabled God's people not only to risk death and to look forward to their heavenly country (eternal life), but also to perform many consequential acts during their earthly lives. So positive is Hebrews about Israel's history that even the reckless and lawless Jephthah and Samson receive praise for faith, alongside Gideon, Barak, David, Samuel, and the prophets.[28] The representatives of God's people Israel "through faith conquered kingdoms, administered justice, obtained promises, shut the mouths of lions, quenched raging fire, escaped the edge of the sword, won strength out of weakness, became mighty in war, put foreign armies to flight" (Heb. 11:33–34).

This positive remembering of Israel's history does not minimize the dreadful sufferings of the people of Israel. Holy Israelites, living by faith in God and the promised reward of eternal life, "were tortured" and "suffered mocking and flogging, and even chains and imprisonment" (Heb. 11:35–36). The Israelites were so impressive in their sufferings that the current suffering of Christians, at least as related by Hebrews, seems to pale in comparison. Hebrews reports the extent of the Israelites' noble, faith-filled suffering for their witness to the true God: "They were stoned to death, they were sawn in two, they were killed by the sword; they went about in skins of sheep and goats, destitute, persecuted, tormented. . . . They wandered in deserts and mountains, and in caves and holes in the ground" (11:37–38).[29] These Israelites were so praiseworthy, so "commended for their faith" (11:39), that Hebrews says that "the world was not worthy" of them (11:38).

Hebrews concludes that followers of Christ should look back to the history of Israel and, with gratitude, should imitate the Israelites: "Therefore, since we are surrounded by so great a cloud of witnesses, let us also lay aside every weight and the sin that clings so closely, and let us run with perseverance the race that is set before us" (12:1). In imitating the Israelites, we are imitating their faith in God's ability to conquer death and to reward the just. Ultimately, the Israelite "cloud of witnesses" bears witness to Christ, who had been promised but was not yet given to them. In this regard, Hebrews states that "God had provided something better so that they [the Israelite heroes of faith] would not, apart from us, be made perfect" (11:40).[30]

Looking back gratefully to Israel's noble past, then, does not compete with "looking to Jesus the pioneer and perfecter of our faith" (Heb

12:2). Jesus Christ is at the center both of our looking back to our (Israel's) past and of our looking forward to eternal life with Christ. Christ has achieved that which Israel's heroes of faith trusted God would accomplish. He is the perfect model of a faith that despises death and trusts in the saving power of God, since "for the sake of the joy that was set before him [Jesus] endured the cross, disregarding its shame, and has taken his seat at the right hand of the throne of God" (12:2). When we look back to Israel's heroes of faith, we learn how to look to Jesus and to cleave to his dying so that we might share in his glorious reward.

Stephen's Speech: Looking Back and Looking Forward in Christian Dying

Ezekiel 20 and Hebrews 11 help us to see that in dying, we must look backward with gratitude at God's work (Heb. 11) and with deep repentance for our sins (Ezek. 20). These texts also remind us that we die as members of God's people, and therefore, in dying, we should remember not only our own lives but also the whole history of God's people, whose center is the crucified and risen Christ. In light of these texts about Israel's past (and ours), let me now turn to the martyr Stephen's historical remembering in Acts 7.[31] I note that although Stephen's speech in Acts 7 precedes his death, the whole speech belongs to his dying.[32] When Stephen remembers his past, he remembers the history of Israel and he speaks to his "brothers and fathers" (Acts 7:2). The emphasis here falls strongly on penitence.

Although Stephen expresses gratitude at the beginning of his speech, he speaks largely in the mode of one remembering in order to repent.[33] We must keep firmly in view that Stephen, like Ezekiel, is speaking in prophetic judgment to his own people (whose past is his own), and also that Stephen confesses his own need for Jesus as Redeemer, thus including himself among those who must repent. Furthermore, Stephen forgives those who stone him; despite the harshness of his prophetic judgment, he concludes on a note of mercy, just as Ezekiel does.

In his speech, Stephen first remembers his (Israel's) past with gratitude. Stephen recalls that God came to Abraham and commanded him to go first to Haran and then to the promised land.[34] Abraham obeyed, but God did not give him an inheritance in the promised land; instead God promised him that his descendants would inherit the land. God also told Abraham that his descendants would be slaves in a foreign country for four hundred years, prior to inheriting the promised land. Stephen observes that Abraham received "the covenant of circumcision" (Acts 7:8) and also received a son, Isaac, whom he circumcised on the eighth day. When combined with the symbolism of circumcision on the eighth day (a new relationship with God that goes beyond the seven days of creation), the promise that Abraham's descendants would undergo a lengthy enslavement before inheriting the promised land already suggests the pattern of dying followed by rising to life with God.[35]

Stephen recalls God's care for Jacob and his sons, especially Joseph. Although through envy his brothers sold Joseph into slavery in Egypt, God "rescued him from all his afflictions" (Acts 7:10) and enabled him to rescue the entire family of Jacob from a deadly famine. Stephen tells this story in a manner that prepares for a rejected Savior. He describes the multiplication of the people of Israel and their enslavement in Egypt, as well as Pharaoh's command that their children be killed. With gratitude, he observes, "At this time Moses was born, and he was beautiful before God" (7:20).[36] In Stephen's remembering, Moses's first encounter with his own people—in which Moses defended an Israelite against an Egyptian but was misunderstood by his own people—becomes another symbolic reference to Jesus, who came to save Israel but was misunderstood.[37] Moses sought to reconcile his people to one another, but they rejected him.

The next scene of Stephen's narration belongs again to grateful remembering: Moses's trembling in awe at the manifestation of God "in the wilderness of Mount Sinai, in the flame of a burning bush" (Acts 7:30). The Lord here appears as Israel's deliverer: "I [the Lord] have come down to rescue them" (7:34). Since the Lord wills to deliver the people through Moses, Stephen draws a clear (though still implicit) connection to Jesus, the deliverer who was rejected but who now is exalted at the Father's right hand as the deliverer of his people: "It was this Moses whom they rejected when they said, 'Who made you a ruler and a judge?' and whom God now sent as both ruler and liberator" (7:35).[38] Positively, Stephen recalls that Moses led the people out of Egypt; and Stephen also remembers Moses's prophecy that "God will raise up a prophet for you [the Israelites] from your own people as he raised me up" (7:37; cf. Deut. 18:15). In Stephen's view, though he does not say so yet, this prophet who has authority like that of Moses is clearly Jesus.

Having recalled with gratitude God's covenantal works in the past (Stephen's *and* Israel's past), Stephen now approaches Israel's past with deep repentance, from a stance of prophetic condemnation. Stephen's accusation is that the people of Israel rejected God's gifts. Although God appointed Moses as deliverer and Moses "received living oracles [the law] to give to us" (Acts 7:38), the people turned away from Moses. Stephen recalls, "Our ancestors were unwilling to obey him; instead, they pushed him aside, and in their hearts they turned back to Egypt" (7:39). The preeminent example of their rebellion is their making and worshiping a golden calf while Moses was with God on Mount Sinai.[39] Their idolatry did not stop after Moses came down the mountain but only intensified, with the result that God "handed them over" to their chosen path (7:42). They worshiped God but they also equally worshiped many other gods. In this respect Stephen cites the prophetic condemnation expressed by God through Amos: "Did you offer to me slain victims and sacrifices forty years in the wilderness, O house of Israel? No, you took along the tent of Moloch, and the star of your god Rephan, the images that you made to worship; so I will remove you beyond Babylon" (7:42–43; cf. Amos 5:25–27).[40]

Stephen nonetheless still has gratitude for Israel's (and his) past, because God did not stop caring for Israel. On Mount Sinai, God showed Moses the pattern for the "tent of testimony" (Acts 7:44), and Moses constructed the tent so that the people would be able to worship God. God enabled Israel to dispossess the nations that dwelt in the promised land. God loved David, and David's son Solomon built the temple in Jerusalem for the worship of God. But these gifts too did not lead Israel to obey God, in part because "the Most High does not dwell in houses made with human hands" (Acts 7:48; cf. Isa. 66:1–2, quoted by Stephen).[41] An implied contrast with the church of Christ, in which God dwells fully, is observable here.[42]

At this juncture, Stephen moves completely into prophetic condemnation, insisting that remembrance of his (Israel's) past requires deep repentance. Echoing Moses's condemnation of Israel as a "rebellious and stubborn" people (Deut. 31:27)—a passage in which Moses prophesies that Israel will continue to be rebellious—and also echoing the Lord's description of Israel as "a stiff-necked people" (Exod. 33:3 and elsewhere), Stephen calls Israel a "stiff-necked people, uncircumcised in heart and ears" (Acts 7:51).[43] He intensifies this condemnation and his corresponding call for repentance by noting that Israel has *always* resisted the Holy Spirit and that the current generation is no different from their ancestors. Echoing Jesus's words with regard to the persecutions endured by the prophets, Stephen says that the Israelites persecuted and killed the prophets and failed to keep the law. It is not surprising, he concludes, that the present generation has become the "betrayers and murderers" of the Messiah, whom Stephen describes as "the Righteous One" (Acts 7:52).[44]

In his remembering, Stephen looks back always with Jesus Christ in view. Thus his looking back is always also a looking forward, in the sense that Israel's past, for Stephen, contains manifold prefigurings and prophetic announcements of Jesus Christ. Again, since Stephen sees his life primarily as located in the story of Israel/the church, he is looking back on his *own* past when he remembers Israel's past. When Stephen looks back with repentance, he sees Jesus—the deliverer who was rejected by his people, the long-awaited prophet like Moses, the true sacrifice who constitutes the true temple.

Likewise, when Stephen finishes his looking back, he looks forward and sees Jesus in an astounding way. We read that Stephen, "full of the Holy Spirit, . . . gazed into heaven and saw the glory of God and Jesus standing at the right hand of God" (Acts 7:55).[45] This statement, while it can be interpreted in various ways, involves the fulfillment of the messianic prophecy of Daniel 7:13-14, "As I watched in the night visions, I saw one like a human being [lit., 'son of man'] coming with the clouds of heaven. And he came to the Ancient One and was presented before him. To him was given dominion and glory and kingship, that all peoples, nations, and languages should serve him." In Matthew 26:64, Jesus's statement to the high priest—"From now on you will see the Son of Man seated at the right hand of Power and coming on the clouds of heaven"—causes the high priest to tear his robes and accuse Jesus of blasphemy.

When Stephen looks forward, then, he gazes upon the living King, the one who stands "at the right hand of God" and shares in the divine glory. He looks forward in the Spirit to his own full entrance into the kingdom of the Son. In looking back at his past, Stephen emphasizes Moses and the promised land; in looking forward he sees the Christ and the eschatological kingdom (cf. Acts 8:12).[46] As he is being stoned, Stephen commends his spirit to the "Lord Jesus" (7:59), his Redeemer. Imitating Christ's merciful dying, the dying Stephen kneels down and prays for those who are stoning him: "Lord, do not hold this sin against them" (7:60).[47]

Conclusion

I have employed Acts 7 to argue that in dying as Christians, we should recall our life with gratitude and repentance, and we should remember that we are not dying as isolated individuals but as members of the body of Christ, the church. The primary history for which we are to give thanks and offer repentance is the history of the people of God, to which our lives have contributed both positively (through our good acts, due to our co-operation with the indwelling Spirit) and negatively (through our sins).[48] Rather than focusing on ourselves in our dying, we should focus on Christ and on our relationship to Christ in his church. In this way, our looking back takes on its proper dimensions, which otherwise would be far too narrowed by a focus upon our own earthly achievements and failures. In looking forward, we should confess our utter dependence upon Christ for salvation and our joyful hope, in the Holy Spirit, to be united to Christ forever in the glory of Trinitarian friendship. In penitent dying, we must forgive others as Christ forgives us: this is the path of the cross, the path that bridges death and leads to resurrection and the kingdom of God.

Inspired by Stephen, I have suggested that prophetic judgment, prompting deep repentance, must be part of our dying, since our remembering of our past (and thus also of the church's past) must include a real attunement to how we have failed, despite God's great gifts to us. After all, only penitents need a merciful Redeemer. As Jesus says, "Those who are well have no need of a physician, but those who are sick. Go and learn what this means, 'I desire mercy, not sacrifice.' For I have come to call not the righteous but sinners" (Matt. 9:12–13).

For Christians, then, Christ must be central not only to our looking forward but also to our looking back upon our lives. In remembering our lives, we must discern the presence and work of Christ, and we must sorrow for our sins (for which he died) and seek his mercy. We must not measure our lives in terms of transient worldly accomplishments and mutually beneficial friendships, or in terms of the lack of such things. Rather, the true measure of our lives is Christ. A life for which we can be grateful, as we die, is a life in which the love and mercy of Christ can be discerned and identified, even in hidden ways known only to God. When we die, we die primarily as a member of Christ's body. As Paul emphasizes, "If one member suffers, all suffer together; if one member is honored, all rejoice together" (1 Cor. 12:26); and "it is no longer I who live, but it is Christ who lives in me. And the life I now live in the flesh I live by faith in the Son of God, who loved me and gave himself for me" (Gal. 2:20). Even more to the point is Romans 14:7-8: "We do not live to ourselves, and we do not die to ourselves. If we live, we live to the Lord, and if we die, we die to the Lord; so then, whether we live or whether we die, we are the Lord's."

Stephen's prophetic judgment, of course, is directed toward his own people, his own past. To accept Jesus as the Christ does not require interpreting Stephen's statement that his fellow Jews betrayed and murdered Christ as an indictment of the Jewish people more than other peoples. The *disciples* of Jesus—not only Judas but also Peter and the others—betrayed and abandoned Jesus, thereby causing him to be killed by the Romans. Paul himself, who (as Saul) consented to the stoning of Stephen (Acts 7:58; 8:1), states, "None of the rulers of the age understood this [wisdom of God]; for if they had, they would not have crucified the Lord of glory" (1 Cor. 2:8). In making this statement, Paul has both Roman and Jewish leaders in view, and he could also accuse Jesus's own disciples, who betrayed and abandoned their master. Far from condemning the Jewish people as being more responsible than others for killing Jesus, Paul argues that the rejection of Jesus as Messiah by many Jews belongs to God's plan to ensure "that, by the mercy shown to you [Gentiles], they [Jews] too may now receive mercy. For God has imprisoned all in disobedience, so that he may be merciful to all" (Rom. 11:31–32). Stephen, too, indicates his own emphasis on mercy (which is Christ's mission) by means of his final words of forgiveness.

Since we are loath to remember anything with real penitence—thereby depriving ourselves of the mercy that sinners such as ourselves need and require in order to have life with God—Israel's prophets, inspired by God, often remembered Israel's past in ways that emphasized the sins of Israel, as in Ezekiel 20. At the same time, since judgment of Israel's past is not the only true way of remembering Israel's past according to the New Testament, I also explored Hebrews 11 with its descriptions of the heroes of faith. The element of gratitude must also be equally present in our dying, as we remember our life.

In this context, Stephen's speech in Acts 7 is rightly understood not as a bitter rendition of Israel's past, let alone an act of self-righteous or anti-Jewish condemnation, but rather as an exemplar of the prophetic mode of remembering one's past with deep penitence (united with gratitude) in order to render oneself fully open to receiving and sharing God's mercy. Mercy is the way of Christ; mercy is the bridge from death to life. In her *Dialogue*, Catherine of Siena depicts God as saying that those "who travel by the way beneath the bridge"—that is, who consciously reject Christ, the bridge to eternal life—"never turn back to admit their sins or to ask for my mercy."[49] Just as in his prophetic judgment Stephen has in view his own people (Israel, the Jewish people), so also in her equally forceful prophetic judgment Catherine has in view her own people (the church, clerical and lay Christians).

If we are to avoid dying "beneath the bridge," we need to learn how to appreciate Acts 7 on Stephen's dying. In looking back upon our lives as members of the church and looking forward to resurrected life, we need to perceive the presence of Christ with faith, hope, and love. Arguably, the note of deep penitence that Stephen sounds is especially crucial for the dying (and living) Christian, as penitence likewise was in the preaching of the prophets of Israel. Augustine urged that even "exemplary Christians and priests ought not to depart from this life without fitting and appropriate repentance"—a counsel that Augustine put into practice in his own dying, during which he continually prayed the penitential psalms with tears.[50] Both personally and communally, as God's people, we have all betrayed the Lord and been responsible for his dying on account of our sins. But as his messianic suffering shows, the merciful Lord has "no pleasure in the death of anyone" (Ezek. 18:32). In dying, then, let us follow the Lord's urgent command through the prophet Ezekiel: "Repent and turn from all your transgressions; otherwise iniquity will be your ruin" (18:30).

CHAPTER 5

GRATITUDE

The Dying of Macrina

In *Gratitude: An Intellectual History,* Peter Leithart argues that "Christianity infuses gratitude into every nook and cranny of human life. Because *all* comes from God, thanks is offered to him for everything."[1] He insists that we must become people "whose first instinct in every circumstance is to offer praise and thanks to the Father. We must learn what it means to offer a continuous sacrifice of thanksgiving."[2] Leithart approaches the topic as a theologian, seeking to understand all that gratitude requires in our relationships with God and our fellow human beings. By contrast, Nina Lesowitz and Mary Beth Sammons provide a more popular introduction to gratitude in *Living Life as a Thank You.* They describe a cancer survivor who exhibits tremendous gratitude for each new experience that he might not have had if the cancer had progressed. They relay ten "tips for becoming grateful," drawn from the blogger Anne Naylor, including keeping "a gratitude journal" and beginning each day with "a gratitude dance."[3] Indicative of their somewhat impoverished approach is the tenth and last gratitude tip, which urges the reader to be grateful each day for "the goodness of your intent; the caring you express to others; the endeavors you take to be true to your ideals"—since "there is no one else quite like you."[4] Quite rightly, however, Lesowitz and Sammons propose that "if you want to turn your life around, try thankfulness. Finding reasons to be grateful every day is the key to living an abundant life."[5]

This exhortation to thankfulness may be excellent advice for which we should be grateful, but what if we are dying? How can we be grateful when our body is corrupting and, far from living an "abundant life," we are about to lose forever our earthly life? I argue in this chapter that, as

Leithart suggests, the answer consists in thanking God in Christ. In union with Christ, even dying can be cause for gratitude.[6] To die in gratitude requires that we die into a personal future, so that our dying and our living can be joined in one thanksgiving. In Christ, we do indeed die into a personal future. Henri Nouwen well describes our natural fear that in dying we lack such a personal future: "Dying and death always call forth, with renewed power, the fear that we are unloved and will, finally, be reduced to useless ashes."[7] Useless ashes cannot be grateful to anyone, and if dying persons think they are about to permanently become "useless ashes," dying persons can be grateful for their past life and for their coming escape from the pains of disease, but they cannot be grateful for their dying per se.

Nouwen emphasizes, therefore, that dying persons need the assurance of Christ's merciful and enduring love, communally expressed in his church, in order to be able to gratefully die. As Nouwen says, a dying person needs to be like a trapeze artist, trusting in the divine "catcher": "Dying is trusting in the catcher. To care for the dying is to say, 'Don't be afraid. Remember that you are the beloved child of God. He will be there when you make your long jump. Don't try to grab him; he will grab you. Just stretch out your arms and hands and trust, trust, trust.'"[8] Such trust, to be real, requires an underlying gratitude for the love of God that Christ has embodied for us in his dying. John Swinton notes that when, in Christ, we enjoy "abundant life," this means not that we somehow have found a path for avoiding the agony of dying, but rather that we recognize gratefully that, even in dying, we are "perfectly loved by God" and are called by God "to live with God and to continue to love God forever."[9]

I begin this chapter by considering the effort of the late Yale University medical doctor Sherwin Nuland to conceive of gratitude in dying from an atheistic perspective. In his bestselling *How We Die*, Nuland holds that death everlastingly annihilates the dying person, but he still thinks that the dying person can look back *and* look forward in gratitude.[10] In this light, I turn to gratitude in dying as depicted in Gregory of Nyssa's *Life of Saint Macrina*.[11] Macrina exemplifies the gratitude of a dying Christian in remembering her life and looking forward to the fullness of life in Christ. I explore how she understands her dying to be integrated into the church's liturgical life of continual thanksgiving, and I examine how she pairs gratitude with repentance as she prepares to meet Christ. I also emphasize the way in which Gregory's account of her dying draws upon Scripture to present dying as a journey toward resurrected life rather than as a mere flight of the soul from the bonds of flesh.

Nuland's book belongs broadly to the "death awareness movement" that began in the 1960s, insofar as he wants to teach us about the actual physical reality of dying and insofar as he is responding to the "medicalization" of dying.[12] Unlike some earlier proponents of the "death awareness movement," Nuland does not romanticize nature: he knows well how indifferent nature is to the deaths of individual persons, and he details this indifference in lengthy chapters on each of the main diseases that cause human death.[13] Yet he supposes that the forward-looking meaning of our dying can be properly found in nature, namely, in our freely accepting our death as part of the cycle by which new organisms come to be in the ongoing evolutionary unfolding of the cosmos.[14]

In this chapter, I argue that Macrina's hope for a deeper union with Christ in his body encourages real gratitude in dying in a manner that Nuland's expectation of union with the cosmos ultimately cannot. Since humans find fulfillment in interpersonal communion, the prospect of an everlasting separation from interpersonal communion cuts to the heart of who humans are. Donald Heinz speaks of "panic at the closing of the door, terror at the dangerous truth that the capacity to project the self into the future has atrophied"; and Joseph Ratzinger remarks, "Nothing is so unbearable for man as to have no future."[15] Macrina knows in faith that Christ has prepared for his body the church a future of ever deeper interpersonal communion in love, and so she does not feel panic or terror in dying. Her gratitude about the life she has lived fits with her grateful dying, because her dying in faith and love is leading her into the fullness of grateful living. If, as Peter Phan says and Nuland himself affirms, "how we die is how we live," then we need to die into a future in which our gratitude truly persists, a future that is found in Christ's everlasting "sacrifice of praise to God" (Heb. 13:15).[16]

Sherwin Nuland on Dignity and Hope in Dying

In seeking to describe how we die, Sherwin Nuland's central concern is that contemporary medicine can lead dying people to undergo painful and useless treatment that does not allow them to say goodbye properly to their loved ones.[17] As he knows from his clinical experience, many dying people are consumed by their painful and exhausting medical treatment and by their unfounded hopes for staving off their approaching death. In his view, "The clinical objectivity that should enter into our decisions must come from a doctor familiar with our values and the lives we have led, and not just from the virtual stranger whose superspecialized biomedical skills we have called upon."[18] On this basis, Nuland emphasizes that we must not allow our final days to be focused on medical procedures, which too often turn into "well-meant exercises in futility" and merely amplify suffering.[19] Instead, we must find some way of accepting that we are really dying, so that our values are able to shape, insofar as possible, how we die.[20]

Nuland suggests that accepting our dying will generally come through the feeling that our life has been "useful and rewarding."[21] By this phrase, he means more than a life that has included numerous pleasures and that has enabled us to help other humans, though these elements are needed. In the broadest sense he thinks of a "useful and rewarding" life in an ecological and cosmic framework, within which our death serves the larger evolutionary movement whereby new organisms can live and develop. He states in this vein, "If by our work and pleasure, our triumphs and our failures, each of us is contributing to an evolving process of continuity not only of our species but of the entire balance of nature, the dignity we create in the time allotted to us becomes a continuum with the dignity we achieve by the altruism of accepting the necessity of death" (267). From this perspective, if we learn to live by a realistic understanding of the kind of creatures that we are, in the end we can "achieve" a final dignity by freely and altruistically "accepting the necessity of death." As Nuland says, we are offered the choice of embracing the fact that "we die . . . so that others may live" (267).

Nuland warns us not to expect a dignified and serene deathbed experience in which we say goodbye to our loved ones. He makes clear that the process of dying is generally painful and undignified. Most people "are fated to die badly" because of the ravages of the mortal disease (265). In this sense, for almost everyone, "The quest to achieve true dignity fails when our bodies fail" (xvii). In his view, therefore, a dignified death is not measured by the process of dying or the kind of disease, let alone by the deathbed experience, but by the "honesty and grace of the years of life that are ending" (268). Along these lines, he defines dying with dignity as follows: "The greatest dignity to be found in death is the dignity of the life that preceded it. This is a form of hope we can all achieve, and it is the most abiding of all. Hope resides in the meaning of what our lives have been" (242). As he pithily states, "Who has lived in dignity, dies in dignity" (268).

What does "dignity" mean here?[22] In part it refers back to his understanding of a "useful and rewarding" life, marked by accomplishments (as well as inevitable failures) and by relationships of love and service (even when imperfect), as well as by an altruistic acceptance of the evolutionary framework in which we die so that others might live. Can people who for whatever reason have not, by any realistic measure, lived a "useful and rewarding" life die in "dignity"? I am not sure how Nuland would answer this question, but it is significant that for Nuland dying in "dignity" is not only backward-looking (toward the "useful and rewarding" elements of one's life) but also forward-looking (toward the contribution one's death inevitably makes to the natural cycle "by which each generation is to be succeeded by the next," 262). As already noted, Nuland considers it important to affirm that the dying person *achieves* dignity—a dignity that caps the dignity expressed in a "useful and rewarding" life—by giving himself or herself altruistically to the natural cycle of life.

In giving ourselves up to this natural evolutionary cycle, to what precisely are we giving ourselves up? Nuland presents us as giving up our lives for the sake of future organisms. This altruistic gesture achieves "dignity" in part because the other alternative, which many people seem to prefer—namely resisting desperately to the very end—is as futile as it is nonaltruistic. Yet the other alternative also might seem to have a certain dignity, as when the Irish poet Dylan Thomas urges his dying father to "not go gentle into that good night" and to "rage, rage against the dying of the light."[23] The poet argues that his father, and each of us, has too much unfulfilled potential to accept "the dying of the light." There is an accurate sense of the irreplaceable dignity of each human person in Thomas's poem. A human person is more than simply another organism within what Nuland terms the "evolving process of continuity not only of our species but of the entire balance of nature" (267). In the deepest possible sense, each of us can never be *replaced* by new human beings.

Nuland is well aware of the unique dignity of each human person. As he observes, each person has "potential unfulfilled" and, in some sense, "unfinished business"; each person has relationships and promises to others that, when the person is dead, leave a never-fillable gap in others' lives (261). Nuland himself remarks, "My mother died of colon cancer one week after my eleventh birthday, and that fact has shaped my life. All that I have become and much that I have not become, I trace directly or indirectly to her death" (xviii). Could his mother, in approaching her early death, have achieved dignity in dying by altruistically handing herself over to the "evolving process . . . of the entire balance of nature"? Far from handing herself over willingly to this evolving process, would not she have been quite right to have fought against it as a brutal and inhumane process that negates unique and urgently important relationships of interpersonal communion (in her case, with the young children who needed her)?

Despite his urging that dying persons not only look back to "useful and rewarding" lives but also look forward to handing ourselves over to the evolving process of the cosmos, Nuland has some rather negative remarks about this process. In his view, the evolutionary process in relation to which we can achieve dignity in dying is a process that coldly annihilates us. On the first page of his book's introduction, he describes death as "a permanent unconsciousness in which there is neither void nor vacuum—in which there is simply nothing" (xv). Nuland admits that this nothingness "seems so different from the nothing that preceded life" (xv).[24] Although he does not explain this difference, surely it consists in the fact that once we have come into existence, the onset of nothingness everlastingly negates our interpersonal communion, our unique and irreplaceable knowing and loving. In Nuland's view, the process of dying is nothing less than "the disintegration of the dying person's humanity" (xvii).

If so, then how can a dying person achieve "dignity," as Nuland thinks possible, by embracing this evolutionary process and thus embracing his or her own utter annihilation? Is it dignified for a human person to bow down reverently to the brutal stamping out of the person's own unique humanity? Nuland himself advises us "to live every day as though we will be on this earth forever," insofar as to do otherwise, out of fear of leaving "unfinished business," is to become inert or dead while we are still alive (261). But would not Dylan Thomas's advice to "rage against the dying of the light" fit better with living every day "as though we will be on this earth forever," so as to get the very most out of life and to refuse at any point (prior to death) to give ourselves over to the brutal annihilation that is death?

I am probing into why Nuland thinks it necessary to affirm not only that the dying find dignity in the backward-looking remembering of a "useful and rewarding" life, but also in the forward-looking "dignity we achieve by the altruism of accepting the necessity of death" (267). Why does he appeal to the evolutionary process as an aspect of the dignity of dying? My understanding is that he wants something meaningful to which, when dying, he can hand himself over. He takes comfort in giving himself freely back to the evolutionary process that gave him life and that will make future use of his material components. But I question whether the evolutionary process to which he wishes to hand himself over—*if* the process means the permanent annihilation of our interpersonal communion—is truly worthy of human dignity or of dignified self-gift.

I agree with Nuland that, despite the great value of modern medicine, medicine cannot be allowed to take over the dying process, either by extreme attempts to give a dying person a few more days or by the even worse alternative of medical euthanasia.[25] As Nuland says, "the central player in the drama is the dying man," not the doctor, and so technological skills must not overwhelm the personal and relational dimensions of one's final days (256). If the central player of the drama is the dying person, it makes sense that Nuland insists that dying persons must look forward and not merely backward—must see themselves as part of a larger unfolding drama that has meaning. In this sense, it is no wonder that Nuland holds that dignity is achieved in death not only by reflecting upon the contributions we may have made to the human race, but also by giving ourselves altruistically to something even bigger, namely the evolutionary process in which organisms come and go. Nuland recognizes that absent such a bigger reality to which our dying contributes, our dying "drama" would be a tragedy or a farce, since once the emotions and memories of our friends and family have faded our dying would lack meaning.

It may be, however, that even Nuland has doubts about whether the evolutionary process can truly provide suitable forward-looking meaning to dying persons. He reflects briefly on the Catholic sacrament of anointing and on the hope of dying persons "in the existence of God and an afterlife" (256). For Nuland, doctors should not scoff at this hope. At a deathbed, he insists, clergy can accomplish more than doctors can. Quite rightly, he bemoans his hospital's renunciation of its "Danger List," which automatically contacted a Catholic patient's priest. Since he himself does not believe that God exists, he states that when his time comes to die, the object of his hope will be first of all avoiding the needless suffering produced by futile medical procedures, and second avoiding the sadness of having to die alone. Most importantly, he says, his hope will be found in the way he lives his life, "so that those who value what I am will have profited by my time on earth and be left with comforting recollections of what we have meant to one another" (257). Notably, in this list of three ways of hoping that he thinks will console him in his own dying, Nuland does not mention the dignity of "contributing to an evolving process of continuity not only of our species but of the entire balance of nature."

In his emphasis on "those who value what I am," Nuland arguably has pinpointed the significance of human dying: namely, it is not only a personal but an interpersonal drama, since in looking back (and looking forward) we inevitably think of our relationships with concrete persons. Nuland's list of his three hopes ultimately centers upon two interpersonal hopes: not having to die alone or abandoned, and leaving behind friends and relations who will think gratefully and fondly of their relationship with him. These interpersonal hopes befit the unique dignity of a human person, marked by irreplaceable interpersonal communion. But insofar as these hopes look back and not truly forward—insofar as these hopes do not truly reach out beyond the deathbed, except by imagining others' thoughts (which last only briefly)—they are insufficient for a human being. Again, Nuland tacitly admits this when he calls for the dying person to achieve "dignity" by altruistically giving himself or herself over to the cosmic evolutionary process, despite the fact that this process is ultimately the destroyer of all interpersonal communion.

Nuland concludes, "Whatever form it may take, each of us must find hope in his or her own way" (257). But surely his book, which aims to converse with the reader about the modes of dying and the kinds of hope that Nuland himself envisions, is the very opposite of this advice of "to each his own." Instead, Nuland offers a meditation on dying that makes clear that, for the act of dying to accord with our human dignity, we must reach out in a forward-looking way and give ourselves, in dying (as in living), to something greater. Although Nuland does not recognize it, this something greater must truly accord with our unique and irreplaceable human dignity and therefore cannot simply be the rhythm of the brutally annihilating cosmos—here Dylan Thomas is quite right. If our dying is to be truly filled with gratitude, we must give ourselves in a forward-looking way consistent with our knowing and loving, and thus with the irreplaceable uniqueness of our drama that, as Nuland says, "makes each of us see our own existence as a heightened example of universal experience—a life that is somehow larger than life, and felt more deeply" (263).[26]

Joseph Ratzinger asserts, "Man has been made so that he cannot live without a future."[27] The problem for Nuland, and for the many people today who find themselves unable to believe in God, is that there ultimately does not seem to be a future for human beings. Not only will we and all who ever knew us die, but also the earth itself will be consumed by the dying sun and the cosmic evolutionary process will at last wipe away everlastingly every possible memory or mark of our brief existence. As Ratzinger puts the problem, human existence "is oriented wholly toward the future, and yet all future is in the end snatched away from it, for its end is death" (50). Because we are made for a future, to die with gratitude we must be able to reach out to a future worthy of us as relational beings.

Seemingly paradoxically for a Christian theologian, Ratzinger insists: "Man is the hope of mankind" (98). But he adds that this hope, this future, is only possible because of Jesus Christ: "In him, for the first time definitively, is man the hope of humanity" (98). The hope that Christians possess in dying—the Lord to whom we give ourselves in dying—is the same Lord to whom we give ourselves in living; human history and the "afterlife" are intrinsically related to each other. According to Ratzinger, then, Christians must show that "in Christ man has become the hope of humanity, by living our own lives in terms of this model, seeking to become one another's hope and to set upon the future the seal of Christ's features—the features of the coming city [which comes not from our power but rather 'comes down from above'] that will be completely human because it belongs completely to God" (99).

How, in dying, do we press forward in gratitude to this truly human future? Here Gregory of Nyssa's sister Macrina can show us the path.[28]

Christian Dying: Why Macrina Matters

At the heart of Macrina's gratitude in dying is the fact that her life takes its bearings from the church's (and Israel's) grateful liturgical worship and regular prayer. Recall Paul's exhortation, "Do not worry about anything, but in everything by prayer and supplication with thanksgiving let your requests be made known to God. And the peace of God, which surpasses all understanding, will guard your hearts and your minds in Christ Jesus" (Phil. 4:6–7). According to Gregory, even as a young child his sister followed Paul's command to "pray without ceasing" (1 Thess. 5:17). He remarks that "there was none of the psalms which she did not know since she recited each part of the Psalter at the proper times of the day, when she rose from her bed, performed or rested from her duties, sat down to eat or rose up from the table."[29] In this recitation of the psalter, she was living in the rhythm of the church's liturgical life. Through the reciting of the psalter, as Athanasius teaches in his "Letter to Marcellinus," the priests of Israel constantly "summoned the souls of the people into tranquillity, and called them into unanimity with those who form the heavenly chorus," and this has continued in the church.[30]

As the eldest of a family of ten children, Macrina guided her siblings upon the path of holiness. Gregory reports that she was responsible for turning her brother Basil from a life of "self-importance" to a life of freely chosen poverty and service, and for similarly educating her brother Peter (26). After all her siblings were grown, Macrina (with her mother) "put herself on an equal footing with the community of maidens [female servants], so as to share on equal terms with them one table, bed and all the needs of life, with every difference of rank eliminated from their lives" (29). She thereby adopted an early form of monastic life. Without mentioning the biblical passage specifically, Gregory presents Macrina as an exemplar of Jesus's command that his followers "not worry, saying, 'What will we eat?' or 'What will we drink?' or 'What will we wear?' For it is the Gentiles who strive for all these things; and indeed your heavenly Father knows that you need all these things. But strive first for the kingdom of God and his righteousness, and all these things will be given to you as well" (Matt. 6:31–33). Macrina also exemplifies Jesus's pithy warning, "You cannot serve God and wealth" (Matt. 6:24). By her life of generous service and renunciation of her material privileges, Macrina serves God and lives in imitation of Jesus.

When her brother Gregory arrives for a long-delayed visit, he finds her "caught in the grip of a grievous sickness" (34).[31] Although her body is deteriorating rapidly, she continues to live according to the values manifested in her years of health. She recalls with gratitude the events of her life, and she looks forward to eternal life. Like her brother, she enjoys philosophical conversation; thus even in her mortal illness she discusses with Gregory "the reason for life in the flesh, for what purpose man exists, how he is mortal, what is the source of death and what release there is from death back to life again" (36). Her brother reports that her conversation was surely "inspired by the power of the Holy Spirit" dwelling within her (36). Gregory describes her attitude in firmly Pauline terms: "she was already looking towards the prize of her upward calling and all but applying the words of the apostle to herself when he says that 'all there is to come now is the crown of righteousness reserved for me, which the righteous judge will give to me,' since 'I have fought the good fight, I have run the race to the end and I have kept the faith'" (37).[32]

When Gregory returns to the company of his sister after a rest, she looks back with profound gratitude upon her earthly life that is now nearly over. Gregory states that "she took up the story of the events of her life from infancy and retold them all in order as in an historical narrative" (37).

She begins with her memories of her parents. The point of her looking back is not merely to reflect upon a "useful and rewarding" life. Instead, says Gregory, "The aim of her story was to give thanks to God" (38). Gratitude is the measure and purpose of her looking back on her life.

In 2 Corinthians 9:6 and 10, Paul tells his congregation that "the one who sows sparingly will also reap sparingly, and the one who sows bountifully will also reap bountifully," and that "he who supplies seed to the sower and bread for food will supply and multiply your seed for sowing and increase the harvest of your righteousness." This divine bounty certainly fits the story of Macrina's parents. As she recalls, her parents inherited no land or property, because their own parents had undergone persecution for their Christian faith. Macrina's maternal grandfather had been executed and his belongings distributed to others, and Macrina's paternal grandparents "had their possessions confiscated for their profession of Christ" (38). God did indeed repay the grandparents' bountiful sowing through the parents' bountiful reaping—both spiritually and materially. Materially speaking, as Macrina reports (in Gregory's summary of her words), "their livelihood increased to such an extent because of their faith that there was no one more reputed than they were among the people of that time" (38). In fact, like the multiplication of the loaves and fishes, the material bounty that the parents divided among their nine children ended up enabling each of the children to enjoy more material bounty than the parents had enjoyed.

In terms of spiritual bounty, Macrina herself—like her brothers Gregory, Basil, Peter, and indeed all her siblings—showed the effect of the spiritual sowing undertaken by her grandparents and parents. When it came time to divide the inheritance left by her parents, Macrina gave her full portion to the church to distribute in service to the poor. She thereby sought to imitate Matthew 19:21, "If you wish to be perfect, go, sell your possessions, and give the money to the poor, and you will have treasure in heaven; then come, follow me." She built up the church through her charity, as in Acts 4:34-35, "There was not a needy person among them, for as many as owned lands or houses sold them and brought the proceeds of what was sold. They laid it at the apostles' feet, and it was distributed to each as any had need." Obviously, therefore, Macrina's looking back at her life does not involve recalling material ease and comfort. Rather, as Gregory summarizes her deathbed reflections, "she never stopped working her hands in the service of God nor did she ever look to man for help nor through any human agency did there come to her the opportunity for a life of comfort" (38). Her life was one of prayer and work for others; in this respect she imitated Paul's unceasing work in building up the church.

Was her life, then, a misery of drudgery? Gregory interjects at this point; for after she has recalled her parents' and her own life, he begins to complain about the troubles that he has been experiencing, including being exiled by Emperor Valens during the semi-Arian controversy, as well as all the troubles he has endured through disputations and conflicts. Macrina, however, meets Gregory's complaints about his own life of service to Christ's church with a strong reminder to Gregory that gratitude should always be the governing impulse of looking back on one's life. She asks him: "Will you not put an end to your failure to recognise the good things which come from God?" (39).[33] She reminds him that he is even better known as a servant of Christ and pastor than was their father, and that he should be grateful to be able to be of service in this period of controversy among the churches.

Her main point, as with the retelling of her own life, is the fittingness of gratitude for whatever blessings God has bestowed in one's life. Every life can be looked at from various angles: from one angle, a life can seem mere toil and troubles, while from another angle, the blessings (however great or small they may have been) stand out. Macrina urges that life be recalled from the perspective of gratitude for the blessings received. In this regard, as in her regular recitation of the psalter, her life is embedded in the church's liturgical praise and thanksgiving to God.

After Macrina has finished the backward-looking story of her life and blessings, she hears the community choir singing its "evening thanksgiving prayers" (39). The liturgical movement of her life, rooted in gratitude, has reached its "evening." The "day" of her life is passing. Gregory describes his response to listening to her discourse on her life (and to her urging him to be grateful for his own life): "I kept wishing that the day could be lengthened so that she might not cease to delight our hearing" (39). This "day" likely signifies her life, with its liturgical rhythm of grateful prayer, instruction, and service. Her earthly life is coming to an end, but the choir singing thanksgiving prayers as day ends reminds us that in dying, she is entering fully into the "day" in which she has already, in a real sense, been living. In dying, Macrina instructs Gregory in how to live by her own actions: "the great Macrina sent me off to church too and withdrew herself to God in prayer" (39). Macrina makes clear that Gregory's life, too, must constantly be enfolded within the liturgical matrix of the church that offers true thanksgiving to God. By withdrawing herself to pray, Macrina also imitates Christ's withdrawal to pray on the eve of his crucifixion, and shows her configuration to his "not what I want but what you want" (Matt. 26:39).

Having looked backward to her earthly life with gratitude (a gratitude to God that, through its connection to her future with God, goes well beyond mere gratitude to one's parents and society for a "useful and rewarding" life), she is looking forward to her life with God; yet she must first cross the agony of death. When Gregory comes to her room the next morning, he sees that she will not live through another day; her breathing is "shallow and tortured" (39). She makes clear that she does not fear death, since her life has already been given to God in her daily prayer and service, and so she is embracing "what she had chosen for this life, right from the beginning up to her last breath" (40). In dying she lives out the values of her life, and this gives her dying its dignity as a thanksgiving offering to God, connected with the whole church's liturgical offering of eucharistic thanksgiving in Christ.

On seeing Macrina, Gregory says of her that "it was as if an angel had providentially assumed human form, an angel in whom there was no affinity for, nor attachment to, the life of the flesh, about whom it was not unreasonable that her thinking should remain impassible, since the flesh did not drag it down to its own passions" (40).[34] In Acts 6:15, Stephen (approaching his death) is likewise said to assume "the face of an angel." The Neoplatonic implication of Gregory's description is that Macrina, through her chastity and virginity, had managed to avoid the earthliness of the body and thereby had retained a pure soul. Gregory goes on to mention her "pure, divine love of the unseen bridegroom," Christ (40). Just as the church is married to Christ (Eph. 5), so is Macrina. Macrina's self-offering and the church's are intrinsically united.

Gregory here emphasizes how desirous Macrina now is to be free of the body: "she seemed to transmit the desire which was in her heart to rush to the one she longed for, so that freed from the fetters of the body, she might swiftly be with him" (40). Is the body, then, a mere Neoplatonic weight fettering the angel-like soul? I think that the answer is no, although Gregory is obviously influenced by Neoplatonism. His statement about Macrina's desire to be free "from the fetters of the body" resonates with Paul's remarks to the Philippians that "living is Christ and dying is gain" and that "my desire is to depart and be with Christ, for that is far better" (Phil. 1:21, 23; cf. 2 Cor. 5:1–9). Gregory has shown that for Macrina, too, "living is Christ": that is, her life is thanksgiving, instruction, and service.

In dying, her life is also Christ, but when she has died she will be fully united with "the beauty of the bridegroom" (40). As her death approaches, she is looking forward to being with her Beloved and with all those who love him, thereby consummating her ecclesial vocation.

The emphasis on her growing configuration with Christ through her suffering and dying, and on her forward-looking expectation of union with him, is augmented by two further details reported by Gregory. First, her friends turn her bed toward the east, so as to face the risen Lord who will come again from the east at the last judgment. In facing east, she is facing in the direction of the church building and altar. In her dying, then, she is configured physically to the church's eucharistic offering of thanksgiving. The repositioning of her bed expresses her forward-looking expectation of meeting the risen Christ, as she has already met him in the Eucharist. Second, she no longer reflects upon her past life and no longer has time for further instruction of her brother or her friends. Instead, on the verge of dying, she now becomes as forward-looking as she can be. Gregory relates that "she stopped conversing with us and was with God in prayer for the rest of the time, reaching out her hands in supplication and speaking in a low, faint voice so that we could only just hear what she said" (40–41).

In her forward-looking dying, has she now undertaken a flight from the world, a pure soul returning to its origin, shaking the dust of the earth from her feet? As she prays to God in her physical agony, Gregory is able to overhear her prayer. Her prayer, in the stylized form that Gregory presents it, is far from that of a pure soul shaking the dust off. It is a thoroughly Christ-centered prayer, rooted in profound gratitude. She begins by praising the Lord for having "released us . . . from the fear of death," alluding to Hebrews 2:15, which states that Christ "free[d] those who all their lives were held in slavery by the fear of death" (41).[35] She goes on to express the Christian understanding of death as a journey to life: "You have made the end of life here on earth a beginning of true life for us" (41). She looks forward not to a disembodied existence in heaven but specifically to the last judgment and the resurrection of the just. She prays in grateful praise of Christ, "You let our bodies rest in sleep in due season and you awaken them again at the sound of the last trumpet. You entrust to the earth our bodies of earth which you fashioned with your own hands and you restore again what you have given, transforming with incorruptibility and grace what is mortal and deformed in us" (41).

Far from shaking the dust off, then, her forward-looking prayer in dying involves the whole of material reality no less than does Nuland's suggestion that in dying we should altruistically hand our lives over to the cosmic evolutionary process. She envisions the whole of material reality being transformed "with incorruptibility and grace," but it will remain material. Her perspective completely accords with 1 Corinthians 15:42, "So is it with the resurrection of the dead. What is sown is perishable, what is raised is imperishable." She looks forward to the culmination of the entirety of human and cosmic history, when, as Paul says, "we will all be changed, in a moment, in the twinkling of an eye, at the last trumpet. For the trumpet will sound, and the dead will be raised imperishable" (1 Cor. 15:51–52).

Referencing Galatians 3:13 and 2 Corinthians 5:21, Macrina praises God for having "redeemed us from the curse and from sin, having become both on our behalf." The hinge for Macrina's grateful understanding of the defeat of death is not the release of the soul from the body, but rather the historical work of Christ. In dying, therefore, she is moving into the fulfillment of history rather than into the negation of history. In her prayer, she gives thanks to Jesus because he "crushed the head of the serpent who had seized man in his jaws because of the abyss of our disobedience" (41). Her reference is to the very beginning of human history, when God tells the "serpent" after the fall: "I will put enmity between you and the woman, and between your offspring and hers; he will strike your head, and you will strike his heel" (Gen. 3:15).

Macrina also praises Jesus Christ for opening up the path of resurrection through his own death. In his death, she finds the meaning and value of her dying; again she is following Paul: "For if we have been united with him in a death like his, we will certainly be united with him in a resurrection like his. . . . If we have died with Christ, we believe that we will also live with him" (Rom. 6:5, 8). By paraphrasing Hebrews 2:14, which teaches that through his death Christ "destroy[ed] him who has the power of death, that is, the devil," Macrina revels in the meaning that Christ has infused into death. What would otherwise have been a path to deepest exile and alienation (or even, as Nuland thinks, to nonbeing) has become a path to the perfect fulfillment of the church's communion with God.

Macrina does not rely upon words or interior thoughts alone for her forward-looking communion with God. Her prayer refers to the physical sign of the cross. She speaks of "a visible token, the sign of the holy cross," that enables those who are marked by this sign to accomplish "the destruction of the Adversary" (41). The reference here may be to Revelation 7:3, where the angel of God calls to the destroying angels: "Do not damage the earth or the sea or the trees, until we have marked the servants of our God with a seal on their foreheads"—which itself is a reference to Ezekiel 9:4. Even if Macrina is not making such a connection, her insistence upon the sign of the cross shows again that Gregory's earlier comparison of Macrina in her dying to "an angel" should not be interpreted as though Macrina were advocating a merely Platonic escape of the soul from history and physical things.

In her dying prayer, too, Macrina's forward-looking intensity (recall that she no longer speaks with her brother or friends) incorporates some backward-looking elements regarding her life, because otherwise it could not include her grateful devotion to Christ as her Savior. In looking forward to life with Christ, moreover, she recalls her lifelong commitment to Christ. She does so not as a saint but as a sinner. She compares herself to the thief crucified by the side of Christ, and with deep penitence she begs for mercy for her sins. Christ was crucified next to two thieves, and while one reviled him, the other defended him and asked, "Jesus, remember me when you come into your kingdom"—to which Jesus replied, "Truly, I tell you, today you will be with me in Paradise" (Luke 23:42–43). In looking forward, Macrina presents herself to God as one who depends entirely upon Christ.[36] She does not rely on a nameless God or on the soul's immortality (though she certainly believes in the latter), but rather she relies on Jesus. In describing her love for God, she says that during her life she has loved God with all her strength (cf. Mark 12:30) and indeed has consecrated to God her whole bodily life (rather than marrying: cf. 1 Cor. 7). But she says this in a spirit of penitent humility, relying for salvation solely on the power of the cross of Christ. She prays, "You who have cut through the flame of the fiery sword and brought to paradise the man who was crucified with you . . . remember me also in your kingdom" (42).

At the same time, she observes in this prayer that she is not relying on Christ as though she has not previously known him. Like Paul, who states, "I have been crucified with Christ, and it is no longer I who live, but it is Christ who lives in me" (Gal. 2:19–20), she urges that she has "been crucified with you [Christ], for I have nailed my flesh out of reverence for you and have feared your judgements" (42). Like Paul, she has sought to "punish [her] body and enslave it" (1 Cor. 9:27) so as to share in the blessings of the gospel. Nonetheless, Macrina recognizes the threat posed by death and begs Christ for strength to persevere. Dying will seal her ultimate destiny, and so dying is a fearful thing. As Nuland says from a different perspective, but surely with accuracy, "No matter the degree to which a man thinks he has convinced himself that the process of dying is not to be dreaded, he will yet approach his final illness with dread."[37] Macrina prays that God will keep her safe from hell, meaning the everlasting loss of communion with God. Not the immortality of the soul, but rather charity is what bridges us to eternal life; and the strength of our charity does not suffice to make this crossing by our own power. Divine mercy, the forgiveness of sins, is at the center of her consciousness as she looks forward to the fearful journey of death. With the parable of the rich man and Lazarus in view, she prays, "Let not the dreadful abyss separate me from your chosen ones. Let not the Slanderer stand against me on my journey" (42). Dying itself, then, consists not only in a looking backward and a looking forward, but also in a journey that has a precise goal: to reach Christ's "chosen ones," the blessed saints and angels who are filled with love.

For Nuland, the dying person is at the center of the drama. By contrast, the person of Jesus Christ stands at the center for Macrina. She prays for forgiveness, with an urgency that seemingly belies the angelic serenity depicted by Gregory but that in fact flows from what Gregory calls her longing "to rush impulsively to her beloved" (40). Since she cannot fully know her own heart, even though she knows that her life has been devoted to Christ, she prays: "Let not my sin be discovered before your eyes if I have been overcome in any way because of nature's weakness and have sinned in word or deed or thought. You who have on earth the power to forgive sins, forgive me" (42).[38]

The final words of Macrina's prayer emphasize again that her body is dying, and very soon she will be a soul before the judgment of Christ. Only the forgiveness won by Christ will enable her truly to "draw breath again" (42). The journey of dying is therefore both an interpersonal drama and one on which her whole life now hinges. She asks God that she "may be found before you in the stripping off of my body without stain or blemish in the beauty of my soul, but may my soul be received blameless and immaculate into your hands as an incense offering before your face" (42). This liturgical imagery is reflective of her whole life, and she implores God to turn her drama of dying into a pleasing offering, in union with Christ's pleasing offering to God.

To express her bodily union with the cross as well as (by God's grace and mercy) her interior union with the cross, Macrina physically traces "the sign of the cross on her eyes, her mouth and her heart" while she is praying—thereby asking God to forgive whatever sins she may have committed and also to conform her completely to Christ, just as she was configured to Christ in the church's sacrament of baptism, in which the baptized person was signed with the cross (43). Her completion of this act of tracing the sign of the cross brings her prayer to an end, and she immediately breathes her last. Her eyes and mouth are closed and her hands are suitably arranged, so that her bodily dying does not require the usual closing of the eyes and so on. Gregory tells us that "the whole position of her body was so spontaneously and beautifully harmonised that any hand to compose the features was superfluous" (43). Body and soul are here united; in her dying, her whole life has taken its harmonious final form as a liturgical offering of grateful praise, expressive of the church community that her acts of love, in Christ and through the Spirit, have built up around her.[39]

Conclusion

For Nuland, the stylization no doubt present in Gregory's portrait of his sister's death would almost surely undermine its message of gratitude in dying—as would Macrina's confidence in the salvation won by Christ. Nuland points out that (assuming we do not hope for a swift death or to die in our sleep) we often "cling to an image of our final moments that combines grace with a sense of closure; we need to believe in a clear-minded process in which the summation of a life takes place," as it does for Macrina.[40] While acknowledging the psychological power of this ideal image of dying, Nuland states that "the classic image of dying with dignity must be modified or even discarded," because most dying persons face waves of suffering that take away their abilities and leave them at the mercy of the physical "indignities being visited on them"—even if "the hour of death itself is commonly tranquil and often preceded by blissful unawareness" (268).

Nuland states bluntly, "The quest to achieve true dignity fails when our bodies fail," noting that, in his many years of experience, "I have not often seen much dignity in the process by which we die" (xvii).[41] He grants that there are a few exceptions, as Macrina appears to have been. As Nuland puts it (not of course with Macrina in mind), "Occasionally—very occasionally—unique circumstances of death will be granted to someone with a unique personality, and that lucky combination will make it [a digni-fied death] happen, but such a confluence of fortune is uncommon" (xvii). Despite the ravages of the fever that killed her, Macrina seems to have retained her mental capacities to the end and to have been strong enough to sustain grateful and penitent prayer even at the very end of her process of dying.

As we saw, Nuland affirms that "who has lived in dignity, dies in dignity" (xvii). Again, by "dignity" Nuland also means the following: "If by our work and pleasure, our triumphs and our failures, each of us is contributing to an evolving process of continuity not only of our species but of the entire balance of nature, the dignity we create in the time allotted to us becomes a continuum with the dignity we achieve by the altruism of accepting the necessity of death" (267).[42] On this basis, he identifies our principal cause for hope in the face of death: "Hope resides in the meaning of what our lives have been" (242).

Gregory and Macrina complicate this notion of "dignity" and of "hope." Macrina shows that "who has lived in dignity, dies in dignity." But dignity does not reside in our achievements and merely human relationships. Macrina's "dignity" consists primarily in her participation in the church's liturgical life, through which the people of God offer themselves in Christ as a sacrifice of thanksgiving, and which extends itself in works of mercy. Prayerful praise and thanksgiving stand at the core of Macrina's conception of human dignity. Since we cannot rely upon our own strength or our own charity, we must penitently beg for divine forgiveness. But our greatness consists in imitating Christ's self-sacrificial love, a love rooted in humble gratitude for all the gifts that God bestows. Our lives become liturgically enfolded into the sacrificial path of thanksgiving that Christ, in his dying, has established for his followers.

For Nuland, in dying we should look back upon the "useful and rewarding" aspects of our life, including our relationships, and we should look forward altruistically to the onward churning of the cosmic evolutionary process. In Nuland's view, therefore, looking back involves *interpersonal* relationships, but looking forward has to do with an *impersonal* process (beyond the memories that our friends, who will soon die themselves, may have of us). Furthermore, for Nuland, looking back in appreciation of our lives is mainly focused on ourselves and our achievements.

By contrast, Macrina looks back first and foremost to God's creative and redemptive work in Christ (and his church), through which she interprets her own life and the lives of her siblings, parents, and grandparents, and she looks forward to a profoundly intimate union with God, in which "this mortal body puts on immortality" (1 Cor. 15:54) and "the sting of death" (1 Cor. 15:56) is no more.[43] No wonder she dies with so much gratitude. When she looks back with gratitude on her life, she recollects not so much her accomplishments as her union with Christ—as she says, "I too have been crucified with you, for I have nailed my flesh out of reverence for you and have feared your judgments."[44] She looks forward with gratitude to the fullness of sharing in Christ's risen life, by sharing through her suffering and dying—within Christ's community of thanksgiving—in his "path to the resurrection."[45] It is Christ, and our grateful participation in Christ's offering of praise, that is at the center of Macrina's drama in living and in dying.

Macrina's dying fits with her living, as Nuland urges should be the case for each of us. Grateful love and communion embody the true sense of "dignity" that Nuland gropes for and surely values, as when in speaking of his wife he praises her "love" and "unquenchable faith."[46] In Macrina's dying, as in her living, we find the source of Christian dignity: "from his fullness we have all received, grace upon grace" (John 1:16). The words of Elizabeth of the Trinity, written as she approached her death from tuberculosis in 1906, confirm the grateful dying that we witness in Macrina: "If you walk rooted in Christ, strengthened in your faith, you will live in thanksgiving."[47]

CHAPTER 6

SOLIDARITY

Divine Mercy and Redemptive Suffering

It should be apparent that the chapters thus far have formed something of a unity with respect to the process of dying. In the book's first five chapters, I have addressed dying persons' fear of annihilation, unfulfilled desires, and the process of looking back upon their life and looking forward to their future. Almost all dying persons, Christians included, experience these aspects of dying, and I have examined them in light of virtues that they foster and require. On this foundation, the book's final four chapters address troubling and difficult questions that dying persons often have. These questions include what good can come to us or to anyone else from our suffering and dying (ch. 6), and why we have to suffer and die even after Christ has conquered death (ch. 7). The questions also include how Christ, through his church, prepares us as our dying becomes imminent (ch. 8) and whether life in Christ after death will be fundamentally like the present life (ch. 9). Whereas the first five chapters cohere thematically, the final four chapters discuss questions that become pressing especially as death approaches. The virtues that take center stage in the final four chapters—solidarity, humility, self-surrender, and courage—are as import-ant for Christian dying as are the foundational virtues of love, hope, faith, penitence, and gratitude.

The present chapter has to do with the fact that God's people share in solidarity in Christ's suffering and dying, and thus in the suffering and dying of all for whom Christ died. This compassionate solidarity, rooted in the power of Christ's love, has in Catholic theology often been termed "redemptive suffering."[1] I will discuss this phrase further below, but at the outset an urgent question arises. Does "redemptive suffering" necessarily (in the words of Christopher Vogt) "lead to the distorted view that pain and suffering is in itself a good thing"?[2] The New Testament scholar Bart Ehrman comments in this regard, "I know there are people who argue that recognizing the pain in the world can make us nobler human beings but, frankly, I find this view offensive and repulsive. . . . There is a lot of suffering in the world that is not redemptive for anybody."[3]

If Ehrman's point is simply that suffering is not a good in itself for anyone, Christians must (and do) strongly agree. Consider the killing of "all the children in and around Bethlehem who were two years old or under" (Matt. 2:16), or the killing of the innocent man Jesus in obedience to Pontius Pilate's command. In itself, the pain endured by these innocent persons is "offensive and repulsive" in the eyes of God. The victims of violence, natural disasters, and bodily diseases are not God's victims, and God does not rejoice in their suffering (see Wisd. of Sol. 1:13), even if God can use these evils to achieve his own good purposes. Insofar as Ehrman is suggesting that Christians hold suffering to be a good in itself, he is mistaken.[4]

Yet, in the fallen world, even God's most beloved servants endure terrible sufferings, as becomes clear from the outset of Genesis: "Cain rose up against his brother Abel, and killed him" (Gen. 4:8). Scripture does not sentimentalize or overlook the suffering of God's beloved. For example, God loves Jeremiah so much that he tells him, "Before I formed you in the womb I knew you, and before you were born I consecrated you; I appointed you a prophet to the nations" (Jer. 1:5). Yet Jeremiah ends up cursing his very birth: "Woe is me, my mother, that you ever bore me, a man of strife and contention to the whole land!" (15:10). Although Jeremiah is privileged to be the bearer of God's words, nonetheless he asks God: "Why is my pain unceasing, my wound incurable, refusing to be healed? Truly, you are to me like a deceitful brook, like waters that fail" (15:18). After being placed in the stocks due to the stern prophetic warnings he delivered, Jeremiah cries out even more strongly: "Cursed be the day on which I was born! The day when my mother bore me, let it not be blessed! . . . Why did I come forth from the womb to see toil and sorrow, and spend my days in shame?" (20:14, 18).[5]

In saying all this, Jeremiah is not denying that God will eventually triumph. He knows that his suffering and that of his people are temporary. God promises through Jeremiah, "The days are surely coming, says the LORD, when I will raise up for David a righteous Branch, and he shall reign as king and deal wisely, and shall execute justice and righteousness in the land. In his days Judah will be saved and Israel will live in safety" (23:5–6). But if God will triumph, why does God now permit his people, including his most beloved servants, to suffer so much at the hands of evil or ignorant persons?

In the context of the fallen world, God even *encourages* his people to suffer and die in faithful love for God and neighbor. Along these lines, Jesus warns in the Gospel of Matthew, "Do not think that I have come to bring peace to the earth; I have not come to bring peace, but a sword. . . . Whoever does not take up the cross and follow me is not worthy of me. Those who find their life will lose it, and those who lose their life for my sake will find it" (Matt. 10:34, 39).[6] Jesus's followers, then, must embrace their suffering (their "cross"), and they must lose their life—both metaphorically and literally. The world will be a place of conflict for them as they share in the tribulation that Jesus underwent. Rather mysteriously, however, Jesus promises that by bearing his "yoke" and learning from him, his people will find "rest for [their] souls" (11:29). Since his "yoke" is one of suffering, how is it that suffering is positive for Jesus's followers? How do we find this spiritual "rest" in bearing the yoke of suffering?

Paul argues that for Christians, suffering is a salvific participation in Christ's sufferings, by which the body of Christ is built up in the power of love. When the risen and ascended Christ converts Paul, Christ shows "him how much he must suffer for the sake of my name" (Acts 9:16).[7] In spreading the gospel to the Corinthians, Paul proclaims, "just as the sufferings of Christ are abundant for us, so also our consolation is abundant through Christ" (2 Cor. 1:5).[8] Connecting our suffering in Christ with our coming exaltation, Paul states that believers are "heirs of God and joint heirs with Christ—if, in fact, we suffer with him so that we may also be glorified with him" (Rom. 8:17).[9] Suffering is redemptive for Christians, not because suffering (or dying) is good in itself, but because it unites us more deeply with the redemptive suffering of Christ and helps to make Christ manifest to the whole world. In this way, God's "power is made perfect in weakness" (2 Cor. 12:9).[10]

When we suffer in union with Christ, and thus also in union with the neighbor whom Christ loves, we allow the transformative power of his redemptive suffering to be at work in the world. This is the mission of the church. Paul puts this most concretely in Colossians 1:24, "I am now rejoicing in my sufferings for your sake, and in my flesh I am completing what is lacking in Christ's afflictions for the sake of his body, that is, the church."[11] Because his sufferings are part of his ministry of love in Christ,

Paul builds up the church by his sufferings and in this sense "complet[es] what is lacking in Christ's afflictions." For this reason, Paul states that we should be "always carrying in the body the death of Jesus, so that the life of Jesus may also be made visible in our bodies. For while we live, we are always being given up to death for Jesus' sake, so that the life of Jesus may be made visible in our mortal flesh" (2 Cor. 4:10–11).[12] As the New Testament scholar Michael Gorman describes Paul's understanding of Christian suffering (and dying) in Christ: "This corporate character of being in Christ corresponds to the inherently relational character of cruciformity. Cruciform faith is not complete until it issues in cruciform love for others. Cruciform love and power are ways of being for others, expressions of commitment to the weak, to a larger body, and to enemies."[13] Indeed, Gorman goes so far as to speak of our "co-crucifixion" with Christ in building up his body in love.[14]

What kind of masochistic religion, however, would make suffering and dying so central not only to Jesus's redemptive work but to our redemptive participation in it? In the next chapter, I will address this topic in light of Christ's own dying. In the present chapter, I engage the topic by asking whether, in the fallen world, it is appropriate to valorize suffering and dying as the path of true solidarity with and love for God and neighbor in Christ, the path by which the Holy Spirit makes us "heirs of God and joint heirs with Christ—if, in fact, we suffer with him [Christ] so that we may also be glorified with him" (Rom. 8:17).

In what follows, I begin with Jon Sobrino's *Where Is God?* It would seem that Sobrino would oppose attributing a positive value to suffering and dying, since Sobrino—as all Christians must—seeks to eradicate the terrible suffering and early death caused by involuntary poverty. In fact, however, Sobrino appeals to the goodness and indeed necessity of voluntary suffering, when he calls upon Christians to show real solidarity (or co-suffering) with the poor in Christ. This solidarity in suffering, of course, seeks lovingly to ameliorate or heal the suffering and dying of the poor, since as Archbishop Oscar Romero observes, "Many would like the poor to keep on saying that it is God's will for them to live that way. But it is not God's will for some to have everything and others to have nothing. That cannot be of God."[15]

Notwithstanding his insistence upon solidarity with those who suffer, Sobrino generally overlooks the involuntary suffering and dying that even the privileged classes endure—often with great loneliness and despair—on a daily basis. Henri Nouwen, who spent much of his career living and working with the disabled at *L'Arche,* insightfully observes, "We all die poor. When we come to our final hours, nothing can help us survive. No amount of money, power, or influence can keep us from dying. This is true poverty."[16] As a second step, therefore, I examine mortal suffering as depicted in the *Diary* of Saint Maria Faustina Kowalska. Faustina connects her suffering to her divinely given vocation to spread devotion to Christ's divine mercy, and thereby to build up Christ's church in the power of Christ's love. Faustina's mortal suffering is involuntary, and yet Christ uses it to build up her solidarity with his salvific suffering and to show how in suffering with him she can bear witness in love to the world's need for divine mercy as the basis of true communion.

In Gorman's words, we "are called to be holy through ongoing 'co-crucifixion' with Christ by the power of the *Holy* Spirit."[17] The crucified and risen Christ wishes to convey his life to the dying. He works through his cruciform followers, who are called to co-suffer lovingly and actively in solidarity with those who are suffering and dying. Indeed, all love-filled suffering in the body of Christ, no matter how unjust and horrible, is an active co-suffering with our Savior Christ, in solidarity with all who are suffering physically and spiritually. Such co-suffering is rooted in the desire to heal and rectify suffering where possible and to unite sufferers with the wondrous power of Christ's love.[18] Paul says in 1 Corinthians 12:26, "If one member suffers, all suffer together"; and Ruth Ashfield therefore observes that "it is the gift of the dying person to call forth from his community and his culture true compassion . . . as what is necessary for true communion."[19] Pope Benedict XVI sums up this christological reality in his encyclical *Spe Salvi*: "The true measure of humanity is essentially determined in relationship to suffering and to the sufferer."[20]

Jon Sobrino's *Where Was God?*

In a manner that has recently been strongly echoed by Pope Francis in his apostolic exhortation *Evangelii Gaudium,* Jon Sobrino emphasizes that the world needs "the solidarity to bear one another's burdens."[21] With an eye to the political and economic situation of El Salvador, Sobrino argues that "there is no redemption without 'bearing the burden' of sin, barbarity, and injustice" (148).[22] If we truly love other people who are suffering, we will make sacrifices in order to reach out to them and to care for them. We will do things that expose us in some way to the same evildoers and problems that afflict those who are suffering. As examples, Sobrino recalls Archbishop Romero and the Jesuit theologian Ignacio Ellacuría. Although they did not become literally poor, they placed their hearts and minds at the service of the suffering poor. As Sobrino says of Romero and Ellacuría, "the poor wanted them to be different, with the power of the word and the institutional church, the power of reason and the institutional university [and the associated financial resources], that they had and the poor did not" (145). In solidarity with the poor, Romero and Ellacuría accepted vulnerability and ultimately martyrdom. Their words and actions demonstrated that they truly loved their impoverished sisters and brothers rather than simply enjoying their own economic and social privilege. In caring for the poor, Romero "refused to accept personal protection," and Ellacuría came back from Spain during a political crisis in order to serve as rector of Jose Simeon Canas Central American University (145). In such cases, Sobrino allows for "the solidarity of unequals as mutual support between the world of poverty and the world of affluence" (97).[23]

Sobrino focuses on "the people bearing the burden of it all"—in Ellacuría's phrase, "the crucified people," the poor who live and die within structures of sin that crush them to the ground and who more than anyone else suffer the weight of what (economic and political) sinners have done and are doing, as well as the weight of natural disasters and disease (50).[24] He exposes the deep physical and psychological vulnerability of most human beings, and the deadly effects that powerful people's sins have upon poor and powerless bystanders. He illumines the ways in which poor people—and indeed all people who live in impoverished countries—bear tremendous burdens that wealthier people and wealthier societies avoid. As he comments cuttingly, "For the enjoyment of life and human rights it helps to have been born in Bonn or in Boston, rather than in Rwanda or Honduras" (59). Given this situation, he argues that Christians in Bonn or Boston cannot truly have "faith" if they willfully blind themselves to the reality of the suffering condition of their brothers and sisters, or if they refuse to do "justice and righteousness" (40).

For Sobrino, as for Romero, "it is the love of Jesus (and of God) that saves, not bloodshed. The love of Jesus saves human beings, especially victims; love that stays through to the end, even if it leads to a cross. That is what we call redemption" (148).[25] On the cross, Jesus's solidarity with sinners "stays through to the end." Jesus certainly does bear "the burden of evil from within"; as a truly innocent man, he enters into the condition of sinners and bears the cost of sins (149). He exhibits in full "the solidarity to bear one another's burdens" (148). By staying "through to the end" in profound solidarity with us—by sacrificing his own life out of love for us—he "bears the burden of evil from within." Drawing upon Paul, Sobrino states, "On the cross he [Jesus] bore the weight of sin; sin unleashed its power on him and had no power left to do more harm," because he died (149).

Since the present world is filled with human suffering and dying, followers of Jesus must, in love, associate themselves with those who suffer and seek healing and justice for them. By joining them in their suffering, we act as Jesus did and freely undergo suffering ourselves out of love for those who suffer. This suffering with others, insofar as we are willing to stay "through to the end" and to endure others' crosses with them, is a participation in Jesus's love-filled suffering that exhibits the truth of the church's faith. Indebted to Pedro Casaldáliga, Sobrino suggests that "bearing the burden of reality" with others should take place with a context of "confident contemplation, coherent witness, brotherly-sisterly community, an embrace of love and service, prophetic commitment, and paschal hope" (148).[26]

When Sobrino speaks of "solidarity" or "bearing one another's burdens," his emphasis is on the situation of the involuntarily poor. He also argues that indeed there can be no true solidarity so long as humans continue to live in such radically different economic and political conditions on earth. He asks rhetorically: "Is there solidarity on a planet where one child in the First World consumes as many resources as 400 children in Ethiopia? This is a paradigmatic example of reality on this planet, of insolidarity even in normal times" (20).[27] In his view, to be in true solidarity with others who are suffering must involve actively suffering with those who are enduring suffering in (for example) Ethiopia, rather than allowing oneself—if one lives in comparative luxury—to rest content with or enjoy one's privileges. He urges that programs of economic assistance must be lived out by sharing in the life of those whom we (namely, economically privileged people) assist, so that "assistance will be transformed into solidarity, and that it will be *human* solidarity," not only "for each other" but "with each other" (20).[28]

Sobrino rightly says that those who are suffering (those who are "victims") "are signs and sacraments of a mysterious reality, the reality of a God who participates in their suffering" (23).[29] I add that although the wealthy generally obtain more decades of life, they too meet with death and often suffer terribly.[30] We therefore need to be in deep solidarity with those who are dying. Christ has already borne this "burden of evil from within"; he has died for us and shown us the path of love. If we are following Christ, then, we cannot *not* be in solidarity with those who are in the process of dying. When people are in the midst of dying, we must exhibit "the solidarity to bear one another's burdens." Mother Teresa's homes for the dying exemplify this task, but surely it is a task for every Christian (and every local church community), since we all have relatives, friends, neighbors, and fellow parishioners who are dying.[31]

Given his economic focus, Sobrino sometimes downplays the interior sinfulness that afflicts the economically poor—as it also does the economically wealthy, whose sinfulness Sobrino amply recognizes. He speaks of the economically poor as having a natural faith, and of the wealthy as having a faith *obtained from* the economically poor. Along these lines, he argues: "The faith of the 'enlightened' [i.e., the nonpoor] is expressed in their sincere attempts to lower themselves, and in their life-risking struggle for justice; but this faith has been brought out by the primary faith of the crucified people, for whom it is entirely natural to live in humility and to take risks in the struggle for life" (95).[32] I grant that the involuntarily poor can be more open to the message of the gospel (which comes from Christ and his apostles) and to prayerful dependence upon God. But in Sobrino's account of "primordial saintliness and primordial martyrdom," he suggests that simply having to endure "unjustly inflicted suffering"—as all the involuntarily poor do, and as (in a certain sense) mortal illness also involves—establishes persons on the Christian path (78).[33] The danger here is that the notion of "primordial saintliness" may obscure the freedom of the involuntarily poor (and of the dying) to choose for or against the gospel, and may even logically excuse what Pope Francis decries when he states that "the worst discrimination which the poor suffer is the lack of spiritual care."[34]

Given the freedom of persons when it comes to embracing faith and to living in love, I cannot equate, as Sobrino does, the body of the crucified Lord simply with "the poor and crucified peoples" (79), if by this is simply meant the economically and politically powerless. Sobrino grants that "in comparison with Jesus' death, the massacre victims' deaths are *less* reflective of Jesus' praxis of defending the poor and actively struggling against the anti-kingdom; they are also *less* reflective of Jesus' faithfulness in the face of persecution, and of the freedom with which he confronted death" (77). But the massacre victims still deserve regard as Christian martyrs, in his view, because they were poor and defenseless and representative of the way in which impoverished "majorities unjustly bear the burden of the sin that has been destroying them bit by bit in life, and has completely annihilated them in death" (77). In my view, particular members of the impoverished majorities must freely come to possess the interior virtues of faith and charity. The same holds for those who are mortally ill, who find themselves bearing the burden of original sin and its consequences.[35]

Sobrino comments, "These poor people and victims may well be 'holy sinners,' in the conventional understanding of holiness and sin. The poor are also sometimes overcome by the mystery of iniquity" (74). But insofar as the appellation "holy sinners" includes people in a condition of unrepentant rejection of God, the appellation is misleading. Sobrino justifies his phrase by arguing that he is simply speaking of "the saintliness of suffering for the will to live, which is different from—more fundamental than—the saintliness of virtue" (73).[36] The connection between Sobrino's involuntarily poor and all (wealthy or poor) who are dying is clear, since both suffer "for the will to live." Such people exhibit "everyday heroism" by their struggle to live, and they inspire our empathy and in certain ways stand as "the presence of God" and a "sacrament" of Christ for us (73).[37] However, I deny that there is a "saintliness of suffering for the will to live" that is deeper than "the saintliness of virtue." How can the two be separated, since it is precisely in the daily challenges faced by each and every person (whether involuntarily poor or involuntarily dying) that "the saintliness of virtue" either manifests itself or fails to manifest itself?[38]

Well aware of human fallenness, Sobrino states, "Human beings are capable of good, but they are also sinful. That sin involves several ways of 'killing': by assassinating, impoverishing, hurting, insulting. Killing necessarily involves concealment and lying" (41). Yet since he focuses on political and economic sins, he tends to present the involuntarily poor and the oppressed as hardly able to sin in any truly significant way, since they have no (or almost no) political or economic power. But sin dwells in the heart in a fundamental way, as Sobrino himself points out: "the human heart is darkened, and it is given up to all kinds of vice (Rom 1:18–32)" (41).[39] Sins against God and neighbor, and sins against one's own self, therefore need a fuller accounting than Sobrino provides. He adds, "Christian faith does not allow us to trivialize the victims' suffering, even by invoking God" (23). Although I think that we can affirm that God has a plan for the accomplishment of good—and that therefore the victims' involuntarily suffering is not a mere surd—I agree that we must be extremely careful not to insinuate that God is the cause of the suffering and dying of the victims. In my view, an important aspect of respecting the suffering of the poor is to affirm that they too are humans in need of redemption from sin, rather than suggesting that they are above their oppressors in this regard (see Rom. 5:8).[40]

In Christ, as Sobrino underscores, God has taken the side of those who suffer mortally, in weakness and in bodily humiliation.[41] The most valuable contribution of Sobrino is his emphasis on the need to bear the burden of God's "crucified people" to the end, in a co-suffering in love that puts our own lives on the line. Christians cannot treat dying persons as though they are forgotten or unimportant in the current of life. Sobrino sees clearly how easy it is for us to ignore the suffering and dying of others. Once people fall out of the stream of active life, out of the economic and political currents that fuel the powerful of this world, we are apt to forget about them or to pretend that they no longer exist.[42] Although Sobrino does not use the phrase "redemptive suffering," his insights into involuntary suffering as a sharing in Christ's crucifixion, a situation that urgently calls for solidarity in love, are powerfully applicable to the suffering of dying persons.[43] This is so because, as Miguel Romero points out in light of the theology of Gustavo Gutiérrez and the encyclicals of Pope John Paul II, "In a world wounded by sin and the reality of evil, our most magnificent imitation of the One who is *rich in mercy* is a volitional participation in the mystical power of *salvific suffering*," the power of Christ's self-sacrificial love.[44]

Maria Faustina Kowalska's *Diary*

This "volitional participation in the mystical power of *salvific suffering*" in union with Christ's mercy sublimely marked the life of St. Maria Faustina Kowalska. Although she suffered greatly in Christ, I will begin by sketching some of the ways in which she shared "abundantly in comfort" (2 Cor. 1:5 RSV), since Christ comforts us when we take up our cross and follow him. Her spiritual consolations, inseparable from her sufferings, highlight the working out of divine mercy that is important to Sobrino.[45] On the cross, Christ's solidarity with those who suffer exhibits his merciful love, and so suffering pertains to real solidarity. Pope John Paul II, who helped to recognize and implement Faustina's mission in the church, remarks that each person "is called to share in that suffering through which all human suffering has also been redeemed. In bringing about the Redemption through suffering, Christ *has* also *raised human suffering to the level of the Redemption*. Thus each man, in his suffering, can become a sharer in the redemptive suffering of Christ."[46]

Faustina reports that in 1925, while she was making a private vow of chastity, "God filled my soul with the interior light of a deeper knowledge of Him as Supreme Goodness and Supreme Beauty," and she received the grace of experiencing that in her heart she "always kept company with Jesus."[47] She was deeply consoled by the divine love. She recalls, "I came to know how very much God loves me. Eternal is His love for me" (9). In a period of spiritual darkness while a novice in her religious community, she experienced a glorious vision at night: "During the night, the Mother of God visited me, holding the Infant Jesus in Her arms" (14). On Good Friday of 1928, she enjoyed an infusion of Jesus's love. She describes this experience: "Jesus catches up my heart into the very flame of His love. This was during the evening adoration. All of a sudden, the Divine Presence invaded me, and I forgot everything else" (15). Again, in the fall of 1928, she received a powerful encounter with Jesus. She recounts that "when I was praying, Jesus pervaded all my soul, darkness melted away, and I heard these words within me: You are My joy; you are My heart's delight" (15–16). This intimacy with Jesus was so profound that for years thereafter she could feel God's presence within her. She remarks, "From that moment I felt the Most Holy Trinity in my heart; that is to say, within myself. I felt that I was inundated with Divine light. Since then, my soul has been in intimate communion with God, like a child with its beloved Father" (16). She even received a vision of the Trinity itself, with Christ at the center. In her words, "I saw an inaccessible light, and in this light what appeared like three sources of light which I could not understand. And out of that light came words in the form of lightning which encircled heaven and earth. . . . Suddenly, from this sea of inaccessible light came our dearly beloved Savior, unutterably beautiful with His shining Wounds" (17).

In 1931, Faustina heard Jesus saying to her after she left the confessional, "My image already is in your soul. I desire that there be a Feast of Mercy. I want this image, which you will paint with a brush, to be solemnly blessed on the first Sunday after Easter; that Sunday is to be the Feast of Mercy" (24). Later, in October 1934, she had an identical vision of Jesus. She describes it as follows: "I saw the Lord Jesus above our chapel, looking just as He did the first time I saw Him and just as He is painted on the image. The two rays which emanated from the Heart of Jesus covered our chapel and the infirmary, and then the whole city, and spread out over the whole world" (43). The two rays were also seen by one of the young wards of the sisters who was with Faustina at the time, though the image of Jesus was seen only by Faustina. In 1934, Faustina also saw a vision of Jesus (joined by Mary) during eucharistic adoration. Jesus spoke to her and named himself: "I am King of Mercy" (44). Jesus commanded, "I desire that this image be displayed in public on the first Sunday after Easter. That Sunday is the Feast of Mercy. . . . I make known the bottomless depth of My mercy" (44). The "image" mentioned here refers to the vision of Jesus that Faustina received and that Jesus commanded that she have painted on canvas.

During these same years, however, Faustina underwent intense physical and spiritual suffering. She portrays "a shadow" over her soul that deprived her of spiritual consolation in prayer; she felt her deep unworthiness and, suffering greatly, begged God to have mercy on her (12). Entering into her soul, she found "great misery," something quite far from the infinite charity and "holiness of God" (12). Shockingly, though in accord with the experience of other saints who come to discover how much they need God's mercy, she experienced for many days a sense of divine wrath against her. She reports that "there came to me the very powerful impression that I am rejected by God. This terrible thought pierced my soul right through; in the midst of the suffering my soul began to experience the agony of death" (13). Already acquainted with serious illness, she here experienced a spiritual dying, as though she were cast off by God and utterly condemned. She entered into the very heart of mortal agony—the threat that death will put an utter end to our interpersonal communion with God. As she observes, "The dreadful thought of being rejected by God is the actual torture suffered by the damned," even if in actuality it is the damned who are rejecting God, rather than the other way around (13). Even when she attempted to appeal to Jesus's "Wounds" and merciful love, she found no relief but, in fact, only "even greater torture" (13). She begged Jesus to remember that even if a mother could forget her own children, God will never forget his people (see Isa. 49:15). Yet she descended still deeper into suffering, and finally entered into "despair" and "complete darkness in the soul" (13).[48]

For Faustina, then, her spiritual darkness—spiritual suffering—was connected experientially with "the agony of death," even though she was still some years away from her death at age 33. When she entered into despair and darkness, she experienced "deadly fears"; and, as she recalls, "my physical strength began to leave me" (14). The fear of total alienation that we associate with fear of physical dying has spiritual dimensions. She recalls that even at this stage, "Jesus did not hear my cries. I felt my physical strength leave me completely. I fell to the ground, despair flooding my whole soul. I suffered terrible tortures in no way different from the torments of hell" (14). Her suffering was in this way united with Jesus's cry from the cross, "My God, my God, why have you forsaken me?" (Matt. 27:46). As her trial continued, Faustina felt as though she could not speak (for lack of voice). As she describes her experience, her "soul began to agonize again in a terrible darkness," because she felt that God had judged her and condemned her permanently as guilty (14).

In response to her "torment of the soul," she continued to cry out to Jesus and to remind Jesus of his promise to be like a merciful mother (14). At a certain point, she even experienced rage against the God who seemingly rejected her: "A terrible hatred began to break out in my soul, a hatred for all that is holy and divine" (15). Despite this hatred, shared by many who are dying, she still cried out to Jesus to make himself present to her. She reports that she even promised Jesus that she would "suffer silently like a dove, without complaining" (15)—just as Jesus accepted his suffering in silence and gave to Pilate "no answer, not even to a single charge" (Matt. 27:14).

Faustina's spiritual sufferings enabled her to see the depth of our need for divine mercy, and thereby to live in solidarity with those who suffer. In 1928 she experienced "intense yearning—a longing to love God" and "an ardent desire to empty myself for God by an active love" (15). She reports a dream in which, despite the fact that people try to thwart her, she recognizes that she must take her "place on the altar," where she will be in solidarity with Jesus (and with his salvific suffering)—and, like Jesus, she feels "a very special love" precisely for those who try to thwart her in the dream (18). She remains acutely aware of her need for redemption through Jesus. In a vision of the particular judgment, in which the soul meets Jesus, she "saw the complete condition of my soul as God sees it" (19). She recalls, "I could clearly see all that is displeasing to God. I did not know that even the smallest transgressions will have to be accounted for" (19). In the vision, Jesus draws her into union with the salvific power of his suffering in love, so that she (like Paul) has comfort in her afflictions. Jesus tells her, "Now, rest your head on My bosom, on My heart, and draw from it strength and power for these sufferings because you will find neither relief nor help nor comfort anywhere else. Know that you will have much, much to suffer, but don't let this frighten you; I am with you" (19–20).

We could respond to this by asking why the Lord Jesus would allow and even encourage a rather innocent young religious sister to suffer so much. But no human life is without suffering. Faustina's deadly physical illness also began to manifest itself strongly at this time. She reports, "Physical weakness was for me a school of patience. Only Jesus knows how many efforts of will I had to make to fulfill my duty" (20).[49] Faustina also suffered from the fact that her religious sisters did not believe her visions. Her religious sisters were not cruel, but understandably they "treated me with pity as though I were being deluded or were imagining things" (20). The result of her illness and of being disbelieved by her religious sisters was a deeper configuration to Jesus's suffering. She explains, "In order to purify a soul, Jesus uses whatever instruments He likes. My soul underwent a complete abandonment on the part of creatures" (20).

It might seem that for Faustina, God is fundamentally an inflictor of sufferings. But her central realization is the very opposite: God is pure mercy, mercifully filling up what humans lack. She emphasizes that "apart from God there is no contentment anywhere"—a truth that dying persons know (23). Notably, her sharing in Jesus's suffering for the sake of others brings her joy, because it is a sharing in self-emptying love. She reports, "I often felt the Passion of the Lord Jesus in my body. . . . These sufferings set my soul afire with love for God and for immortal souls. Love endures everything, love is stronger than death, love fears nothing" (24). Jesus's sufferings arise from his pure merciful love for sinners who, as Faustina found in her own soul, have "great misery" due to their alienated condition and even have "a hatred for all that is holy and divine" (13, 15). Our rejection of God wounds us deeply, and it is this wound that Christ's cross heals from within, as an act of his divine mercy.[50]

In this context of suffering with Christ in love, Faustina received the command from Jesus to bring it about that the Sunday after Easter be "the Feast of Mercy" and that "priests proclaim this great mercy of Mine [Jesus's] towards souls of sinners" (24). Having given her a deep awareness of solidarity with needy sinners and an equally deep awareness of solidarity with his own sufferings in love, Jesus tells Faustina: "Let the sinner not be afraid to approach Me. The flames of mercy are burning Me—clamoring to be spent; I want to pour them out upon these souls" (24–25). Faustina describes the meaning of redemptive suffering in a manner that connects explicitly with what we found in Sobrino, even if Faustina in many ways goes deeper: "I want to share compassionately in the sufferings of my neighbors. . . . Suffering is a great grace; through suffering the soul becomes like the Savior; in suffering love becomes crystallized" (29). This compassionate sharing in the sufferings of our neighbors, rooted in Christ's powerful and transformative love, is what Sobrino urges us to undertake by staying "through to the end" and bearing the burden of God's "crucified people."

As noted above, Faustina states that during the period of the first open onset of her tuberculosis, while she was still a novice, her physical suffering was joined to a spiritual darkness. Her religious superior quite sensibly commanded her "to stop tormenting [herself] for no reason," but Faustina nonetheless felt that she was not pleasing to God; indeed, as she recalled, "a deathly sadness penetrated my soul to such an extent that I was unable to hide it. . . . I lost hope" (35). Again, enduring mortal illness often involves such darkness. Although not only her religious superior but also her confessor urged her that the darkness was not a sign of lack of grace, she felt it as such. Her confessor urged her to be gentle with herself: "It is a very great grace, Sister, that in your present condition, with all the torments of soul you are experiencing, you not only do not offend God, but you even try to practice virtues" (35). Faustina tells us precisely how she tried to practice virtue: "I imitated the blind man who entrusts himself to his guide, holding his hand firmly, not giving up obedience for a single moment, and this was my only safety in this fiery trial" (35–36). Our suffering with Christ in times of spiritual darkness and mortal illness is not likely to feel particularly triumphant. It is more likely to feel like a tremendous effort in order simply to be able to say with Christ, "Father, into your hands I commend my spirit" (Luke 23:46).

The burden of mortal illness is nicely summed up by Faustina: "Only Jesus knows how burdensome and difficult it is to accomplish one's duties when the soul is so interiorly tortured, the physical powers so weakened and the mind darkened" (36). This moves us beyond a romantic notion of sharing in Christ's sufferings through a triumphant accomplishment of our own, such as through a wondrously inspiring dying process. It is a tremendous effort to accept that we are dying, that we are powerless, and that even though it feels as though we are abandoned sinners, God is with us in Christ. By clinging to the divine love and mercy during our suffering, we enter into real solidarity with Christ in his merciful love for others.

Describing her experience of such solidarity, Faustina first depicts her desolation: "When people spoke to me about God, my heart was like a rock. I could not draw from it a single sentiment of love for Him. When I tried, by an act of will, to remain close to Him, I experienced great torments, and it seemed to me that I was only provoking God to an even greater anger" (39). She then notes that "blind obedience was for me the only path I could follow and my very last hope of survival" (39–40). Abandoning herself to God's will, like Christ at Gethsemane, she prayed, "Do what You will with me, O Jesus; I will adore You in everything. May Your will be done in me, O my Lord and my God, and I will praise Your infinite mercy" (40). When she relies entirely upon Christ and not at all upon any resources in herself that she can perceive, Christ reveals himself to her in a perfect solidarity of love: "Suddenly I saw Jesus, who said to me, 'I am always in your heart.' An inconceivable joy entered my soul, and a great love of God set my heart aflame" (40).

Why is it, however, that Christ seemingly waits to the last moment? Why is it that such physical and spiritual suffering must be undergone? The answer that Faustina gives is that (as God told her) "it is precisely through such misery that I want to show the power of My mercy" (74). This does not mean that God causes misery (by no means!), but rather that acquaintance with misery (whether our own or that of others with whom we suffer in love) opens us to the power of God's merciful love in Christ. When we see miserable people in the world, we too often turn away, scared to be contaminated.[51] In the depths of her existential solidarity with sinners, Faustina herself feared that "it seems that You do not associate intimately with such wretched people as I" (74). When God revealed to her that the very opposite is the case, she rejoiced with love: "Oh, how good it is to abandon oneself totally to God and to give Him full freedom to act in one's soul!" (74).

When at the outset of her vocation Faustina received a vision of the suffering that she would endure if she embraced God's call to profound solidarity with Christ, she realized that, like Christ, "my name is to be: 'sacrifice'" (75). Christ did not force this path upon her, but when she freely embraced it and subjected herself entirely to God's will, she discovered that at the core of solidarity is not suffering but tremendous joy. She recalls: "God's presence pervaded me. My soul became immersed in God and was inundated with such happiness that I cannot put in writing even the smallest part of it" (76). She felt as though she had finally learned how to live, as indeed she had.

When we encounter mortal suffering, that of our loved ones or ourselves, how will we deal with it? Will we truly be able to stay "through to the end" without rebelling against the terribleness and the humiliation of it all?[52] Faustina's message is that Christ calls us to solidarity with him in the very depths of our soul, where we must set up no barriers to the powerful, merciful love that is Christ. Why does Christ not fix the world's problems in an easier way? The answer appears to be that we must learn to love with

God's self-emptying love, and in our fallen and mortal condition this true solidarity will entail sharing in Christ's suffering through charitable and merciful service to others. Even though suffering in itself is an evil, therefore, God turns it to his own purposes through merciful love. In solidarity with Christ, offering herself fully to God's will, Faustina proclaims: "I felt I was transformed into love; I was all afire, but without being burned up. I lost myself in God unceasingly" (79). In solidarity with Christ in love, profoundly aware of human neediness, she found herself able to help to build up the whole church with Christ's mercy.

Conclusion

The *Life of St Dunstan*, an early biography of a tenth-century archbishop of Canterbury, records that God "finally decided in His mercy that the end of Dunstan's laborious struggles should come to pass. Now, joining the blessed troops of angels, he would be rewarded in heaven with the pay for which he so often sweated while he bore God's light burden on earth."[53] In general, the *Life of St Dunstan* does not cast a friendly eye upon "the insatiable maw of greedy death," but in this case death was a relief from the suffering that is every person's lot on earth.[54] Archbishop Dunstan, however, spent most of his life with the nobility and with the powerful. Why then was he acclaimed a saint? Like Archbishop Romero, Archbishop Dunstan paid dearly for his faithfulness to Christ. After confronting the newly crowned King Eadwig, who was having sex with a mother and her daughter rather than attending to his duties at his coronation, Dunstan was exiled from England and, in imitation of Christ, endured the betrayal of his student-disciples.[55]

All people have to suffer, especially if they are poor—and also, in Dunstan's case, if they are brave enough to accept the task of correcting the powerful of this world. As Sobrino makes clear, we must accompany those who are poor and suffering, assure them by our presence and love that they are not worthless or useless, show them the love of Jesus, refuse to abandon them, and bear the crushing reality of their situation with them so that we suffer in solidarity with them. Pope Benedict XVI makes a similar point in his encyclical *Spe Salvi*, where he teaches that "to accept the 'other' who suffers means that I take up his suffering in such a way that it becomes mine also."[56] The Pontifical Council for the Promotion of the New Evangelization warns that "we can sin by omission regarding this love for the poor and needy, since mercy transcends justice ... being, in turn, more radically sensitive to and in solidarity with all kinds of poverty and marginalization."[57] All this has been summed up by Pope Francis in *Evangelii Gaudium*, when he insists, "We incarnate the duty of hearing the cry of the poor when we are deeply moved by the suffering of others."[58] If the general lack of many visitors to modern hospitals and nursing homes is any indication, many of us are sinning "by omission" with respect to the dying, who are (as Nouwen states) "languishing in hospitals and lonely rooms" in a society that is "preoccupied with ... accomplishments" and often cares only for those who can now exercise power and influence.[59]

When we are mortally ill, we will almost inevitably be beset by a variety of spiritual sufferings, including fear of alienation from God and fear of annihilation. Faustina's experience shows that physical suffering (especially that rooted in a mortal illness) and spiritual suffering are almost inevitably connected. Jesus's physical and spiritual sufferings enact the powerful divine mercy for those who are suffering. By freely uniting his or her sufferings with those of Jesus, who died in solidarity with us to heal and restore the whole world, the dying person can share in Jesus's work of mercy for the sake of others, and be transformed by the power of Christ's cross. Faustina's message conveys how deeply we need divine mercy, and also that when we discover our true neediness, we joyfully discover the depth of Jesus's solidarity with all those who need him.[60]

At its root, sharing in Jesus's sharing and dying consists in a surrender of the self to God. Like Sobrino, Henri Nouwen urges that we learn this surrender precisely from the poor: "In a mysterious way, the people dying all over the world because of starvation, oppression, illness, despair, violence, and war become our teachers."[61] When we see people dying from starvation in Somalia or from oppression in Guatemala (two countries named by Nouwen), we realize that we are their brothers and sisters, not only in the sense that we must act in solidarity with them to relieve their suffering, but also in the sense that we are in an even deeper solidarity with them because "we will die as they do."[62] Nouwen points out that we will only be generous with our lives on behalf of the suffering poor "when we are willing to let their dying help us to die well," when we fully admit that we ourselves share in the same destiny of death, where all will be united in a shared "poverty" and no one will be the "exception."[63] In this "intimate solidarity with all the people on this planet,"[64] all of whom must die, we find ourselves in solidarity with (as Benedict XVI says) the merciful God who, in Christ, "experiences and carries that suffering *with* us" and who will undo for all victims "the injustice of history."[65]

The dying, therefore, are tremendously important members of the living. Nouwen recalls his words to a dying friend, "Please trust that the time ahead of you [the final days of earthly life] will be the most important time of your life, not just for you, but for all of us whom you love and who love you."[66] This is because a dying person has a once-in-a-lifetime opportunity to share fully in Christ's "great 'compassion' [suffering-with]" and to contribute to "the treasury of compassion so greatly needed by the human race" by gifting the world with the power of a love-filled dying in union with the saving death of Christ.[67] Inevitably, dying involves a painful loneliness, but given that death is our common destiny—and given Christ's own dying—dying involves solidarity more than it involves loneliness.

Kristine Rankka observes that "if Job's experience can be used as a guide, we are brought, in and through suffering, to an encounter with God that results in a greater state of blessedness."[68] This is not because suffering in itself is good, but because, when we suffer and die in love, the Source of blessing is with us and we are with him, inhabiting his "community of cruciform generosity and justice" and "participating *now* in the life and mission of the triune cruciform God."[69] Indeed, as the Orthodox theologian John Behr reminds us, what is at stake is nothing less than becoming truly and fully human: "for us to become human requires . . . our own *martyria.*"[70] In Christ, we become fully human in solidarity with the dying.

CHAPTER 7

HUMILITY

Jesus's Dying and Ours

According to Servais Pinckaers, it can seem that the virtue of humility—a central virtue in Scripture and in patristic tradition—"receives an overly modest position" in Thomas Aquinas's *Summa theologiae*, in which Aquinas classes humility under the virtue of modesty.[1] This seems to make humility a less important virtue than temperance, since as Aquinas remarks, "temperance moderates those matters where restraint is most difficult, whereas modesty moderates those that present less difficulty."[2] Yet as Pinckaers recognizes, the true importance of humility becomes apparent in Aquinas's treatment of pride.[3] Rationally speaking, pride *should* be easy to restrain. In this vein, Aquinas remarks that once pride is "discovered by reason, it is easily avoided, both by considering one's own infirmity, according to Ecclus. x. 9, *Why is earth and ashes proud?* and by considering God's greatness, according to Job xv. 13, *Why doth thy spirit swell against God?* as well as by considering the imperfection of the goods on which man prides himself"—for example, the fact that we must die, as noted by Isaiah 40:6, "All people are grass, their constancy is like the flower of the field" (II-II, q. 161, a. 6, ad 1). Although pride should be easy to avoid, however, Aquinas finds that it turns out to be "the *queen and mother of all the vices*," and indeed, the "most difficult to avoid" (II-II, q. 162, a. 8; II-II, q. 162, a. 6, obj. 1).[4] Even when we are practicing the virtues, pride can come upon us and in a hidden way lead us to exalt ourselves and to refuse to be "subject to God and his rule" (II-II, q. 162, a. 5). Our deepest disorder consists in our constant wish to overstep our creaturely limits, as though there were "a good which is not from God" or as though grace were "given to men for their merits" (II-II, q. 162, a. 4, ad 1).

The central place of humility, then, consists in that it "properly regards the subjection of man to God," whereas "pride properly regards lack of this subjection," leading to an "aversion from God" in the proud person who scorns to be subject to God and "scorns to be subject to a creature for God's sake" (II-II, q. 162, a. 5; II-II, q. 162, a. 7, ad 2).[5] Given that humility is central to the enactment of the kingdom of God, the link between humility and dying should not surprise us.[6] Jesus urges that "whoever does not take up the cross and follow me is not worthy of me. Those who find their life will lose it, and those who lose their life for my sake will find it" (Matt. 10:38–39).[7] Jesus's kingdom involves the profound humility of the cross. It is not for nothing that, as Christopher Vogt observes, "It is a part of ordinary Catholic pastoral practice to urge those approaching death to make a conscious connection between their own dying and that of Jesus Christ."[8]

Granted the value of humility, however, it remains the case that God has "no pleasure in the death of anyone" (Ezek. 18:32).[9] Although I accept the context of original sin—whose just punishment is death—I still wonder why suffering and dying, on such a massive scale (billions of people, each of whom God knows and loves), should be so integral to God's plan, rather than being a mark of divine powerlessness to conquer sin by a means that does not perpetuate the grim cycle of suffering and dying.[10]

This chapter engages this troubling problem by means of two steps. First, I set forth Brant Pitre's historical-critical research into late Second Temple belief in the imminence of a decisive "eschatological tribulation."[11] Like N. T. Wright and others, Pitre argues that on the cross, Jesus understood himself to be the Messiah of Israel undergoing the eschatological tribulation on behalf of Israel and all nations, so that through his paschal blood they would be spared God's definitive punishment for sin and would arrive at the goal of the new exodus—although they would have to share in the tribulation. Second, I examine some of Aquinas's theological reflections on Jesus's dying and ours, in light of Aquinas's theology of humility. My contention is that the reason why God, in Christ, has chosen suffering and dying as the path of salvation for his people has to do with humility, with the interior reversal of the self-deifying pride that is at the root of human violence, greed, lust, and oppression—the earthly city that is the opposite of the kingdom of God.

Jesus "humbled himself and became obedient to the point of death— even death on a cross" (Phil. 2:8). In dying, we are called to learn the depths of humility in the same way, and, stripped of "the pride of life"

(1 John 2:16 RSV), to embrace God in the full realization that "the world and its desire are passing away, but those who do the will of God live forever" (1 John 2:17). As John Behr observes, "Adam took his life to be his own possession to do with as he pleased, and trying to secure his own immortality he ends up dying. Yet, through the work of Christ, our very mortality now becomes the very means by which we learn to live the life of God—through our experience of weakness."[12]

Jesus and the Tribulation: Brant Pitre on Jesus's Dying

Historical-critical Jesus research proceeds by historical hypotheses and reconstructions that seek to account for why the Jesus of the Gospels says and does the things that he says and does. In *Jesus, the Tribulation, and the End of Exile*, Brant Pitre takes up the stream of Jesus research that emphasizes Jesus's eschatological worldview. Pitre focuses on Second Temple Jewish expectations of an eschatological tribulation, and he argues that "the tribulation may have had a much wider impact on the Jesus tradition than is usually recognized, one that goes well beyond the Olivet Discourse of Mark 13."[13] Specifically, Pitre links Jesus's emphasis on the kingdom of God with the view that Jesus sought to inaugurate the kingdom by undergoing the eschatological tribulation expected by many Second Temple Jews. As Pitre describes his approach: "Because there is a virtual consensus among New Testament scholars that the kingdom of God was a central theme of Jesus' message, it is imperative that we determine whether the expectation of eschatological tribulation is present in sayings of Jesus regarding the kingdom itself" (131).

In his final summative chapter, Pitre concludes—much like Albert Schweitzer and N. T. Wright, and on the basis of extensive argumentation—that it is historically quite likely that "Jesus taught that he as Messiah (the 'Son of Man') would give his life in the tribulation (drink the 'cup' and be 'baptized') in order to bring about the release (the 'ransom') of scattered Israel (the 'many') from exile" (514). Thus he finds that "the notion of an atoning death" is likely not the invention of the early church but rather stems from Jesus's own eschatology (518). When Pitre discusses Jesus's dying, he urges that we first think in terms of the people of Israel's enslavement in Egypt, the Passover, and the exodus. Given the central place of the exodus in Israel's worldview, it makes sense that to understand Jesus's dying—and also to understand why death has such a central place in God's plan to give his people life—we need to reflect upon the exodus narrative.[14] Let me undertake this task briefly, with a focus on the significance of dying.

As the book of Exodus begins, the people of Israel are in mortal peril; Pharaoh has commanded the killing of all the male children of the Israelites, and Pharaoh has multiplied their burdens of work. Moses, an Israelite raised within the court of Pharaoh, kills an Egyptian whom he found "beating a Hebrew" (Exod. 2:11). When Pharaoh hears what Moses had done, "he sought to kill Moses" (2:15). The specter of death—the death of God's people—looms large.

Moses flees to the land of Midian, where he marries and settles down. However, God hears Israel's "groaning under their slavery" and "cry for help," and "God remembered his covenant with Abraham, Isaac, and Jacob" (Exod. 2:23–24). When God prepares to send Moses to liberate the people from "their sufferings" and "to bring them up out of that land to a good and broad land" (3:7–8), God shows his power to Moses by demonstrating divine power over death. First, God turns Moses's staff into a poisonous snake, and then God makes Moses temporarily leprous. Despite God's power, Pharaoh refuses to listen to Moses, and so God sends ten plagues, culminating (after Pharaoh threatens Moses with death [10:28]) in the terrible plague of the death of the firstborn: "About midnight I [the Lord] will go out through Egypt. Every firstborn in the land of Egypt shall die, from the firstborn of Pharaoh who sits on his throne to the firstborn of the female slave who is behind the handmill. . . . Then there will be a loud cry throughout the whole land of Egypt, such as has never been or will ever be again" (11:4–6). This is death-dealing indeed; the threat that death will cut off our lives and our families is fully expressed here.[15]

God promises Israel radical deliverance from this terrible plague. Due to the blood of the Passover lamb, the people will be spared the deaths that come upon the idolatrous Egyptians. Moses instructs the people that "the LORD will pass through to strike down the Egyptians; when he sees the blood on the lintel and on the two doorposts, the LORD will pass over that door and will not allow the destroyer to enter your houses to strike you down" (12:23). But although God thereby shows his sovereign power over life and death, God does not offer to liberate Israel from the eventual ordeal of dying. On the contrary, the Israelites still have to die. The exodus itself is marked by the constant threat of death, and indeed a whole generation (including Moses) dies before entering the promised land.

It follows that the exodus narrative contains two paramount elements with respect to death and dying: the overcoming of death due to the blood of the Passover lamb, and a journey to the promised land that involves death. God draws Israel out of mortal peril by the blood of the Passover lamb, but God does not exempt Israel from the difficult and deadly journey. In my view, this already tells us something about why it is that we die even after Christ died: there must be something about the *journey* of dying that is important for us spiritually, in preparing us for the promised land (eternal life).

We can return now to Pitre. In discussing Mark 10:45, "For the Son of Man came not to be served but to serve, and to give his life a ransom for many," Pitre notes that this verse appears in the context of the request by the disciples James and John to sit by Jesus when he enters into his glory. As Pitre points out, "It is the restoration of Israel, with Jesus at its head and the twelve at his side, that is directly presupposed by James and John's request" (390). James and John have in view a restored Davidic kingdom, and they probably also have in view Daniel 7's prophecy of "one like a son of man" (RSV) and his royal court sitting in judgment in his everlasting kingdom. According to Daniel 7, there will first be a period of tribulation before "the kinship and dominion and the greatness of the kingdoms under the whole heaven shall be given to the people of the holy ones of the Most High" (7:27). Pitre connects this point with Jesus's reference, in responding to James and John, to "the cup that I drink" and "the baptism that I am baptized with" (Mark 10:38). Jesus will undergo the eschatological tribulation, and his followers will share in it.

With this background, Pitre hones in upon the meaning of Jesus giving "his life a ransom for many" in Mark 10:45. Pitre argues that while there is a connection here with the Suffering Servant text of Isaiah 53, there is also a particularly significant connection with Daniel 7 and 9. He focuses upon Daniel 9:24–27, which shows that the goal is "to finish the transgression, to put an end to sin, and to atone for iniquity, to bring in everlasting righteousness" (9:24) and that an "anointed one [messiah], a prince" (RSV), will come and will "be cut off" (9:25–26) with a "flood," "war," and "desolations" (9:26). Pitre finds that 9:24–27 "prophesies *that the Messiah will die during the tribulation*," and that his death will somehow atone for sin (401).

On this basis, Pitre develops the argument that in Mark 10:45, Jesus intends to reveal that "he will give his life, in a kind of new Passover, in order to bring about the New Exodus" (405). Pitre connects Jesus's words about "a ransom for many" offered by the "Son of Man" with the end of exile and the restoration of Israel. Exploring the Greek and Hebrew terms for "ransom" in the Old Testament, he notes that these terms are often used to describe a payment that accomplishes release from exile. Indeed, the "'ransom' terminology [*lytroō*] is used over and over again in the Old Testament to depict two prominent events in salvation history: Israel's past deliverance from exile in Egypt in the Exodus, and Israel's future deliverance from exile in the 'New Exodus,' the ingathering of the scattered elect from among the nations" (407). In the Greek Septuagint and in the Masoretic Hebrew text, the words for "ransom" (or "redeem"; Greek *lytroō*; Hebrew *pdh* and *g'l*) appear in Exodus 6:6, Micah 6:4, Psalm 78:42, and Isaiah 51:10–11—all passages that speak of God's leading the people out of Egyptian slavery and into the promised land. Pitre lists many other examples of the same connection between "ransom" and the exodus, including Exodus 15:13, 16; Deuteronomy 7:8; 9:26; 13:5, 15:15; 24:18; Psalms 74:2; 77:15; 106:10; and 136:24.

Turning to texts that apply "ransom" to the eschatological new exodus, Pitre first treats Isaiah 43, where the Lord tells Israel, "Do not fear, for I have redeemed [ransomed] you. . . . Do not fear, for I am with you; I will bring your offspring from the east, and from the west I will gather you" (Isa. 43:1, 5). In this new exodus, the Lord will gather together not only all Israel but also the Gentiles and show them that the Lord alone is God and that he is "about to do a new thing" (43:19). Pitre finds the same connection in Isaiah 52, which announces that the Lord has "redeemed" or "ransomed" Israel and instructs the people to "go out from there" (52:3, 11). The Lord assures Israel that, as at the first exodus, so now "the LORD will go before you, and the God of Israel will be your rear guard" (52:12). This text from Isaiah immediately precedes the depiction of the Suffering Servant, who "shall be exalted and lifted up" despite his humble and "marred" appearance (52:13–14).

Jeremiah 31 is another passage that explicitly makes the link between "ransom" (as in Mark 10:45) and the eschatological new exodus. God "has saved his people" (Jer. 31:7 RSV) and will gather them anew from "the farthest parts of the earth" (31:8). Ransom, new exodus, and the restoration of Israel appear together in 31:11–12: "For the LORD has ransomed Jacob, and has redeemed him from hands too strong for him. They shall come and sing aloud on the height of Zion, and they shall be radiant over the goodness of the LORD." Likewise, Micah's prophecy of the eschatological restoration of Israel (the ingathering of the twelve tribes) and the flowing of the Gentiles to Israel bears the note of "ransom." Pitre observes that Micah 4:1–2 draws together Israel and the Gentiles: "In days to come the mountain of the LORD's house shall be established as the highest of the mountains, and shall be raised up above the hills. Peoples shall stream to it, and many nations shall come and say: 'Come, let us go up to the mountain of the LORD . . . that he may teach us his ways, and that we may walk in his paths.'" This eschatological restoration will come about through a release or ransom from exile: "Writhe and groan, O daughter Zion, like a woman in labor; for now you shall go forth from the city and camp in the open country; you shall go to Babylon. There you shall be rescued, there the LORD will redeem [ransom] you from the hands of your enemies" (Mic. 4:10). I note that when they are redeemed, the people will finally obey God's command "to do justice, and to love kindness, and to walk humbly with your God" (Mic. 6:8).

As a final text that draws together "ransom," the restoration of Israel, the new exodus, and the tribulation, Pitre treats Zechariah 10. The ingathering of the twelve tribes will come about through the Lord redeeming or ransoming Israel: "I will signal for them and gather them in, for I have redeemed [ransomed] them, and they shall be as they were before. Though I scattered them among the nations, yet in far countries they shall remember me, and they shall rear their children and return" (Zech. 10:8-9). Though Egypt is not the only foreign nation that the Lord mentions in this prophecy, the prophecy refers to the exodus, demonstrating that a new exodus is envisioned: "They shall pass through the sea of distress, and the waves of the sea shall be struck down" (10:11; cf. also v. 10). The redeemed will be given a humble "spirit of compassion and supplication" (12:10).

In light of the prophetic texts about "ransom," Pitre proposes that Jesus does not envision his death simply as atoning for sins, but specifically as atoning for sins in order to accomplish "the *redemption of all Israel from exile*" (412).[16] The restoration of the people Israel is paramount, and this involves a new exodus, as the people move from their current exiled condition to the heights of Zion. This new exodus will occur through an eschatological tribulation. Turning to Isaiah 53, Pitre notes that the Suffering Servant will "make many righteous" and will bear "the sin of many" (53:11-12). According to Daniel 9:27, furthermore, the Messiah or "anointed one" will "make a strong covenant with many"; and "There shall be a time of anguish [tribulation], such as has never occurred since nations first came into existence. . . . Many shall be purified, cleansed, and refined" (Dan. 12:1, 10). The eschatological consummation, marked by the general resurrection from the dead, will follow the tribulation: "Many of those who sleep in the dust of the earth shall awake, some to everlasting life, and some to shame and everlasting contempt" (Dan. 12:2). First, however, the Messiah and those who follow him will have to endure the tribulation.[17]

In his discussion of the authenticity of Mark 10:45 in light of the criterion of coherence, Pitre links Mark 10:45 to Jesus's Last Supper. Most notably, he argues that Jesus understood the Last Supper to be "*a reconfigured Passover meal*. . . . Jesus is replacing the 'flesh' of the Passover lamb (Exod 12:8) with his own body and the 'blood' of the Passover lamb (Exod 12:13, 22–27) with his own blood. Hence, by means of this final enacted sign, Jesus is *prophetically reconstituting the Passover sacrifice around his own suffering and death*" (443).[18] According to Pitre, Jesus is presenting himself as the new Passover lamb as part of "setting in motion a final Passover, an *eschatological Passover*, that would both precede and somehow bring about the coming of the eschatological kingdom of God" (444).[19] Liberated and sustained by the new Passover meal (a sharing in Jesus himself), his followers are enabled to endure the tribulation and ultimately to arrive at the new promised land (the final consummation, at which Christ's followers will be vindicated).

Reflecting upon Mark 14:24, where Jesus says, "This is my blood of the covenant," Pitre connects these phrases with a number of exodus and new exodus texts (including Exod. 24:8; Isa. 42:6; 49:8; 55:3; Jer. 31:31; Bar. 2:34; and Ezek. 37:26). He directs particular attention to Zechariah 9:9–12. In Zechariah 9, God urges Israel to rejoice, because God is sending the messianic and victorious Davidic king who will redeem Israel "because of the blood of my covenant with you" (9:11) and who will restore Israel by means of a new exodus (see 10:11). Summing up, Pitre concludes that "the tribulation in which Jesus expected to die is nothing less than an eschatological Passover which will precede the New Exodus and the End of the Exile" (450).[20]

Pitre responds briefly to scholars who hold that if Jesus intended to die in this way, then Jesus must have been a fanatic. He defends Jesus on the grounds that he would have been thinking along lines that were widely shared in his time—even if Jesus went further by striving to undertake the messianic labor himself.[21] Could it be, however, that not only Jesus but also his contemporaries had fanatically deluded themselves into thinking that God willed to redeem and restore Israel through a *tribulation*? The answer depends in large part on whether we think that God appropriately wills a path of salvation that centrally involves suffering and dying, both for Jesus and for his followers. In favor of such a path, it seems reasonable that our suffering and dying (in Christ and aided by his Spirit) help to strip us of our exilic cleaving to the "fleshpots" of Egypt (Exod. 16:3), that is, to strip us of our "proud glory" (Lev. 26:19).

Employing the image of a new Passover, Paul urges that believers must learn to live as Christ lived, in "sincerity and truth," because "our paschal lamb, Christ, has been sacrificed" (1 Cor. 5:7–8). Paul says this in the context of warning the Corinthians about their "boasting" (5:6) and stating: "And you are arrogant! Should you not rather have mourned?" (5:2). Later in his letter, Paul suggests that Christ was already mysteriously present in the first exodus and that the deadly trials undergone by the Israelites on the first exodus "were written down to instruct us, on whom the ends of the ages have come" (10:11). On our journey, we will be strengthened by partaking in "our paschal lamb," the true manna: "The cup of blessing that we bless, is it not a sharing in the blood of Christ? The bread that we break, is it not a sharing in the body of Christ?" (10:16). Paul notes that in suffering and dying, we become fully configured to Jesus: "we suffer with him so that we may also be glorified with him" (Rom. 8:17). Sharing in Jesus's tribulation and strengthened for the new exodus by his Passover sacrifice, we find that our journey across "the valley of the shadow of death" is entirely God's gift: "Then what becomes of boasting? It is excluded" (Rom. 3:27; see Ps. 23:4).[22]

Thomas Aquinas on Jesus's Dying and Ours: A Brief Sketch

Pitre makes sense of Jesus's dying in terms of a historical-critical reconstruction of Jewish expectations for an eschatological tribulation. In Pitre's view, Jesus understands himself as undergoing this tribulation in a representative manner on behalf of the whole people, but Jesus also recognizes that his followers will have to share in the tribulation until the final consummation. Pitre depicts all this in terms of a new Passover, with Jesus understanding himself to be the new Passover lamb whose blood will protect his followers from the wrath of the tribulation and lead them on a new exodus to the true promised land. I have suggested that the reason behind our sharing in the eschatological tribulation by suffering and dying consists in our need to be fully configured to the one who "humbled himself and became obedient to the point of death" (Phil. 2:8), so that we might share in his exaltation and put fully behind us the pride that caused humanity's alienation from God.

Thomas Aquinas's theological reflections about why God wills a path of salvation that includes suffering and dying complement and enrich Pitre's insights. Like Pitre, Aquinas highlights the tribulation that Jesus freely endured out of love for his people. He argues that Christ's pain in dying was "greater than all other pains."[23] There has never been a suffering like Christ's suffering in terms of intensity and scope. Aquinas suggests that this point is already anticipated in Lamentations 1:12, which he reads as being prophetically about Christ: "Look and see if there is any sorrow like my sorrow, which was brought upon me" (III, q. 46, a. 6, *sed contra*).[24] The extent of the suffering endured by Christ can be measured in terms of both internal sorrow and bodily pain. In terms of the latter, Aquinas notes the severity of crucifixion. People who are crucified "are pierced in nervous and highly sensitive parts—to wit, the hands and feet; moreover, the weight of the suspended body intensifies the agony; and besides this there is the duration of the suffering because they do not die at once" (III, q. 46, a. 6). Since the Holy Spirit fashioned Christ's body, Christ would have felt bodily pain more sensitively than other people do.

With regard to interior pain or sorrow, Aquinas observes that Christ bore "all the sins of the human race" in the sense that he knew those sins, knew the goodness of God violated by those sins, and suffered deliberately for those sins (III, q. 46, a. 6). Because his soul was free of sin (which obscures the apprehension of goodness), Christ "apprehended most vehemently all the causes of sadness" (III, q. 46, a. 6). Furthermore, Christ did not choose to avoid any of his suffering, as we often do by stepping back from the cause of our suffering and reasoning calmly about it. Instead, Christ gave himself fully to his suffering, because he came for the purpose of bearing the penalty of sin. In his grief, says Aquinas, "Christ surpassed all grief of every contrite heart, both because it flowed from a greater wisdom and charity, by which the pang of contrition is intensified, and because he grieved at the one time for all sins" (III, q. 46, a. 6, ad 4). Not only does greater charity and wisdom mean greater sorrow over sin—because Christ truly knew the goodness (of God and of true human flourishing) that sinners reject—but also Christ appears to have refused any mental consolation whatsoever during his passion. Unlike martyrs who are consoled in their suffering by the thought of God's love, Christ concentrated upon the sins for which he died. Aquinas states in this regard, "In other sufferers the interior sadness is mitigated . . . from some consideration of reason, by some derivation or redundance from the higher powers into the lower; but it was not so with the suffering Christ" (III, q. 46, a. 6).[25] In his passion, Christ does not allow his higher contemplation (his intimate, inexpressible communion with his Father) to intrude upon his focus upon the sins that he freely bears for us, and so his sorrow is voluntary and "proportionate" to the accomplishment of our redemption (III, q. 46, a. 6).[26]

Aquinas adds that Christ underwent all the different classes of suffering. This does not mean that Christ suffered all the painful events possible for humans to suffer. This would of course be impossible, "since many are mutually exclusive, as burning and drowning" (III, q. 46, a. 5). Nonetheless, Christ endured suffering from the whole of humankind. He suffered from Jews and from Gentiles, from men and from women (Aquinas notes that there were "women servants who accused Peter"), from rulers and servants, from the general populace and from his own friends (III, q. 46, a. 5). Christ also endured all the different kinds of suffering that humans fear. He endured suffering "from friends abandoning Him; in His reputation, from the blasphemies hurled at Him; in His honor and glory, from the mockeries and the insults heaped upon Him; in things, for He was despoiled of His garments; in His soul, from sadness, weariness, and fear; in His body, from wounds and scourgings" (III, q. 46, a. 5). Many other people have had friends abandon them and have had their reputations unjustly destroyed and their lives unjustly taken, but no one other than Christ has been the innocent Lord enduring such dreadful things. Aquinas notes that Christ also endured severe suffering in all of his bodily members and bodily senses.

Yet, if Christ has "borne our griefs and carried our sorrows," as Aquinas holds to be the case, then why do his followers suffer and die (III, q. 46, a. 6, obj. 1 and ad 4)? Aquinas thinks that baptism intrinsically has the power to take away the penalty of death from the baptized. Christ does not will for baptism to do this, however, because people would then seek "to be baptized for the sake of impassibility in the present life, and not for the sake of the glory of life eternal" (III, q. 69, a. 3).

Even if followers of Christ must still die, why must dying continue to be so painful and difficult physically and spiritually? Why must our road be so "hard and rough," even if Christ's had to be so (III, q. 45, a. 1)? Aquinas's answer draws upon Paul's use of the metaphor of athletic training and competition. Paul compares our life in Christ with how an athlete seeks a prize: "Do you not know that in a race all the runners compete, but only one receives the prize? Run in such a way that you may win it. Athletes exercise self-control in all things; they do it to receive a perishable wreath, but we an imperishable one" (1 Cor. 9:24–25). Along these lines, Aquinas states that our suffering and dying has the purpose of "spiritual training:

namely, in order that, by fighting against concupiscence and other defects to which he is subject, man may receive the crown of victory" (III, q. 45, a. 1). A similar argument appears in Hebrews 12, which compares God to a father who disciplines his children so that they can reach maturity in Christ: "he [God] disciplines us for our good, in order that we may share his holiness. Now, discipline always seems painful rather than pleasant at the time, but later it yields the peaceful fruit of righteousness to those who have been trained by it" (Heb. 12:10–11; cf. Prov. 3:11–12).

But was not Christ himself afraid of dying? The Synoptic Gospels indicate that in the garden of Gethsemane, on the night before his arrest, Jesus prayed to the Father to "remove this cup from me; yet, not my will but yours be done" (Luke 22:42). An angel came and strengthened Jesus, but Jesus's anticipation of his dying remained agonized: "In his anguish he prayed more earnestly, and his sweat became like great drops of blood falling down on the ground" (Luke 22:44). Aquinas considers that all persons feel something like this agony when consciously confronted with dying. All humans (and indeed all creatures) naturally abhor death, since it is a severe bodily trial that attacks our very constitution. Although Jesus's rational will conformed to his Father's will and his sensitive appetite did not obstruct the purposes of his rational will, he fully manifested the natural emotion of fear of death, since dying indeed is a fearful thing (III, q. 18, a. 6).

Among his reasons for the fittingness of Christ's passion as the way of salvation, Aquinas states that Christ thereby "set us an example of obedience, humility, constancy, justice, and the other virtues displayed in the Passion, which are requisite for man's salvation" (III, q. 46, a. 3).[27] He cites 1 Peter 2:21, "Christ . . . suffered for you, leaving you an example, so that you should follow in his steps."[28] The virtue that I find especially instructive with regard to the fittingness of our suffering and dying is humility, because suffering and dying undercut our pride. Aquinas calls pride "the most grievous of sins," on the grounds that it involves both "conversion to a mutable good" (oneself or other things of this world) and a deliberate "aversion from the immutable good . . . simply through being unwilling to be subject to God and his rule" (II-II, q. 162, a. 6). He agrees with Augustine that the humility of Jesus is the remedy to our pride, which prevents us from cleaving to God (III, q. 1, a. 2).[29]

In discussing humility, Aquinas quotes James 4:6, itself a quotation of Proverbs 3:34: "God opposes the proud, but gives grace to the humble" (see II-II, q. 161, a. 5, ad 2). On this basis, Aquinas argues that humility is "the foundation of the spiritual edifice" (II-II, q. 161, a. 5, ad 2). He points out, "The reason why Christ chiefly proposed humility to us, was because it especially removes the obstacle to man's spiritual welfare consisting in man's aiming at heavenly and spiritual things, in which he is hindered by striving to become great in earthly things" (II-II, q. 161, a. 5, ad 4). In the "spiritual warfare" in which Christ's cross plays the decisive role, our temptation consists in focusing on the goods of this world (II-II, q. 161, a. 5, ad 4). Suffering and dying help to foster humility because the process of dying weakens our grasp upon the goods of this world (II-II, q. 161, a. 3). Thus Aquinas describes humility as assisting our "untrammeled access to spiritual and divine goods" (II-II, q. 161, a. 5, ad 4). In suffering and dying, we follow the path of Christ and receive the opportunity to grow in Christlike humility, thereby being made open to "divine goods."

Commenting on Philippians 2:8, "he humbled himself and became obedient to the point of death," Aquinas draws the connection to Matthew 11:29, "learn from me; for I am gentle and humble in heart." What we must learn from Jesus is not only that we must humble ourselves, but more specifically that this humility requires becoming "obedient to the point of death." Aquinas observes that "it is characteristic of the proud to follow their own will, for a proud person seeks greatness."[30] In pride, we want to rule others, not to be ruled by anyone, even by God. Jesus, however, acts in the opposite way: he shows his humility by obediently accepting his cross and thereby doing the will of God.

Aquinas recognizes that in general "the human will tends toward two things, namely, to life and to honor."[31] Dying persons, of course, have to give up both life and worldly honor.[32] After all, the power and positions of dignity that we enjoy while living will not be ours when dead; and a dying person is subject to numerous bodily indignities that detract from the person's worldly honor. Suffering and dying, then, are profoundly humbling, and as Aquinas recognizes, the issue is whether we will accept this humbling with a free and loving obedience to God's will, accepting that our time has come to die. Only if we die obediently in this sense can the humbling associated with death become in us true humility. By stripping away our life and honor, suffering and dying provide a great opportunity for Christlike humility, a reversal of the pride that turns us away from the love of God. As Adrian Walker puts it, dying "conceals a medicinal mercy, an opportunity to come to our senses, to wake up from the perverse illusion of godlike autonomy without God."[33]

Indeed, Aquinas goes so far as to argue, in his commentary on Matthew 11:29, that "meekness and humility"—the conditions of being gentle and lowly of heart—constitute that in which "the whole New Law consists."[34] This is a very strong claim, but a justified one: the "New Law," by which the kingdom of God is ruled, evinces itself in humility and is the obverse of pride. Aquinas comments that humility properly orders our relationships with God, self, and neighbor, and he adds that "humility makes a man capable of being filled with God."[35] In this life, humble persons who are filled with the Holy Spirit, and who therefore build up God's kingdom of love, desire to share ever more deeply in God and his kingdom. Thus Aquinas points out that "the meek are not quieted in the world," since "the fulfillment of [their] desires" is not possible in this life.[36] Suffering and dying open us even further to this truth about rightly ordered human desire, and thereby open us to the real humility that enables us to receive that which God wishes to give us: himself, in union with all the blessed, in "the kingdom prepared . . . from the foundation of the world" (Matt. 25:34).

Arguably, then, the reason why God works salvation by enabling us to share with Jesus in the eschatological tribulation is not that God loves to see us suffer, let alone that Jesus did not conquer sin and death, but that in our fallen condition we need help in letting go of this world, in trading the "pride of life" (the root of all sin) for a real humility that configures us to Jesus and enables us to be filled with his divine life. From this perspective, suffering and dying play a positive role in our new exodus journey, which is nourished by the heavenly manna that is the Eucharist.

Aquinas finds the Gospel accounts of Jesus's baptism to be filled with references to the exodus, and thus also to the new exodus. In this vein, Aquinas remarks: "It was through the river Jordan that the children of Israel entered into the land of promise. Now, this is the prerogative of Christ's baptism over all other baptisms: that it is the entrance to the kingdom of God, which is signified by the land of promise" (III, q. 39, a. 4). It might seem, says Aquinas, that the connection to the exodus would have been made more clearly by having Jesus baptized in the Red Sea, since the drowning of the Egyptians can be typologically linked with the blotting out of our sins at baptism. In Aquinas's view, however, the eschatological signification of Christ's baptism is best symbolized by the river Jordan, because it was only when they reached the river Jordan that the Israelites were almost in the promised land. He explains, "The crossing of the Red Sea foreshadowed baptism in this—that baptism washes away sin: whereas the crossing of the Jordan foreshadows it in this—that it opens the gate to the heavenly kingdom: and this is the principal effect of baptism" (III, q. 39, a. 4, ad 1).[37] Baptism into Christ's death—his profound humbling and his supreme humility—enables us to journey even now to the open gate of "the heavenly kingdom" without any "complaining against the LORD" (Exod. 16:7) and with "a willing heart" (35:22), eager to commune with God "face to face, as one speaks to a friend" (33:11). As Joseph Ratzinger observes, "Baptism means the union of our death with Christ's death. It means that we enter into the change in value that human death underwent through the death of Christ. . . . The whole process of dying is, if we accept it in faith, the realization of our being baptized."[38]

Conclusion

This chapter addressed the problem of why, when Jesus Christ has "abolished death" (2 Tim. 1:10), suffering and dying continue. As we saw, Pitre contends that the Second Temple Jewish concept of an eschatological tribulation involves the related concepts of a new Passover and a new exodus. If Jesus's dying is that of the true Passover lamb—atoning for sins and releasing us from exilic (sinful) slavery to the goods of this world—then it is no wonder that discipleship involves a temporal *training* whereby we follow the crucified Jesus on a new exodus, strengthened by water from the rock (baptism) and the heavenly manna (the Eucharist). Having instituted a new exodus to the promised land of the new Jerusalem, Jesus leaves in place the tribulation of the exodus whereby the people learn humility— even while he also makes clear that for those who are united to him, death has lost its "sting" (1 Cor. 15:55). By sharing in Christ's tribulation, believers find the path of peace, gradually overcoming the exilic habit of loving self over God.

With this portrait of the eschatological tribulation and the new exodus in view, I turned to some theological insights of Aquinas into Jesus's dying and our own. Reflecting upon Christ's passion, Aquinas makes clear his awareness of the profundity of the suffering that Jesus freely endured for our sake. The humility of the divine Son in becoming man is a humility that empowered him to conquer sin and death, and thus a humility that demonstrates that the divine "power is made perfect in weakness" (2 Cor. 12:9). Just as Aquinas looks realistically at the intensity of Christ's sufferings, so also he does not minimize how "hard and rough" the journey of the new exodus is for Jesus's followers. He accepts that humans have a natural horror of dying, and he recognizes that people would do a great deal to avoid death. He argues, therefore, that Jesus's cross does not and indeed must not take away our participation in his cross through our own suffering and dying, because we need to be trained in holiness. Having to undergo suffering and dying in Christ fosters Christlike humility, since dying persons can no longer plausibly strive in pride "to become great in earthly things" and must recognize their utter dependence upon God. As Stephen Pardue observes, "When humans act humbly, confessing their own limitations and creatureliness, they are liberated to see beyond those boundaries"—and thus to share in God's own humility, which is the power and path of salvation.[39] The process of dying serves to encourage the humility that we need in order to overcome our pride and fully embrace Christ's redemptive and deifying love.

Thomas Joseph White remarks, "Through his cry of agony and desire, Jesus intends (through his consciousness of himself as the eschatological Son of Man) to inaugurate the kingdom of God (Mk 14:62)."[40] But in the inaugurated kingdom, followers of Jesus today still have to walk the dark path of suffering and dying, because we need to do so in order to learn to humbly love God rather than trying violently and ridiculously to exalt ourselves in pride.[41] When given a choice between God's kingdom and (the illusion of) our own, we too often choose the latter—a path that leads not to life but to spiritual death, because it is fueled by a desire for greatness that rejects the only true greatness, which is divine humility and divine love. A true relationship with God in his inaugurated kingdom requires humility, since as Edward Sri remarks, "Humility is the foundation of all prayer."[42] More graphically, Ratzinger explains that God must "[tear] away from us our selfish, self-seeking, egotistical existence so as to reshape us according to his image."[43] Despite the grimness and agony of the process of dying, and despite the fact that we must give up our very life, suffering and dying are our path to union with Christ in his Passion and thus, at the same time, to union with the exalted Christ in his kingdom.[44] Jesus teaches, "Those who love their life lose it, and those who hate their life in this world will keep it for eternal life" (John 12:25). The humbling journey of the new exodus liberates us from the fleshpots of Egypt in order to enable us to have the humility, both in the present time and everlastingly, that God wills for his beloved people, to whom he feeds the new manna that is Christ.[45]

CHAPTER 8

SURRENDER

Anointing the Sick

When Richard John Neuhaus lay dying of colon cancer—though he did not die but lived another fifteen years—a priest came to give him the sacrament of anointing of the sick. According to Neuhaus, the reception of the sacrament had a businesslike quality about it; it was a preparation, making him ready for his journey. During this time, he wondered deeply about dying, especially about the moment of death and what the transition could possibly be like. He recovered, but (of course) he did not lose his sense of the mystery of dying, which as he says involves both "your self . . . being taken from you" and "you . . . surrendering yourself."[1] On the one hand, he felt helpless, since his body was corrupting whether he agreed to it or not. His experience was that death was attacking him and he could not escape it or do anything in relation to it by any act of his own. On the other hand, he nonetheless recalls that "I *was* surrendering myself," and he describes this as a "wrenchingly wonderful truth."[2]

Years later, when faced with the cancer that killed him, Neuhaus's final published writing included a moving testimony to self-surrender: "Who knew that at this point in my life I would be understanding, as if for the first time, the words of Paul, 'When I am weak, then I am strong'? . . . The entirety of our prayer is 'Your will be done'—not as a note of resignation but of desire beyond expression."[3] This desire for self-surrender to God's will (which alone fulfills all desire) comes about in us in union with Christ and with "all the saints and angels who accompany us each step through time toward home."[4] But Neuhaus never pretended that surrendering himself was not wrenching and difficult. Henri Nouwen observes that "dying is not a sweet, sentimental event; it is a great struggle to surrender our lives completely. This surrender is not an obvious human response. To the contrary: we want to cling to whatever is left."[5]

In this chapter, I argue that the sacrament of anointing of the sick serves to help dying persons embody self-surrender. Colman O'Neill remarks that "the sick and the dying" have a "special place . . . in the church" as a sign of Christ, since they "enter personally into the mystery of the suffering Christ."[6] In charitable union with Christ, dying involves a free self-surrender that is a supreme enactment of love. The sacrament of anointing of the sick assists this final self-surrender by purifying the sick and dying person of the remnants of rebellious pride, through what O'Neill calls "a deeper healing of [our] personality" by which God fits us for an otherwise unthinkable journey to a direct encounter with Christ.[7] As the Orthodox theologian Vigen Guroian observes, in "the sacrament of holy unction" God "may or may not heal our physical infirmities," since God's greater purpose is to bring about "the final surrender to death of the sinful self as repentance opens onto the ineffable divine light."[8]

The Mennonite theologian Johann Christoph Arnold makes clear in *Be Not Afraid: Overcoming the Fear of Death* that Protestants also have a stake in the sacrament of anointing of the sick, even if they do not practice it as a "sacrament." Arnold describes a hospital visitation that he made to a dying woman named Xaverie: "One day when my wife and I came to see her, she asked for the laying on of hands, a blessing described in James 5, which reads, 'Are any among you sick? They should call for the elders of the church and have them pray over them, anointing them with oil in the name of the Lord.'"[9] In response to her request, Arnold organized "a service for Xaverie," and he notes, "We all felt the presence of eternity in our midst," and her face was "shining with expectancy and joy."[10] Arnold recalls, "As I laid my hands on her, she looked at me trustingly and said, 'With God, everything is possible!' But while she was certain that she could be healed if that was God's plan, she was also completely ready to die."[11] According to Arnold, the laying on of hands marked the final step in her complete self-surrender to God. The Presbyterian theologian Amy Plantinga Pauw points out, "Many Protestant communions have adopted rituals of . . . anointing for the sick. The significant convergence between Catholic and Protestant practices of dying well is a hopeful sign for the future of the Christian community."[12]

In making the case within Catholic theology that this sacrament should be celebrated for imminently dying persons (without denying that it should be celebrated for any seriously ill person who requests it), this chapter proceeds in two steps. First, I briefly review two representative contemporary Catholic theological perspectives on the sacrament of anointing of the sick, along with the summation given in the *Catechism of the Catholic Church*. Second and equally briefly, I retrieve insights of Thomas Aquinas that help to situate the sacrament within the context of sin, the divine mercy, and the healing that dying persons need in order finally to surrender their lives fully to God, freed of the remnants of rebellion. My purpose is to encourage dying persons to receive the sacrament of anointing of the sick in their last days or hours, as part of their final preparation for "ascend[ing] the hill of the LORD" (Ps. 24:3).[13]

Contemporary Catholic Approaches to Anointing of the Sick

John Kasza: An Anointing for Healing

In his 2007 study of the sacrament of anointing of the sick, John Kasza comments, "As a result of the theological reflection done prior to the Second Vatican Council, it is no longer possible to restrict reception only to the *moribundi* (dying). Moreover, the shift in terminology from *Extreme Unction* to *sacrament of the sick* opened a window of opportunity for discussing the issue of serious illness."[14] For Kasza, the fundamental reality addressed by the sacrament of anointing is not the reality of dying, but the reality of sickness. He emphasizes that "sickness is alienating. The sacrament of the sick is designed to break through this alienation and bring the sick person back into the community" (xii). He explains that in the sacrament of anointing of the sick (which he terms "the sacrament of the sick"), "the community of faith goes to the sick person, celebrates the rite and 're-incorporates' him or her back into the life of the church" (xii).[15] The reincorporation involves activity on both sides; the person who is ill is not merely passive. Rather, precisely by his or her illness, the person who is sick "gives an impetus to the community to pray, to engage in pastoral care, and to minister in faith" (xii). In turn, the community ministers to the person who is sick and assures that person that "he or she is not alone" (xii). Kasza observes, "The community has compassion (literally 'suffers with') for the sick person. By their physical presence, the members of the community reflect the omnipotent presence of the crucified and risen Lord" (xii).[16]

Kasza bemoans the fact that, "unfortunately, despite the efforts of theologians and pastors, people still wait until the waning moments of a patient's life before inviting the church to intervene" (xiii). Laypeople still treat the sacrament of anointing along the preconciliar theological lines of "extreme unction," intended for the dying. Kasza notes that in 1989, more than twenty years after the council, the hospital chaplain Miguel Monge conducted a survey that showed that "despite the change in the terminology of the sacrament and the desire of the church that her seriously ill members receive sacramental Anointing early in their illnesses, 'the pair Extreme Unction–death is still very much alive in the popular mind and in that of many pastors'" (3).[17] At the time, Monge anticipated that it would take another generation and extensive catechesis in order to change the popular conception of the sacrament as being mainly for the dying, but even today this popular conception remains largely in place.

Kasza criticizes Thomas Aquinas for the medieval shift from a sacrament for the sick to a sacrament for the dying. Although Kasza finds a baleful influence of Thomistic thought in church teaching at the sixth Council of Benevento (1374), the General Council of Florence (1439), and the Council of Trent (1551), he nonetheless perceives some positive remnants of the earlier focus on the sick rather than on the dying. Among these positive signs is the repeated exhortation that priests should administer the sacrament of "extreme unction" *prior* to the dying person's loss of consciousness. Positively, the Council of Trent also speaks of the sacrament's effect of the healing of body and mind, thereby signaling that the sacrament is for others besides those who are definitely going to die. But as Kasza notes with concern, during the medieval period the church "shifted its focus from healing the sick to preparing the dying person for eternal glory. The sacrament, while retaining its healing function, became a last Anointing which 'sealed' and 'signed' the person as a member of the body of Christ as he or she left this world for eternal life" (55).

From this perspective, Kasza defends the postconciliar shift from the sacrament of anointing as the "last rite" to viaticum as the preferred last rite. Kasza observes that today, "in the event that the patient is in the process of actively dying (and thus not able to receive the Eucharist [viaticum]), the 'last rite' becomes the Commendation of the Dying" (198).[18] This commendation consists in the recitation of a set of scriptural texts, the reading of a passage from Scripture, a litany of the saints, and prayers of commendation.[19] Yet, Kasza also affirms that the sacrament of anointing of the sick serves dying persons by preparing them for eternal life. He states in a quite traditional manner, "The effects of sacramental anointing include the strengthening of the person, the joining of the patient's sufferings to those of Christ, the healing of their ailment if it is conducive to the healing of their soul, the forgiveness of sins, and the preparation for the passing from this life to the next."[20] But Kasza's emphasis is on the "need to re-appropriate the tradition of caring for *all* the sick, not just those who are seriously ill or near death" (201).

Lizette Larson-Miller: An Anointing for Dying?

In *The Sacrament of the Anointing of the Sick*, Lizette Larson-Miller takes her bearings from Vatican II's *Sacrosanctum Concilium*, §73, which reads: "'Final anointing,' which can also and better be called 'anointing of the sick,' is not a sacrament exclusively for those who are involved in the final crisis of life and death. There can therefore be no doubt that the point when a Christian begins to be in danger of death, either through illness or old age, is already a suitable time to receive it."[21] From this text in *Sacrosanctum Concilium*, Larson-Miller observes, much followed: "In the revisions of the rite for anointing the sick and its deliberate move away from extreme unction, a great deal of energy was expended on designing language that would remove any association with the last rites."[22] She finds that in many cultures, this revision has proven to be highly appreciated and valued. But she also expresses the concern that "there is an almost studied avoidance of death in many celebrations [of the sacrament of anointing] that seems to have a great affinity with the cultural inability to talk about or deal with death" (120).[23]

Given that the rite of the sacrament of anointing of the sick does not mention death or dying (although it does mention Christ's death), Larson-Miller states that she wishes to make "a tentative suggestion to consider expanding the official circumstances of anointing of the sick to include the dying" (121). While insisting that "Viaticum remains, rightly, the primary sacrament for the dying," she nonetheless considers that "there are newer considerations arising from the interplay between medical technology and culture that beg the question be raised again" (121).[24] Raising the question involves admitting that Catholic believers often do not want the sacrament of anointing prior to the diagnosis of a mortal illness. In this regard she turns to the work of Kristiaan Depoortere. As Larson-Miller notes (121), Depoortere has observed, "Doesn't the stubborn association of anointing and dying mean that the sick want to reserve that gesture for the last moment?"[25] Without advocating a return to "extreme unction," Depoortere goes so far as to say that the Catholic faithful today "are asking vitally and viscerally for a rite of transition, certainly for the last passage. Too early an anointing robs them of this. People do not want to be anointed unless they themselves—or their families—really feel that it is now or never."[26] Furthermore, Depoortere challenges the supposition that viaticum can suffice as the rite for the dying: "In our Christian hospitals many believers communicate twice a week. So at an anthropological level the supreme sacrament does not work as a ritual of transition."[27]

After approvingly quoting these passages from Depoortere, Larson-Miller adds the point that given the realities of modern medicine and hospitalized dying, consciously consuming the Eucharist (viaticum) is no longer possible for many or even most dying people. In such situations, "There is no opportunity for communion under either species . . . but only touch, prayer, and blessing, and commendation when timely. But the faithful and fearful gathered around the patient, and perhaps the patient him- or herself whose cognizance is often underestimated, understandably want something to be done [by the priest]" (122). In this light, Larson-Miller proposes that the church should "consider an extraordinary rite of anointing when all other substantial rituals of transition are not possible"—that is, mainly when viaticum is not possible (122). She concludes with a question that offers a promising avenue for reflection: "Are medical changes surrounding the way we die an invitation to reconsider an anointing for the dying with appropriate texts and rituals?" (122).[28]

The Catechism of the Catholic Church: A "Sacramentum Exeuntium"

The 1997 Catechism of the Catholic Church begins by noting that the church, obeying Christ's command to "heal the sick" (Matt. 10:8), does so not only by taking care of the sick and interceding in prayer, but also by the sacrament of anointing of the sick. This sacrament has the goal of strengthening those who are ill, and it is "not a sacrament for those only who are at the point of death," as the catechism observes by quoting §73 of Sacrosanctum Concilium.[29] In enumerating the effects of the sacrament, however, the catechism emphasizes the need to give the sacrament to persons who are in the midst of the actual dying process. Thus the catechism observes, "If the sacrament of anointing of the sick is given to all who suffer from serious illness and infirmity, even more rightly is it given to those at the point of departing this life; so it is also called sacramentum exeuntium (the sacrament of those departing)" (§1523). The sacrament of anointing is the *sacramentum exeuntium,* says the catechism, because it "completes our conformity to the death and Resurrection of Christ, just as Baptism began it. It completes the holy anointings that mark the whole Christian life" (§1523).[30]

According to the catechism, the effects of the sacrament include a strengthening gift of the Holy Spirit (healing the soul and potentially also the body), a deeper union with Christ's passion, and a grace that distinctively unites the sick person to the whole church in the church's configuration to Christ's self-offering to the Father. The sacrament's effects also include preparing the sick person for his or her final journey, the journey of death. Citing with appreciation the Council of Trent, the catechism states, "This last anointing fortifies the end of our earthly life like a solid rampart for the final struggles before entering the Father's house" (§1523). It follows that this sacrament is indeed a sacrament to be given to the dying.

At the same time, of course, the catechism attends carefully to viaticum. The catechism remarks: "In addition to the Anointing of the Sick, the church offers those who are about to leave this life the Eucharist as viaticum. Communion in the body and blood of Christ, received at this moment of 'passing over' to the Father, has a particular significance and importance" (§1524). This final reception of the Eucharist underscores the Eucharist's eschatological significance, its relationship to eternal life. At the moment of dying or "passing over," we consume in faith "the seed of eternal life" (§1524). The catechism here recalls John 6:54, "those who eat my flesh and drink my blood have eternal life, and I will raise them up on the last day." As the sacrament of Christ's Paschal Mystery, the Eucharist is the sign of Christ's Passover and the sign of our passing over to eternal life as members of Christ's body. As the catechism puts it, "The sacrament of Christ once dead and now risen, the Eucharist is here the sacrament of passing over from death to life, from this world to the Father" (§1524). Viaticum has an important place in Christian dying because it supremely unites us with Christ in his death and resurrection, and thus draws dying persons fully into his Passover.

Thomas Aquinas on the Sacrament of "Extreme Unction"

As we saw, Kasza considers Thomas Aquinas to be a pivotal figure in the theological corruption of the sacrament of anointing of the sick. Given the teaching of the catechism about the *sacramentum exeuntium* and the numerous points raised by Larson-Miller (drawing upon Depoortere), however, I think that Aquinas's connection of the sacrament with Christian dying—and with the healing of the remnants of sin that impede our full self-surrender—deserves retrieval. For brevity's sake, I will focus on Aquinas's treatment of the sacrament of anointing of the sick (or "extreme unction") found in the supplement to his *Summa theologiae.*[31]

At the outset of his discussion, Aquinas connects the sacrament of "extreme unction" with human sinfulness, on the basis of James 5:14–15. In this biblical foundation for the sacrament of anointing of the sick, James teaches: "Are any among you sick? They should call for the elders of the church and have them pray over them, anointing them with oil in the name of the Lord. The prayer of faith will save the sick, and the Lord will raise them up; and anyone who has committed sins will be forgiven."[32] The reference to "raise them up" and to the forgiveness of sins indicates that the anointing has as much to do with the eternal life (in Christ) of the sick man as it does with his restoration to earthly bodily health.[33]

Aquinas explores the fittingness of the oil of anointing in light of the analogy between bodily healing and spiritual healing. As he notes, oil "has a softening effect, it penetrates to the very heart of a thing, and spreads over it" (Suppl., q. 29, a. 4).[34] Likewise, spiritual healing "ought also to be gentle, lest hope, of which the dying stand in utmost need, be shattered rather than fostered" (Suppl., q. 29, a. 4).[35] Aquinas quotes Isaiah 1:6 as a hinge for his argument. In Isaiah 1, the Lord complains through the prophet that Israel is a "sinful nation, people laden with iniquity" (1:4). The Lord compares the people of Israel to a physical body whose "bruises and sores and bleeding wounds . . . have not been drained, or bound up, or softened with oil" (1:6). Bodily healing, in Isaiah 1, is intimately related to the spiritual healing that the Lord yearns to bring to his people, if only they repent and surrender themselves to him rather than continuing to rebel against him.

As we are dying, we can expect Christ (who is at the right hand of the Father) to help us, but we cannot expect him to make himself present in the direct and unmediated way that he did (for example) to the ten lepers during his earthly ministry (see Luke 17). Aquinas observes that by consecrating the oil with regard to both its material element and its use, the church ensures that Christ's healing power—the power of his cross and resurrection—can flow to us through the oil.[36] The bishop consecrates the oil, because this reflects the way in which Christ works through his hierarchical ministers in the church's sacraments. Through consecration, God makes the oil to be "the instrument of a divine operation" (Suppl., q. 29, a. 6, ad 2).[37] The oil can thereby sacramentally mediate the saving power of Christ.

Since persons can be anointed with oil for various reasons, a bodily anointing on its own could obviously not suffice for a sacrament. Aquinas holds that the anointing is specified as a sacrament by words spoken by the priest that beg for pardon of sins on behalf of the recipient. This "form" of the sacrament has its roots in what James specifies will be the effects of the anointing: "the Lord will raise them up; and anyone who has committed sins will be forgiven" (James 5:15). That begging for forgiveness is the "form" of the sacrament is especially appropriate for dying persons, not least because they can be tempted to rest their hope upon medical doctors rather than turning with spiritual seriousness to God. How fitting it is for the priest to beg not medical doctors but God for the grace of healing—a healing that must inevitably be primarily from sin. The power that operates in the sacrament, Aquinas observes, is "the mercy of God" (Suppl., q. 29, a. 9).

If the recipient of the sacrament of anointing of the sick is not in a state of grace or is not repentant, of course, the sacrament cannot work its merciful effects; the sacrament of reconciliation must then be requested first. Aquinas explains, "Now just as a bodily cure presupposes bodily life in the one who is cured, so does a spiritual cure presuppose spiritual life. Hence this sacrament is not an antidote to those defects which deprive man of spiritual life, namely, original and mortal sin" (Suppl., q. 30, a. 1). Instead, the effect of the sacrament of anointing of the sick is to remove the remnants of sin that impede us from fully giving ourselves to God. Aquinas states that the sacrament "is a remedy for such defects as weaken man spiritually, so as to deprive him of perfect vigor for acts of the life of grace or of glory; which defects consist in nothing else but a certain weakness and unfitness" (Suppl., q. 30, a. 1).[38] He recognizes that "bodily health is not the principal effect of this sacrament" (Suppl., q. 30, a. 2, ad 1). If it were so, then we would anticipate a bodily healing almost every time the sacrament is celebrated, whereas experience shows that this does not happen. Nonetheless, he insists that the sacrament does indeed have "the effect of a bodily remedy, namely a healing of the body" (Suppl., q. 30, a. 2). Unlike baptismal water that necessarily washes the body, however, the anointing oil does not necessarily heal the body. The bodily healing comes about through the sacramental oil only when God wills it do so.

It would seem that since this sacrament takes away the remnants of sin, everyone should receive it regularly. Aquinas considers that the "sacrament is a spiritual healing . . . and is signified by way of a healing of the body" (Suppl., q. 32, a. 1).[39] If one does not need bodily healing, therefore, one *cannot* receive the sacrament because the necessary signification would not be present. Aquinas adds that not all kinds of sickness make a person a suitable recipient of the sacrament. In his view, only "sickness that brings man to the extremity of his life" fits a person for the sacrament (Suppl., q. 32, a. 2). Although this position goes too far, I think that he is on solid ground when he states that the sacrament is for persons whose illness is "of such a nature as to cause death, the danger of which is to be feared" (Suppl., q. 32, a. 2). After all, it is generally through the potential to cause death, or at least to contribute significantly to its coming by seriously incapacitating a person, that an illness is distinguished as serious. Aquinas is right to conclude that "the principal effect of this sacrament is that immunity from disorder which is needed by those who are taking their departure from this life and setting out for the life of glory" (Suppl., q. 32, a. 2 ad 2). Freed from the remnants of rebellious disorder, dying persons are prepared to surrender their lives.

In the sacrament of anointing of the sick, Aquinas does not think that the whole body should be anointed, as happens in baptism by immersion.[40] Instead, he argues that it is fitting that the sacramental oil be applied "to those parts where the root of the disease is seated"—and by "disease" he here means "spiritual sickness" (Suppl., q. 32, a. 5). The bodily parts that should be anointed include the eyes, nose, ears, lips, hands, and feet. It may seem that the head, breast, and loins should also be anointed, since many sins come forth from the mind, heart, and sexual passions. Aquinas comments, however, that it suffices to focus the anointing upon the five sensory organs and the feet. He notes that some churches anoint the loins on account of the sexual appetite, but he considers this unnecessary since the disorders of the sexual appetite flow first from the sensory organs. Naming the bodily sites "where sin originates in us first," Aquinas lists "the eyes . . . on account of the sight, the ears on account of hearing, the nostrils on account of the smell, the mouth on account of the taste, the hands on account of the touch which is keenest in the finger tip," and finally the feet since "they are the chief instrument" of the motive power (Suppl., q. 32, a. 6). Anointing these places is appropriate for signifying healing from the remnants of sin and directing dying persons to self-surrender in and with Christ.

In accordance with Scripture, Aquinas holds that Christ ascended to the right hand of his Father in order to lift us up with him, to prepare "the way for our ascent": "since he is our Head the members must follow whither the Head has gone" (III, q. 57, a. 6). The ascension of Christ directs "the fervor of our charity to heavenly things," so that we surrender our hearts to God rather than to earthly things (III, q. 57, a. 1, ad 3; see Matt. 6:21). Yet God can and in certain cases does restore bodily health through the sacrament, and humans can be mistaken about whether a particular illness is indeed going to cause death. Thus Aquinas gladly affirms that the sacrament of anointing of the sick can be repeated (unlike baptism). For diseases that are long in duration, resulting in a dying process that has more than one episode in which the person seems about to die, he encourages the repetition of the sacrament.

The fundamental purpose of the sacrament of anointing of the sick is not to help believers to escape from death, but to help believers escape from everlasting death marked by permanent refusal to give oneself to the Giver of life. When, with the help of the sacrament, dying persons are freed of all impediments to surrendering themselves to God, they discover, in Andrew Davison's words, "what it means to share in Christ"—and thus in his dying—"*right to the end*."[41]

Conclusion

Tears are appropriate for dying, but for some dying persons tears flow solely because they are being cut off so abruptly and scarily from this-worldly friendships, status, and pleasures.[42] In this context, the focus of the sacrament of anointing of the sick on spiritual healing, signified by bodily healing, assists dying persons in surrendering themselves to God by freeing them from the remnants of rebellion against God. John Boyle points out that for Aquinas anointing of the sick is not merely ordered to spiritual and bodily health, but rather is ordered to "*robustness* of health," primarily "robustness of spiritual life."[43] In this sense, the sacrament of anointing of the sick "is the medicine that attends to the various remains of sin that weaken or limit a healthy but not vigorous spiritual life."[44] Especially in dying, though also in living, we need the "vigorous spiritual life" that consists in fully surrendering ourselves to God.

During the dying process, of course, people often undergo a fierce spiritual battle. In the Venerable Bede's *Life of Cuthbert*, the dying monk

Cuthbert decides to separate from others for a short period in order to prepare himself to accept death. Describing this experience of separation, Cuthbert does not make light of the spiritual struggle that he endures during his period of trial: "My assailants [demons] have never tempted me so sorely as they have during the past five days."[45] A less harrowing experience of dying, but one still marked by spiritual battle, is presented in the *Life of Wilfrid*. Here we find the compassion of the church fully manifested to Wilfrid as he lies dying in his bed: "The brethren chanted round the bed day and night, weeping as they sang."[46]

Aquinas recognizes that in dying, we confront—generally whether we wish to do so or not—the deep "marks and scars" of sin, in the words of Marilyn Chandler McEntyre, and we bear these "marks and scars" in our bodies.[47] Since this is the case, the sacrament of anointing of the sick addresses the root of the situation of the dying person.[48] Anointing oil involves physical contact, and it is gentle. The oil anoints the sick person's body through the ministry of Christ's body. This act of ecclesial compassion mediates the power of Christ's salvific compassion, and its gentleness penetrates into our bodies with a healing touch, in accord with the unity of the sacrament's power of bodily healing with its primary power of spiritual healing. The sacrament readies the person to lose his or her life in the name of Christ and while fully united to Christ's own dying. Thus the church gives this sacrament (the "*sacramentum exeuntium*") not only to the seriously sick but "even more rightly . . . to those at the point of departing this life."[49] As Andrew Davison remarks, the sacrament of anointing of the sick has to do with "salvation completed."[50]

Writing for dying persons in the voice of a dying person, Marilyn McEntyre conveys the fruits of her wide experience in caring for the dying when she remarks from a Protestant perspective: "I need people now who know when and how to touch me. . . . Only certain ones bring that gift of touch. I need to ordain them to that task."[51] Similarly, the Episcopalian theologian Megory Anderson remarks that she often uses "oil in rituals with the dying," since anointing with oil "involves intimacy and touch" and helps the dying "person feel the sacred in her body and . . . experience purification and blessing for the journey ahead."[52] In the sacrament of anointing of the sick, the "gift of touch" is connected with the saving, raising, and forgiveness promised by James 5:14–15. On the journey of Christian dying, we here find the most tangible expression of the compassion of Christ and of his mystical body for the person who is being fully configured to Christ's own mortal suffering. Thus I agree with the Catholic theologian Michael

Drumm when he comments, "Illness and old age are not disasters waiting to befall us but are part of our paschal destiny" that "must be integrated into the life of the local Christian community."[53]

Drumm affirms that "the pastoral care of the dying revolves around the Eucharist, reconciliation, and anointing," and he recognizes that "many people close to death naturally desire to receive absolution and to be anointed."[54] At the same time, much like Kasza, he urges that for dying persons "anointing is the least significant of the three sacraments" and viaticum is the most important.[55] The church today teaches in the "Rite for Emergencies" that "Christians in danger of death are bound by the precept to receive communion. If there is still sufficient time, the anointing of the sick may then be celebrated."[56] With the *Catechism of the Catholic Church*, and in accord with the extensive experience of many Catholics as well as Protestants such as Arnold and McEntyre, I have emphasized the importance, whenever possible, of the dying person (including the imminently dying person) receiving the sacrament of anointing of the sick.[57]

In the final sentence of *The Denial of Death*, a bestselling work of cultural anthropology, Ernest Becker concludes: "The most that any of us can seem to do is to fashion something—an object or ourselves—and drop it into the confusion, make an offering of it, so to speak, to the life force."[58] By contrast, in the faith-filled reception of the sacrament of anointing of the sick, Christ makes dying persons into a holy offering to the God who loves them, as befits members of his body. Just as Christ was royally anointed for his dying by the woman who "brought an alabaster flask of ointment" with which to anoint his feet (Luke 7:37), so now dying persons are royally anointed by Christ himself (through his church) and prepared to surrender their lives, freed from sinful rebellion, when Christ calls them to be "at home with the Lord" (2 Cor. 5:8). Here we find the heart of the sacrament of anointing, which is, as Therese Lysaught puts it, "an act of worship" and "an act of Christ's body" that "must always reflect Christ's work, which was to relentlessly point to and draw us to the Father."[59] By making possible the final surrendering of that which in believers says "no" to God, the sacrament of anointing of the sick strengthens sick and dying persons—in the words of Hans Urs von Balthasar about life in Christ—"in clinging in the midst of suffering to the unconditional will of the One who suffers out of love and outlasts suffering through love."[60]

CHAPTER 9

COURAGE

Goodbye to This World

Christians know that God will completely conquer death. Indeed, the prophet Isaiah states that God "will destroy on this mountain [Zion, Jerusalem] the shroud that is cast over all peoples, the sheet that is spread over all nations; he will swallow up death forever. Then the Lord God will wipe away the tears from all faces, and the disgrace of his people he will take away from all the earth" (Isa. 25:7–8).[1] Later in the book of Isaiah, we find the promise that God will "create new heavens and a new earth" (65:17) that will be marked by an absolute lack of violence or calamity: "The wolf and the lamb shall feed together, the lion shall eat straw like the ox. . . . They shall not hurt or destroy on all my holy mountain" (65:25).[2] Likewise, in light of Christ's death and resurrection, the seer of the book of Revelation foretells that Death will be thrown into "the lake of fire" to emerge no more (Rev. 20:14). After a vision of the "new Jerusalem" (the glorified church) "coming down out of heaven from God," the seer hears that God "will wipe every tear from their eyes. Death will be no more; mourning and crying and pain will be no more, for the first things have passed away" (21:2, 4). God himself states the death-defeating conclusion: "See, I am making all things new" (21:5).

On the one hand, dying Christians can look forward to this radical transformation with joyful anticipation. It will be wonderful for the blessed to discover "what God has prepared for those who love him" (1 Cor. 2:9; cf. Isa. 64:4). On the other hand, most dying Christians also face this future with trepidation. Along these lines, despite his firm faith in Christ, Henri Nouwen asks himself doubtfully whether he is prepared "to let go of everything and be carried into the completely unknown."[3] Similarly, from a standpoint of faith in the life to come, Carol Zaleski recognizes the scary profundity of the change: "Considering how radically we are changed by every critical crossing of the stream of life, it stands to reason that the translation to eternal life must be far more wonderful and more terrible than anything we have dared to wish. But it must also exact a correspondingly higher price. We pay not just with our flesh . . . but with the very surrender of ourselves."[4] Even as a renewed creation—indeed precisely as a renewed creation—eternal life will necessarily be quite different from the present earthly life that we know and love. This radically transformed mode of existence means that in dying, we say a final goodbye to the familiar mode of life that we have enjoyed in our earthly lives.

My rather simple argument in this concluding chapter is that undertaking this goodbye requires courage. Christian thinkers, of course, have not been entirely immune to what Zaleski (drawing upon consolation literature of the Victorian era) calls "the banal domestic vision of heaven—complete with smoking jacket and golden retriever."[5] We tend to want to imagine eternal life as simply part two of our present life, but without its more obvious imperfections. Miguel de Unamuno sums up this perspective bluntly: "What we really long for after death is to go on living this life, this same mortal life, but without its evils, without its tedium—and without death."[6] Thus many dying persons fearfully anticipate not only dying and death, but also what the atheist philosopher Raymond Tallis calls the "unthinkable" and "elusive notion of continuation in being despite utter transformation."[7] Tallis notes that if dying meant entering into the "gaze" of an all-knowing God, he could hardly "bear the self-knowledge that would come with that gaze."[8] As the Letter to the Hebrews says, "It is a fearful thing to fall into the hands of the living God" (Heb. 10:31).

We need great courage, therefore, to accept a truly radical transformation as we die.[9] In this chapter, I first survey portraits of life after death that, in my view, tend to deny this need for courage by turning life after death into a mere enhanced continuation of a pleasurable earthly life. In this vein, I briefly examine depictions of eternal life offered by Plato (or Socrates), the Qur'an, and N. T. Wright. These depictions diverge in important ways, but they are united by a strong emphasis on continuing with an enhanced version of the work and enjoyments of the present life. I then investigate in more detail Richard Middleton's biblical argument for greater continuity between this life and the life to come, and I contrast his position with Paul Griffiths's insistence upon much greater discontinuity. Both scholars affirm that there will be continuity, since we will retain our knowing and loving and our bodiliness, and since the whole creation will remain in existence in a renewed form. But given Griffiths's insistence that many of the central elements that characterize our daily lives will no longer be present and that the new center of our lives will be God, it is clear that Griffiths has in view a mode of life that differs from ours so much as to be almost inconceivable. Agreeing with this latter viewpoint, I argue that dying means a real rupture, a real goodbye to this world, a transition to something that "no eye has seen, nor ear heard, nor the human heart conceived" (1 Cor. 2:9). In preparing to enter the true promised land, dying persons must "be strong and bold," trusting boldly and bravely in "the LORD who goes before you" and who "will be with you" (Deut. 31:7–8).[10]

A Realm after Death in Which Our Familiar Life Continues

In a number of cultures, including our own, dying persons have anticipated a blessed realm after death in which life continues along essentially the same lines that we experience in earthly life, but in an exalted and much happier way. In Plato's *Gorgias*, for example, Socrates offers a story—which he recognizes to be mythic in character but which he nonetheless holds to be true—whose fundamental point is that "the man who has led a godly and righteous life departs after death to the Isles of the Blessed and there lives in all happiness exempt from ill, but the godless and unrighteous man departs to the prison of vengeance and punishment which they call Tartarus."[11] In Plato's *Phaedo*, Socrates provides a fuller explanation of these realms and modes of life. During our lifetimes, Socrates argues, "we do not realize that we are living in its [the earth's] hollows, but assume that we are living on the earth's surface."[12] According to Socrates, these hollows of the earth are much less beautiful than is the real surface of the earth. Socrates observes that "this earth [which we see around us] and its stones and all the regions in which we live are marred and corroded, just as in the sea everything is corroded by the brine" (110a, p. 91).

By contrast, Socrates imagines that on the real surface of the earth, which we cannot now see, "The mountains too and the stones have a proportionate smoothness and transparency, and their colors are lovelier. The pebbles which are so highly prized in our world—the jaspers and rubies and emeralds and the rest—are fragments of these stones, but there everything is as beautiful as they are, or better still" (110d, p. 91). Socrates proposes that the real surface of the earth also has animals and humans, as well as "sanctuaries and temples which are truly inhabited by gods, and oracles and prophecies and visions and all other kinds of communion with the gods occur there face to face" (111b, p. 92). According to Socrates's story, after death "those who are judged to have lived a life of surpassing holiness . . . are released and set free from confinement in these regions of the earth, and passing upward to their pure abode, make their dwelling upon the earth's surface" (114b, p. 94). Although Socrates adds that the holiest persons dwell there without bodies, the main point is that earthly life goes on—now, however, on the far more beautiful surface of the earth rather than in the hollows where we now live (or in the deeper cavities where those undergoing punishment live).

Somewhat similarly, the Qur'an's prophecies about the afterlife repeatedly promise the continuation and enhancement of the most pleasurable aspects of bodily life.[13] In Sura 37, God teaches that the blessed will endlessly and joyfully dwell in "gardens of delight," lying on couches, enjoying the favors of women "with modest refraining glances," and drinking wine that does not oppress the senses.[14] In Sura 44, likewise, God teaches that after death "the pious shall be in a secure place, amid gardens and fountains, clothed in silk and richest robes, facing one another: thus shall it be: and we will wed them to the *virgins* with large dark eyes: therein shall they call, secure, for every kind of fruit; therein, their first death passed, shall they taste death no more; and He shall keep them from the pains of Hell" (335).[15] In Sura 52, God promises that amid "gardens and delights shall they dwell who have feared God, rejoicing in what their Lord hath given them" (355). Having sacrificed and suffered on earth, they will have plenty to eat and drink, and "on couches ranged in rows shall they recline; and to the damsels with large dark eyes will we wed them" (356). They will also be reunited with those of their earthly children who were faithful during their earthly lives. Very similar portraits of life after death appear in Sura 55 and 56,[16] and Sura 78 concludes that "for the God-fearing is a blissful abode, enclosed gardens and vineyards; and damsels with swelling [i.e., youthful] breasts, their peers in age, and a full cup: there shall they hear no vain discourse nor any falsehood: a recompense from thy Lord— sufficing gift!" (406).[17]

In *The Remembrance of Death and the Afterlife*, book 40 of his *The Revival of the Religious Sciences*, the Sufi Muslim theologian Abu Hamid al-Ghazali (1058–1111) devotes a section to the everlasting "Vision of the Divine Countenance, which is the greatest of all delights, and which shall cause one to be quite oblivious of the pleasures of the people of Heaven."[18]

Al-Ghazali argues that compared to the vision of God, none of the physical pleasures of heaven will count for anything. He downplays the experience of the other delights of heaven as "no more than that of a beast let loose in a pasture."[19] On the other hand, he does not fail to describe the clothes, dwellings, horses, camels, food, drink, and sex that the blessed will enjoy, including a promise that each man will be united in marriage with 12,500 women possessed of various degrees of sexual experience, and that sexual intercourse with each of these women will last for as long as a lifetime on earth, since each man will each day have the sexual energy of seventy men on earth.[20] In polemical writings, medieval Christian theologians criticized the Qur'an and Muslim thinkers for holding to a conception of eternal life that promised these bodily pleasures.[21]

At the same time, Muslim thinkers such as al-Ghazali give more centrality to the vision of God than do many Christians today. For example, in *Surprised by Hope: Rethinking Heaven, the Resurrection, and the Mission of the Church*, N. T. Wright proposes that for the blessed, life after death will be a fundamentally recognizable extension of the daily tasks and pleasures of the present life, just as the whole new creation will be recognizably like the present one. He observes that in the general resurrection, God will give us a new (risen and immortal) body so that we can "rule wisely over God's new world. Forget those images about lounging around playing harps. There will be work to do and we shall relish doing it."[22] This work, he thinks, will accord with the abilities that we have discovered in ourselves during our earthly life, and it will also give us a chance to explore everlastingly the other talents that we have but that we did not find time or opportunity to employ during our earthly life. As he puts it, "All the skills and talents we have put to God's service in this present life—and perhaps too the interests and likings we gave up because they conflicted with our vocation—will be enhanced and ennobled and given back to us to be exercised to his glory" (161).[23]

Whereas the images in the Qur'an promise rest on couches with beautiful women and plentiful food and drink, Wright suggests that the New Testament indicates that we will need to (and will want to) continue working.[24] He emphasizes that since "the biblical view of God's future is of the renewal of the entire cosmos, there will be plenty to be done, entire new projects to undertake" (161).[25] In this presumably everlasting movement from project to project, he underscores the primary duty of tending and naming "the garden," that is, of ruling over all creation (161). In his view, everlasting life will be temporal, even if time "may well itself be transformed in ways we cannot at present even begin to imagine" (162).[26]

Wright affirms that in eternal life, the blessed will "enjoy God's immediate presence."[27] But his larger emphasis is on life after death as a continuation of the work of the present life. If so, then death is not really a goodbye to this world, and those who are dying are not, in fact, leaving the well-worn paths that they love. If no goodbye is necessary, then those who die in a holy condition will "awake"—at least at the general resurrection—to a life that is fundamentally familiar in its central aspects, even if also transformed in certain ways. If no goodbye is really necessary, then dying may still be difficult, but it does not require the special courage that is otherwise needed.

Richard Middleton and Paul Griffiths: Contrasting Portraits of the Eschatological State

Richard Middleton: Strong Continuity

The Reformed theologian Richard Middleton's position on this topic reflects N. T. Wright's. Middleton opens *A New Heaven and a New Earth* with a story from his youth in Jamaica. He states: "I remember once, on a climbing trip to Blue Mountain Peak, the highest point on the island, watching a breathtaking sunrise at 7,500 feet above sea level. After some minutes of silence, my friend Junior commented wistfully, 'This is so beautiful; it's such a shame that it will all be destroyed some day.' I still remember the dawning awareness: *I don't think it will be.*"[28] Speaking simply in terms of natural science, the earth prior to the eschaton will not only continue to undergo massive topological changes due to plate tectonics and erosion, but also the earth will be burned up by the dying sun in due time. Middleton knows this, but in his view God will ensure that this beautiful world, as we now know it, will not perish forever but will be restored in "the new heaven and the new earth" (12). The eschatology of George Eldon Ladd, who focused on "the redemption of creation" rather than "the unbiblical idea of being taken out of this world to heaven," made a strong impression upon the young Middleton (13).[29]

Middleton notes that among Christian pastors, "'Heaven' tends to be conceived in two main ways. First, heaven is understood as a transcendent realm beyond time and space. Second, heaven is characterized primarily by fellowship with and worship of God" (23). Critically reviewing a num-

153

ber of classic hymns (as well as contemporary revisions of these hymns), Middleton shows that they promote a "notion of a perpetual worship service in an otherworldly afterlife" (28). By contrast, he notes that Jamaican Rastafarian religion and Seventh-Day Adventism have avoided these notions of otherworldly escape. He blames Augustine in particular for dealing "the main blow to the vision of a renewed cosmos" (291).[30] According to Middleton, Augustine overlooks that God created humans not for the ethereal or spiritual task of worshiping God, but for "the responsible exercise of power on God's behalf over our earthly environment" (39).

This responsible ruling over the earth does not preclude worship; indeed, it is worship. Augustine holds that to reign with God is to participate worshipfully in God's triune life. In this sense, all creatures, including inanimate ones, are created for the worship of God. Middleton states, however, that "the human creature is made to worship God in a distinctive way: by interacting with the earth, using our God-given power to transform our earthly environment into a complex world (a sociocultural world) that glorifies our creator" (41). This is precisely what fallen humans have generally failed to do, but it remains our task today and forever in the "cosmic temple" that is God's creation.[31] Middleton notes that Genesis 1 and 2 closely unite creation and eschatology in their vision of the human being: "By our faithful representation of God, who is enthroned in the heavens, we extend the presence of the divine king of creation even to the earth, to prepare the earth for God's full—eschatological—presence, the day when God will fill all things" (49).[32] The new creation will not be otherworldly; rather, it will be *this* world, *this* cosmos, filled by God, and with humans as his royal representatives, charged with ensuring "shalom, generosity, and blessing" (52).

Turning to the narrative of salvation history, Middleton observes that God's election of Israel was always intended for the liberation or earthly flourishing of all peoples.[33] Furthermore, the blessings that God attaches to the people's obedience include earthly blessings such as "the fruitfulness of crops and herds, with regular rains," thereby demonstrating "the link between the moral and cosmic orders" (97). Middleton shows that the wisdom literature contains the same kinds of instruction for "holistic earthly flourishing," for "restoring the whole of life to what it was meant to be" for both humans and nonhumans (102). He also emphasizes that "the salvation of humanity . . . has ramifications for the restoration of the non-human world" (106).[34] Jesus's goal, as the second Adam, is for the whole human race to "once again utilize their God-given power and agency to rule the earth as God intended—a renewal of the human cultural task, but this time without sin" (70).

Middleton investigates various biblical passages that cut against the grain of his view of the eschatological goal. For example, he considers Isaiah 51:6, "Lift up your eyes to the heavens, and look at the earth beneath; for the heavens will vanish like smoke, the earth will wear out like a garment, and they who dwell in it will die like gnats; but my salvation will be forever." How is it that salvation can be "forever," if the earth and heavens no longer exist? Middleton answers that Isaiah is employing hyperbolic language to describe God's judgment. Such language aims to describe something far out of the ordinary, and so it should not be interpreted literalistically as though God planned actually to obliterate the very heavens and earth that God is redeeming. This observation is confirmed, Middleton thinks, by the image of God's "refining fire" (123). As in Isaiah 60, God's judgment "radically transforms without totally destroying what is judged" (124).

Middleton observes that until a relatively late stage, the texts that came to be the Old Testament did not envision life after death but instead considered "Sheol" to be a place of oblivion.[35] Later texts such as Psalm 73 press against this vision of death, and Isaiah 25 offers a particularly strong insistence upon God's conquest of death. Daniel 7 and 12 link the resurrection of the just with their receiving "the kingdom that is rightfully theirs" (140). God intends for his people to be rulers over creation, just as they were created to be. Second Temple Jewish writings highlight the expectation that in the new creation the blessed will be everlastingly "reigning and executing judgment on earth" (143).[36] Paul teaches that "the saints will judge the world" and will "judge angels" (1 Cor. 6:2–3), and Jesus speaks of the apostles sitting "on twelve thrones, judging the twelve tribes of Israel" (Matt. 19:28).

This rule, of course, will involve love and service rather than arbitrary power or domination, which are the marks of fallen human rule. As Hebrews 2:5–9 shows, God created humans to rule all things, and in Christ God is making it possible for humans finally to attain their proper (holy) rule. Second Timothy 2:12 promises that we will "reign" with Christ, and Middleton emphasizes that this is not merely a spiritual reign. Rather, even now we share in the battle against "the cosmic powers of this present darkness" (Eph. 6:12), and the book of Revelation shows that our final condition will involve God dwelling on earth, a new Jerusalem come down from heaven, and God's risen people not only worshiping God but also reigning "forever and ever" (Rev. 22:5).

Middleton concludes that resurrection of the dead aims to reverse and "rectify a situation in which death has impeded God's purposes for blessing and shalom" (153). Earthly life for humans finally will become what it was always meant to be: the full expression of "the royal status of humanity and our commission to image our creator in loving and wise stewardship of the earth," or, put another way, "the holistic flourishing of embodied people in the entirety of their earthly, cultural existence" (154). The church can and must strive, in Christ and through the Holy Spirit, to nourish this "holistic flourishing" even now.

Middleton adds a cosmic dimension to the holistic flourishing or reign of the blessed on earth. Citing Acts 3:21's testimony to a "universal restoration" and Ephesians 1:10's testimony to God's plan to unite in Christ "things in heaven and things on earth," Middleton comments that "heaven and earth" here means the entirety of creation, since "in the beginning God created the heavens and the earth" (Gen. 1:1). The same emphasis on cosmic redemption appears in Colossians 1:20, Romans 8:19–23, 2 Peter 3:10–13, and Revelation 21:1.[37] For Paul, Middleton observes, "The first step in the process of redemption . . . is that the oppressors (the human race) must be liberated from their own sin. Then the redemption of the nonhuman world can begin, when it will be set free from the bondage of sinful human rule" and will instead enjoy righteous human rule (160). Middleton comments that traditional translations of 2 Peter 3:10 ("burned up") depend upon the presence of the verb *katakaēsetai*, but in Codex Vaticanus and Codex Siniaticus, which are "two of the oldest and most reliable of the ancient Greek manuscripts," the verb is *heurethēsetai*, whose literal translation is "will be found" (162). Middleton holds that the imagery of the elements being "dissolved with fire" (which precedes the disputed verb in 2 Pet. 3:10) is a hyperbolic way of describing the divine judgment and the resulting purification from sin.

Indeed, the eschatological task of humans will be to "fill the earth" (Gen. 1:28) with God's presence, which previously was only in "heaven." When "the Lord God the Almighty and the Lamb" (Rev. 21:22) make themselves so perfectly present in the new Jerusalem that no temple is needed any longer, then not only has heaven come to earth, but also the consequences are cosmic.[38] Middleton states, "The center of God's governance of the cosmos from now on will be permanently established on a renewed earth" (170). That the new Jerusalem is the fulfillment of the creation—and thus has implications not only for the earth but for the heavens—is shown by the imagery of the river that flows from God's throne in the new Jerusalem, just as a river flowed from Eden (see Gen. 2:10).

Middleton does not speculate upon how the renewed earth, on which God will dwell, will relate to the vast spaces of the cosmos. Instead, he draws out the significance of the movement from a garden (Gen. 2) to a city (Rev. 21). Cultural production and cultural diversity will belong to the new creation. As evidence, he cites Isaiah 60:11, "Your gates shall always be open; day and night they shall not be shut, so that nations shall bring you their wealth, with their kings led in procession" (173). On this basis, Middleton urges again that "we need to drop pious ideas of a perpetual worship service as our ultimate purpose in the eschaton" (174).[39] Instead, humans are to "reign" (Rev. 22:5) in a variety of ways.

Middleton reads passages that seem to foretell the destruction of the present cosmos as expressing the intensity of God's judgment upon sin. He addresses quite a number of such texts, including Matthew 24:35 ("Heaven and earth will pass away"), 2 Peter 3:10 ("the heavens will pass away with a loud noise"), and Revelation 21:1 ("the first heaven and the first earth had passed away"). He interprets these texts as indicating a perfect refining and purification of the present cosmos. Just as our corruptible body must be changed to an incorruptible body—while remaining the same body—so also the cosmos must be changed in a transformative rather than destructive way. Middleton explains, "This understanding of passing away as transformation and not as simple obliteration and replacement is supported by the pattern of Scripture, which assumes a parallel between the redemption of persons (including the body) and the redemption of the nonhuman world" (206). He also emphasizes that the "new creation" will be *new*, since "heaven" (where God dwells) will truly come to earth, in the sense that God will fully dwell on earth: "the heavenly city is coming here, and it will be unveiled at the last day" (219). In this context, Middleton contests the popular dispensationalist view of the "rapture" and argues (by contrast to N. T. Wright) that there is no clear biblical teaching of an "intermediate state" in which disembodied souls await the resurrection of the dead (234).[40]

The kingdom of God preached by Jesus, says Middleton, is the same thing as "eternal life" in the Gospel of John. Both the kingdom and eternal life are already present in a certain way, but not yet *fully* present. Middleton emphasizes that the kingdom of God should not be thought to be "basically equivalent to the church," as Augustine and many others have supposed; nor should the kingdom of God be imagined to be instantiated in a nonearthly realm rather than on earth (247).[41] Rather, the kingdom involves a redemptive healing of both personal and social brokenness and sin, including the healing of our bodies and of our relationship to the earth. The kingdom requires "concrete reconciliation between people" and is meant to include the whole human race (269).

Paul Griffiths: Discontinuity and Continuity

In *Decreation: The Last Things of All Creatures*, Paul Griffiths portrays the world to come as being radically unlike our current life, even if he also faults the classical theological tradition for in certain ways underestimating the connection between this world and the world to come.[42] Like Middleton, Griffiths recognizes the present world's need for renewal; indeed, he underscores its fallenness more than does Middleton.[43] In favor of the familiarity of the life to come, Griffiths recognizes that we will exercise intelligence and love in eternal life, and he thinks that all plants and animals will be present and restored. But his overall emphasis points strongly in the direction of a truly radical transformation. Characteristic of Griffiths's emphasis on transformation is his account of the "time" of eternal life. He proposes that eternal life remains temporal, but not in the "metronomic" mode of temporality that we experience in this life, which can be "timed by a clock" (217). In eternal life, says Griffiths, time will possess a "systolated" or "ingathered" mode (217). As he puts it, "In the timespace that is heaven . . . the systolation of time is complete, and the repetitive stasis already evident in the liturgical life is brought to consummation" (217). Arguably, this position fits with the rhythmic and symbolic portrait of "time" around the divine throne that we find in Revelation 4: "whenever the living creatures give glory and honor and thanks to the one who is seated on the throne, who lives forever and ever, the twenty-four elders fall before the one who is seated on the throne and worship the one who lives forever and ever; they cast their crowns before the throne" (Rev. 4:9–10).

Griffiths proposes that in the liturgical "time" of eternal life, the blessed enjoy the vision of God, and beyond this inexhaustible vision "lies nothing new to come" (218).[44] Nothing new is to come because the blessed are utterly filled by the glory of praising the name of the Lord; it follows that no further "history" can take place, because the inexhaustibly rich goal of all history has been found and is being enjoyed in the deepest possible sense (235).[45] In addition, Griffiths argues that the blessed will be entirely ordered toward God in such a way as not to be at all ordered toward themselves: "Their existence will, grammatically, be entirely dative—they will be constantly addressed by the LORD's voice, and constantly confronted by his face; and their response will be exclusively one of adoration, to which experience does not and cannot belong" (236).[46] By contrast to our experience of consciousness in this life, he suggests that the focus of the blessed upon God will negate their self-awareness—an opposition that I think unnecessary, given that the blessed can maintain self-awareness without ceasing humbly to "cast their crowns before the throne" (Rev. 4:10). Griffiths adds that in eternal life, since we will be open fully in love to everyone, "it is likely that we are as close to those who were . . . our enemies as to our friends and lovers" (239).[47] In my view, the charitable relationships that we enjoy in this life will remain of distinctive value in eternal life,[48] but we will be fully loving toward all, including those who were our enemies.

With regard to the similarity of the new creation and the original one, Griffiths criticizes Thomas Aquinas for arguing that, in the new creation, plants and animals will not be present in their characteristic forms. As Griffiths notes, Aquinas holds that all the material of which plants and animals are made will still be present in the new creation, but now in a nonorganic though immensely beautiful form—much like Revelation 21's focus mainly upon humans and precious jewels.[49] Although I can understand why Aquinas arrives at his position, I think that Griffiths's position is the more fitting one. Admittedly, it may be solely an image when Revelation 22:2 speaks of the presence of "the tree of life with its twelve kinds of fruit, producing its fruit each month." Although the tree of life is symbolic, however, the new creation would be missing a great deal if there were absolutely nothing like trees or fruit. Revelation 19, similarly, speaks of horses and birds being on the side of Christ. In the context of the book of Revelation, these are obviously symbolic images, but I expect that the new creation will contain at least most of the distinctive and irreplaceably unique perfections that we find in the plant and animal kingdoms, just as it will contain our own perfected bodies.

For Aquinas, as Griffiths explains, one problem is that glorified plants and animals could not really be themselves in eternal life; plants could no longer grow or do some other characteristic plant things, and animals could no longer eat flesh or vegetation and do some other characteristic animal things. On these grounds, Aquinas excludes them from a living participation in the new creation. But I think that just as with our own bodies, God can find a way to transform plant and animal bodies into the incorruptible new creation, without making them unrecognizably different (as would happen if they were simply dissolved into their elements, as Aquinas holds to be the case).[50] Aquinas strongly affirms a new creation rather than a mere destruction or discarding of the material creation, but he is not sufficiently attuned to the enduring value and beauty of plant and animal life, both in itself and in its relationships with human beings. Admittedly, plants and animals *cannot* be resurrected, if by this one means raising from the dead the same plant or animal.[51] Since plants and animals do not possess immaterial souls (note that neither Griffiths nor Middleton supposes that immaterial souls exist at all), plants and animals have no principle that can bridge the chasm opened up by material death and decay. Lacking such a principle, a dog (for example) in the new creation cannot be the same dog that existed in the original creation; it can at most be a replica of the original dog.[52]

For Griffiths, if I understand him correctly, the healing of our violent and destructive relationships with specific plants and animals requires that the same plants and animals be in the new creation in a healed state. I do not think this possible, and I also deny that the corruptibility of organic things, with the violence and death attendant upon organic cycles, is in itself a consequence of sin. It follows that I do not think that God owes resurrection (even if it could be done) to animals that have suffered pain.[53] In my view, that plants and animals cannot be resurrected, but can only at best be replicated in a glorified form, is a good thing. It saves us from being tempted to think that literally all plants and animals—all the species that have ever lived and all the members of those species—must be present in the new creation, since they were present in the original creation. The surpassing power of the resurrection does not require holding (with Griffiths) either that "plants or animals are resurrected for eternal life" or that "all plant and animal kinds, with all their individual members" that have ever existed are to be found in the new creation (289, 293). Even so, given the beauty and significance of plants and animals (and given biblical images such as the wolf dwelling with the lamb; see Isa. 11:6), we can expect that God will include a vast number of glorified plants and animals in his new creation. As Griffiths says, each creature's existence "glorifies the LORD," and the new creation "is the world healed, the world made beautiful as cosmos" (293).

Griffiths's constructive portrait of the new creation, with "the LORD" at its center and "time" concentrated liturgically, and with the full panoply of creatures glorified and at peace, accords with the scriptural testimony to the "eternal weight of glory beyond all measure" (2 Cor. 4:17). In his account of the world, which he calls "the devastation," he is more negative than I am: his way of looking at the world seems to look forward to dying as a release from the "charnel house," whereas in my view—having enjoyed many wonderful gifts in this life, alongside many sufferings too—it will be difficult to leave this world by dying (4). But his portrait of the new creation, although he only very rarely quotes Scripture, is more scriptural than Middleton's because it is more open to the promises about sharing in God that Scripture makes about eternal life. By affirming the beatific vision in its constituent character as worship, Griffiths bridges the scriptural promises about bodily resurrection and new creation with the scriptural promises about knowing God as he knows us and sharing intimately in the Son's relationship to the Father.[54] The royal glory of eternal life, in which all our actions are worship, means that dying persons need courage to say goodbye to the comforts of our familiar world and to dare to enter into the divine light of the new creation, the "kingdom" in which God will "be everything to every one" (1 Cor. 15:24, 28 RSV).

Conclusion

The contemporary poet and essayist Christian Wiman has rightly observed, "It's not that conventional ideas of an afterlife are too strange; it is that they are not strange enough."[55] When Middleton holds that "we need to drop pious ideas of a perpetual worship service as our ultimate purpose in the eschaton," he exemplifies this problem, because he has not grasped the true strangeness—and thereby the true greatness—of the worship made possible by deification.[56] He needs to give deeper attention to the mysteries opened up by 2 Peter 1:4 ("participants of the divine nature"), 1 Corinthians 13:12 ("then I will know fully, even as I have been fully known"), 2 Corinthians 4:17 ("an eternal weight of glory beyond all measure"), 1 John 3:2 ("what we will be has not yet been revealed. What we do know is this: when he is revealed, we will be like him, for we will see him as he is"), John 14:23 ("Those who love me will keep my word, and my Father will love them, and we will come to them and make our home with them"), Revelation 3:12 ("If you conquer, I will make you a pillar in the temple of my God; you will never go out of it. I will write on you the name of my God, and the name of the city of my God, the new Jerusalem that comes down from my God out of heaven, and my own new name"), Revelation 3:21 ("To the one who conquers I will give a place with me on my throne, just as I myself conquered and sat down with my Father on his throne"), and Revelation 4:8 ("Day and night without ceasing they sing, 'Holy, holy, holy, is the Lord God the Almighty, who was and is and is to come'"). These biblical texts, and others like them such as those that describe the final consummation as a marriage between God and his people, challenge simple conceptions of eternal life that are overly modeled on our present existence. The biblical texts instead point toward a mysterious eternal *participation* in the divine life, a real communion with infinite tripersonal Life, Wisdom, and Love.[57] To reign with the triune God on his throne means to be elevated, in a body-soul communion that embraces the whole people of God along with the renewed cosmos, into the joy and beatitude of God—and thereby to arrive at the glorious and inexpressible fulfillment of cosmic history, not to continue on with cosmic history and temporal labor. Here Middleton could learn from Griffiths.

In addition to neglecting the biblical texts that undergird the doctrine of deification, Middleton does not give sufficient place to texts that indicate that the cosmos will be utterly transformed. When he treats passages such as Matthew 24:35 ("Heaven and earth will pass away"), 2 Peter 3:10 ("the heavens will pass away with a loud noise"), and Revelation 21:1 ("the first heaven and the first earth had passed away"), he implies that the new version of the heavens and earth will be fundamentally like what we now have. But although we know what a "physical body" is and looks like, we cannot yet fully know what a "spiritual body" (1 Cor. 15:44). God tells the seer of the book of Revelation that "death will be no more" and that "I am making all things new" (Rev. 21:4–5). How could this be done if there are still plants that grow and decay, and animals that need food and employ digestive tracts? Surely a radical transformation of the material cosmos is necessary for there is truly to be no death, no more violence. Jesus teaches that "when they [humans] rise from the dead, they neither marry nor are given in marriage, but are like angels in heaven" (Mark 12:25). How could this be, if our sexual desires are still as strong as they often are in the present life? The description of "the holy city Jerusalem coming down out of heaven from God. It has the glory of God and a radiance like a very rare jewel, like jasper, clear as crystal" (Rev. 21:10–11), makes clear that it is radically different from an ordinary city. Indeed, the sun will no longer be needed, since our light will come directly from God, and "there will be no more night" (Rev. 22:5). The images here suggest a profound and unfathomable change. As Dale Allison remarks, "The discontinuity between now and then must be extreme."[58]

Dying, then, is truly a goodbye to this world. Even though we will recognize continuity between the present creation and the new creation, the dissimilarity will be far greater, and in dying we must let go of this world and of our earthly mode of being. Everything is going to be reconfigured around charity, and so charity is the only thing we securely can take with us across the passage of death. Rather than hoping for a resumption of our cultural tasks, we must heed Paul's warning about that which passes away and that which does not. Paul instructs the Corinthians: "Love never ends. But as for prophecies, they will come to an end; as for tongues, they will cease; as for knowledge, it will come to an end. . . . And now faith, hope, and love abide, these three; and the greatest of these is love" (1 Cor. 13:8, 13). Everything else belongs to this world, and we must not cleave to it; in dying, we must say goodbye, fearful (even if also exciting) as this is. In saying goodbye, we must not pretend that the present earthly life gives us a "lasting city" (Heb. 13:14). In some way, of course, we will get back what we freely leave behind—we will "receive a hundredfold, and will inherit eternal life" (Matt. 19:29)—but we cannot expect to get it back in a familiar form. It is not for nothing that Jesus warns in this very context that "it will be hard for a rich person to enter the kingdom of heaven" and that "it is easier for a camel to go through the eye of a needle than for someone who is rich to enter the kingdom of God" (Matt. 19:23–24), since riches make us loath to say goodbye to the good things that we have.

The dying person, then, must be like those who (in Jesus's words) have freely "left houses or brothers or sisters or father or mother or children or fields, for my name's sake" (Matt. 19:29). We must embrace what Donald Heinz calls "a thrill of hope that is *totaliter aliter*—unlike anything we know."[59] This action requires courage. Madeleine L'Engle puts the matter in simple terms: "Death is change, and change is always fearful as well as challenging, but until we can admit the fear, we cannot accept the challenge. Until we can admit the fear, we cannot know the assurance, deep down in our hearts, that indeed, we are *not* afraid."[60] According to Thomas Aquinas, this courage in the face of mortal fear can be given to us by God. Craig Titus sums up Aquinas's teaching about the divinely "infused" virtue of courage by noting that it "participates in divine strength, in the midst of human fear, trials, and weakness."[61]

In dying, then, let us make life in God our "eager expectation and hope" and undertake "with all boldness" (Phil. 1:20) to suffer with Christ so that we might be wondrously glorified with him in his renewed and transformed cosmos as "heirs of God and joint heirs with Christ" (Rom. 8:17).

Conclusion

I have written many words about dying in this book, but in the face of death, we are often struck utterly silent. This reaction is clearly not wrong. Awe-filled silence belongs to the heart of any sane encounter with dying. Yet a painful and even despairing silence—a "choked and beaten silence"[1]—can arise from shock at the sheer brutality of dying, at the viciousness with which it renders dying persons prone and helpless. Can we really say, with truth rather than merely with the desire to draw a curtain over the misery of dying, that the dying person "does not fade into mist but is carrying out one of the major tasks of his human existence"?[2] Realistically, Christopher Vogt comments that "what people find most troubling and difficult to deal with is the fact that they see . . . living through the experience of dying as yielding no benefit to themselves, their loved ones, or the world."[3]

In response, I have argued in this book that for our dying to be a major task of our living rather than a mere collapse that we experience as meaningless, we need the gifts that come from Jesus Christ. Not only do we need his cross to free us from our sinfulness, but also we need the strength of his Spirit to unite us in gratitude, humility, solidarity, and self-surrender to his supreme act of love. We do not have the strength to repent without God's help, and even our deepest penitence cannot suffice to rectify things without the forgiveness won by Christ. Otherwise, the wounds we have inflicted upon other people and ourselves, due to our own rebellions against God, would render our dying merely a final discovery of our helpless humiliation. To understand our dying as an act of grateful living characterized by virtues, we need Christ.

164

Here it is important to appreciate that Christ's dying, like ours, has a context—as Ephraim Radner puts it, "a gathering, a communion, a historical reach" that "is made up of people who were born, lived, grew, weakened, and died, suddenly, or only quickly, or more gradually, though all in short order and finally."[4] As Hebrews 11 indicates, the communal context of Christ's dying can be seen in the holy Israelites who chose to suffer for the sake of fidelity to the God of the covenant. In this context, patient endurance of dying shows that we embrace our status as "strangers and foreigners on the earth" who look toward "a better country, that is, a heavenly one" (Heb. 11:13, 16). Yet, like the deacon Stephen, Radner knows that the existence of the heroes of faith, no matter how many there have been, does not justify Christian or Israelite self-congratulation.[5] In the marred history of the church, God has allowed weeds to grow along with the wheat (Matt. 13:25), an image that refers not simply to the difference between the good and the wicked but also to our own divided hearts. The *Catechism of the Catholic Church* comments that "because God is holy, he can forgive the man who realizes that he is a sinner before him," and it adds that "unless man acknowledges that he is a sinner he cannot know the truth about himself . . . and without the offer of forgiveness he would not be able to bear this truth."[6] We know that we are sinners. But in this same context we also know God's forgiveness, by his mercy in Christ that shapes us into Christ's body the church through the grace of the Holy Spirit.

As Christians, Karl Rahner emphasizes, our entire life should be a continuous dying to self. Rahner describes "our participation in Christ's death through our own real death, which is enacted throughout our lives and consummated in the actual death of the Christian."[7] Yet, no matter how sincere and devout this lifelong participation is, we face something new when it comes to our final days, to our "actual death." What is this reality that we call dying, and where is it really leading us? Coming face-to-face with our "actual death" will test every fiber of our being. Indeed, the present book is not for those who anticipate easy deaths, but for those who anticipate the opposite, who accept that "dying for most of us will be a messy, painful business."[8] Here Eberhard Jüngel wisely points out, "There is a great danger that edifying speeches on the subject of death may serve only to explain away the bitter inevitability of our own death and also the pain we feel at the death of another."[9] By giving contexts to particular virtues of dying, I have sought to uphold concrete ways of living the trial of our dying, ways that are offered to the church by Christ through his Spirit.

Although this book treats nine virtues, Christian dying is not simply for those who in spiritual things have *already* "become rich" or who are *already* "strong" (1 Cor. 4:8, 10). These virtues are God's gracious *gifts*, for which, against all Pelagianism or presumption, we must continuously ask. In light of his own experience of cancer, Todd Billings asks God: "Will you fulfill your purpose in me when I feel too listless to hope in your coming kingdom?"[10] His point is that our hope can only be in God and his mercy, not in any virtues that we imagine ourselves to possess "on our own." All our virtues would be nothing if they were not enlivened personally by Christ's Spirit uniting us to communion with God the Father. Facing death, we are surely like the tax collector of Jesus's parable who, knowing his own guilt and neediness, can only "beat his breast" and say, "God, be merciful to me, a sinner!" (Luke 18:13). We are beggars—and the virtues of dying are God's merciful alms.

David Bentley Hart has pointed out that there are moments in our life when "we stand amazed before the gratuity of being and the luminosity of consciousness and the transcendental splendor that seems to shine in and through all things."[11] As the book of Job shows, however, this amazement in itself could not suffice if dying ended our conscious existence. Job makes clear that we could not rightly accept the everlasting obliteration of our conscious communion, if that were what death is, without profound protest. Dying and living ultimately have no meaning if all things simply return to the brutal and mindless unfolding of the cosmic life force, plowing onward endlessly into a temporal eternity.[12] Hart observes that "death runs contrary to the whole orientation of human consciousness— or, rather, cuts entirely across its grain," because "our orientation toward the future is part of the very essence of our humanity."[13] The approaching end of our earthly life and the shrouding of our future "threatens us with the possibility of nothingness, the futility of all enterprises, the overthrow of all hopes."[14]

Is it possible to be more optimistic about death, on secular grounds? Rather boldly, Arthur Imhof has proposed to develop a modern *ars moriendi* that assists the dying person in declaring himself or herself "fulfilled by life, and not just tired of it," and able happily to "let go even without the prospect of any continuation."[15] But in fact the wonders of interpersonal communion do not allow for this kind of satiation; Imhof's counsel is a path to despair or, at best, to an anesthetized dulling of human desire. After all, as Imhof recognizes, even if we have experienced an enjoyable life and are remembered for a while by friends and family, the continuing cosmic process will eventually, sooner rather than later, destroy even the tiniest trace of the fact that we once lived. How could such annihilation be welcomed as a satiated fulfillment of our interpersonal communion? Thus the Muslim scholar Abul A'la Maududi is quite right that "belief in a life after death is the greatest deciding factor in the life of a human being," since the meaningfulness of a human life cannot be squared with annihilation.[16]

In this book, I have argued that by obeying in faith Jesus's command to take up our cross and follow him (Matt. 10:38) through the Spirit, we can die well. Like Paul, as we approach our dying we can be "of good courage" and, insofar as "we walk by faith," we can prefer to "be away from the body and at home with the Lord" (2 Cor. 5:7–8). In preparing for dying, we can already anticipate receiving "the crown of righteousness" alongside "all who have longed for his appearing" (2 Tim. 4:8), namely, the "great multitude that no one could count, from every nation, from all tribes and peoples and languages" (Rev. 7:9). Girded by the virtues of dying, we can look forward to meeting all these blessed saints and angels, and to rejoicing and reigning with them in the new creation, when "the marriage of the Lamb has come" (Rev. 19:7) and the whole cosmos shines forth with everlasting, infinite love. Even now, we yearn for the wondrous, unimaginable fulfillment of Christ's promise: "To the one who conquers I will give a place with me on my throne, just as I myself conquered and sat down with my Father on his throne" (Rev. 3:21).

Yet virtuous dying can still be agonizing and, to all outward appearances, miserable and humiliating. We know in faith that if we die in Christ, who "loves us and freed us from our sins by his blood" (Rev. 1:5), he will give us "the crown of life" (2:10). We know that our lives in Christ, as members of his body the church, prepare us for this final completion of our Passover, which involves not the glorification of death but its conquest in and through the agony of dying.[17] As Vogt observes, "It is by a lifelong effort to nurture faith, hope, patience, compassion, and all the virtues of the good Christian life that we best prepare ourselves for the time of our dying."[18] This preparation itself, however, is Christ's gift through his Spirit, and it does not mean that we will be able to traverse the path of dying with earthly "dignity." There will be no shame in moaning with the psalmist, "I am poured out like water, and all my bones are out of joint; my heart is like wax; it is melted within my breast; my mouth is dried up like a potsherd, and my tongue sticks to my jaws; you lay me in the dust of death" (Ps. 22:14–15).

Notably, however, the very first words of this psalm are spoken by Jesus during his dying on the cross: "My God, my God, why have you forsaken me?" (Ps. 22:1; Matt. 27:46; Mark 15:34). When we are dying, when our "heart is like wax" (Ps. 22:14), our faith and love unite us with "the offering of the body of Jesus Christ" (Heb. 10:10), and we are preparing "to enter the sanctuary by the blood of Jesus" (Heb. 10:19). Thus Vigen Guroian, recognizing that we are baptized into Christ's death (see Rom. 6:4), points out that "each of us is called to be the priest of our own death," in a manner that "cannot be disconnected from the community of faith."[19] United to Christ, the dying person and the whole community gathered around him or her "assumes a priestly sacrificial role as sufferers and co-sufferers under the sign of the cross."[20] This priestly offering of the dying person in Christ has in view the "new life of resurrection" that the risen Christ has promised, which will consist in "communion with God in eternity and with all the persons to whom we were bound in love during our temporal lives" and with all the blessed.[21]

The virtues of dying are those that enable us to exercise this priestly offering, as dying members of Christ's body. Since dying does not destroy the creative Word who is the "life" that is "the light of all people" (John 1:4), and also since "God so loved the world that he gave his only Son, so that everyone who believes in him may not perish but may have eternal life" (John 3:16), dying is something that humans, without losing themselves, can rightly do.

After all, the cosmos is too wondrous,[22] and too wondrously contingent, to be the fruit of cold lifelessness rather than the fruit of transcendent love. So we should hardly be surprised that Christ has transformed the fallen path of dying into "the gateway to eternal life" for those who believe in him and embrace his mercy.[23] Without glorifying dying as though it were intrinsically good, we can even affirm that in this fallen world "the painful process of breaking [dying] is the way in which God shapes the new thing," since "God breaks the old Adam (collectively and individually) so as to form the new Adam out of him; bit by bit he breaks our willfulness and self-sufficiency so as to recast us for the freedom of his love."[24]

In Christ, therefore, and without being ashamed of our fear, let us "put on the whole armor of God" (Eph. 6:11)—love, hope, faith, penitence, gratitude, solidarity, humility, self-surrender, and courage. In this way, in our dying we will not "grieve as others do who have no hope" (1 Thess. 4:13), nor will we suppose that we can understand or articulate all that the good God wills to draw from the evil of our dying. In our dying, we go to meet our merciful judge and redeemer, who has borne the "wages of sin" (Rom. 6:23) for us and who will "not disappoint us, because God's love has been poured into our hearts through the Holy Spirit that has been given to us" (Rom. 5:5).[25] In dying, our scattered words, including the many words of this book, find their meaning in the merciful Word, in whom "every one of God's promises is a 'Yes'" (2 Cor. 1:20). "Be silent, all people, before the LORD; for he has roused himself from his holy dwelling" (Zech. 2:13).[26]

Notes

Notes to the Introduction

1. Since this book is a work of Catholic theology, I presume the authority of Christian Scripture. At the same time, I am interested in how all peoples and religions have approached dying. Here it is worth noting that, as John Bowker observes, "The earliest history of religions, both east and west, to which we have access makes it clear that religion did not originate in an offer of worthwhile life after death" (*The Meanings of Death* [Cambridge: Cambridge University Press, 1991], 37). Bowker notes that "such widely influential people as J. G. Frazer (of *The Golden Bough*) were profoundly wrong when they tried to locate the origin of religion in the superstitious ignorance of primitive people. . . . The religious exploration of death is a great deal more profound and interesting than that, since it is, basically, an assertion of value in human life and relationships which does not deny, and is not denied by, the absolute fact and reality of death. In place of the widespread and current view of religious origins (that religions derive their original and basic power over human lives from their 'sales pitch' on life after death) we have to recognise that the earliest religious explorations of death were focused much more on the disruption and disorder of death, and on how to maintain order in the face of chaos and malevolence and the deliberate willing of evil" (37–38).

2. William Greenway, *For the Love of All Creatures: The Story of Grace in Genesis* (Grand Rapids: Eerdmans, 2015), 149.

3. Anthony C. Thiselton, *Life after Death: A New Approach to the Last Things* (Grand Rapids: Eerdmans, 2012), 3. Greenway seems to overlook this point when, construing faith in an anthropocentric fashion, he states: "All the dynamics of awakening to the fact that we have been seized by love for every creature, including ourselves, recognition of the asymmetry and personal realization of the glory of living life in the saving light of the transcending 'yes' of grace, that is, the glory of living faith that is

the gift of grace—absolutely all of this stands even if our deaths mark totally, without exception and forevermore, the end of our lives" (Greenway, *For the Love*, 150).

4. Georges Florovsky, *Creation and Redemption*, Collected Works of Georges Florovsky 3 (Belmont, MA: Nordland, 1976), 106, 111.

5. Dumitru Staniloae, *The World: Creation and Deification*, trans. and ed. Ioan Ionita and Robert Barringer, vol. 2 of *The Experience of God* (Brookline, MA: Holy Cross Orthodox Press, 2000), 202. Vigen Guroian adds the point that from a Pauline perspective, "death as we know it in a fallen world is not the same thing as the natural cessation of life that Adam and Eve might have experienced had they not sinned" (*Life's Living toward Dying: A Theological and Medical-Ethical Study* [Grand Rapids: Eerdmans, 1996], 43). Guroian goes on to explain, "Human experience is now suffused with the typically vague but sometimes acute sense that everything of value and joy in life is disintegrating and being despoiled. We all experience moments when the harmony of the body-and-soul union is assaulted or severely weakened, moments when our body or mind seems out of control and our identity and relationship with the world seem to be at risk. These descents into sickness are what dying in sin is ultimately about" (47). Here Guroian cites appreciatively William F. May, "The Sacral Power of Death in Contemporary Experience," in *On Moral Medicine: Theological Perspectives in Medical Ethics*, ed. Stephen E. Lammers and Allen Verhey (Grand Rapids: Eerdmans, 1987), 175–84.

6. Bartholomew J. Collopy, SJ, "Theology and the Darkness of Death," *Theological Studies* 39 (1978): 42. Collopy "presses theology to cast off all conceptual presumptuousness, all assumptions that would make God a calculated and obvious comfort, that would make death a test fulsome with piety" (50). In my view, Collopy goes too far: why must theology know absolutely nothing, and why cannot death be a trial enriched by piety? For Collopy, the theology of death "must show that faith simply waits for God to be God, *on God's terms*, in a freedom of being beyond all human sight and experience" (50). But what if God has already revealed his "terms," which include Christ, the firm faith and hope of Paul and of the martyrs facing death, and the existence of a "soul" that is not killed when the body is killed (Matt. 10:28)? Collopy is allowing Heidegger, or perhaps Rudolf Otto, to set the terms. Collopy affirms Jesus's resurrection "as a shocking and scandalous counterclaim" to death (53).

7. Thomas Aquinas, *Summa theologica* II-II, q. 142, a. 3, trans. Dominican Fathers of the English Province (Westminster, MD: Christian Classics, 1981).

8. Certainly Christian fear of dying should not be exactly the same as the fear experienced by nonbelievers. As Athanasius says in *On the Incarnation*, trans. and ed. a religious of CSMV (Crestwood, NY: St. Vladimir's Orthodox Seminary Press, 1993), "All the disciples of Christ despise death; they take the offensive against it and, instead of fearing it, by the sign of the cross and by faith in Christ trample on it as on something dead. Before the divine sojourn of the Saviour, even the holiest of men were afraid of death, and mourned the dead as those who perish. But now that the Saviour has raised His body, death is no longer terrible, but all those who believe in Christ tread it underfoot as nothing, and prefer to die rather than to deny their faith

in Christ, knowing full well that when they die they do not perish, but live indeed, and become incorruptible through the resurrection. . . . Every one is by nature afraid of death and of bodily dissolution; the marvel of marvels is that he who is enfolded in the faith of the cross despises this natural fear and for the sake of the cross is no longer cowardly in face of it" (57–58). I feel much more "cowardly" than Athanasius, but on the other hand I can testify to the great difference Christ makes in the face of death. Athanasius himself admits that the "natural fear" of death still exists even for the martyr who "despises" this fear.

9. Hans Urs von Balthasar, *Life out of Death: Meditations on the Paschal Mystery*, trans. Martina Stöckl (San Francisco: Ignatius, 2012), 9. I have left out Balthasar's extensive discussion of dying in his trilogy. See, for example, his profound reflections on "The Theme of Death" in world literature, in *Prolegomena*, trans. Graham Harrison, vol. 1 of *Theo-Drama: Theological Dramatic Theory* (San Francisco: Ignatius, 1988), 369–408; as well as his discussion of dying (and living) in Christ, in *The Last Act*, trans. Graham Harrison, vol. 5 of *Theo-Drama: Theological Dramatic Theory* (San Francisco: Ignatius, 1998), 323–46. In the latter volume, Balthasar engages—critically and appreciatively—Martin Heidegger's theology of death: "Basing himself on Scheler's insight that human life, if it is to be capable of genuine, that is, definitive, moral decisions, must be finite and hence mortal, Heidegger realized that the immanence of death in human existence is precisely what enables it to escape from the void of 'everyday facticity' and attain freedom to pursue its 'ultimate possibility,' namely, 'self-surrender.' Within this ultimate possibility the acts of existence (which—since they have ethical value—can be evaluated) participate in the quality of this self-surrender. It is a fact, of course, that in Heidegger this 'ultimate possibility' is acted out in the face of the unresolved enigma of being (for Heidegger, being is essentially veiled), and so it cannot have any discernible meaning for the totality; accordingly this has a negative effect on the ethical acts initiated in life. It seems that the only way to avoid this effect would be to mask life's radical end by some kind of premature flight into the supratemporal realm, or into the supra-individual realm of the 'universal'" (323–24). See Martin Heidegger, *Being and Time*, trans. Joan Stambaugh, rev. Dennis J. Schmidt (Albany: State University of New York Press, 2010), especially the section on "The Possible Being-a-Whole of Dasein and Being-toward-Death," 227–55, in which Heidegger unfolds his view of "an existentiell, authentic being-toward-death" (255).

For further Christian assimilation of Heidegger's critique, seeking "to allow death to be death," see Emmanuel Falque, "Suffering Death," in *The Role of Death in Life: A Multidisciplinary Examination of the Relationship between Life and Death*, ed. John Behr and Conor Cunningham (Eugene, OR: Cascade, 2015), 47. Falque insists that the Christian stance before death must not seek to mask death's fearfulness, a fearfulness that even (and indeed supremely) Christ experienced. Though I agree with Falque in this respect, I think that he mistakenly sidelines the view that Christ understood his death in sacrificial terms (as "satisfaction" for sin) and that he also is mistaken to minimize Christ's knowledge of his coming resurrection and of the achievement of his cross. In my view, Aquinas handles these matters better by holding that Christ on the cross gave himself entirely and without any reserve to his suffering.

10. Balthasar, *Life out of Death*, 9.

11. Balthasar, *Life out of Death*, 15–16.

12. Balthasar, *Life out of Death*, 19. As David S. Crawford observes, therefore, "when we think of death, it is right to think not only of the entry into eternal life, but also of personal disaster. . . . Even with Christian faith the tragic character of death remains" ("The Gospel of Life and the Integrity of Death," *Communio* 39 [2012]: 373–74).

13. Hans Urs von Balthasar, *You Have Words of Eternal Life: Scripture Meditations*, trans. Dennis Martin (San Francisco: Ignatius, 1991), 231.

14. Balthasar, *You Have Words*, 231. See also Balthasar, *Two Sisters in the Spirit: Thérèse of Lisieux and Elizabeth of the Trinity* (San Francisco: Ignatius, 1992), where he explores Elizabeth of the Trinity's doctrine of "heaven on earth" (which comes about when the Trinity dwells in our soul): "If, from the perspective of faith, the Christian life is an abiding, a refusal to depart from the eternal, from the perspective of pure creatureliness, it is a once-for-all entry into this eternal circle. . . . It is not God who is fixed in place; it is not God who has moved; rather it is the soul who has arrived at the place of God, because the veils and distances between her and God have fallen away and because she has come in from the 'outside' and has left her estrangement to come home, not to herself, but to her homeland and her natural center in God. *God in the soul* has acquired the deeper meaning of *the soul in God*" (398, 444–45).

15. Christopher P. Vogt notes that for the sixteenth-century theologian William Perkins, "the question was essentially 'what must I do to be saved?'" and the answer was found in "reconciling oneself to God, attaching oneself to Christ, and striving to live rightly" (*Patience, Compassion, Hope, and the Christian Art of Dying Well* [Lanham, MD: Rowman & Littlefield, 2004], 82–83). Certainly by the seventeenth century (and indeed, I would argue, well before), the question of annihilation was a live one for Christian thinkers, as can be seen for example in Pascal's wager. See Blaise Pascal, *Pensées*, trans. A. J. Krailsheimer, rev. ed. (London: Penguin, 1995), §418, pp. 122–25. Pascal goes on to say, "All our actions and thoughts must follow such different paths, according to whether there is hope of eternal blessings or not, that the only possible way of acting with sense and judgement is to decide our course in the light of this point, which ought to be our ultimate objective. . . . I can feel nothing but compassion for those who sincerely lament their doubt [in God, Christ, and the soul's immortality], who regard it as the ultimate misfortune, and who, sparing no effort to escape from it, make their search their principal and most serious business. . . . Nothing is so important to man as his state: nothing more fearful than eternity. Thus the fact that there exist men who are indifferent to the loss of their being and the peril of an eternity of wretchedness is against nature" (§427, pp. 128–29, 131).

Vogt points out that for the contemporary theologian Jürgen Moltmann, "despair arises from an acute awareness of the depth and strength of social sin and evil in the world," an acute awareness that makes one doubt whether "the future will hold anything but more of the same legacy of evil and human misery" (*Patience, Compassion, Hope*, 83; with reference to such works as Moltmann's *Is There Life after Death?* [Milwaukee: Marquette University Press, 1998]). Even deeper than social sin, however, is personal sin; and with regard to the future the deepest apparent threat for a meaningful future is the apparent possibility of the everlasting annihilation of all human communion due to the ongoing cosmic unfolding (whose telos appears to be the heat death of the universe). In *Is There Life after Death?*, Moltmann proposes that we find hope by giving ourselves to the kingdom of God—a point with which I would agree only insofar as we are thereby giving ourselves to the person of Jesus Christ rather than to a divine project. I certainly agree with Moltmann that God alone can be the source of true hope for human healing.

16. Hans Urs von Balthasar, *The Moment of Christian Witness*, trans. Richard Beckley (San Francisco: Ignatius, 1994), 26.

17. Balthasar, *Moment of Christian Witness*, 26-27. On Christ's transformation of death into a "blessing" for those who die in Christ, see Paul O'Callaghan, *Christ Our Hope: An Introduction to Eschatology* (Washington, DC: Catholic University of America Press, 2011), 271. As O'Callaghan says, "Life itself . . . is meant to become for the Christian a process of gradually dying, dying to self, dying to the world. In this way, death acquires, in union with Christ, a special coredemptive value, for Christians 'always carry in the body the death of Jesus, so that the life of Jesus may also be manifested in our bodies' (2 Cor 4:10)" (272).

18. Balthasar, *Moment of Christian Witness*, 27; for a similar insight see Balthasar, *Love Alone Is Credible*, trans. D. C. Schindler (San Francisco: Ignatius, 2004), 139–40. See also Balthasar's contention (partly in response to Heidegger's "being-toward-death") in *Last Act* that "genuine liberation from the tragedy of death" consists "in the fact that the human destiny of death is undergirded by the death of Jesus Christ. What does his death tell us? First, that it bears all the essential characteristics of human death. . . . He who says, 'My hour is not yet come' (John 2:4), is constantly aware that everything is moving toward his death; only by conscious anticipation of the death he was personally to undergo could he take responsibility for both the radical quality of his words and demands and the eschatological content of his deeds (forgiving sins, healing)" (325). For Balthasar, given his theology of the cross, it is important to say that Christ's death (which is "absolute love") "takes the place of all sinful deaths; it involves self-surrender to God-forsakenness and powerlessness, thereby undergirding every possible instance of God-forsakenness and powerlessness on the part of sinners. In his surrender to death, he brings the deaths of all sinners with him; he envelops them in his uniquely definitive death and gives them a changed value, thereby changing the value of all life destined for a similar death" (327). I agree with much of this, but I would emphasize that the "God-forsakenness" undergone by Jesus differs from the God-forsakenness that is the result of sinful rejection of God. In my view, Jesus' love and his free choice to suffer the penalty (death) that fallen humans owe in justice are the best path for understanding his cross.

19. Terence Nichols, *Death and Afterlife: A Theological Introduction* (Grand Rapids: Brazos, 2010), 13. Nichols tells the story of his friend Diane, who died in her mid-forties of leukemia, and died well: "Contrary to usual expectations, her passing was joyful. She was sure that her family would be taken care of and that she was going home to God. If one is going to die in the prime of life and leave behind a beloved family, one could hardly manage it more gracefully than did Diane. . . . Three things made Diane's death joyful: she was confident about an afterlife with God, she was prepared emotionally and spiritually for death, and she died close to her loved ones and to God in an atmosphere of prayer" (9–10). Nichols grants, however, that "not many people die like Diane. Many people die unsure about God or any future life with God, unprepared to meet death, depressed, uncertain, afraid, and often alone" (10). He adds, "I often find in my students a deep uncertainty about afterlife and a fear of death. These are connected" (10).

20. J. Todd Billings, *Rejoicing in Lament: Wrestling with Incurable Cancer and Life in Christ* (Grand Rapids: Brazos, 2015), 2–3, 157; Dale C. Allison Jr., *Night Comes: Death, Imagination, and the Last Things* (Grand Rapids: Eerdmans, 2016), 10–11.

21. Billings, *Rejoicing in Lament*, 89, 109. William F. May insightfully observes, therefore, that Christians *must* speak of death and dying: "To preach about death is absolutely essential if Christians are to preach with joy. Otherwise they speak with the profound melancholy of men who have separated the church from the graveyard. They make the practical assumption that there are two Lords. First, there is the Lord of the Sabbath, the God who presides over the affairs of cheerful philistines while they are still thriving and in good health. Then there is a second Lord, a Dark Power about which one never speaks, the Lord of highway wrecks, bedside squabbles, hospitals, and graveyards who handles everything in the end. The Christan faith, however, does not proclaim two parallel Lords. The Lord of the church is not ruler of a surface kingdom. His dominion is nothing if it does not go at least six feet deep" ("The Metaphysical Plight of the Family," in *Death Inside Out*, ed. Peter Steinfels and Robert M. Veatch [New York: Harper & Row, 1975], 60).

22. See Billings, *Rejoicing in Lament*, 107–9.

23. My book thus has similarities with Kerry Walters's valuable and inspiring *Art of Dying and Living: Lessons from Saints of Our Time* (Maryknoll, NY: Orbis, 2011). In seven chapters, Walters explores the dying of seven contemporary Christians, and she identifies a virtue for each chapter: trust (Joseph Bernardin), love (Thea Bowman), gratitude (Etty Hillesum), obedience (Jonathan Daniels), courage (Dietrich Bonhoeffer), patience (John Paul II), Christing (Caryll Houselander). Her book has its foundation in the point that "the best way to learn how to be virtuous is by observing and emulating virtuous persons as they go about the business of living and dying" (xix). For discussion, see especially her section on "Virtues for Dying Well" in her book's first chapter, 12–16. Walters owes a debt, as do I, to books by Christopher Vogt and Henri Nouwen.

24. Thus Amy Plantinga Pauw observes that the Christian answer to fear of death

"is not merely a matter of interior, personal conviction. It takes concrete form through the patterned life of the Christian community, molding the way we live as well as the way we die. . . . The Christian practices surrounding the passage of death echo the regular rhythms of worship and fellowship in the Christian life. Dying well grows out of the Christian community's attempts to live well before God in the present" ("Dying Well," in *Practicing Our Faith: A Way of Life for a Searching People*, ed. Dorothy C. Bass [San Francisco: Jossey-Bass, 1997], 163–64, 177). Pauw compares dying to infant baptism: "Like our birth into Christian faith, our dying well draws strength from the entire community. We live by grace, and we also die by grace" (176).

25. Herbert McCabe, OP, *God, Christ and Us*, ed. Brian Davies, OP (London: Continuum, 2003), 145; Dinesh D'Souza, *Life after Death: The Evidence* (Washington, DC: Regnery, 2009), 3. D'Souza accurately captures the prevailing viewpoint among the Western intellectual elite, a viewpoint with which he disagrees: "there is no life after death, and it is silly to suggest otherwise. We have this life, and that's it. We know this because science has shown us our true nature—and our true nature, like that of other animals, is mortal. Moreover, we are material creatures in the world—creatures with material bodies—and when these bodies disintegrate there is nothing left to live on. 'Once we die,' writes philosopher Owen Flanagan, 'we are gone.' As for the soul, well, science has looked and looked and found nothing like a soul inside of us" (*Life after Death*, 8; citing Owen Flanagan, *The Problem of the Soul* [New York: Basic Books, 2002], 12).

26. Billings, *Rejoicing in Lament*, 143, 176; see also xiii, 77–78, 125, 134–35, 166, 173; Balthasar, *Moment of Christian Witness*, 23, 25. See also Billings, *Union with Christ: Reframing Theology and Ministry for the Church* (Grand Rapids: Baker Academic, 2011).

27. Balthasar, *Life out of Death*, 87.

28. Henri J. M. Nouwen, *Our Greatest Gift: A Meditation on Dying and Caring* (New York: HarperCollins, 1994), xiii.

29. Walters, *Art of Dying and Living*, 4. Since we seek everlasting personal communion—which a loving God can give us—Walters rightly observes, "While it's not the case that all religious faith is motivated solely or even mostly by death-fear, it would be foolish to deny that it plays a significant role. Typically, religion promises that physical death isn't the end of *us*, but only of our *bodies*. That which is most vitally us—soul, spirit, personal identity—somehow endures. But even for people whose faith assures them of an afterlife, death remains frighteningly uncanny. How, for example, can I possibly remain myself in the absence of a body?" (5). The resurrection of the body is a deeply significant aspect of divine revelation.

30. Thérèse of Lisieux, *Her Last Conversations*, trans. John Clarke, OCD (Washington, DC: ICS, 1977), 228.

31. Let me reiterate the point that fear of dying, far from being egotistical, is rooted in love. Joseph Haroutunian insightfully points out, "Concern about death in human beings arises out of a love of life which is essentially a love of our fellowman and a love of ourselves as fellowmen. . . . It is love that provides the peculiar shock of human death, and the only way not to feel the sting of death is to deny the love which

is our life. . . . For the *human* meaning of death is bound up with the question of love. Where love is, there is a rational and salutary and inevitable concern with nothingness" ("Life and Death among Fellowmen," in *The Modern Vision of Death*, ed. Nathan A. Scott Jr. [Richmond, VA: John Knox, 1967], 88, 94). Haroutunian adds that the love that overcomes death comes from "Jesus of Nazareth, who is the source of this gift among us, and the heart of it" (95).

32. Nicholas Berdyaev, *The Destiny of Man* (New York: Harper & Row, 1960), 263; cited in Guroian, *Life's Living toward Dying*, xxv. As Guroian says, for Berdyaev "all valuation and judgment in a Christian ethics must begin with the fact that death claims every human being and would nullify every human effort to achieve happiness and meaningful existence were it not for the fact that Jesus Christ triumphed over death for our sakes through his own freely offered death on the cross" (*Life's Living toward Dying*, xxv).

33. Plato, *Phaedo* 67e, in *The Collected Dialogues of Plato*, ed. Edith Hamilton and Huntington Cairns (Princeton: Princeton University Press, 1961), 50.

34. See Samuel Johnson, *Rasselas* (New York: Penguin, 1976).

35. Vogt, *Patience, Compassion, Hope*, 2. Vogt recognizes that "many virtues pertain to the experience of dying," and he offers a persuasive explanation of his decision to focus on three virtues.

36. I treat compassion under the rubric of solidarity and patience under the rubric of surrender, but Vogt brings out further dimensions of compassion and patience. His reflections on compassion have his critique of euthanasia in view, and he explores patience in the context of "the suffering that results from anticipatory grieving of one's own death" (*Patience, Compassion, Hope*, 5) and in the context of hope. By exploring particular virtues within the context of reflections on dying, I affirm Joseph Ratzinger's observation that "questions like those about life and death can in the final analysis never be answered simply with a formula but, rather, find their true answer only in the lived appropriation of the formula" (*Dogma and Preaching: Applying Christian Doctrine to Daily Life*, trans. Michael J. Miller and Matthew J. O'Connell [San Francisco: Ignatius, 2011], 244).

37. Vogt, *Patience, Compassion, Hope*, 4.

38. *Patience, Compassion, Hope*, 6; citing William Perkins, *A Salve for a Sicke Man*, in *The English Ars Moriendi*, ed. David William Atkinson (New York: Lang, 1992), 127–63.

39. Balthasar, *Life out of Death*, 86–87.

40. Jay F. Rosenberg, *Thinking Clearly about Death*, 2nd ed. (Indianapolis: Hackett, 1998), xvii. For Rosenberg, one's own death, as an event, is not to be feared, "for such attitudes are logically appropriate only to historical events which one could, in principle, *live through*—and one's own death is necessarily not such a historical event" (310). I agree with Rosenberg that the person who dies cannot "live through" death— since the separated soul is not the person, but awaits reunion with the body at the resurrection of the dead. But I think that death, as an event, is certainly to be feared.

Rosenberg's strict materialism, while in his view the fruit of common sense, actually reduces in irrational ways the mysteries of existence and consciousness. Rosenberg points out that some dyings are not dreadful, since some persons are killed in an instant and do not suffer. Strict materialism also appears in Fred Feldman, *Confrontations with the Reaper: A Philosophical Study of the Nature and Value of Death* (Oxford: Oxford University Press, 1992), 105: "Most of us will continue to exist after we die. The bad news is that though we will survive death, and will continue to exist after we die, each of us will then be dead. We will have no psychological experiences. We will just be corpses. Such survival may be of little value." If we are simply material bodies, then it makes sense to suppose that we must continue as material corpses. This essential equation of living bodies with corpses, since both are just matter, indeed undermines materialism as a common-sense project.

41. Jaroslav Pelikan, *The Shape of Death: Life, Death, and Immortality in the Early Fathers* (Nashville: Abingdon, 1961), 5. Pelikan's book treats five figures and connects each with a particular geometric model of death in relation to creation/time and salvation/eternity: Tatian (arc), Clement of Alexandria (circle), Cyprian of Carthage (triangle), Origen (parabola), and Irenaeus (spiral). Commenting on Irenaeus, Pelikan states: "Nowhere is a man more alone than when he dies, yet nowhere does he have more in common with all men. The death of a man is unique, and yet it is universal. The straight line would symbolize its uniqueness, the circle its universality. . . . Christianity declares that in the life and death of Jesus Christ the unique and the universal concur" (101–2). For Pelikan, however, the best figure for understanding death is the cross.

42. Peter C. Phan notes the difference between writing on eschatology (or the "last things") in one's twenties and thirties and writing on it later in life: "Then death was someone else's, now it is *mine*. Then the afterlife was an object for scholarly reflections, now it is a reality to *live* everyday. Then heaven and hell were theological possibilities for all, now either is the destination for *me* at the end of my earthly journey" (*Living into Death, Dying into Life: A Christian Theology of Death and Life Eternal* [Hobe Sound, FL: Lectio, 2014], viii). I share this sense of personal existential urgency, and therefore I resonate with Phan's description of the intended audience of his book: "In a real sense, its primary targeted reader is none other than myself, trying to put into words the meaning and purpose of my own life" (viii)—although in my case the task involves exploring the mystery of death in such a way as to learn the virtues of Christian dying.

43. Even if we differ from him, most of us can resonate with the words of Hillel Halkin, who compares the prospect of death to a terrifying prison in which each day some prisoners are taken at random and shot, and who is amazed at how fast his life has gone by. See Hillel Halkin, *After One-Hundred-and-Twenty: Reflecting on Death, Mourning, and the Afterlife in the Jewish Tradition* (Princeton: Princeton University Press, 2016), 206–7.

44. Pope John Paul II, *To the Elderly*, Vatican translation (Boston: Pauline Books & Media, 2000), §14, p. 30. John Paul II answers, "Christ, having crossed the threshold of death, has revealed the life which lies beyond this frontier, in that uncharted 'territory' which is eternity" (§15, p. 31).

45. Thus the New Testament scholar Dale Allison comes to the conclusion about his own beliefs: "I decline to go along with the notion that, without a soul or some functional equivalent, eternal life is nonetheless possible. Some things just can't be" (*Night Comes*, 38). Allison explains that "because resurrection is our return," we must "be something more than what the undertaker handles," since if you are "your body and only your body, and if that body disintegrates, aren't you gone for good?" (38). Allison is quite right in this regard, since without a soul as the principle of continuity, a restored body—even were it possible to restore it with exactly the same matter—would be a replica of me but not me. Allison cites Mark Johnston, *Surviving Death* (Princeton: Princeton University Press, 2010), 1–125; and he critiques (as I have also done, in ch. 6 of *Jesus and the Demise of Death: Resurrection, Afterlife, and the Fate of the Christian* [Waco, TX: Baylor University Press, 2012]) the exegetical and theological persuasiveness of Oscar Cullmann's *Immortality of the Soul or Resurrection of the Dead? The Witness of the New Testament* (New York: Macmillan, 1958) and Joel B. Green's *Body, Soul, and Human Life: The Nature of Humanity in the Bible* (Grand Rapids: Baker Academic, 2008). As Allison says, "the New Testament doesn't anticipate modern physicalism. Matthew, Mark, the author of Luke-Acts, John, and Paul as well as the authors of Hebrews, James, 1 Peter, 2 Peter, and Revelation all believed that the self or some part of it could leave the body and even survive without it" (*Night Comes*, 33). Simon Tugwell, OP, has helpfully pointed out that "any tendency to insist heavily either on the immortality of the soul or the resurrection of the body is the product of an essentially false problematic" (*Human Immortality and the Redemption of Death* [Springfield, IL: Templegate, 1991], xi).

46. See Charles de Foucauld, *Charles de Foucauld: Writings*, ed. Robert Ellsberg (Maryknoll, NY: Orbis, 1999), 54–55.

47. Romano Guardini, *Rilke's Duino Elegies: An Interpretation*, trans. K. G. Knight (Chicago: Regnery, 1961), 298.

48. Certainly living forever on earth would soon become unbearable, but that means simply that we are called to a higher interpersonal communion, not that destruction is good for us.

49. Guardini, *Rilke's Duino Elegies*, 302.

50. Guardini, *Rilke's Duino Elegies*, 301. Elsewhere Guardini contests the well-known view that "to wish to go on living beyond the end is folly; it is also unmanly and dishonorable. The very inevitability of the end makes life great and glorious" (*The Last Things: Concerning Death, Purification after Death, Resurrection, Judgment, and Eternity*, trans. Charlotte E. Forsyth and Grace B. Branham [New York: Pantheon, 1954], 16). Such a view, present in Heidegger, underestimates the value of interpersonal communion.

51. Alexander Schmemann, *O Death, Where Is Thy Sting?*, trans. Alexis Vinogradov (Crestwood, NY: St. Vladimir's Seminary Press, 2003), 18. In the same discussion, Schmemann observes that it would be equally foolish to require life after death to be empirically provable, which it could only be if it were already contained in this world.

52. Schmemann, *O Death*, 28. In light of Schmemann, Conor Cunningham comments: "Christianity is not, therefore, about reconciling us to death. On the contrary, Christianity reveals death to be what it is: abominable, or unnatural" ("Is There Life before Death?," in *The Role of Death in Life: A Multidisciplinary Examination of the Relationship between Life and Death*, ed. John Behr and Conor Cunningham [Eugene, OR: Cascade, 2015], 144).

53. Ephraim Radner, *A Time to Keep: Theology, Mortality, and the Shape of a Human Life* (Waco, TX: Baylor University Press, 2016), ix, 5.

54. Radner, *Time to Keep*, x.

55. Radner, *Time to Keep*, 8.

56. Radner, *Time to Keep*, xi.

57. Guroian, *Life's Living toward Dying*, 48–49.

58. Vogt, *Patience, Compassion, Hope*, 9.

59. See also Hans Urs von Balthasar, *Unless You Become like This Child*, trans. Erasmo Leiva-Merikakis (San Francisco: Ignatius, 1991), as well as the valuable study of Balthasar's perspective by Jeffrey O. Njus: "From a Mother's Smile to Our Father's Embrace: Filiation and Mission at the Heart of Hans Urs von Balthasar's Theology" (STD diss., University of Saint Mary of the Lake, 2016).

60. Nouwen, *Our Greatest Gift*, 14.

61. Alasdair MacIntyre, *Dependent Rational Animals: Why Human Beings Need the Virtues* (Chicago: Open Court, 1999), 8, 161. I am applying MacIntyre's terminology to my own focus upon dying persons, and thus my account of "virtues of acknowledged dependence" differs from his (his is focused upon practical reasoning and upon "social relationships that are informed by the norms of giving and receiving" [162]). According to MacIntyre, the (tragic) achievement of Friedrich Nietzsche consisted in striving to reject any virtue of acknowledged dependence: "Nietzsche in a heroic series of acts isolated himself by ridding himself, so far as is humanly possible, of the commitments required by the virtues of acknowledged dependence. . . . Nietzsche's claim is that to be able consistently to avoid the bonds of obligations that do not arise from one's own voluntary willing is much more difficult than might be supposed. It requires a hardness and a steeling" (162–63).

62. Nouwen, *Our Greatest Gift*, 15–16.

63. Nouwen, *Our Greatest Gift*, 17.

64. J. Warren Smith, *Passion and Paradise: Human and Divine Emotion in the Thought of Gregory of Nyssa* (New York: Crossroad, 2004), 109. Smith is here discussing Origen's understanding of the fall and of Christ.

Notes to Chapter 1

1. Joseph Ratzinger, "Appendix 1: Between Death and Resurrection: Some Supplementary Reflections," in *Eschatology: Death and Eternal Life*, trans. Michael

Waldstein with Aidan Nichols, OP, 2nd ed. (Washington, DC: Catholic University of America Press, 2007), 259. For the same point see Vigen Guroian, *Life's Living toward Dying: A Theological and Medical-Ethical Study* (Grand Rapids: Eerdmans, 1996), 21: "Death would not be so bitter were it not that love makes life so sweet. Nor would death inspire such fear and dread were it not that it cuts us off from those whom we love and who love us. Love creates communion and produces joy, but death can throw us into desolation and despair." See also C. S. Lewis, *A Grief Observed* (repr., New York: HarperCollins, 2001).

2. John Bowker proposes "affirming the worth and value of the entire universe which cannot *be* on any other terms than those of death; and affirming that death is the necessary condition of new thresholds and new opportunities of life. . . . For Christians, the death and resurrection of Jesus are the singularity (the event and fact) which initiates the new environment, attained through death, in which we are able, now and already, to begin to live. But the crucifixion is a deep statement, enacted in truth, that there cannot be this new life, in a universe like this, without death; and that God, in drawing us freely to himself, has accepted the necessity of death into himself, into his body on a tree" (*The Meanings of Death* [Cambridge: Cambridge University Press, 1991], 229). Bowker thus suggests that human death is due to the internal necessities of creation, and that God enters into history to save us from the (ugly) internal necessities of creation and to undergo them himself so as to show that he does not make his creatures do what he himself will not do. I think that the biblical portrait of the relationship of sin and human death, and of the redemption from sin accomplished by Christ's cross, demands our adherence both in faith and as part of the doctrine of the goodness of God's created order.

3. Bowker, *The Meanings of Death*, 228.

4. Jon D. Levenson, *Resurrection and the Restoration of Israel: The Ultimate Victory of the God of Life* (New Haven: Yale University Press, 2006), 68. (Hereafter in this section, page references from this work will be given in parentheses in the text.) According to Levenson, then, the book of Job has to do with whether God can rescue the innocent from devastating suffering. In his apostolic letter *Salvifici Doloris*, Pope John Paul II, like many exegetes, presents the book of Job as a meditation on whether suffering is always a justified punishment: "The conviction of those who explain suffering as a punishment for sin finds support in the order of justice, and this corresponds to the conviction expressed by one of Job's friends: 'As I have seen, those who plow iniquity and sow trouble reap the same' [Job 4:8]. Job however challenges the truth of the principle that identifies suffering with punishment for sin. And he does this on the basis of his own opinion. For he is aware that he has not deserved such punishment, and in fact he speaks of the good that he has done during his life. In the end, God Himself reproves Job's friends for their accusations and recognizes that Job is not guilty. His suffering is the suffering of someone who is innocent; it must be accepted as a mystery" (*Salvifici Doloris*, Vatican translation [Boston: St. Paul Books and Media, 1984], §§10–11, p. 15).

5. Levenson finds two kinds of passages about Sheol in the Hebrew Bible, and he argues that there is a "contradiction between those passages that assert that Sheol is indeed the destination of all human beings and those more numerous passages that affirm the possibility of a fortunate end to life. That the former passages are so few and that the differentiation of terminology is so thoroughgoing is remarkable and suggests that the inconsistency is best seen as a tension between two competing theologies. The one that sees Sheol as the universal destination comports well with ancient Mesopotamian and Canaanite notions of human destiny as finally one of pure gloom. This conception survives in the Hebrew Bible, especially in Wisdom literature, the category to which most of those exceptional passages belong. But it is very much at odds with most of the relevant texts, which instead assume a distinction between those who go to Sheol and those who die blessed, like Abraham, Moses, and Job. Another way to state this is to say that the Hebrew Bible displays a tension between an older notion of Sheol as the ultimate destination of all mankind, on the one hand, and a bold and younger affirmation of the Lord as savior, on the other. This second assertion eventually culminated in a proclamation of the God of Israel as the one who is powerful even over the gloomy netherworld and the forces that impel people toward it. But the development toward that point was neither inevitable nor linear, and the remnants of the older view remained, even in relatively late texts" (*Resurrection and Restoration*, 75).

6. Levenson's position can be compared and contrasted with views such as that of the nineteenth-century liberal religious thinker Ernest Renan, though Levenson does not cite Renan. Renan remarks that for "the Semitic mind," "death did not call forth any idea of sadness, when the hour came when a man should rejoin his fathers and when he left behind him numerous children. In this respect no difference existed between the Hebrews and the other peoples of remote antiquity. The narrow horizons that bounded life left no room for our uneasy aspirations and our thirst for the infinite. But the mind of everyone was troubled when catastrophes such as that of Job were recounted in the text, up till then free from such stumbling blocks. . . . The book of Job is the expression of the incurable trouble that seized the conscience at the epoch when the old patriarchal theory, based exclusively upon the promises of the terrestrial life, became insufficient. The author perceives the weakness of this theory; he is, with good reason, shocked at the crying injustice that an artificial interpretation of the decrees of providence brings with it; but he can discover no outlet from the closed circle from which man can only free himself by a bold appeal to the future" ("The Cry of the Soul," in *The Dimensions of Job: A Study and Selected Readings*, ed. Nahum N. Glatzer [repr., Eugene, OR: Wipf & Stock, 2002], 119—an excerpt from Renan, *The Book of Job*, trans. A. F. G. and W. M. T. [London: W. M. Thomson, 1889]). For Levenson, the book of Job does indeed prepare for the Jewish doctrine of the resurrection of the body, but the book of Job's ending is nonetheless a happy one without need for personal immortality. It should be noted that Renan's summary comment about "the other peoples of remote antiquity" is of course inaccurate, since many ancient Near Eastern cultures professed a belief in life after death. I also differ sharply from Renan's conclusion, refuted by

Levenson, that "the Jewish mind left to itself has never completely broken through that fatal circle" ("Cry of the Soul," 120).

7. For a similar position offered in a work of contemporary philosophy, see Samuel Scheffler, *Death and the Afterlife*, ed. Niko Kolodny (Oxford: Oxford University Press, 2013). Scheffler states, "I believe that biological death represents the final and irrevocable end of an individual's life" (15), but he argues that "our continuing to regard things as mattering to us in our worldly lives is more dependent on our confidence in the survival of humanity [for a long time, even if in the end the universe will burn out] than it is on our confidence in our own survival" (76). In Scheffler's view, "the personal afterlife has seemed important to people for (at least) the following reasons. It has seemed to offer them the prospect of personal survival, of relief from the fear of death, of being reunited with their loved ones, of seeing cosmic justice done, of receiving a satisfying explanation for some of life's most troubling features, and of gaining assurance that their lives have some larger purpose or significance" (68). I think that Scheffler does not specify a key aspect: that we are relational beings and yearn for communion with God and neighbor, with the result that the everlasting quashing of our desire to actively know and love God and neighbor would mean the everlasting crushing of who we are at our deepest core. See also Miguel de Unamuno, *The Tragic Sense of Life*, trans. Anthony Kerrigan, ed. Martin Nozick and Anthony Kerrigan (Princeton: Princeton University Press, 1972).

In response to Scheffler, Susan Wolf argues that all that we need for meaningful action is a community that has "a past and a present" ("The Significance of Doomsday," in Scheffler, *Death and the Afterlife*, 124). Wolf grants that nothing makes "a *permanent* difference to the world," but concludes that this does not matter (127). Responding to Scheffler in the same volume, Harry G. Frankfurt also finds that everything that "we value for its own sake" would continue to matter to us in the present even if we knew that the whole human race, including ourselves, was about to be extinguished ("How the Afterlife Matters," in *Death and the Afterlife*, 135).

8. Against the view of Frank Moore Cross and others that Job presents a less personal God, I agree with J. Gerald Janzen (and Levenson) about the book of Job: see Janzen, *Job* (Atlanta: John Knox, 1985), 10, discussing Cross's *Canaanite Myth and Hebrew Epic* (Cambridge: Harvard University Press, 1973). Janzen further argues, "The book of Job was written during a time (speaking in evolutionary terms) when humankind had not long emerged from a predominantly group consciousness only flickeringly and incipiently qualified by individual self-awareness and when the distinctions between self and world and between the diverse modalities of physical and mental existence were much less sharply drawn. By the time of Habakkuk and Jeremiah, Job and Second Isaiah and Ezekiel, one is able to discern in Israel an intensification of concern to explore and to assess the status of solitary self-consciousness in the community and in the world before God" (47). Whether there ever was as little "individual self-awareness" as Janzen posits, it is certainly the case that Job is deeply interested in "the status of solitary self-consciousness."

9. Jean Daniélou contends that "the essential theme" of the book of Job is the "testing of [Job's] righteousness" alongside "a debate upon the mystery of suffering," given "the insupportable character of suffering" ("Job: The Mystery of Man and God," in *Dimensions of Job*, ed. Glatzer, 103–4—an excerpt from Daniélou's *Holy Pagans of the Old Testament*, trans. Felix Faber [London: Longmans, Green, 1957], 86–103). For Daniélou, "Job's suffering reveals the mystery of man, because it does away with the pretension on man's part to claim any right. In a most radical way it prevents him from regarding his relations with God as a form of commutative justice. And thus, by stripping him of all pretension, it brings to light his natural creature condition, that is to say his basic poverty of being, which takes away from him the right to lay claim to anything since he possesses nothing except as a wholly gratuitous gift" (105–6).

I think that the matter is more complex. In my view, given that God has created him, Job lays claim to the right in justice to not be annihilated by God. Yet I agree with Daniélou that Job brings to light our "basic poverty of being," in the sense that we are utterly dependent upon the divine Giver of being and upon the fidelity and goodness of this Giver. I also agree with Daniélou that "when Jesus, stripped of his garments, covered with bruises, encompassed with shame, stands before the judgment seat of Pilate," Jesus "is mankind itself reduced to the nakedness of its tragic condition; and Job was its most perfect prefiguration. Thus there is a real and mysterious link between Job and Jesus. Job is the question, Jesus the answer. . . . Jesus is the immediate answer to Job because he shares his suffering and is the only one to do so. Suffering encloses a man in solitude, puts him outside communion with his fellow men" (109). I agree with this, but the context of death still seems to me to be the heart of the matter.

10. In this regard, with particular attention to the revelation of God's presence, see Martin Buber, "Job," in *On the Bible*, ed. Nahum N. Glatzer (New York: Schocken, 1982), 188–98.

11. In the introduction of *Job*, 3rd ed. (Garden City, NY: Doubleday, 1973), Marvin H. Pope recognizes the problem of annihilation as one that plagues Job (xvii–xviii), even though later in his introduction he identifies the focus of the book of Job as "the tragic predicament of humanity, especially . . . individual suffering" (xli). Ultimately, Pope agrees with notable earlier twentieth-century commentators that the book of Job responds to the problem "of seemingly unmerited or purposeless suffering, and especially the suffering of a righteous man," that is, the unsolvable problem of "theodicy" (lxviii). Against the notion that "a hope of recompense in a future life would have sustained Job and solved his problem," Pope argues that although this hope "would have mitigated the difficulty considerably," nonetheless it is not likely that "the prospect of future bliss gives one the strength and consolation to bear present pain, a pain that is meaningless and unjustified" (lxxi). Similarly, David J. A. Clines holds that the "major question" of the book of Job is either "the problem of suffering" or "the problem of the moral order of the world," by which he means "whether there is any rule whereby goodness is rewarded and wickedness punished" (*Job 1–20* [Dallas: Word, 1989], xxxviii–xxxix)—although Clines also recognizes (in light of Job 9) that the question is

whether God "is by settled design hostile to his creation" (xliii). For David B. Burrell, CSC, "the book's primary role in the Hebrew canon will be to correct that characteristic misapprehension . . . displayed by Job's friends, as their 'explanation' of his plight turns on reading the covenant as a set of simple transactions. That is, good things are in store for all who abide by the Torah, while affliction attends anyone who does not" (*Deconstructing Theodicy: Why Job Has Nothing to Say to the Puzzled Suffering* [Grand Rapids: Brazos, 2008], 16).

Although such a misunderstanding of theodicy is indeed an important theme in the book of Job, I think that the standing of humans before death—the threat of annihilation—is the greater theme. Burrell would quite possibly agree with me, since he goes on to emphasize that "in the measure that the covenant is gift, it must be intended to lead those to whom it is given to the giver" (18). Job does indeed lead us directly to the Giver, with the poignant question of whether the Giver intends to annihilate the persons whom he has gifted into being. Gustavo Gutiérrez presents Job as rebelling "against the suffering of the innocent, against a theology that justifies it, and even against the depiction of God that such a theology conveys. . . . Job the rebel is a witness to peace and to the hunger and thirst for justice" (*On Job: God-Talk and the Suffering of the Innocent*, trans. Matthew J. O'Connell [Maryknoll, NY: Orbis, 1987], 14). Without denying that Job cries out against unjust suffering, I hold that Job goes even deeper into the human condition shared by rich and poor, oppressor and oppressed alike. Gutiérrez goes on to argue that Job perceives that "the real issue . . . is the suffering and injustice that mark the lives of the poor. Those who believe in God must therefore try to lighten the burden of the poor by helping them and practicing solidarity with them" (16). I do not see in the book of Job a focus on economic poverty or political oppression. Yet the book of Job can certainly help us to "discover the features of Christ in the sometimes disfigured faces of the poor of this world" (17). Pope helpfully reviews various parallels to the book of Job in ancient Near Eastern literature, including Sumerian and Babylonian (Akkadian) texts (there is also an Indian parallel found in the Markandeya Purana).

12. I can agree, then, with Thomas Aquinas's view, widespread among medieval thinkers, that the book of Job is ultimately a defense of God's providence: see Aquinas, *The Literal Exposition on Job: A Scriptural Commentary Concerning Providence*, trans. Anthony Damico (Atlanta: Scholars Press, 1989). For Aquinas, however, passages such as Job 3:11–19, where Job speaks about the realm of the dead, indicate Job's belief that "man, by reason of his soul, remains in existence after death" (107). Aquinas thinks that Job believes in a future life, with a heaven and a hell as conceived in Catholic doctrine. For Aquinas, "Job had the right opinion about divine providence but had been so immoderate in his manner of speaking that scandal was produced from it in the hearts of the others when they thought that he was not showing due reverence to God" (415). Similarly, Aquinas considers that "Job did not base his hope on recovering temporal prosperity but on achieving future happiness" in eternal life (472). Aquinas's viewpoint is especially clear in his commentary on Job 14:3–7, where he argues: "Job

had wondered at the divine esteem for men, since man is still of such frail and wretched condition if the state of the present life is considered, but this wonder would cease if it were considered that after this life another life is reserved for man in which he remains forever. From this point on, then, he [Job] tires to show this fact" (224). Aquinas's view that Job argues for the resurrection of the dead and for everlasting life strikes me as erroneous, even if the book of Job includes important developments that lead toward the (Jewish) doctrine of the resurrection of the dead.

13. Gutiérrez translates this text differently: "I repudiate and abandon (change my mind about) dust and ashes" (*On Job*, 86). He argues: "The new translation illumines the whole of Job's second response and makes it more coherent. The Hebrew verb *m's*, 'reject, repudiate,' is no longer left hanging without an object; it refers, as does the verb 'repent' (taken in the sense of 'change one's mind'), to Job's attitude of protest and reproach. . . . This means that in his final reply what Job is expressing is not contrition but *a renunciation of his lamentation and dejected outlook*. Certain emphases in his protest had been due to the doctrine of retribution, which despite everything had continued to be his point of reference. Now that the Lord has overthrown that doctrine by revealing the key to the divine plan, Job realizes that he has been speaking of God in a way that implied that God was a prisoner of a particular way of understanding justice. It is this whole outlook that Job says he is now abandoning" (87).

While I demur from Gutiérrez's translation of this verse and from his view that Job's primary concern is "the doctrine of retribution" (let alone "solidarity with the poor" [88]), I think that Gutiérrez is right to emphasize that Job has gained a new trust in God's gratuitous love and thereby no longer needs to lament bitterly about his situation. Gutiérrez goes on to praise "the gratuitousness and universality of God's *agapeic love*. Nothing can limit or contain this love, as Yahweh makes clear to Job in the revelation of what Yahweh has established as the fulcrum of the world" (94). For Gutiérrez, the message is that believers should be led "to a preferential option for the poor and to solidarity with those who suffer wretched conditions, contempt, and oppression, those whom the social order ignores and exploits" (94). I find that the message is that all of us, since we have to die, will eventually be as nothing in the eyes of the world—a fact that should indeed produce "solidarity with those who suffer wretched conditions, contempt, and oppression."

14. For a recent philosophical approach to the problem of death, see John F. X. Knasas, *Aquinas and the Cry of Rachel: Thomistic Reflections on the Problem of Evil* (Washington, DC: Catholic University of America Press, 2013). Knasas's book is particularly helpful because it surveys numerous prior approaches to the problem, including those of Marilyn McCord Adams and Eleonore Stump. Knasas argues philosophically that "if we remember our natural status, viz., principal parts in a cosmos naturally fraught with contingency and with a psyche of similar nature, how can we demand that we be exempt from evil, even of the most horrendous kinds? Does not that insight remove anger and replace it with an honest resignation? Also, does not knowledge that the creator will not leave *quandoque* evil unordered to good engender some sense of

justice, just as it engendered some sense of solace?" (291). Theologically, Knasas takes note of the fact that, indeed, "the creator relates to us in a more personal manner" (292).

I think that Knasas's insights here are right, although his view depends upon God's decision to create a whole (the cosmos) whose parts, insofar as they are material, come and go in a fashion that manifests their contingency and corruptibility—a decision whose goodness must be accepted rather than demonstrated (even if we can demonstrate on other grounds that God is infinitely good). Although he recognizes that "God intended to free Adam from death," Knasas emphasizes that for Aquinas death is "a natural corruption" rather than "a *quandoque* evil" (75–76), and he also points out that death "is not so evil that God fails to will it" (74). As Michel René Barnes puts it, "we are fragile collections of messy bits of flesh, and . . . the laws of death are written in physics" ("Snowden's Secret: Gregory of Nyssa on Passion and Death," in *A Man of the Church: Honoring the Theology, Life, and Witness of Ralph del Colle*, ed. Michel René Barnes [Eugene, OR: Pickwick, 2012], 121; cf. Jacques-Marie Pohier, "Death, Nature and Contingency: Anthropological Reflections about the Postponement of Death," trans. David Smith, in *The Experience of Dying*, ed. Norbert Greinacher and Alois Müller [New York: Herder & Herder, 1974], 78).

In my view, the revealed truth that the Creator God did not will human death as we now know it—and that after original sin God wills human death as a punishment (or in Christ's case as a free act of taking upon himself our punishment)—needs emphasis, because the very fact that God did not create humans for death as we now experience it tells us something quite significant about dying. See also Marilyn McCord Adams, *Horrendous Evils and the Goodness of God* (Ithaca, NY: Cornell University Press, 1999); Eleonore Stump, *Wandering in Darkness: Narrative and the Problem of Suffering* (Oxford: Oxford University Press, 2010).

15. Pope Benedict XVI, *Spe Salvi* (Vatican City: Libreria Editrice Vaticana, 2007), §26.

16. I recognize that, as the activist-theologian Daniel Berrigan, SJ, observes in his commentary on Job, "The text of Job is a daunting thicket of what experts call 'variant readings'" (Berrigan, *Job: And Death No Dominion* [Franklin, WI: Sheed & Ward, 2000], xix). All books in the Bible have places where the manuscript tradition is simply unclear, but this is true to a particularly significant extent for the book of Job. See also Pope, *Job*, xxxix: "The book of Job is textually the most vexed in the Old Testament, rivaled only by Hosea."

17. In his introduction to his translation of the book of Job, Stephen Mitchell remarks, "Compared to Job's laments (not to mention the Voice from the Whirlwind), the world of the prologue is two-dimensional, and its divinities are very small potatoes. . . . The author first brings out the patient Job, his untrusting god, and the chief spy/prosecutor, and has the figurines enact the ancient story in the puppet theater of his prose. Then, behind them, the larger curtain rises, and flesh-and-blood actors begin to voice their passions on a life-sized stage. Finally, the vast, unnameable God appears. . . . The

god of the prologue is left behind as utterly as the never-again-mentioned Accuser, swallowed in the depths of human suffering into which the poem plunges us next" ("Introduction," in *The Book of Job*, trans. Stephen Mitchell [New York: HarperCollins, 1992], xi–xii). Mitchell argues that the theme of the book is why humans suffer: "Job has become Everyman, grieving for all of human misery. He suffers not only his own personal pain, but the pain of all the poor and despised. He is himself afflicted by what God has done to the least of these little ones" (xvi).

My view is that death-as-annihilation most concerns Job. For Mitchell, as for Berrigan (or perhaps even more than Berrigan), a radically negative or apophatic theology is a key to interpreting the book of Job: "During their dialogue, Job and the friends agree about the limits of human understanding, but none of them suspects how absolute those limits are. In order to approach God, Job has to let go of all ideas about God: he must put a cloud of unknowing (as a medieval Christian author expressed it) between himself and God, or have the Voice do this for him" (xix). Yet Mitchell ends up arguing strongly that the message of the book of Job is that there is no "moral God," since God has a "destructive Shiva-aspect" (xxiv). In Mitchell's view, moreover, the book of Job ends up embracing annihilation as a good: "Job's comfort at the end is in his mortality. The physical body is acknowledged as dust, the personal drama as delusion. It is as if the world we perceive through our senses, that whole gorgeous and terrible pageant, were the breath-thin surface of a bubble, and everything else, inside and outside, is pure radiance.... The very last word is a peaceful death in the midst of a loving family. What truer, happier ending could there be?" (xxviii, xxx).

18. Berrigan comments on Job 1:21, "And the end; the dribble of a handful of clay on a coffin lid.... Life is a gift, better, a loan; on this basis we proceed, now firm of step, now faltering, toward—eventuality. Every debt comes due; alas, even (or perhaps especially) this one. Death is the calling in of the debt" (*Job*, 21). Berrigan's lament here about death and his description of life as moving toward an amorphous "eventuality" fit with what I find to be Job's concern about annihilation, although Berrigan's focus in his commentary is on political events from the 1990s, as, for example, when he extends Job 1:19 to apply to American missile strikes against Iraq: "The 'great wind from the wilderness' was no catastrophe in nature. Nothing of that. Rather, a cruise missile 'struck the four corners of the house, so that it collapsed upon the young people and they died.' The literal, horrific scene was enacted in the bomb shelter in Baghdad in 1996. The missile struck, a multitude were incinerated" (23). Berrigan later makes clear that he thinks that Job believes in some form of life after death (as distinct from annihilation). Commenting on Job 3:17–22, he states, "Job longs for an end of it all; for death. Not extinction; death. The man Job, living (or as he might say, 'so to speak, living') conjures images of a 'postlife,' images both somber and wonderful. What might Sheol be like? The images speak of a great longing, of a heart broken in pieces, a dropped pottery— and he striving to gather and repair the shards.... It sounds like paradise. Beautiful, we think, plangent, seductive. And finally impossible, this longing, this dream of a postworld world, in which the dead enjoy a surrogate life, a life 'of sorts'" (41–42).

To my mind, the images contained in Job 3:17–22 speak of a "rest" and "ease" that is nonexistence. Berrigan holds that "negative" or "apophatic" theology undergirds the book of Job: "As for Job, nothing of Second Isaiah, that gospel of comfort. He knows only darkness. If this must be, he will dwell in the dark. But his perfervid questioning, summoning, indicting—these he will not cease from uttering. And for his pains, he is granted little of surcease, let alone of approval, whether from his interlocutors or from God. His world is a death before death. . . . Darkness is Job's (and God's) native element, while time lasts. In contrast, the 'light' of the adversaries, their confidence in their own powers, their sere logic and abusive rhetoric, their obsessive claiming of a god who sides with them against Job—such 'light' is a mirage" (176, 240).

19. H. H. Rowley remarks in this regard: "By insisting that there is such a thing as innocent suffering, the author of Job is bringing a message of the first importance to the sufferer. The hardest part of his suffering need not be the feeling that he is deserted by God, or the fear that all men will regard him as cast out from God's presence. If his suffering is innocent it may not spell isolation from God, and when he most needs the sustaining presence of God he may still have it. Here is a religious message of great significance, and it is by his religious message, which matches the magnificence of his literary gift, that the author of our book created his masterpiece" ("The Intellectual versus the Spiritual Solution," in *Dimensions of Job*, ed. Glatzer, 125—an excerpt from Rowley's *From Moses to Qumran* [London: Lutterworth, 1963], 175–83). Although I hold with respect to human death that "God did not make death" (Wisd. of Sol. 1:13) and that "sin came into the world through one man, and death came through sin" (Rom. 5:12)—as I explain in ch. 6 of *Engaging the Doctrine of Creation: Cosmos, Creatures, and the Wise and Good Creator* (Grand Rapids: Baker Academic, 2017)—I agree with Rowley about the crucial significance of differentiating the suffering that comes upon us because of our sins from the suffering that so frequently comes upon us through no fault of our own.

20. As Burrell observes, Job here is complaining "to the very One whom he identifies as his persecutor" (*Deconstructing Theodicy*, 30). In Burrell's view, the fact that Job speaks to God is crucial: "What the voice from the whirlwind [the divine voice] commends is . . . the inherent rightness of Job's mode of discourse: speaking (however he may speak) *to* rather than *about* his creator" (109; cf. 115–16).

21. As Pope comments on Job 14:13–15, "Job here gropes toward the idea of an afterlife. If only God would grant him asylum in the netherworld, safe from the wrath which now besets him, and then appoint him a time for a new and sympathetic hearing, he would be willing to wait or even to endure the present evil" (*Job*, 108).

22. Carol Zaleski observes regarding our desire for ongoing communion with God: "We know that our strongest wishes and desires cloud our judgment; it is therefore sensible to be cautious about indulging them. There is a nobility to the heroic realism and ascetic rationality of the Freudian tradition. We should be suspicious of any easy confidence in immortality. On the other hand, we also know that our strongest wishes and desires reveal to us a world of meaning and possibilities to which premature skepticism would block our access. We may be justified, then, in wagering on them.

We may make an argument from desire" (*The Life of the World to Come: Near-Death Experience and Christian Hope* [New York: Oxford University Press, 1996], 39).

For this argument for personal immortality based on desire for communion with God, see Miguel de Unamuno, *The Tragic Sense of Life in Men and Nations*, trans. Anthony Kerrigan (Princeton: Princeton University Press, 1972), 43–64, 255–81; on 39–40 of her book Zaleski cites Unamuno (281), where he insists (quite rightly in my view): "We must believe in the other life, in the eternal life beyond the tomb, and in an individual and personal life, a life in which each one of us senses his own consciousness and senses that it is joined, without being confounded, with all others in their consciousness within the Supreme Consciousness, in God; we must believe in that other life in order to live this life and endure it and endow it with meaning and finality." Zaleski affirms Unamuno's position, and cites in its favor William James's affirmation of the rationality of the will to believe, Immanuel Kant's practical postulate, and John Henry Newman's cumulative reasoning on the basis of probabilities (as well as Blaise Pascal's wager). Unamuno is deeply critical of Catholicism, at least in the condition in which he found it in the early twentieth century. Arguing in favor of fideism in the face of divine mysteries, he bemoans "the triumph of Thomist theological rationalism. It is no longer enough to believe in the existence of God; anathema falls on anyone who, though he believe in His existence, does not believe it is demonstrable by rational arguments or believes it has not so far been irrefutably demonstrated by rational arguments" (*Tragic Sense*, 85). The latter view is in fact not anathematized by Vatican I.

23. I may be misinterpreting this, since Pope argues that what Job means in 14:21–22 is that "although man is deprived of knowledge by death, he is still subject to pain" (*Job*, 111). Against Pope's interpretation, note Job 14:12: "mortals lie down and do not rise again; until the heavens are no more, they will not awake or be roused out of their sleep." This certainly appears to be a complete lack of consciousness, and therefore no conscious bodily suffering or pain would be possible for the dead person.

24. Pope suggests that Job is complaining simply about his "cruel sufferings" (*Job*, 141) but I think that it is death (understood as annihilation) that Job has primarily in view.

25. The Hebrew of Job 19:25–27 contains irresolvable problems for translation, but the passage may nonetheless be a strong ray of hope within what is otherwise a strong lament about approaching annihilation. The NRSV translates Job 19:25–27 as follows: "For I know that my Redeemer lives, and that at the last he will stand upon the earth; and after my skin has been thus destroyed, then in my flesh I shall see God, whom I shall see on my side, and my eyes shall behold, and not another." Pope comments that "these lines are extremely difficult, the text having suffered irreparable damage. It is clear that Job expects to be vindicated, but it is not certain whether he expects his vindication to come in the flesh or after his body has disintegrated" (*Job*, lxxvi). Although Pope recognizes that Job 14 (among other passages) makes clear that "the only prospect is extinction" and that there is no consciousness after death (xviii), he nonetheless also thinks that 19:25–27 shows that "Job never completely gives up his conviction

that justice must somehow triumph. Even if his flesh rots away and his body turns to dust, in his mind's eye he sees his ultimate vindication and expects to be conscious of it when it comes, though it be beyond this life in the dust of the netherworld" (lxxvii). For a similar interpretation, see Janzen, *Job*, 140–45. Indeed, Janzen argues that 19:25–27 "portrays Job as seeing God from a newly embodied state. . . . The redeemer acts, and resurrection occurs, to serve the restoration of the relation between Job and God. It is not simply life that Job hopes for. As the threefold repetition of verbs in the last three lines underscores (see, see, behold), Job's hope reaches toward a restored vision of God, a God no longer estranged from him. The vision is thoroughly covenantal" (144–45). If so, then 19:25–27 anticipates what I find in the book of Job's concluding chapters.

In his annotation on 19:25 in *The Jewish Study Bible*, however, Mayer Gruber comments that the Hebrew for "Redeemer" or "Vindicator," *gō'ēl*, here means not God but "a future kinsman who will vindicate him, who will take revenge on God for what God has done to Job" (*The Jewish Study Bible*, ed. Adele Berlin and Marc Zvi Brettler [Oxford: Oxford University Press, 2004], 1529). See also Robert Gordis, *The Book of Job: Commentary, New Translation, and Special Studies* (New York: Jewish Theological Seminary of America, 1978), 204–6, 526–29.

26. Pope capitalizes "Death" here and argues that the word should here "be taken as the proper name of the ruler of the infernal region, Mot" (*Job*, 223). I think that Job simply has in view everlasting destruction or unconsciousness.

27. I am not trying to overemphasize the word *friendship*. Pope's translation of this verse reads: "As I was in the prime of my life, when 'Aliy [God] founded my family" (*Job*, 207).

28. The meaning of the Hebrew words here translated "clouds" and "mists" is uncertain, but the basic point seems clear nonetheless.

29. Contemporary exegetes tend to emphasize the arbitrary divine power entailed by God's response and Job's submission. Thus Pope remarks: "The content of the divine answer from the storm is something of a surprise and, on the face of it, a disappointment. The issue, as Job had posed it, is completely ignored. No explanation or excuse is offered for Job's suffering. . . . The complete evasion of the issue as Job had posed it must be the poet's oblique way of admitting that there is no satisfactory answer available to man, apart from faith. God does not need the help or advice of impotent and ignorant men to control the world, any more than he needed such to create it. God cannot be summoned like a defendant and forced to bear witness against himself. No extreme of suffering gives mere man license to question God's wisdom or justice as Job had done. It is apparently on this very point that Job repents and recants" (*Job*, lxxx).

Clines similarly argues: "All Job has been speaking of are the principles on which the world is, or should be, governed; he thought they were pretty straightforward matters of justice and fairness, but the way Yahweh tells it, everything in the world is a marvel, and Job had better accept that justice and fairness too, like the structure of the physical universe, and the ways of Yahweh in rain and wind, are 'marvels' beyond his comprehension or understanding. Redefining cosmic justice as a 'marvel' puts it outside any realm that humans can access or have rights in. . . . If cosmic justice is God's business, then it is whatever he decides it is. . . . It is not a rule, the knowledge of which is shared by Yahweh and humans. It is yet another sphere of divine might, another instance of the truth that Yahweh can 'do anything'" (*Job 38–42* [Nashville: Nelson, 2011], 1214–15).

The interpretation offered by Pope and Clines might be right if the key question of the book of Job is why humans suffer, rather than (as I think) whether death annihilates the human person—in which case God's pointing to his power and wisdom as Creator would be quite an appropriate answer rather than merely an assertion of arbitrary will. Pope's eloquent words near the end of his introduction indicate his awareness of the centrality of the question of death for the book of Job: "The issues raised are crucial for all men and the answers attempted are as good as have ever been offered. The hard facts of life cannot be ignored or denied. All worldly hopes vanish in time. The values men cherish, the little gods they worship—family, home, nation, race, sex, wealth, fame—all fade away. The one final reality appears to be the process by which things come into being, exist, and pass away. This ultimate Force, the Source and End of all things, is inexorable. Against it there is no defense. Any hope a man may put in anything other than this First and Last One is vain. There is nothing else that abides. This is God. He gives and takes away. From Him we come and to Him we return. Confidence in this One is the only value not subject to time. But how can a man put his faith in such an One who is the Slayer of all? Faith in Him is not achieved without moral struggle and spiritual agony. . . . The transition from fear and hatred to trust and even love of this One—from God the Enemy to God the Friend and Companion—is the pilgrimage of every man of faith. Job's journey from despair to faith is the way each mortal must go. Almost invariably there must be initial shock and disappointment to bring a man to the realization of his predicament" (*Job*, lxxxii–lxxxiii).

30. Katherine Sonderegger, *The Doctrine of God*, vol. 1 of *Systematic Theology* (Minneapolis: Fortress, 2015), 326.

31. For the opposite view, see Timothy P. Jackson, "Must Job Live Forever? A Reply to Aquinas on Providence," *The Thomist* 62 (1998): 1–39. I evaluate Jackson's argument and respond to it in ch. 3 of *Betrayal of Charity: The Sins That Sabotage Divine Love* (Waco, TX: Baylor University Press, 2011).

Notes to Chapter 2

1. Terence Nichols, *Death and Afterlife: A Theological Introduction* (Grand Rapids: Brazos, 2010), 10.

2. Nichols, *Death and Afterlife*, 11.

3. David Rieff, *Swimming in a Sea of Death: A Son's Memoir* (New York: Simon & Schuster, 2008), 78–79. (Hereafter in this section, page references from this work will be given in parentheses in the text.) See also the portrait of the dying Sontag in Katie

Roiphe, *The Violet Hour: Great Writers at the End* (New York: Random House, 2016), ch. 1. Roiphe treats Sontag, Sigmund Freud, John Updike, Dylan Thomas, Maurice Sendak, and James Salter. All of them, so far as I can tell, conceived of themselves as headed to annihilation, with the possible exception of Salter and the likely exception of Updike, who, in planning his funeral, had asked for a passage from the end of one of his stories to be read, a passage in which the character is looking at dead pigeons' feathers: "He was robed in this certainty: that the God who had lavished such craft upon these worthless birds would not destroy His whole Creation by refusing to let David live forever" (cited in Roiphe, *Violet Hour*, 158).

4. Christopher P. Vogt remarks along lines possible for believers in a loving God, "The task of dying is not that of learning to bear misfortune without grimacing. It is to learn the truth about ourselves—that we are not the center of the universe, able to exist indefinitely and independently by the sheer force of our own will. We are social creatures ultimately dependent upon God" (*Patience, Compassion, Hope, and the Christian Art of Dying Well* [Lanham, MD: Rowman & Littlefield, 2004], 133). Sontag knew intellectually that she could not exist indefinitely by force of will, but she could conceive of no alternative other than the unacceptable one of annihilation. For this reason, Vogt's emphasis on prayer—an option for Sontag as for anyone—is particularly helpful. See also Richard Payne, "Hope in the Face of Terminal Illness," in *Living Well and Dying Faithfully: Christian Practices for End-of-Life Care*, ed. John Swinton and Richard Payne (Grand Rapids: Eerdmans, 2009), 205–25. Payne's essay, largely focused on the duties of medical palliative caregivers, argues for the need to be frank with people about their terminal diagnosis and to assist them in identifying paths for hope.

5. Reference not given.

6. Intriguingly, according to the medical doctor Daniel B. Hinshaw, "in many organs, healthy fully differentiated cells respond to a program for cell death (apoptosis) and undergo a highly choreographed dying process so that their host, the larger organism, might live. Cancer to some extent represents a failure to respond to the 'kenotic' program for death, a cellular act of autonomous 'rebellion' that seeks immortality, but in the process brings death to its host along with the tumor. When individual cells lose their ability to respond to the apoptotic program and eventually are transformed by unrestrained signals for growth they also lose their connectedness, their *koinonia*, with the larger community of cells in their tissue of origin. The behavior of cancer cells is a powerful metaphor for the isolation that affects the whole organism when it seeks purely its own interest and no longer responds to the other, to the non-self. Self-absorption, pride, and ultimately presumption of the divine prerogative—the worst of the passions are spiritual forms of the cancer state" ("The Kenosis of the Dying: An Invitation to Healing," in *The Role of Death in Life: A Multidisciplinary Examination of the Relationship between Life and Death*, ed. John Behr and Conor Cunningham [Eugene, OR: Cascade, 2015], 161).

7. Oliver Sacks, *Gratitude* (New York: Knopf, 2015), 18. This list of things to do contrasts importantly with the popular movie *The Bucket List*, which presents two

old men "who go about spending their money on fun and dangerous things" (Jeffry Hendrix, *A Little Guide for Your Last Days* [Plano, TX: Bridegroom, 2009], 13). As the Catholic author Hendrix warns, following the movie's notion of a "bucket list" "drops you right back to square one—distraction from awareness of your gifted knowledge. Do not under any circumstances fall for this ruse. At best, you will come out of the experience with that sinking realization that nothing has changed. At worst, you will provide the keepers of pop culture with yet another example of how to distract yourself to death" (13–14). Instead, Hendrix recommends taking a monastic retreat as a "way to reorient your life and your impending death to the glory of the One Who made you, gave you life, sustained you, redeemed you, and will sanctify you all the way to Heaven" (43). In Hendrix's view—he was writing his book as he prepared to undergo chemotherapy for a recurrence of cancer—the key to dying well is, in gratitude for life, to work on forgiving others and on seeking forgiveness from God. What turns out not to be meaningful are human ambition and merely human squabbles or games.

    8. Sacks, *Gratitude*, 26–27.

    9. See Sacks, *Gratitude*, 45.

    10. Ian Brown, *Sixty* (New York: Experiment, 2016). See also the assumption that death is an "eternal silence" in Willard Spiegelman, *Senior Moments* (New York: Farrar, Straus and Giroux, 2016).

    11. Steven Luper, *The Philosophy of Death* (Cambridge: Cambridge University Press, 2009), 58.

    12. Raymond Tallis, *The Black Mirror: Looking at Life through Death* (New Haven: Yale University Press, 2015), 1–3, 337. As he remarks, "*In memoriam* will give way to *In amnesiam* and 'RT [Raymond Tallis]' will be a lost signal in the noise of the universe. . . . Less than a blink of the eternal eye separates the days when the book of condolence is opened, when the last signature collected, when the volume is archived, when it is pulped, and when the pulp dissolves in the universal solvent of change. The last bubble from the wake marking his passage through the world will pop, the last current will lose its identity, the last ripple will break on the shore, into wavelets too small to cause even a paper boat to bob. Death outlasts all that would preserve the dead" (331–32). At the same time, Tallis states in the third person: "The possibility of some sort of afterlife on the far side of the grave owed what little power it had over his [Raymond Tallis's] imagination to his awareness of the profound difference between the It [corpse] in the bed and the He who had lived as I, the distance between the organism that had been RT's body and the person RT who had lived RT's life. One of his most enduring preoccupations had been a mighty gap in our understanding; namely that we have no idea how consciousness, mind, self-consciousness, the sense of the past and of the future, could have arisen out of, fitted into, and acted upon the physical world to which his body had belonged. . . . Physical laws could not explain how one bit of the material world had formed the concept of 'matter' and uttered the word 'world.' And it had seemed to him that mankind could not be entirely a creature of thermodynamics if it had been able to conceive the notion of 'entropy.' And so he

had been close at times to succumbing to the temptation to think that, if the embodied subject that was RT could continue as a subjectless body, as a corpse, it might also be continuing as a bodiless subject in another place: that his death had been merely the parting of the ways of RT-the-body and RT-the-person. If he had resisted this temptation it was on the grounds of the asymmetry of the relationship between the two RTs. A body in good working order had been a necessary condition for RT's existence as a person; but RT's continuation as a person had not been a necessary condition for the body to be in some kind of working order" (333–34).

I think that Tallis's effort to resist simple dualism is correct—see further his *Aping Mankind: Neuromania, Darwinitis and the Misrepresentation of Humanity* (Durham, Eng.: Acumen, 2011)—but he could have recourse to better philosophy that would aid him in this resistance while still affirming the immateriality and incorruptibility of consciousness. For better philosophical options, see Edward Feser, *Philosophy of Mind: A Beginner's Guide* (Oxford: Oneworld, 2006); Feser, *Aquinas* (Oxford: Oneworld, 2009); David Braine, *The Human Person: Animal and Spirit* (Notre Dame: University of Notre Dame Press, 1992); Braine, *Language and Human Understanding: The Roots of Creativity in Speech and Thought* (Washington, DC: Catholic University of America Press, 2014).

13. Carlos Eire, *A Very Brief History of Eternity* (Princeton: Princeton University Press, 2010), 11. As Tallis states, "Each journey from I-hood to thing-hood and onwards to loss even of thing-hood is unique. This transition from somewhere to nowhere, from someone to no-thing, is beyond the grasp of particular thoughts entertained by a particular person on a particular morning, afternoon, evening or night. Truly to think your extinction, you would have to become the equal in your thoughts of the sum total of yourself that is cancelled. So, while fear may be important, something deeper than fear stops us fixing our attention on our end. It is its inconceivability" (*Black Mirror*, 2). This inconceivability suggests, in my view, that God does not will it. See also, for a view similar to Tallis's, Thomas Nagel, *The View from Nowhere* (Oxford: Oxford University Press, 1986), 223–31.

14. Eire, *Very Brief History of Eternity*, 19; cf. 222–23, where he critiques contemporary philosophy and argues that the loss of eternity means a loss of charity, even if it also means a decrease in religiously motivated violence: "Given the uncertainty of which we [contemporary educated Westerners] are so certain concerning eternity, perhaps only a post-postmodern turn can save us from being overwhelmed by our impending doom, our terminal temporality. Philosophy offers all sorts of alternatives, but little consolation. Analytic, anyone? Or would you prefer Continental? Which brand? Phenomenology? Positivism? Existentialism? Nihilism? How about a custom blend, a potpourri? . . . It's a mixed blessing. Men who do not expect to cavort forever in some eternal paradise with eternal virgins in exchange for some horrific self-immolation that kills thousands in the name of the Almighty tend not to fly aircraft filled with passengers into tall, crowded buildings. But then, again, men who believe that they will suffer eternal torment for failing to love their neighbor usually shy away from doing that sort

of thing too. Normally they also avoid building extermination camps where human beings can be turned into ashes and soap very quickly, by the hundreds of thousands, or millions, with industrial efficiency—something that Martin Heidegger assented to, openly and shamefully, as he thrilled deep thinkers everywhere with his *Da-sein* and his *Ent-wurf* and his *Un-zu-hause*."

15. Eire, *Very Brief History of Eternity*, 152–53. He adds, "I am not suggesting an immediate causal relationship, but merely pointing to a clear trajectory over several centuries. Whether or not the secularization of the West is due mainly or even solely to Protestants is not the issue. Lest we forget, Rabelais could speak of a 'great perhaps' in 1553, when Protestantism had not yet made serious inroads in France. And Machiavelli's *Prince* may have been published in 1532, but it was written before Martin Luther ever thought about taking on John Tetzel's traveling indulgence carnival. . . . Moreover, if we listen to the complaints of reforming clergy, we can come away with the impression that unbelief was rampant, as in this allegation from 1620: 'A great number of Christians, even of Catholics, do not believe that there is an eternity in Hell and in Heaven; that is to say, they would certainly live otherwise if they truly did believe it.' Apparently, then, there was already some unbelief and some 'secularization' at work in sixteenth-century Europe, gnawing at the status quo from within. But there is no denying the fact that, on the whole, zealous Protestants did much more than Machiavelli to dismantle those social, political, and economic structures that reified eternity for early modern Western Europeans. After all, the vast majority of Italians continued offering masses for the dead for centuries, and many do so still, even in our own day. But the vast majority of Saxons and Zurichers, and Englishmen and Scots, stopped praying for their dead altogether nearly five centuries ago" (153–54). The interior quotation is from Jeremias Drexelius, SJ, *Considerations on Eternity*, trans. Marie José Byrne (New York: Pustet, 1920), 162. See also Jared Wicks, SJ, "Applied Theology at the Deathbed: Luther and the Late-Medieval Tradition of the *Ars Moriendi*," *Gregorianum* 79 (1998): 345–68; Austra Reinis, *Reforming the Art of Dying: The Ars Moriendi in the German Reformation (1519–1528)* (Aldershot: Ashgate, 2007).

16. Carol Zaleski, *The Life of the World to Come: Near-Death Experience and Christian Hope* (New York: Oxford University Press, 1996), 81. She points out: "Genuinely religious hope does not evade but rather consecrates that consciousness of death which is pivotal for the development of self-consciousness in human beings. Along with language (and intimately related to language), awareness of death uniquely marks our species" (8). Part of her project involves critically evaluating near-death experiences as culturally shaped, but not thereby unworthy of attention. She notes that "what we call near-death experience today is nothing new. Stories of people who return from death, bringing back eyewitness testimony about the other world, can be found in nearly every religious tradition, and although they have many similar features, such reports invariably portray this experience in ways that conform to cultural expectations" (20). Zaleski's aim is to defend "the revelatory potential of the religious imagination," and thereby to take seriously the "visionary encounter" even if (as scientists say) the person

was not dead (34). As she asks: "If God is willing to descend into our human condition, may he not also, by the same courtesy, descend into our cultural forms and become mediated to us in and through them?" (35).

17. Jacques Derrida argues that in the work of the Czech philosopher Jan Patočka, "The Christian themes can be seen to revolve around the *gift* as gift of death, the fathomless gift of a type of death: infinite love (the Good as goodness that infinitely forgets itself), sin and salvation, repentance and sacrifice. What engenders all these meanings and links them, internally and necessarily, is a logic that at bottom (and that is why it can still, up to a certain point, be called a 'logic') has no need of *the event of a revelation or the revelation of an event*. It needed to think the possibility of such an event but not the event itself" (*The Gift of Death*, 2nd ed., in *The Gift of Death and Literature in Secret*, trans. David Wills [Chicago: University of Chicago Press, 2008], 49–50). Whatever the case with Patočka's (or Derrida's) philosophy, the opposite is needed for Christian hope; the *events* of divine revelation are necessary. On Christian faith, see especially Romanus Cessario, OP, *Christian Faith and the Theological Life* (Washington, DC: Catholic University of America Press, 1996). See also N. T. Wright's defense of the credibility of Jesus's resurrection in *The Resurrection of the Son of God* (Minneapolis: Fortress, 2003).

18. John Swinton and Richard Payne, "Attending to God in Suffering: Re-Imagining End-of-Life Care," in *Living Well and Dying Faithfully*, ed. Swinton and Payne, 273. For their account of imagination, Swinton and Payne are indebted to Stanley Hauerwas; and their goal is to "re-fund the imagination of Christian caregivers in ways that are liberative, transformative, and healing" (273).

19. See Lester L. Grabbe, *Wisdom of Solomon* (New York: T. & T. Clark, 2003), 87–90. Grabbe concludes that the most likely date is "the reign of Augustus" (90).

20. For background to Wisd. of Sol. 2 in Greco-Roman philosophical schools and literary culture, see David Winston, *The Wisdom of Solomon* (Garden City, NY: Doubleday, 1979), 114–19. Winston points out that Wisd. of Sol. 2:12 is "virtually a quotation from the LXX version of Isa 3:10, where the Hebrew is quite different. It is quoted by many of the Church Fathers, following its citation in Barnabas 6:7, as referring to Christ" (119).

21. Winston notes that a similar view of the immortality of the soul is held by Philo as well as by a wide variety of other Second Temple (nonbiblical) texts (*Wisdom of Solomon*, 125). As Winston points out, too, "Josephus presents us with a radically dualistic anthropology very similar to that of Philo: 'All of us, it is true, have mortal bodies, composed of perishable matter, but the soul lives forever, immortal; it is a portion of the Deity housed in our bodies' (*J.W.* 3.8.5); cf. the words placed by Josephus in the mouth of the Zealot leader Eleazar at Masada: 'Life, not death, is man's misfortune. For it is death which gives liberty to the soul and permits it to depart to its own pure abode, there to be free from all calamity, but so long as it is imprisoned in a mortal body and tainted with all its miseries, it is, in sober truth, dead, for association with what is mortal ill befits that which is divine' (*J.W.* 7.8.7)" (125–26). In addition, as Winston remarks, "In the extrabiblical apocalyptic

literature, the dead are no longer described as 'shades' but as 'souls' or 'spirits' and survive as individual conscious beings who may either enjoy a blissful existence as a reward for their righteousness or receive punishment for their wickedness" (126).

See also Wright, *Resurrection of the Son*, 162–75. Wright concludes: "The Wisdom of Solomon certainly does teach 'immortality,' but it is (a) an immortality which is *attained* through wisdom, not innate in a pre-existent soul (leaving 8.19–20 as a remaining puzzle, but not allowing it to veto what the rest of the work, in form and shape as well as content, actually says); and (b), probably more important, an immortality which would ultimately consist not in a disembodied soul but in a renewed bodily life, when at last the soul is given a body to match it (9.15). The time when 'the souls of the righteous are in god's hand' (3.1) is simply the temporary period of rest during which they are looked after, like Daniel going to his 'rest,' or the souls under the altar in Revelation, until the time when they, like him, rise for their reward, and indeed for their rule over the world. There is no 'tension' here between two different doctrines. To suggest such a thing is simply to fail to see how the story works, and how those who believe in a final resurrection necessarily believe in an intermediate time when those to be raised in the future are kept alive not by an innate immortality but by the power and love of Israel's god" (174).

For my part, I see no reason to deny an "innate immortality" of the soul, since this does not mean that the soul no longer depends utterly upon God for the sustaining of its existence. Otherwise, however, I entirely agree with Wright. Wright adds (quite correctly) that "it seems probable that the emerging belief in resurrection (grounded, as we have seen, in the same belief in YHWH as creator as characterized ancient Israel) precipitated further reflection on the continuing identity of the people of YHWH in between bodily death and resurrection. For that task, Hellenistic language about the soul lay ready to hand. It was capable of being imported without necessarily bringing all its latent Platonic baggage with it" (175).

22. Josef Pieper, *In Defense of Philosophy: Classical Wisdom Stands Up to Modern Challenges*, trans. Lothar Krauth (San Francisco: Ignatius, 1992), 25. See also Pieper, *The Philosophical Act*, published in *Leisure, the Basis of Culture*, trans. Gerald Malsbary (South Bend, IN: St. Augustine's Press, 1998), 61–134; Pieper, *In Tune with the World: A Theory of Festivity*, trans. Richard and Clara Winston (South Bend, IN: St. Augustine's Press, 1999); Pieper, *Abuse of Language, Abuse of Power*, trans. Lothar Krauth (San Francisco: Ignatius, 1992), 52–53.

23. Pieper, *In Defense of Philosophy*, 38.

24. Pieper, *In Defense of Philosophy*, 54. Note that this is quite different from mere optimism or failure to perceive the real extent of evil in the world. As Pieper comments in *In Tune with the World*, the greatest Christian thinkers "held that man has so shamefully disgraced the earth and himself and plunged both into such a deplorable state that return to nothingness, total *annihilatio*, might well appear an act of justice. Compared with such a view, it is the height of naïve optimism to believe that the evil in the world is a matter of specific social systems or 'dark ages'" (82).

25. Josef Pieper, *Hope and History: Five Salzburg Lectures*, trans. David Kipp (San Francisco: Ignatius, 1994), 35.

26. See Pieper, *Hope and History*, 89.

27. Pieper, *In Defense of Philosophy*, 75. Likewise, in *The Philosophical Act*, Pieper states: "When the world is no longer looked upon as creation, there can no longer be *theoria* in the full sense" (79). He adds that "the world that is related to the spiritual being is the sum-total of existing things; this is so much the case that this set of relations belongs as well to the nature of spirit; the spirit is the power of comprehending the totality of being, as it belongs to the nature of existing beings themselves: 'to be' means 'be related to spirit.' . . . But man is not pure spirit; he is finite spirit so that both the nature of things and the totality of things are not given in the perfection of a total understanding, but only in 'expectation' or 'hope'" (89, 92).

28. Pieper, *In Defense of Philosophy*, 54.

29. Pieper, *In Defense of Philosophy*, 54. In *In Tune with the World*, Pieper remarks similarly: "I really do not know how an incorruptible mind, faced with the evil in the world, could keep from utter despair were it not for the logically tenable conviction that there is a divinely guaranteed Goodness of being which no amount of mischief can undermine. But that *is* the point of view of the man who sees the world as *creatura*" (82).

30. Pieper, *In Defense of Philosophy*, 76. For further discussion see my *Proofs of God: Classical Arguments from Tertullian to Karl Barth* (Grand Rapids: Baker Academic, 2016).

31. See Josef Pieper, *Death and Immortality*, trans. Richard and Clara Winston (South Bend, IN: St. Augustine's Press, 2000). In addressing this theme, Pieper aims to engage the existential viewpoint on death put forward by philosophers such as Martin Heidegger and Karl Jaspers. For discussion see especially Berthold Wald, "Martin Heidegger, Josef Pieper und die neue Thanatologie," in *Tod und Unsterblichkeit: Erkundungen mit C. S. Lewis und Josef Pieper*, ed. Thomas Möllenbeck and Berthold Wald (Paderborn: Schöningh, 2015), 81–95. For a summary and critique of Heidegger's philosophy of death, see Bernard N. Schumacher, *Death and Mortality in Contemporary Philosophy*, trans. Michael J. Miller (Cambridge: Cambridge University Press, 2011), 61–84; cf. 111. In response to Heidegger, Schumacher points out that "the fact that the *Dasein* is constituted as a Being essentially ahead-of-itself does not logically imply that it is a Being-towards-the-end, a Being-mortal: it only makes it a Being radically open to the indeterminate future of possibilities. . . . Heidegger's notion of Being-towards-death is based on an *a priori* decision to think of death in terms of an ontology of a radically finite temporality and to take the *here* as the point of departure for the analysis" (80–81). For a critique of "Heidegger's absolute immanentism" (225), see David Bentley Hart, *The Beauty of the Infinite: The Aesthetics of Christian Truth* (Grand Rapids: Eerdmans, 2003), 214–29. For succinct critical summaries of views of death proposed by Heidegger ("being to the end"), Sartre (absurdity), and Jaspers (fulfillment), see Hans Küng, *Eternal Life? Life after Death as a Medical, Philosophical, and Theological Problem*, trans. Edward Quinn (New York: Doubleday, 1984), 35–41. Küng goes on

to discuss the influential atheistic position of Ernst Bloch (the "great perhaps"; see 44–46). Küng's positive conclusions at the end of his book are deeply moving (230–34). On Sartre, Jaspers, and Heidegger, see also Jacques Choron, *Death and Western Thought* (New York: Collier, 1963), 225–54.

32. Ephraim Radner, *A Time to Keep: Theology, Mortality, and the Shape of a Human Life* (Waco, TX: Baylor University Press, 2016), 153.

33. See Raymond Hain, "Aquinas and Aristotelian Hylomorphism," in *Aristotle in Aquinas's Theology*, ed. Gilles Emery, OP, and Matthew Levering (Oxford: Oxford University Press, 2015), 48–69; Thomas S. Hibbs, *Virtue's Splendor: Wisdom, Prudence, and the Human Good* (New York: Fordham University Press, 2001), 44–55; Patrick Toner, "St. Thomas Aquinas on Death and the Separated Soul," *Pacific Philosophical Quarterly* 91 (2010): 587–99. If the person dies, can the separated soul be the same person (in the intermediate state), given that a human person is a body-soul composite rather than merely a soul (i.e., the soul of Peter is not Peter)? Hain notes that in *Summa theologica* II-II, q. 83, a. 11, ad 5, "Aquinas appears to accept that the saints themselves do not pray for us; only their souls do" ("Aquinas and Aristotelian Hylomorphism," 65). It seems to me that since separated souls preserve their ordering to their bodies, separated souls (while not the person in a proper sense) are not a new entity and can still rightly be called by their personal name. The same point applies to the term *human* or *man*. Aquinas observes that given the separation of the soul from the body (death), "to say that Christ was a man during the three days of his death simply and without qualification, is erroneous. Yet it can be said that he was *a dead man* during those three days" (III, q. 50, a. 4).

34. Although death is the natural result of human materiality and in this sense is not opposed to human nature, death is not the natural result of the spiritual soul as the form of the body. Pieper argues that "death can only be called outrightly unnatural or contrary to nature insofar as in it the forming of the body is violently interrupted and destroyed contrary to the innermost intention of the soul and of the man himself" (*Death and Immortality*, 62–63). See also Randall S. Rosenberg, "Being-toward-a-Death-Transformed: Aquinas on the Naturalness and Unnaturalness of Human Death," *Angelicum* 83 (2006): 747–66; David Albert Jones, *Approaching the End: A Theological Exploration of Death and Dying* (Oxford: Oxford University Press, 2007), ch. 5: "In One Way Natural, in Another Unnatural: Death in the Thought of Thomas Aquinas."

35. Pieper, *Death and Immortality*, 47; cf. 65. I discuss human death as a just punishment of original sin in ch. 6 of my *Engaging the Doctrine of Creation: Cosmos, Creatures, and the Wise and Good Creator* (Grand Rapids: Baker Academic, 2017).

36. As Pieper comments: "what seems merely something to be suffered, might truly be transformed into something freely chosen, so far as is humanly possible—but chosen without all the fierceness and gloom of false heroics; chosen rather under the very human auspices of stout-hearted cheerfulness of soul" (*Death and Immortality*, 72). A similar emphasis on the act of dying is advocated by Marjorie Casebier McCoy, in her embarrassingly titled *To Die with Style!* (Nashville: Abingdon, 1974). Unfortunately,

McCoy has positive words for the Euthanasia Educational Council, mistakenly seeing in it only the desire of dying persons to be free of heroic medical treatments and to receive pain-suppressing medication.

37. For critical responses to this viewpoint—which Gisbert Greshake character-izes as the view that dying involves "the final and supreme active expression of [one's] freedom"—see Greshake, "Towards a Theology of Dying," trans. Robert Nowell, in *The Experience of Dying*, ed. Norbert Greinacher and Alois Müller (New York: Herder & Herder, 1974), 81; Paul O'Callaghan, *Christ Our Hope: An Introduction to Eschatology* (Washington, DC: Catholic University of America Press, 2011), 269. Greshake notes that the view is by no means original to Pieper, but can be found already in H. E. Hengstenberg, *Einsamkeit und Tod* (Regensburg: Pustet, 1938); and in R. W. Gleason, "Toward a Theology of Death," *Thought* 23 (1957): 39–68; Karl Rahner, SJ, *On the Theology of Death*, trans. Charles H. Henkey (Freiburg: Herder, 1961); and Ladislaus Boros, SJ, *The Mystery of Death* (New York: Seabury, 1973).

Greshake raises the following problems with this view of death: it "escapes expe-rience and verification" and therefore does not really address actual dying persons; it overlooks the possible connection between dying and the fundamental passivity present in being born; it asserts that dying, despite most appearances, is the locus of the highest meaningful activity; it asserts that life finds its complete meaning at the moment of death and therefore *prior* to meeting God; and it privileges the moment of death and thereby devalues "the significance of concrete human life (including dying as the concluding phase of life)" ("Towards a Theology of Dying," 83–84).

I think that Greshake's concerns here are generally on target, although I am still willing to believe that in many cases the act of dying can be decisive in the ways outlined by Pieper. I also agree with Greshake's *positive* point that Pieper's position helpfully reminds us that the process of dying "shows the concentration and sharpening of what has already always existed in the fulfilment of human life" (84) and thereby that Pieper's position has value in making clear that dying belongs to (and indeed is in certain ways the supreme expression of) our living. As Greshake says, here in firm agreement with the main lines of Pieper's perspective, "the biological process of dying remains still a situation of radical decision where man is asked how he has understood himself and his life and now—in retrospect—wishes to understand it. The time immediately before the end, the process of dying, provides a last possible way for man, who is essentially free, to determine the pattern of his life. . . . It is the latest moment for accepting that life does not belong to one and that it cannot bring about its own consummation and perfection by means of however extended a prolongation in time. In this way dying gives man his last chance to break out of himself, to leave his life, in which he formerly did not want to die with Christ, and to go forward towards God's future" (91, 96).

For concerns that echo Greshake's (in response specifically to Rahner), see David Jones's remarks that "it is not legitimate to conclude that, because death brings life to a stop, it therefore brings it to a fulfilment" and that "if the 'act of dying' is separated too much from individual acts in this life, then individual acts lose their significance"

(*Approaching the End*, 174, 178). Jones also rightly notes, "The act of renunciation, by which death is willingly accepted, is never as such the cause of death, so the phrase 'act of dying' is one that should be treated with extreme caution. Nevertheless, Rahner is right to see the renunciation of life by the martyrs as the completion of that dying-to-self which is a necessary part of accepting the grace of God. . . . Yet, even in this case, death itself is not an act of fulfilment nor is it to be seen as something desirable in itself, but circumstances have arisen that require, or at least allow, life to be forfeited for the sake of holding fast to God" (180).

Bartholomew J. Collopy, SJ, criticizes Boros's and Rahner's position for its "methodological bias against death's disabling aspects, its incoherence, its brutish tearing through order and explication" ("Theology and the Darkness of Death," *Theological Studies* 39 [1978]: 38). Collopy also rejects Pieper's *Death and Immortality*, on the grounds that Pieper's commitment to the spiritual soul undermines the real gravity of death. For an enthusiastically Rahnerian position, see Robert Ochs, SJ, *The Death in Every Now* (New York: Sheed & Ward, 1969).

38. Pieper, *Death and Immortality*, 84.

39. Pieper, *Death and Immortality*, 92. Edward Schillebeeckx, OP, helpfully specifies that "death is not an act but the attitude of mind in which we accept death can give it the value of an act" ("The Death of a Christian II: Our Personal Approach," *Life in the Spirit* 16 [1962]: 335).

40. See especially Oscar Cullmann, *Immortality of the Soul: or, Resurrection of the Dead? The Witness of the New Testament* (New York: Macmillan, 1958).

41. Pieper, *Death and Immortality*, 104. See Moses Mendelssohn, *Phädon, or On the Immortality of the Soul*, trans. Patricia Noble (New York: Lang, 2006). As Jonathan M. Hess points out, Mendelssohn was "one of the preeminent voices of the German Enlightenment" and his "*Phaedon, or On the Immortality of the Soul* (1767) was translated into Dutch, French, Danish, Italian and Russian during his lifetime and earned him fame across Europe as the 'German Socrates'" (*Germans, Jews and the Claims of Modernity* [New Haven: Yale University Press, 2002], 93). See also Aaron W. Hughes's treatment of Mendelssohn's *Phädon* in Hughes, *The Art of Dialogue in Jewish Philosophy* (Bloomington, IN: Indiana University Press, 2008), ch. 6. According to Hughes, "*Phaedon* . . . secured for Mendelssohn a predominant place in Enlightenment thought and brought him into intimate contact with the luminaries of that intellectual tradition, individuals such as Nicolai, Lessing, and Kant" (139). Hughes holds that *Phädon* is "a polemical work designed to demonstrate to a predominantly Christian audience that Christianity was not a prerequisite to the felicity of the soul after corporeal death. . . . Moreover, reading *Phaedon* from the perspective of his later works, we hear in the utterances of Socrates the echo of later articulations in which Mendelssohn argues that it is Judaism, requiring neither dogma nor faith, that alone enables its practitioners to live well" (140). Hess notes that Mendelssohn's writings on Judaism were generally not known to his Christian contemporaries (see *Germans, Jews*, 93).

For further reflection on Plato's *Phaedo*, emphasizing Socrates's valuation of death as a passage of mind to the Idea as the perfection of life, see Romano Guardini, *The Death of Socrates: An Interpretation of the Platonic Dialogues: Euthyphro, Apology, Crito and Phaedo,* trans. Basil Wrighton (Cleveland: Meridian, 1962). See also Simon Tugwell's critical reflections on whether the *Phaedo* holds the soul to be the living person: *Human Immortality and the Redemption of Death* (Springfield, IL: Templegate, 1991), 22–37. Tugwell concludes negatively: "The *Phaedo* makes death an achievement, the supreme achievement of this life, but . . . it does so by making immortality an alternative to life, rather than, as in more traditional Greek parlance, an alternative to death" (42).

42. Pieper, *Death and Immortality,* 115. For discussion of this point in light of contemporary science, see ch. 4 of David Bentley Hart, *The Experience of God: Being, Consciousness, Bliss* (New Haven: Yale University Press, 2013). See also Tallis's *Aping Mankind.* As Tallis puts it, "If consciousness *were* simply brain processes, it would not be able so to distance itself from brain processes to discover, or imagine that it has discovered, that it is brain processes" (338). Against the overzealous claims of contemporary neuroscience, Tallis points out that "unless we *were* at a great distance from the kind of activity revealed in our brains and unless our shared lives were profoundly different from the kinds of animal aggregations seen in the natural world, then the *voluntary* adoption of social policies, influenced or not by the latest whizz-bang neuroscience, would be impossible; for there would be no outside from which policies could be dreamed up, judged and tested. The notion that our brains are calling the shots and that, most of the time, we don't know what the shots are, is equally vulnerable on this account. If this were true, how could the brains of (for example) neuroscientists ever come to know just how clever the brain is and, indeed, how reality differs from the way our brains present it to us: how 'red' light energy, for example, is not red in itself? How could neuroscientists outwit their own vastly superior brains to unmask what they are up to, and what do they outwit it with?" (339–40). For an early statement of the same point, see the evolutionary theorist J. B. S. Haldane, "When I Am Dead," in *Possible Worlds and Other Essays* (London: Chatto & Windus, 1932), 204–10. Like Hart, Tallis's central claim is that materialism cannot now and never will be able to account for human intentionality (without thereby denying that a functioning brain is needed for intentionality). Unlike Hart and Pieper, however, Tallis does not believe in spiritual realities, and so he arrives at a fully agnostic conclusion about the sources of consciousness. For an excellent defense of the Christian (and biblical) doctrine of the spiritual soul in light of a wide variety of contemporary viewpoints, see T. Nichols, *Death and Afterlife,* ch. 6. Nichols emphasizes that "the immortality of the soul is a gift from God and is due to its relation to God" (131).

43. Zaleski, *Life,* 42.

44. Zaleski, *Life,* 43. Zaleski sees our immortality as coming not from the spiritual soul but from "an eschatological transformation that happens to the whole person" (45)—and indeed our immortality as body-soul persons does indeed come in this way. Nonetheless, she argues in favor of imaginative construals of life after death that include

imagining "oneself as a soul" (46), and she believes that we possess a spiritual soul. Although she lacks Pieper's grasp of the philosophical arguments for the existence of an indestructible soul (whose indestructibility depends, of course, upon God's sustaining it in being), Zaleski approvingly cites the Congregation for the Doctrine of the Faith's "Letter on Certain Questions Concerning Eschatology," in *L'Osservatore Romano* (July 23, 1979): 7–8, where the church teaches that "a spiritual element survives and subsists after death, an element endowed with consciousness and will, so that the 'human self' subsists."

See also Joseph Ratzinger's response to this text by the Congregation of the Doctrine of the Faith, published in English as "Appendix 1: Between Death and Resurrection: Some Supplementary Reflections," in *Eschatology: Death and Eternal Life*, trans. Michael Waldstein with Aidan Nichols, OP, 2nd ed. (Washington, DC: Catholic University of America Press, 2007), 241–60. Ratzinger affirms: "Immortality does not inhere in a human being but rests on a relation, on a *relationship*, with what is eternal, what makes eternity meaningful. This abidingness, which gives life and can fulfil it, is truth. It is also love. Man can therefore live forever, because he is able to have a relationship with that which gives the eternal. 'The soul' is our term for that in us which offers a foothold for this relation. Soul is nothing other than man's capacity for relatedness with truth, with love eternal" (259).

I agree with this, even while I think that more can be said about the soul. Indeed, Ratzinger says a good bit more, including his excellent (intentionally Thomistic) description of the relationship of the separated soul to its body: "It is thoroughly obvious from this starting-point (of Thomas') that man throughout his life 'interiorizes' matter. Consequently, even in death he does not relinquish this connection. Only so can his relation to resurrection be meaningful. But by the same token, one does not need to disavow the concept of soul, nor to substitute in its place a new body. It is not that some kind of body holds the soul fast, but that the soul itself, in its continuing existence, retains within itself the matter of its life, and therefore tends impatiently towards the risen Christ, towards the new unity of spirit and matter which in him has been opened for it" (258). Zaleski appreciatively cites Ratzinger's *Eschatology* (*Life*, 61–62).

45. Robert Jay Lifton, *The Broken Connection: On Death and the Continuity in Life* (New York: Simon & Schuster, 1979), 3. Lifton's book, which relies heavily (though not uncritically) upon Sigmund Freud, addresses "our present preoccupation with absurd death (and by implication, absurd life) and unlimited technological violence" (4–5), and treats the tendency of persons and cultures to seek self-perpetuation by victimizing and scapegoating others (the Nazi movement being one example). Lifton grants that "we are unable to imagine—that is, experience through imagery—our own nonexistence," since in imagining such a thing "we" still exist as imagining it (8). But as Lifton points out, "I can very well imagine a world in which 'I' do not exist" (8). For Lifton, the answer to the problem involves ongoing culture, in which we (though dead and nonexistent) still participate through the contributions to culture that we made during our lifetime. He distinguishes between "literal perpetuation of the intact self—

an illusion and frequently a dangerous one—and imagined (symbolized) perpetuation of elements of the self through connection with larger forms of human culture" (8). In his view, the latter suffices for meaning. In my view, nothing but God and communion with God can uphold the meaning of a human life, since everything in this world is passing away and will come to nothing.

46. See John Henry Newman, *An Essay in Aid of a Grammar of Assent* (repr., Westminster, MD: Christian Classics, 1973). Newman has in view "assent" rather than "belief," but his terms evoke what I am trying to describe here.

47. Zaleski, *Life*, 47. She cites Colleen McDannell and Bernhard Lang, *Heaven: A History* (New Haven: Yale University Press, 1988), for evidence that "the history of heaven is the history of the projection of humanly constructed ideals" (*Life*, 47). In her view, "it is true that such imaginings will at present tell us more about our own assumptions and longings than they do about the heavenly society" (48). I think that this is true, but only up to a point. The New Testament contains divinely revealed images that, while reflecting the culture of its day, nonetheless give us a basis for imagining eternal life in ways that are not simply culturally dependent. While remaining culturally inflected images, they do more—though certainly not less—than "offer the individual a wider cosmos within which to dwell, nourished by a rich network of social, natural, and spiritual connections" (48). Zaleski grants that "there are tawdry, banal forms of imagination about the afterlife" (48).

48. Aidan Nichols, OP, *The Thought of Pope Benedict XVI: An Introduction to the Theology of Joseph Ratzinger*, 2nd ed. (London: Continuum, 2007), 128. For background to Ratzinger's eschatology (inseparable from his liturgical theology, as my student Roland Millare has made clear to me), see Thomas Marschler, "Perspektiven der Eschatologie bei Joseph Ratzinger," in *Joseph Ratzinger: Ein theologisches Profil*, ed. Peter Hoffmann (Paderborn: Schöningh, 2008), 161–88; Michael Kunzler, "Die kosmische Dimension der Eucharistiefeier: Zu Fragen ihrer liturgischen Gestalt bei Joseph Ratzinger," in *Der Logos-gemäße Gottesdienst: Theologie der Liturgie bei Joseph Ratzinger*, ed. Rudolf Voderholzer (Regensburg: Pustet, 2009), 172–204.

49. Herbert McCabe, OP, *God, Christ and Us*, ed. Brian Davies, OP (London: Continuum, 2003), 145.

50. I note that this hope does not separate us from love of neighbor and from the church on earth, since as Scott Hahn points out, "There are *not* multiple churches—one in heaven, one on earth, and one in purgatory. Christians have traditionally believed in one church that is both heavenly and earthly. . . . To think like a Catholic is to have this sense of the 'communion of saints'—both the 'saints' in the pews (Col 1:2) and 'the saints in light' (Col 1:12)" (*The Creed: Professing the Faith through the Ages* [Steubenville, OH: Emmaus Road, 2016], 151).

51. Bellarmine's book belongs to the tradition of *ars moriendi* that began in the fifteenth century. On this tradition, see Allen Verhey, *The Christian Art of Dying: Learning from Jesus* (Grand Rapids: Eerdmans, 2011), 85–171, in which Verhey constructively surveys *Crafte and Knowledge for to Dye Well*, a 1490 English translation of the widely

circulated *Tractatis Artis Bene Moriendi*, which was based upon a section of Jean Gerson's brief pastoral handbook *Opusculum Tripertitum*. See *Crafte and Knowledge for to Dye Well*, in *The English Ars Moriendi*, ed. David William Atkinson (New York: Lang, 1992); Johannes Gerson, *Opusculum Tripertitum*, in *Opera Omnia*, ed. Louis Ellier Du Pin (Hildesheim: Olms, 1987), 1:425–50. In pages 173–385 of his book, Verhey develops his own contemporary Christian *Ars Moriendi*. For historical background to the *ars moriendi* tradition, see Mary Catherine O'Connor, *The Art of Dying Well: The Development of the Ars Moriendi* (New York: Columbia University Press, 1942).

52. In treating Bellarmine and de Sales, I am not proposing that the seventeenth century was a placid Christian age by comparison to our own "postmodern" age. On the contrary, Jacques Choron, in *Death and Western Thought* (New York: Collier, 1963), is quite right to locate what he terms "The Crisis of the Christian View of Death" (ch. 9 of his book) in the late Middle Ages and the Renaissance humanist period. Bellarmine and de Sales were not living in a placidly Christian age, if indeed there ever was such a thing.

53. Zaleski, *Life*, 12.

54. Robert Bellarmine, SJ, *The Art of Dying Well*, in *Spiritual Writings*, trans. and ed. John Patrick Donnelly, SJ, and Roland Teske, SJ (New York: Paulist, 1989), 243. Hereafter in this section, page references from this work will be given in parentheses in the text.

55. Zaleski comments with respect to hell: "Christians may also dare to hope, as Hans Urs von Balthasar has argued, for the eventual salvation of all humankind. For the hope that all may be saved is not the same as the optimistic assertion of an *apokatastasis pantōn* (universal restoration) that cancels human freedom by denying all possibility of loss. What shall we say, then, of the proliferation of imaginative scenarios [not least in the New Testament] for the judgment of the dead and the eternal condemnation of the wicked? As Balthasar suggests, the problem with these scenarios has been their deployment by a theological tradition that tried to know too much, and took pleasure from the torment of the unjust" (*Life*, 68; drawing upon Balthasar's *Dare We Hope "That All Men Be Saved"? with a Short Discourse on Hell*, trans. David Kipp and Lothar Krauth [San Francisco: Ignatius, 1988]; and Brian E. Daley, SJ, *The Hope of the Early Church: A Handbook of Patristic Eschatology* [Cambridge: Cambridge University Press, 1991], 168–204).

In noting the unseemliness of Christians—who are followers of the Lord who came to forgive sinners—taking anticipatory "pleasure from the torment of the unjust," Zaleski puts her finger on a sad problem. It is tremendously sad that the atheist writer Christopher Hitchens, when he was dying of cancer, received from some Christians the message that this was God's revenge on him and that God would delight in tormenting him everlastingly in hell (many more Christians, fortunately, sincerely prayed for Hitchens and wished good things for him): see Hitchens, *Mortality* (New York: Twelve, 2012), 12–14. I agree with Paul O'Callaghan's formulation: "The object of Christian hope is twofold: the glorious *Parousia* of Christ at the end of time and the salvation of each one of the elect. . . . However, even though the hope of Christians should include

NOTES TO PAGES 39–40

trust in God's benevolence toward every human being, it simply cannot include their response to God's grace, for this is the exclusive right and duty of each Christian believer, of each person. In brief, the believer's act of hope includes ipso facto their own trusting response to God, but not the personal response of others. It is fair to say that Christians can and should desire the salvation of all, in that God seeks it (1 Tim. 2:4). Besides, they should strive to achieve salvation under God's grace and attempt to communicate it to the rest of humanity. Yet the salvation of each and every person cannot as such be considered an object of Christian hope in the strict sense of the word. If God himself had no intention of supplanting or suppressing the free will of each Christian, on what basis should other humans be in a position to do so?" (*Christ Our Hope: An Introduction to Eschatology* [Washington, DC: Catholic University of America Press, 2011], 221). For a more appreciative appropriation of Balthasar, though well aware that Satan is irrevocably lost, see Reinhard Hütter, *Dust Bound for Heaven: Explorations in the Theology of Thomas Aquinas* (Grand Rapids: Eerdmans, 2012), 181. I note that since punishment in hell orders humans to divine justice, hell is not an eternal evil principle warring against God's eternal goodness.

56. Skepticism about the existence of immaterial (and thus nonempirical) realities flourished during Bellarmine's lifetime. Renaissance thinkers retrieved the philosophy of the ancient Skeptics (or Academics) in a way that proved persuasive to many, including most influentially Michel de Montaigne. See Montaigne, "Apology for Raymond Sebond," in *The Complete Works: Essays, Travel Journal, Letters*, trans. Donald M. Frame (New York: Knopf, 2003), 387–556. See also Richard H. Popkin, *The History of Scepticism from Savonarola to Bayle* (Oxford: Oxford University Press, 2003).

57. I note that the doctrine of merit does not oppose the fundamental truth that, as Richard John Neuhaus says, "When I come before the judgment throne, I will plead the promise of God in the shed blood of Jesus Christ. . . . I will plead no merits other than the merits of Christ, knowing that the merits of Mary and the saints are all from him" (*Death on a Friday Afternoon: Meditations on the Last Words of Jesus from the Cross* [New York: Basic Books, 2000], 70). Merit or reward belongs to us only insofar as we depend (and have depended) utterly upon Christ and his Spirit dwelling within us, and thus the person who has truly merited will plead only Christ's merits. For biblical and theological insight into what is meant by meriting, see Gary A. Anderson, *Sin: A History* (New Haven: Yale University Press, 2009); Charles Raith II, "Calvin's Critique of Merit, and Why Aquinas (Mostly) Agrees," *Pro Ecclesia* 20 (2011): 135–53; Raith, "Aquinas and Calvin on Merit, Part II: Condignity and Participation," *Pro Ecclesia* 21 (2012): 195–210.

58. A comparison with the Eastern desert fathers (through the mid-seventh century) may be worthwhile here. Jonathan L. Zecher notes that the "memory of death" involves "two types of contemplative practice: meditation on one's inevitable but unknowable demise, and contemplation (even figuration) of the divine judgment that follows. Both practices are simultaneously paraenetic and existential: they bespeak the reality of ascetics' moral condition, and urge them away from vices and toward virtues

that divine judgment picks out as particularly salient" (*The Role of Death in the Ladder of Divine Ascent and the Greek Ascetic Tradition* [Oxford: Oxford University Press, 2015], ix). The same points apply to Bellarmine's (and de Sales's) work. Of course, the ascetic life of the monks for whom John Climacus wrote went well beyond the asceticism advocated by Bellarmine and de Sales for nonmonastic Christians.

59. On Scripture's teaching about the intermediate state (and thus the existence of the soul, whether or not one calls it by the name "soul"), see my *Jesus and the Demise of Death: Resurrection, Afterlife, and the Fate of the Christian* (Waco, TX: Baylor University Press, 2012), chs. 1 and 6. N. T. Wright argues in favor of the New Testament's testimony to the intermediate state both in *The Resurrection of the Son of God* and in *Surprised by Hope: Rethinking Heaven, the Resurrection, and the Mission of the Church* (New York: HarperCollins, 2008), 162, 172. For the view that God preserves "something" of us after death but that this something need not be called the "soul"—a view that is presumed by Wright, who wishes to move as far away from Plato as possible—see Simon Tugwell, OP, *Human Immortality and the Redemption of Death* (Springfield, IL: Templegate, 1991), 164; cf. 77.

60. For an account of the fulfillment of the central elements of the inaugurated kingdom of God in the consummated kingdom, see my *Jesus and the Demise of Death*, ch. 7 (paired with ch. 4 of that book). In his *Decreation: The Last Things of All Creatures* (Waco, TX: Baylor University Press, 2014), Paul J. Griffiths proposes that the death of the human person involves a "temporary annihilation" (since neither the soul nor the body, when separated from each other, is the human person), and he argues that unrepentant sinners can, through the corruption of sin, annihilate themselves: "when the soul is sufficiently corrupted, it ceases to be" (175, 200). In this way Griffiths addresses the mystery of how God could permit humans and angels to lock themselves permanently in a hellish state of alienation from God. The biblical testimony to an everlasting hell seems to me to be conclusive, since I do not think that God himself would annihilate his rational creatures or that created spirits can annihilate themselves. The fallen angels have irrevocably alienated themselves from God; on this point see the *Catechism of the Catholic Church*, 2nd ed. (Vatican City: Libreria Editrice Vaticana, 1997), §393. I briefly discuss the biblical testimony in *Predestination: Biblical and Theological Paths* (Oxford: Oxford University Press, 2011), 192–94. See also the biblical arguments in *Four Views on Hell*, ed. Preston Sprinkle (Grand Rapids: Zondervan, 2016).

61. For emphasis that such works of charity display much more than a "utilitarian calculation" (as indeed works of charity do for Bellarmine, though he is not above trying to persuade his readers by utilitarian arguments), see Gary A. Anderson, *Charity: The Place of the Poor in the Biblical Tradition* (New Haven: Yale University Press, 2013), 6.

62. Although it is true that "hell" serves the good of justice, and is therefore not strictly incompatible with God's goodness, Peter C. Phan rightly specifies that "God does not and cannot create hell as a kind of Abu Ghraib and then hurl evil people in there after their death to be eternally punished and tortured for their sins. Rather, God

offers us *only one* reality, namely, 'heaven,' that is, the eternal and infinite life and love uniting the three Persons of the Trinity and constituting them the one God. This divine life, or heaven, is what God gives to each and every human being. By contrast, hell is nothing more than the result of a person's irrevocable decision to refuse God's gift of love and cannot be understood except as the contradiction of heaven" (*Living into Death, Dying into Life: A Christian Theology of Death and Life Eternal* [Hobe Sound, FL: Lectio, 2014], 68). For Phan, "Christians must preach heaven, and not hell" (68), but in my view the kind of warnings issued by Bellarmine (and Jesus Christ) are salutary in reminding us of the eternal stakes of our actions. As Moses says in the book of Deuteronomy (speaking about life in the promised land as the reward for obeying God's law), "I call heaven and earth to witness against you today that I have set before you life and death, blessings and curses. Choose life so that you and your descendants may live, loving the LORD your God, obeying him, and holding fast to him" (Deut. 30:19–20).

63. Bellarmine owes a debt here to Ignatius of Loyola. In the First Exercise of his *Spiritual Exercises*, Ignatius calls upon us to think of the angels' sin, to think of Adam and Eve's sin, and to think of how easy it is to go to hell. He invites us to imagine ourselves in the presence of Christ on the cross, and to contemplate what Christ has done for us and to ask ourselves what we have done for Christ. This is a preparation for thinking of all our sins in the Second Exercise. It may seem that Ignatius is following an overly guilt-ridden path, but the purpose of thinking of the enormity of sin (especially our own) is to rejoice in God's mercy, insofar as God has borne with his creatures and borne with me rather than blotting us out in justice. The Third and Fourth Exercises urge us further to recognize our sins and to be freed of attachment to worldly things. The Fifth Exercise then places us in hell, which we are urged to experience concretely with each of our five senses. The biblical images here include fire, wailing, smoke, tears, and flames. Each person undertaking the exercises learns to say of himself or herself that God "has shown me, all through my life up to the present moment, so much pity and mercy" (*The Spiritual Exercises*, trans. George E. Ganss, SJ, in *The Spiritual Exercises and Selected Works*, ed. George E. Ganss, SJ [New York: Paulist, 1991], 142).

64. The influence of Plato's *Phaedo* seems to be indirectly present here, since Plato too locates a heavenly realm above the present earthly realm. In Plato's *Phaedo*, Socrates proposes that we presently "live in a hollow of the earth," although "we assume that we are living on the surface" (in *The Collected Dialogues of Plato*, ed. Edith Hamilton and Huntington Cairns [Princeton: Princeton University Press, 1961], 109d, p. 91). See also 111a-c, p. 92; 114b-c, p. 94.

65. Christopher Vogt rather strongly criticizes Bellarmine's *Art of Dying Well* on the grounds that "what stands out most noticeably in Bellarmine's description of the theological virtues is how they are kept at some distance from God's compassion. . . . Bellarmine makes a connection among faith, hope, and God's mercy, but then goes on to make the matter of whether one has purified oneself of sin via penance the test of whether hope is genuine. . . . The emphasis in Bellarmine's *Art of Dying Well* is more upon human purity and an almost mechanical removal of sin via penance rather than

upon the free exercise of divine mercy" (*Patience, Compassion, Hope*, 33). In my view, given that Bellarmine certainly has divine mercy in view, it is reasonable that he urges us to imitate the divine mercy and generosity toward the poor and to seek out Jesus's mercy in the sacrament of penance, where God freely has willed to apply the mercy of Christ. Vogt complains about "the sheer quantity of scriptural references" as well as patristic references (31), but I think that these references are a highlight of his work, which seeks to connect the reader to the scriptural narratives as interpreted by the fathers. Vogt adds: "One leaves this work with a sense that the best that one can generally hope for is to avoid sin in a world pervaded by it. Intimate union with God and spiritual perfection are well beyond the horizon" (32). In fact, Bellarmine's images (in the passage that I quote from *Art of Dying Well*, 337) of riches, pleasures, honors, and dignities are descriptive, as his readers well knew, of precisely the everlasting intimate union with God that—for Bellarmine—is accessible, in part, even in this life. Bellarmine's insistence upon the pervasiveness of sin in the present world should be praised as realistic, and we should also appreciate his emphasis upon the sins of wealthy (literate) people against the poor.

While I certainly do not mean to claim that every aspect of Bellarmine's approach is beyond criticism, I do think that the sharp contrast between Vogt's negative view of Bellarmine's book and Vogt's positive view of the *ars moriendi* books of the Catholic humanist Desiderius Erasmus, the Puritan William Perkins, and the Anglican Jeremy Taylor has more to do with the contemporary Catholic theological tendency to treat Bellarmine as a Baroque whipping boy than with the actual merits of the works in question (all of which strike me as praiseworthy in their diverse ways). See also Erasmus, *Preparing for Death (De praeparatione ad mortem)*, trans. John M. Grant, in *Spiritualia and Pastoralia*, ed. John W. O'Malley, SJ, Collected Works of Erasmus 70 (Toronto: University of Toronto Press, 1998), 389–450; Perkins, *Salve for a Sicke Man*, 127–63; Jeremy Taylor, *Holy Living and Holy Dying*, ed. P. G. Stanwood (Oxford: Clarendon, 1989).

66. Francis de Sales, *Introduction to the Devout Life* (New York: Vintage, 2002), xxxvii. (Hereafter in this section, page references from this work will be given in parentheses in the text.) For a sixteenth-century work of spiritual guidance that, like Ignatius of Loyola's *Spiritual Exercises*, influenced Francis de Sales, see Louis of Granada, OP, *The Sinner's Guide*, trans. a Dominican father (Rockford, IL: TAN, 1985). Drawing on Jesus's parable of the wise and foolish virgins (Matt. 25:1–13), in which Jesus calls upon his followers to be alert for the sudden coming of the kingdom of God, Louis urges us to lead lives of love and to meditate upon our approaching death. He portrays the dismay with which we will greet our imminent dying, unless we begin to prepare now by cultivating repentance and charity: "You will find yourself distracted with pain, filled with anguish and terror at the approach of death and at the thought of the eternal sentence which is about to be pronounced upon you" (209). This existential terror, whether connected with damnation or with annihilation, is indeed commonplace.

67. As Louis of Granada says, "Life is short; every moment brings us nearer to death. Why, then, lay up so much provision for so short a journey? Why burden yourself with so many possessions which must necessarily impede your progress? . . . Death will rob you of all your earthly possessions; your works, good and bad, will alone accompany you beyond the tomb. If this dread hour finds you unprepared, great will be your misfortune. All that remains to you will then be distributed into three portions, your body will become the food of worms; your soul the victim of demons, and your wealth the prey of eager and perhaps ungrateful or extravagant heirs. Ah! Dear Christian, follow the counsel of Our Saviour; share your wealth with the poor, that it may be borne before you into the kingdom which you hope to enjoy. What folly to leave your treasures in a place of banishment whither you will never return, instead of sending them before you to that country which is intended for your eternal home!" (*Sinner's Guide*, 270–71). He congratulates the charitable person on how well prepared he or she will be for dying: "When you will have reached the end of your earthly pilgrimage, poor in this world's goods, your wealth of real treasure will far exceed that of the covetous, whose lives have been spent in accumulating riches. How different will be the account exacted of you, and how readily you will part from the little you may have of the goods of earth, because you always esteemed them at their true value!" (270).

68. See Griffiths, *Decreation*, 166–69, 193–98. Griffiths observes: "The flesh's eros under the metronome [time] gets bored quickly. Driven by desperation to enact its desires, always with a tincture of expropriation and domination, it finds what it wants and what it does repetitive. . . . What was once, the first time or the first dozen times, an almost unmixed delight, received at least in part as the gift it is, becomes with the deadening repetition of the metronome no longer enough, or even something no longer pleasing at all in its first form. The boredom of repetition in the sphere of the flesh's eros has in part to do with the attempt to expropriate and dominate. The extent to which an object of fleshly eros is subjugated in those ways is exactly the extent to which it becomes a bore because it cannot any longer offer what is really needed, which is the free response of the unsubjugated" (167–68).

69. Jean-Pierre de Caussade, SJ, *Abandonment to Divine Providence*, trans. John Beevers (New York: Doubleday, 1975), 22. Hereafter in this section, page references from this work will be given in parentheses in the text.

70. On the meaning of "the gospel," see Scot McKnight, *The King Jesus Gospel: The Original Good News Revisited* (Grand Rapids: Zondervan, 2011); as well as my "What Is the Gospel?," in *Theological Theology: Essays in Honour of John B. Webster*, ed. R. David Nelson, Darren Sarisky, and Justin Stratis (London: Bloomsbury, 2015), 149–66.

71. Verhey, *Christian Art of Dying*, xiii.

72. Similarly, Anthony C. Thiselton observes that "God is in control of time. If the kingdom of God or the world really needs the completion of what we are doing, God will give us time to finish it. This is not to devalue or to forget the real pain of disability, or degenerative illnesses. But if it is *purely* an investment of self-centered hopes,

for ourselves or others, it may seem to be cut short. Pannenberg rightly reminds us that this is a matter of *trust*. We all aim at some kind of security, but our 'relationship [with God] is ... destroyed when a person tries to replace trust with security'" (*Life after Death: A New Approach to the Last Things* [Grand Rapids: Eerdmans, 2012], 5, citing Wolfhart Pannenberg, *What Is Man? Contemporary Anthropology in Theological Perspective*, trans. Duane A. Priebe [Philadelphia: Fortress, 1970], 35).

73. See Verhey, *Christian Art of Dying*, 11: "Philippe Aries begins his classic study of death with the stories of the deaths of Roland and the Knights of the Round Table. The stories, he said, displayed deaths that not only were typical of death in the early Middle Ages but also expressed traditions surrounding dying that were already centuries old. Death was then simple and public. . . . The rituals were simple enough. After acknowledging the imminence of death with a certain ambivalence, expressive at once of regret and resignation, the dying person said good-by to his family and friends, forgiving them and asking forgiveness, blessing them and instructing them, and commending them to God's care and protection. Having said his farewells, the dying person would pray, confessing his sins and commending his soul to God." We will see a similar deathbed scene in ch. 5, which focuses on Gregory of Nyssa's account of the death of his sister Macrina. Verhey is drawing upon Philippe Ariès, *The Hour of Our Death*, trans. Helen Weaver (New York: Knopf, 1981), especially 14–18.

For a sociologist's assessment of Ariès's argument here, concluding that "the individualised conception of dying did grow in significance as Aries has argued, if unevenly, and it was indeed to become a major force in world thinking, though only in a very specific and rather urban pathway," see Allan Kellehear, *A Social History of Dying* (Cambridge: Cambridge University Press, 2007), 121. In my view, Kellehear does not pay enough attention to the impact of Christian faith, and to the concerns about death felt by all people, when he states (citing Simone de Beauvoir as evidence), "The fatalism and acceptance of death so common in pastoral peoples so familiar with dying and the brevity of life in general were not adopted by the longer-living, professionally serviced middle classes" (143). Kellehear goes on to criticize Ariès by noting that "Aries viewed 'traditional' death as tame and modern ideas about death as 'wild' and therefore in need of 'taming.' In fact, however, the process of taming death, of its domestication as it were, is a fascinating record of its shift from earlier and eventually failing methods to tame it (with good-death religious images and observances) to a more urban and recently accelerated secular method (with medical and legal observances)" (176).

I agree with Kellehear's conclusion, focused on the contrast between religious faith and lack of it, that "death became wild, not because doctors, lawyers or hospitals appeared on the scene but because the old place of death (the afterlife) became questionable, even evaporated before the eyes of an increasingly sceptical urban elite" (177). Yet he ends by conceiving the matter again from a purely sociological viewpoint, arguing that the key to diverging understandings of death is "a social diversion, even evolution, in the way elites related to death compared to their peasant and early farming forebears" (178). Interestingly (somewhat like Jesus!), Kellehear assumes that wealth means atheism: "This is a longstanding feature of all urban elites where wealth, distancing social position and long life-expectancy and experience create serious questions and doubts about otherworld journeys, or at least, if these doubts do not exist, an additional anxiety about optimising successful outcomes for that journey when dying" (179).

74. In his *Scars: Essays, Poems and Meditations on Affliction* (London: Bloomsbury, 2014), Paul Murray, OP, gives an example of just such an acceptance of dying, in the experience of his friend Sr. Joan McNamara. Describing their epistolary correspondence, Murray reports two instances of his friend's acceptance of what God was allowing to happen to her. First, she writes: "'In a strange way, Paul, I feel *cocooned* into God. Strange image. I can find no other words. Silenced. At first the word frightened me a little. Cocoon is so fragile. Then a kind friend said: 'But only your resistance can break the cocoon, Joan.' And so many things fell into place!'" (78). Here we see the insight, powerful in Sr. McNamara's life, that we must embrace what God is permitting in our lives, even while seeking medical care and doing what we can to allow God to heal us if it is his will. In a second letter, she offers a similar perspective, as described by Murray: "She spoke briefly of her attempt to understand what was happening to her 'in this amazing time.' But then she said: 'I don't think "understanding" is the right word. I think it is more like "not resisting" or "embracing"'" (78).

75. Pope Benedict XVI, *Last Testament: In His Own Words*, trans. Jacob Phillips (London: Bloomsbury, 2016), 11.

76. Pope Benedict XVI, *Last Testament*, 11.

77. Katy Butler, *Knocking on Heaven's Door: The Path to a Better Way of Death* (New York: Scribner, 2013), 213.

78. For discussion see Romanus Cessario, OP, *The Virtues, or the Examined Life* (London: Continuum, 2002), ch. 2; and Hütter, *Dust Bound for Heaven*, ch. 8: "'In Hope He Believed against Hope'—The Unity of Faith and Hope in Paul, Thomas, and Benedict XVI." See also the treatment of the virtue of hope in Vogt's *Patience, Compassion, Hope.* Vogt sums up his perspective, with which I agree: "Christian hope is rooted deeply in an abiding faithfulness in God. This faith steers the Christian away from despair by affirming that God's love is more powerful than death. This faith also moves the Christian away from a facile or 'cheap' hope by linking God's promises of eternal life to a simultaneous challenge to conversion. Christian hope does not promise the continuation of the status quo after death, but rather offers a *new* life with God at its center" (78).

79. For the images present in contemporary popular culture, and for the impact of religious pluralism upon contemporary views, see also Greg Garrett, *Entertaining Judgment: The Afterlife in Popular Imagination* (Oxford: Oxford University Press, 2015); Lisa Miller, *The Visions of Heaven: A Journey through the Afterlife* (New York: TIME, 2014); Miller, *Heaven: Our Enduring Fascination with the Afterlife* (New York: HarperCollins, 2010). See also Jeffrey Burton Russell, *A History of Heaven: The Singing Silence* (Princeton: Princeton University Press, 1997); and Russell, *Paradise Mislaid: How We Lost Heaven—and How We Can Regain It* (Oxford: Oxford Univer-

sity Press, 2006)—the last book being a broader response to secular despisers of Christian doctrine.

80. Griffiths, *Decreation*, 166–67. On the importance of thinking of the things of this world in terms of "gift" (grounded in the Holy Spirit, who is divine Gift in the Trinity), see Antonio López, *Gift and the Unity of Being* (Eugene, OR: Cascade, 2014).

81. Verhey, *Christian Art of Dying*, 120, 122.

82. See, for example, Augustine, *On Free Choice of the Will*, trans. Thomas Williams (Indianapolis: Hackett, 1993), 3.6–8, pp. 83–87.

83. For an insightful critique of the view that hoping for everlasting life is egotistical, responding in part to Krister Stendahl's contention (from a Christian perspective) that it is egotistical, see Dale C. Allison Jr., *Night Comes: Death, Imagination, and the Last Things* (Grand Rapids: Eerdmans, 2016), 1–2 and 73–83, citing Stendahl's "Immortality Is Too Much and Too Little," in *End of Life*, ed. J. D. Roslansky (Amsterdam: North-Holland, 1973). For another Christian view similar to Stendahl's, see Timothy P. Jackson, *Love Disconsoled: Meditations on Christian Charity* (Cambridge: Cambridge University Press, 1999). Indebted to Ludwig Wittgenstein and Simone Weil (but much less mystically attuned than either of them), D. Z. Phillips argues that the "religious conception of dying to the self" forms a stark contrast with "the desire for compensation" that, in his view, pertains to any doctrine of an actual, existentially real life after death (*Death and Immortality* [London: Macmillan, 1970], 53). For Phillips, it is enough to know that "the soul which is rooted in the mortal is the soul where the ego is dominant in the way which Simone Weil describes in such penetrating detail in her works. The immortality of the soul by contrast refers to a person's relation to the self-effacement and love of others involved in dying to self. Death is overcome in that dying to the self is the meaning of the believer's life" (54). In other words, we have "immortality" if at the end of our lives we achieve dying to self, so that dying to self accurately describes our lives—even though, existentially speaking, death means that we never again exist.

Phillips accomplishes a similar inversion with regard to what it means to speak of the existence of God: "In learning by contemplation, attention, renunciation, what forgiving, thanking, loving, etc. mean in these contexts, the believer is participating in the reality of God; *this is what we mean by God's reality.* This reality is independent of any given believer, but its independence is not the independence of a separate biography. It is independent of the believer in that the believer measures his life against it" (55). On this view, existentially speaking, God does not have distinct existence of any kind. Phillips has underestimated the philosophical case for God's existence, and he has also instantiated a deeply hopeless (though nobly Stoic) form of dying to self, in large part because of his misidentifying desire for ongoing interpersonal communion (love) as an egotistical desire. For a better approach, see Louis Roy, OP, *Self-Actualization and the Radical Gospel* (Collegeville, MN: Liturgical Press, 2002). See also the main concern of Francesca Aran Murphy, *God Is Not a Story: Realism Revisited* (Oxford: Oxford University Press, 2007).

84. Pope Benedict XVI, *Spe Salvi*, §31.
85. Pope Benedict XVI, *Spe Salvi*, §31.
86. Mother Teresa, letter to Sr. Joan McNamara, quoted in Murray, *Scars*, 81.

Notes to Chapter 3

1. Quotations in the first two paragraphs are from *Gaudium et Spes*, in *The Conciliar and Post Conciliar Documents*, vol. 1 of *Vatican Council II*, ed. Austin Flannery, OP, rev. ed. (Northport, NY: Costello, 1996), 903–1001.

2. Raymond Tallis, *The Black Mirror: Looking at Life through Death* (New Haven: Yale University Press, 2015), 339.

3. For this view, see also Elisabeth Kübler-Ross, *Death: The Final Stage of Growth* (New York: Simon & Schuster, 1986). Indebted to his grandfather, the Mennonite theologian Johann Christoph Arnold adopts this perspective, despite his Christian commitments: "my grandfather, writer Eberhard Arnold, says that our flesh, blood, and bones are not, in the truest and deepest sense, our real selves. Being mortal, they die. Meanwhile the real seat of our being, the soul, passes from mortality into immortality, and from time into timelessness. It returns from the body it was breathed into back to its author, God. That is why, my grandfather says, the human soul longs perpetually for God, and why, instead of merely dying, we are 'called into eternity' and reunited with him" (*Be Not Afraid: Overcoming the Fear of Death* [Farmington, PA: Plough, 2002], 189).

This view of dying strikes me as not adequate to the terrible reality of the separation of body and soul. Most importantly, for Christians our "real self" is not our soul, but rather is the body-soul composite that God has created us to be. In a welcome fashion, Arnold adds, "For those of us who call ourselves Christians, it is impossible to contemplate such a future without recalling the resurrection of Jesus, the 'Son of Man,' and the price he paid for it. . . . His death was not just an isolated historical event, but (as he himself indicated by saying, 'Follow me') the unavoidable gateway through which each of us must pass if we want to share everlasting life with him" (189). For further examples of viewing dying as a good in itself, see Robert E. Neale, *The Art of Dying* (repr., New York: Harper & Row, 1977); Roger Troisfontaines, SJ, *I Do Not Die*, trans. Francis E. Albert (New York: Desclée, 1963); Maggie Callanan and Patricia Kelley, *Final Gifts: Understanding the Special Awareness, Needs, and Communications of the Dying* (New York: Bantam, 1993); Daniel R. Tobin, *Peaceful Dying* (Reading, MA: Perseus, 1999). Christopher P. Vogt rightly warns that "the vision of hope proposed by Kübler-Ross and others today is heavily dependent upon the *denial* of the negativity of death. Even at an experiential or existential level, denial cannot be ultimately satisfying" (*Patience, Compassion, Hope, and the Christian Art of Dying Well* [Lanham, MD: Rowman & Littlefield, 2004], 79–80). For the similar point that dying cannot be treated simply as a natural part of living, see Helmut Thielicke, *Death and Life*, trans.

Edward H. Schroeder (Philadelphia: Fortress, 1970), 14; Bartholomew J. Collopy, SJ, "Theology and the Darkness of Death," *Theological Studies* 39 (1978): 22–54. Collopy offers an excellent critique of Kübler-Ross, Neale, and Troisfontaines. Regarding the view that dying "is simply being set free for what is authentic," Joseph Ratzinger observes critically: "Not infrequently over the course of history, this image of death as friend, the idealistic image of death, has been confused with the Christian image of death. . . . Man is 'authentic,' is himself, precisely in the body" (*Dogma and Preaching: Applying Christian Doctrine to Daily Life*, trans. Michael J. Miller and Matthew J. O'Connell [San Francisco: Ignatius, 2011], 245).

4. Kathleen Dowling Singh, *The Grace in Dying: How We Are Transformed Spiritually as We Die* (New York: HarperCollins, 1998), 22.

5. David Kuhl, *What Dying People Want: Practical Wisdom for the End of Life* (New York: PublicAffairs, 2002), 271.

6. Carol Zaleski, *The Life of the World to Come: Near-Death Experience and Christian Hope* (New York: Oxford University Press, 1996), 36–37. She adds, "Studies conducted by Andrew M. Greeley and his colleagues at the National Opinion Research Center and the International Social Survey Program indicate that people (indeed, the overwhelming majority of those surveyed) believe in life after death above all because they believe that they are loved" (37). Interestingly, she reports, "A similar transformation has taken place with respect to the classical Indian doctrine of *saṃsāra* (rebirth). Especially in its recent imported forms, the doctrine of rebirth has come to be seen as the consoling promise of many lifetimes. In its classical forms, however, it described a sorrowful state of human bondage within which, impelled by one's own karma, one must undergo an endless series of judgment days" (37).

7. Allen Verhey, *The Christian Art of Dying: Learning from Jesus* (Grand Rapids: Eerdmans, 2011), 65. As Verhey suggests, a "generic spirituality" encourages the notion that our dying is solely about "an internal and individual search for meaning," and it also tempts us (including in its Christian forms) to "domesticate the Mystery, rendering the inscrutable not only scrutable but serviceable to [our] own projects" (65).

8. Singh, *Grace in Dying*, 1. (Hereafter in this section, page references from this work will be given in parentheses in the text.) See also Kenneth Kramer's conclusion that "the world's sacred traditions teach that the person who is able to appropriate death from the future into life, who is able to die anticipationally and spiritually, and thereby to be reborn or awakened, is able to face death with a transformed attitude" (*The Sacred Art of Dying: How World Religions Understand Death* [Mahwah, NJ: Paulist, 1988], 200).

9. Somewhat similarly, in *The Tibetan Book of the Dead*—which Singh counts among her most prominent sources—we find the promise that as soon as the dying person stops breathing, "a naked awareness will arise, not extraneous, but radiant, empty and without horizon"—and the dead person should "recognise this brilliant essence of your own conscious awareness to be the buddha" (*The Tibetan Book of the Dead*, trans. Gyurme Dorje, ed. Graham Coleman with Thupten Jinpa [London: Penguin,

2005], 228, 231). The book calls upon caregivers to urge the dying person to "meditate on the generation of loving kindness, compassion and an altruistic intention," and the book also urges that the dead (but still conscious) person must not "be attached to this life" or "cling to this life" and must "abandon pride" (230, 235, 241) as part of the overcoming of self (and of the cycle of reincarnation). For a succinct discussion of *The Tibetan Book of the Dead* and the tradition from which it arises, see Elisabeth Benard, "The Tibetan Tantric View of Death and Afterlife," in *Death and Afterlife: Perspectives of World Religions*, ed. Hiroshi Obayashi (New York: Praeger, 1992), 169–80.

10. Her experience is that "by and large, people die in solemnity, peace, and transformed consciousness, radiating energy that can only be described as spiritual" (3). Citing William James and Mircea Eliade, along with *The Tibetan Book of the Dead*, Buddhist viewpoints, Thomas Moore, and others, Singh describes the way in which the spiritual energy that she has witnessed indicates the connecting of our earthly consciousness with higher spiritual dimensions.

11. For stories (rooted in hospice ministry) about what they term "Nearing Death Awareness," see Maggie Callahan and Patricia Kelley, *Final Gifts: Understanding the Special Awareness, Needs, and Communications of the Dying* (New York: Bantam, 1993). Their stories describe dying persons turning outward in reconciliation and love because they know that they are about to die; the value of dying at home is also a recurrent theme. Joel H. Baron and Sara Paasche-Orlow observe that in the Jewish tradition, "caring for a person at the time of death and for the body after death is considered among the greatest acts of kindness" (*Deathbed Wisdom of the Hasidic Masters: The Book of Departure and Caring for People at the End of Life*, trans. and annotated by Joel H. Baron and Sara Paasche-Orlow [Woodstock, VT: Jewish Lights, 2016], 64).

12. It is unclear to me whether for Singh, as for process theology influenced by Alfred North Whitehead, it is accurate to say that (in the words of the Catholic process theologian Robert L. Kinast) "God receives the life experience of each person as a real contribution to God's becoming," so that "the final outcome or satisfaction [accomplished at death] can then be a real contribution to the whole, to the all-inclusive experience of God's becoming. The discrete events arise out of and contribute back to the whole. For the term of their own becoming, they are radically atomistic, but precisely in this phase of their becoming their experience is isolated. Through perishing, an entity satisfies its urge toward definiteness and becomes valuable for the whole" (*When a Person Dies: Pastoral Theology in Death Experiences* [New York: Crossroad, 1984], 114). Certainly Singh agrees with this emphasis upon the movement from the "atomistic" to the all-inclusive "whole."

13. For the origins of the "life review" as a therapeutic tool, see Robert Butler, "The Life Review: An Interpretation of Reminiscence in the Aged," *Psychiatry* 26 (1963): 65–76. See also Donald Heinz's observation: "It may be that in a decadent consumer society, it will be the life of Elizabeth Taylor or Paul Newman or Madonna that is more arresting than our own. Or perhaps, in our final days, we will as our last request desire to know how the plots of our favorite soap operas are going to turn out.

If the concept of life review is to be redeemed as the first act of a last career, we will have to rescue it from the trivialities that have accrued to it. Life review is best done over time, grieving or rejoicing as scenes from the past insistently present themselves or are carefully retrieved. We recover ourselves through memory, retrace how we have come to our present stature, fill in the history that has poured into the mold our present self. . . . We look with some wonder, some disappointment, some gratitude at the eddies of our existence, especially as we near the mouth of the river and our journey out to sea" (*The Last Passage: Recovering a Death of Our Own* [Oxford: Oxford University Press, 1999], 96).

14. Cf. 265 and elsewhere. Singh proclaims: "Everything that had obscured the nondual nature of Spirit-as-Spirit has been dissolved, dissipated, relaxed—releasing us into vastness. In splendor and in peace, we remerge with the luminous Ground of Being from which we had once emerged" (267). Describing the death of her Catholic uncle in the early 1990s, Singh shows awareness of Christianity. Regarding self-surrender and detachment, she states: "This is called, in Buddhist tradition, dying to the 'I.' In the Christian tradition, this is known as 'living in the Mystical Body of Christ'" (278). She goes on to say: "The Noble Eightfold Path is the Buddhist formulation of the Jewish concept of *kiddush hashem*, daily living as sanctification of the Divine Name, the 'Work of God.' It is the Buddhist formulation of the Christian concept of living in, living the, Presence of God" (279).

15. By contrast, Ratzinger points out that generally "death is experienced by man, not as a friend, but as a foe," simply because of death's "sheer dreadfulness," which even Jesus Christ and the saints have not avoided (*Dogma and Preaching*, 246). Ratzinger adds quite rightly, "The inherent fragility of the idealistic interpretation of death is one decisive reason why in the modern era it has been increasingly displaced by the materialistic explanation of death. . . . This explanation rules out the spiritual component and maintains that in death an organism ceases to be, just as it once began to be" (247). The Christian approach to death is that of neither idealism nor materialism.

16. Kuhl, *What Dying People Want*, xviii. (Hereafter in this section, page references from this work will be given in parentheses in the text.) For true stories of persons whose dying involved spiritual growth for themselves and for their families and friends, see Arnold, *Be Not Afraid*.

17. See also Edmund D. Pellegrino, "Euthanasia and Assisted Suicide," in *Dignity and Dying: A Christian Appraisal*, ed. John F. Kilner, Arlene B. Miller, and Edmund D. Pellegrino (Grand Rapids: Eerdmans, 1996), 105–19. Already in 1996, Pellegrino points to "the very significant advances made in pain control in recent years" (108). Pellegrino's Christian concerns about euthanasia are worth citing in response to the vision of autonomy promoted by euthanasia advocates: "For the Christian, this is a distorted sense of freedom that denies life as a gift of God over which we have been given stewardship as with other good things. This kind of freedom violates the truth of God's creative act and providential purpose for each individual's life. . . . Most of all, the secularized notion of freedom fosters a radical moral solipsism, a supreme act of pride, that

denies that our lives, however difficult, may be instruments in God's hands to shape the lives of those among whom we reside. . . . Christians are called upon to relieve pain and suffering. But, because suffering has meaning, even though a mysterious one, Christians can offer something more than extinction to the suffering person" (109–10, 112).

18. As Paul Meyendorff observes, "Sick persons are often reduced to the status of a dependent child. They begin to doubt that they can contribute to the lives of others, particularly to those to whom they were close before. This often leads to guilt, because we live in a society where productivity has become the measure of human worth. . . . The one who falls sick is thus depersonalized" (*The Anointing of the Sick* [Crestwood, NY: St. Vladimir's Seminary Press, 2009], 75). Kuhl's recommendations aim to show the dying person that there are still important things to be done.

19. Vogt notes that whereas earlier *ars moriendi* texts often focused on physical pain, "for contemporary readers . . . the main difficulty to be endured in dying is no longer pain so much as vulnerability or a sense of meaninglessness" (*Patience, Compassion, Hope,* 132)—due to the success, at least in relatively wealthy areas of the world, of pain management through opiates.

20. Here the danger consists in imagining that we ourselves can determine the meaning of our lives, as though we could know such a thing, and as though whatever meaning that we determined could be an enduring (and therefore objectively true) one. The psychoanalyst Ignace Lepp proposes, "Since the meaning of life, and therefore of death, depends on man's free choice, it follows that he who is not capable of such a choice cannot give meaning to either his life or his death. Thus we are forced to conclude that only those who are capable of freedom can give meaning to their life and death. As for others, we must admit that we cannot, at least in the present state of our knowledge, understand the meaning of their life or death. Perhaps we are to see them as inevitable lapses in the process of creative evolution" (*Death and Its Mysteries,* trans. Bernard Murchland [New York: Macmillan, 1968], 147). It seems that in this case it is the overarching process of evolution, not individual human freedom, that truly assigns whatever "meaning" a human being might have—which is absurd given that humans (by contrast to the evolutionary process) enjoy an interpersonal communion of knowing and loving. Lepp asserts, "For the man who uses his life well, death seems spontaneously, without the least pretense, to come not as the destruction, but as the fulfillment of life" (146). How can annihilation (reabsorption into the cosmic evolutionary process) be the "fulfillment" of interpersonal communion?

21. Heinz observes similarly: "Dealing with guilt may be an inevitable and long-overdue dimension of life review. Postponed intentions, buried animosities, unfinished business, or moral turpitude may lie in wait. . . . No wonder, then, that some will seek to mythicize their pasts rather than struggle to make sense of them. Instead of laboring for insight or taking heavy responsibility, they embrace self-justification as their only task. A finally authentic self is a goal, but not a guaranteed attainment" (*Last Passage,* 98, 101).

22. See also Megory Anderson's heartbreaking account of a dying eleven-year-old girl's guilt and fear of God "find[ing] out what I've done" (*Sacred Dying: Creating*

Rituals for Embracing the End of Life [New York: Marlowe, 2004], 101). The girl finds emotional/spiritual relief in confessing to her family members the times that, in her view, she acted badly toward them. Mortified by her confession, her family members held her and prayed for her, and Anderson—who was present as a spiritual counselor—concluded the group prayer by stating, "God wants us all to know how much we are loved. We can be sure that God is waiting for Katy right now, with open arms" (103). Anderson's positive conclusion (refusing to criticize the girl's desire for forgiveness) strikes me as correct: "Sometime during that night, Katy died. There were many tears, but the reconciliation she experienced with her family and most of all, with God, led her peacefully through that journey" (104). Anderson reports more broadly, "Time after time I see people holding on to things done and things left undone. I see fear and guilt overwhelm the dying person to the point where she cannot let go and die a peaceful death. Most of the guilt has to do with relationships with loved ones. Most of the fear has to do with God. With the help of rituals and various confessional opportunities or prayers, we may enable the dying person to experience freedom from the internal burdens. However, to let go of the emotional pain, he must also experience reconciliation with loved ones and with God" (104).

Anderson, an Episcopalian, tries to encourage dying persons from every religious tradition in the terms of their own tradition. I appreciate the intention of this approach even though I hold that the particular fulfillment of the dying person's needs brought by Jesus Christ should be recognized and, when appropriate, offered. Anderson comments somewhat agnostically (though it seems clear that she believes in God), "No one can tell us what is on the other side of death, but those of us here left to care for the dying can reassure the dying person and make her feel secure at this time. In all the sacred traditions there are many wonderful words from holy texts and scriptures that will help comfort the person dying. We read of God's mercy and love in the Qur'an or of God's presence in the Hebrew Bible or the assurance in the Christian Gospels that Jesus will not leave us. The Hindu words from the Bhagavad Gita are beautiful and reassuring, and *The Tibetan Book of the Dead* helps a person cross over into death" (112; cf. 131).

23. Anderson remarks poignantly, "I have also seen loved ones refuse to discuss anything to do with the past. They cannot handle the feelings and emotions buried in their family history. If the person dying wants to bring up concerns within the family, I've seen children or spouses literally walk away from the bed and out of the room" (*Sacred Dying*, 113).

24. See also Anderson, *Sacred Dying*, 121–23.

25. Somewhat like Singh, however, Heinz rightly warns, "Untranscended ego-preoccupation can simply become the narcissism of old age: the withering of any taste for the other or for larger concerns" (*Last Passage*, 101).

26. From a different vantage point, Heinz comments that, for many modern persons, "Judgment is out of the question, and mercy is unnecessary. . . . It is not easy to restore the moral component of death and dying to public discussion and cultural attention. Modern understandings of death focus on technical, physical, and psycholog-

ical aspects and ignore the moral component—the dimension of human responsibility in relationships. As life draws to a close only an immature person would want to ignore questions about the moral life one has led—responses one has made to relations and situations, accountability for interaction, and solidarity with the human community" (*Last Passage*, 102). Kuhl's study helpfully shows that most dying people still want to engage these questions. Heinz adds, "Once deathbed penance was a ritual prescription," and he indicates that this was a good idea (102).

27. See also Anderson, *Sacred Dying*, 115. From a historical perspective, Philippe Ariès argues that "by the beginning of the nineteenth century . . . belief in hell had disappeared. It was no longer conceivable that the dear departed could run such a risk. At most, among Catholics, there still existed a method of purification: time in purgatory, shortened by the pious solicitude of survivors. No sense of guilt, no fear of the beyond remained to counteract the fascination of death, transformed into the highest beauty. . . . The next world becomes the scene of the reunion of those whom death has separated but who have never accepted this separation" (*The Hour of Our Death*, trans. Helen Weaver [New York: Knopf, 1981], 611). Kuhl's reference to "without judgment" may indicate such a lack of belief in the possibility of hell, and indeed most modern Christians do not believe that they or their loved ones will be condemned to hell. Kuhl may also be signaling the graciousness of God's gift of reconciliation.

28. N. T. Wright observes, "In Second Temple Judaism, resurrection is important but not that important. Lots of lengthy works never mention the question, let alone this answer. It is still difficult to be sure what the Dead Sea Scrolls thought on the topic. But in early Christianity, resurrection has moved from the circumference to the center. You can't imagine Paul's thought without it. You shouldn't imagine John's thought without it, though some have tried. Take away the stories of Jesus's birth, and all you lose is four chapters of the Gospels. Take away the resurrection and you lose the entire New Testament" ("Can a Scientist Believe in the Resurrection?," in *Surprised by Scripture: Engaging Contemporary Issues* [New York: HarperCollins, 2014], 47). See also Wright, *The Resurrection of the Son of God* (Minneapolis: Fortress, 2003). After making a multilayered case for the historical plausibility of Christ's resurrection, Wright gladly grants that "although the historical arguments for Jesus's bodily resurrection are truly strong, we must never suppose that they will do more than bring people to the questions faced by Thomas and Peter, the questions of faith and love. We cannot use a supposedly objective historical epistemology as the ultimate ground for the truth of Easter" ("Can a Scientist Believe," 63). Instead, Wright holds that "love is the deepest mode of knowing, because it is love that, while completely engaging with reality other than itself, affirms and celebrates that other-than-self reality" (63). Here he draws upon the thought of Bernard Lonergan, SJ.

29. On "implicit" faith in Christ, see my *Christ's Fulfillment of Torah and Temple: Salvation according to Thomas Aquinas* (Notre Dame: University of Notre Dame Press, 2002), 23–24, 92–93.

30. Singh, *Grace in Dying*, 201–2.

31. Kuhl, *What Dying People Want*, 270.

32. N. T. Wright, *Small Faith, Great God: Biblical Faith for Today's Christians*, 2nd ed. (Downers Grove, IL: IVP Books, 2010), 155.

33. David Kessler, *Needs of the Dying* (New York: HarperCollins, 2000), xxii. See also the section on "For Those Who Wish to Help People Dying Alone," in Anderson, *Sacred Dying*, 200–203.

34. Mother Teresa, *Total Surrender*, ed. Br. Angelo Devananda (Ann Arbor: Servant, 1985), 41.

35. Mother Teresa, *Total Surrender*, 40.

Notes to Chapter 4

1. Thomas Aquinas, *Summa theologica* III, q. 85, a. 2, ad 1, trans. Fathers of the English Dominican Province (Westminster, MD: Christian Classics, 1981). The novelist Walker Percy warned repeatedly against the cultural loss of a sense of personal sin, and it is worth quoting here the Orthodox ethicist Vigen Guroian's commendation of Percy's perspective in his last novel, *The Thanatos Syndrome*, in which the character of Fr. Simon Smith presides over a church community for which the killing of the unwanted has become the norm: "Looking out over those parishioners as he preaches a sermon at the close of the novel, Fr. Smith is halted by their complacency and their inability to comprehend their complicity in the evil surrounding them. 'I don't see any sinners here,' he says. 'Everyone looks justified. No guilt here! . . . Not a guilty face here.' These wry words belie the reason Fr. Smith climbed the fire tower in the first place. At least one of his parishioners sees through the irony, however: 'For God's sake. Like Jonah, I mean, really. Has it ever occurred to anybody that he might be up there for a much simpler, more obvious reason? . . . He could be doing vicarious penance for the awful state of the world.' His parishioners view Fr. Smith as anything from a hopeless eccentric to a dangerous lunatic" (Guroian, *Life's Living toward Dying: A Theological and Medical-Ethical Study* [Grand Rapids: Eerdmans, 1996], xiv–xv; citing Percy, *The Thanatos Syndrome* [New York: Farrar, Straus and Giroux, 1987], 112–13, 360–61).

2. *Summa theologica* III, q. 85, a. 3.

3. *Summa theologica* III, q. 85, a. 4, *sed contra*.

4. See Jörgen Vijgen, "St. Thomas Aquinas and the Virtuousness of Penance: On the Importance of Aristotle for Catholic Theology," *Nova et Vetera* 13 (2015): 601–16; Maria C. Morrow, "Reconnecting Sacrament and Virtue: Penance in Thomas's *Summa theologiae*," *New Blackfriars* 91 (2010): 304–20. Vijgen notes that the Greco-Roman philosophers tended to present penance as merely an emotion rather than a virtue (or habit of the soul). He points to "the saying of the Presocratic philosopher Democritus: 'Penance (*metameleia*) over shameful deeds is one's own salvation in life (*biou soteria*).'" What Democritus is saying here, however, is merely that the emotion, the pathos of *metameleia*, is not without significance for the moral life: it prevents a person from exhibiting a moral apathy regarding

his past and from making the same mistakes in the future. The value of retrospective shame at one's misdeeds lies merely in the fact that it is a prerequisite for progress" (603; citing *Die Fragmente der Vorsokratiker*, ed. Walther Kranz, 6th ed. [Berlin: Weidmann, 1952], 55A43–84). As Vijgen points out, the key element in these philosophical approaches is that penance "remain[s] merely an emotion that stands in the way of a morally good life," and that must "be overcome" (604). Aristotle, too, treats penance as "more like a passion than a habit," and therefore not a virtue (605). Even William of Auxere and Albert the Great hold that "in the proper sense of the word, penance is not a virtue" (610). For Aquinas, Vijgen explains, penance is a virtue that "is not about canceling what one has done, but about freely and actively accepting what one has done and all its consequences and being willing to make amends" (613).

5. Christopher P. Vogt, *Patience, Compassion, Hope, and the Christian Art of Dying Well* (Lanham, MD: Rowman & Littlefield, 2004), 99. Vogt goes on to note, quite importantly, "Many interpreters also read it [Luke's passion narrative] as an attempt to locate Jesus within the Israelite tradition of the martyr—one who suffers innocently for his or her religious convictions and who dies a model of patience and forgiveness. Parallels between Luke's passion narrative and writings about the martyrs of Israel exist at both a linguistic and a thematic level" (100). Vogt here draws upon Brian E. Beck, "*Imitatio Christi* and the Lucan Passion Narrative," in *Suffering and Martyrdom in the New Testament*, ed. William Horbury and Brian McNeil (Cambridge: Cambridge University Press, 1981), 28–47; and Raymond E. Brown, SS, *The Death of the Messiah: From Gethsemane to the Grave* (New York: Doubleday, 1994), 187–88.

For contemporary martyrs, see Robert Royal, *The Catholic Martyrs of the Twentieth Century: A Comprehensive World History* (New York: Crossroad, 2000); Charles E. Moore and Timothy Keiderling, eds., *Bearing Witness: Stories of Martyrdom and Costly Discipleship* (Walden, NY: Plough, 2016). In his encyclical *Ut Unum Sint* (1995), Pope John Paul II states: "In a theocentric vision, we Christians already have a common *martyrology*. This also includes the martyrs of our own century, more numerous than one might think, and it shows how, at a profound level, God preserves communion among the baptized in the supreme demand of faith, manifested in the sacrifice of life itself" (§84, in *The Encyclicals of John Paul II*, ed. J. Michael Miller, CSB [Huntington, IN: Our Sunday Visitor, 2001], 822). Although most Christians do not die as martyrs, one of my purposes in the present chapter is to suggest that the martyrs teach us how to die—not as self-righteous people who stand over against their murderers, but as members of Christ's penitent people who die bearing witness to Christ's mercy and love and to our (and their own) need for Christ's mercy.

6. Craig S. Keener remarks that "Jewish thought included categories of corporate personality foreign to modern Western individualism. Thus Jewish people confessed the sins of their ancestors and pleaded that God not hold these against them. They recognized that they could suffer for the sins of their own ancestors and could seek atonement for their ancestors' sins as well as their own" (*Acts: An Exegetical Commentary*, 4 vols. [Grand Rapids: Baker Academic, 2012–15], 2:1426). For a survey of

literature discussing "corporate personality" in ancient Israel, see Joseph C. Atkinson, *Biblical and Theological Foundations of the Family: The Domestic Church* (Washington, DC: Catholic University of America Press, 2014), 161–92. Admittedly, N. T. Wright issues a salutary caution (though not refutation) here: "Earlier sweeping proposals on this subject [corporate personality] have retreated in the face of sharp critique, though that may simply mean that the theories were unworkable, not that there was no data to be explained" (*Paul and the Faithfulness of God*, book 2, parts 3 and 4 [Minneapolis: Fortress, 2013], 827).

7. Karen D. Scheib, "'Make Love Your Aim': Ecclesial Practices of Care at the End of Life," in *Living Well and Dying Faithfully: Christian Practices for End-of-Life Care*, ed. John Swinton and Richard Payne (Grand Rapids: Eerdmans, 2009), 43.

8. David A. Lambert "identifies, among ancients and moderns, a practice of reading 'repentance' into the Bible," which he calls "the 'penitential lens'" (*How Repentance Became Biblical: Judaism, Christianity, and the Interpretation of Scripture* [Oxford: Oxford University Press, 2016], 3). He argues that the Hebrew Bible does not have a concept of "repentance," which in his view enters into the Jewish worldview only in late Second Temple writings (due to Hellenistic influence) and "in the writings of rabbinic Judaism and early Christianity" (187). While Lambert finds repentance throughout the New Testament (although he does not discuss Acts 6–7), he argues that we should interpret the prophets not as calling for repentance but as proclaiming divine power (and their own power). He states that "we need to look again at the question of the efficacy of prophetic utterances and to recognize the ways in which the prophets are effective agents, interested parties, in the running conflict between a people and their deity. Part of the issue at stake has to do with the representation of the deity, taking seriously its anthropopathism. As portrayed by the prophets, divine anger, as a mode of rectification, aims at the destruction, not the edification, of its object. Rebellion against the deity requires a reactivation of divine power through acts of mastery. As a discourse, prophetic speech attaches the impotence imposed upon the nation by events to the power of their deity, affirming his potency and justifying his actions by developing an account of collective guilt" (117). I think that Lambert, while insightful in his reading of certain texts, offers a deeply reductive account of prophetic discourse and of the relationship between Israel and YHWH.

9. Amy Plantinga Pauw, "Dying Well," in *Practicing Our Faith: A Way of Life for a Searching People*, ed. Dorothy C. Bass (San Francisco: Jossey-Bass, 1997), 173.

10. Richard Hays argues that for Hebrews, the new covenant in Christ is not the negation of Israel but the fulfillment of Israel; in other words, Hebrews in its original context is an instance of Jewish eschatology, not an instance of anti-Judaism. See Richard B. Hays, "'Here We Have No Lasting City': New Covenantalism in Hebrews," in *The Epistle to the Hebrews and Christian Theology*, ed. Richard Bauckham, Daniel R. Driver, Trevor A. Hart, and Nathan MacDonald (Grand Rapids: Eerdmans, 2009), 151–73. For Hebrews as an exemplar of a Jewish-Christian text prior to the firm division between "Christianity" and "Judaism," see Pamela Eisenbaum, "Locating Hebrews within the

Literary Landscape of Christian Origins," in *Hebrews: Contemporary Methods—New Insights*, ed. Gabriella Gelardini (Leiden: Brill, 2005), 213–37. See also George H. Guthrie, "Hebrews' Use of the Old Testament: Recent Trends in Research," *Currents in Biblical Research* 1 (2003): 271–94.

11. See also such texts as Pss. 78, 105, and 106.

12. Joseph Blenkinsopp suggests that we read Ezek. 20 in light of Israel's "increasing need to seek explanation of the current crisis in the past" (*Ezekiel* [Louisville: John Knox, 1990], 86). He dates Ezek. 20 to 591 BCE, a few years prior to the Babylonian siege of Jerusalem in 588 and the Babylonian exile in 586. The basic idea of Ezek. 20, according to Blenkinsopp, is that the judgments of God against his people's infidelities have finally reached the boiling point, so that the infidelity of the present generation will unleash the long-deserved punishment of exile. Blenkinsopp states, "Ezekiel is presenting present and future disasters as the climax of a history of estrangement but a climax that also entails an unanticipated new beginning (vs. 33–44). And this remains true even if, as seems plausible, much of this last section was added after the judgment had become unmistakably clear with the Babylonian conquest and ensuing exile" (87).

13. For the point to which Ezekiel is responding, see Exod. 34:7, where the Lord describes himself as "visiting the iniquity of the parents upon the children and the children's children, to the third and the fourth generations." See also the contrary legal teaching in Deut. 24:16: "Parents shall not be put to death for their children, nor shall children be put to death for their parents; only for their own crimes may persons be put to death." Blenkinsopp comments, "Ezekiel's teaching on moral accountability in chapter 18 served to forestall an objection arising out of his theology of history. By choosing freely to replicate the conduct of their forebears, they, unlike the son who sees the sins of his father yet does not do likewise (18:14), place themselves within that historical pattern and so perpetuate it" (*Ezekiel*, 87).

14. Here Blenkinsopp reflects upon what "life" entails: "This assurance of life, in the context, means rather more than a promise of survival in the coming holocaust (which would then demand a date before the fall of Jerusalem). It also implies rather less than eternal life in the usual sense of postmortem existence—though that dimension cannot be absolutely excluded at least at the implicit level. Life here has the broader and less precise connotation of association with God, some sense and intimation of which is available for the person who desires it in the act of worship. Here . . . a reading of those psalms which speak of the divine presence as life-giving and joy-conferring would be appropriate. The death which is the absence of that association is the lot of the son who chooses evil" (*Ezekiel*, 83–84).

15. See, for example, David Noel Freedman, with Jeffrey C. Geoghegan and Michael M. Homan, *The Nine Commandments: Uncovering the Hidden Pattern of Crime and Punishment in the Hebrew Bible*, ed. Astrid B. Beck (New York: Doubleday, 2000). For the view that Ezekiel presents an antiteleological view of history, see Lyle Eslinger, "Ezekiel 20 and the Metaphor of Historical Teleology: Concepts of Biblical History," *Journal for the Study of the Old Testament* 23 (1998): 93–125.

16. Blenkinsopp notes that "Ezekiel follows priestly tradition according to which the divine name is first revealed in Egypt (Exod. 6:2–3, 28–29). This is quite different not only from other traditions about the origin of the divine name (see Gen. 4:26; Exod. 3:13–15) but from the alternative account according to which Moses had to retreat into the wilderness of Midian to encounter Yahweh" (*Ezekiel*, 88).

17. Blenkinsopp points out that "nowhere else [in the Bible] is the history of apostasy traced back to these Egyptian beginnings. Worship of Egyptian gods may have been suggested by the—for Ezekiel—baleful influence of Egypt on Judah during the last decades of its independent existence. . . . It is, nevertheless, a bold move which goes significantly beyond previous historical reinterpretations, as, for example, that of Hosea, for whom Israel's deviation began with settlement in the land and the establishment of the monarchy" (*Ezekiel*, 88).

18. With respect to God acting for the sake of his name, Blenkinsopp observes that this is a "way of expressing the intense reciprocal involvement of Israel and its God. To speak of the name in this context is to say that Israel exists not for itself but to fulfill the divine purpose in history" (*Ezekiel*, 88). Blenkinsopp also contrasts Hosea's "idyllic" portrait of the wilderness period with Ezekiel's view of it "as a time of infidelity and judgment" (89). I note that the anthropomorphic characterizations of God in Ezek. 20 are corrected elsewhere in Scripture, as well as in the theological tradition.

19. Attempting to understand this claim (or at least to understand how Ezekiel could have justified it), Blenkinsopp reasons that "the story of the 'binding of Isaac' in Genesis 22 could be read as recommending the substitution of an animal [for the Israelite firstborn], and this could be taken to imply that the practice was not unknown in early Israel" (*Ezekiel*, 89–90). See also Jon D. Levenson, *The Death and Resurrection of the Beloved Son: The Transformation of Child Sacrifice in Judaism and Christianity* (New Haven: Yale University Press, 1993). Commenting on Ezek. 20:25–26, Levenson argues that God gives bad laws as *just* punishment that the people deserved: "because the people in their rebellion refused to obey YHWH's life-promoting laws (especially those governing the Sabbath [vv 21–24]), he, in turn, saddled them with bad laws that would, nonetheless, ultimately serve his sovereign purpose. The product of his punishment is . . . *the laws themselves*" (7). Thus Levenson holds that "there is no reason to think that he [Ezekiel] regards the practice of the sacrifice of the first-born as contrary to God's will in the time for which God ordained it," since the law commanding the offering of the firstborn was "YHWH's retaliation for idolatry" without being in itself idolatrous (7). For Levenson, there was probably an "older normative tradition" according to which "YHWH once commanded the sacrifice of the first-born," in order to punish Israel for its idolatry (8). In obeying this law that YHWH commanded as a punishment of its idolatry, Israel was punished; the law served as "a means to bring about the death of those who had turned away from the means to abundant life" (8). On these grounds, Levenson advocates a literal interpretation of Exod. 22:29, "The firstborn of your sons you shall give to me."

See further the position of the Lutheran exegete Horace D. Hummel, who distinguishes God's "positive will" from his "punitive will": "The 'not good' statutes were 'independent of Yahweh's positive will' but yet were 'enclosed within the purview of his punitive will' and were indeed given by God. Impervious to positive attempts to teach them to know and recognize God (Ezek 20:5, 7, 12, 19), the people finally had to encounter God in a life-negating judgment 'so that they might know that I am Yahweh' (20:26)" (*Ezekiel 1–20* [Saint Louis: Concordia, 2005], 599). In my view, it is crucial to maintain that God is infinite goodness and innocence: God does not deliberately lead his people astray, even as an act of punishment. For a helpful discussion of biblical texts in which "God himself is the cause of apparently evil actions," including Ezek. 20:23–26 (although he focuses on other texts), see Matthew J. Ramage, *Dark Passages of the Bible: Engaging Scripture with Benedict XVI and Thomas Aquinas* (Washington, DC: Catholic University of America Press, 2013), 181–95 (quotation on 182). See also Jean-Miguel Garrigues, OP, *Dieu sans idée du mal: Méditations sur la miséricorde*, 3rd ed. (Geneva: Ad Solem, 2016).

20. Literally, these words contradict the origin of Israel from Abraham and Sarah, who were neither Amorites nor Hittites. Arguably, therefore, Ezek. 16:3 puts in the mouth of the Lord something that was not considered to be literally true—namely that Israel descended from the conquered, despised, and idolatrous Amorites and Hittites—as a way of conveying what Israel would have been like without God's covenantal election and thus also what Israel *will now become* if Israel continues to turn away from God. In accord with the genre of prophetic judgment, God's statement that Israel descended from Amorites and Hittites has a metaphorical truth. If so, then Ezek. 20:25–26 need not be read as contradicting 16:21, since the metaphorical truth is that Israel now worships a god who gives evil precepts and demands child sacrifice. The real God does precisely the opposite, just as in fact Israel descends from Abraham and Sarah. But in the prophetic judgment, God paints things as it were from Israel's perspective: if their idolatry means that they descend from Amorites and Hittites, then their god must be an idol who gives evil precepts and requires that they kill their children to appease him, since the gods of the Amorites and Hittites required child sacrifice. For the view that 20:25–26 refers to pagan laws, see Moshe Greenberg, *Ezekiel 1–20* (Garden City, NY: Doubleday, 1983), 368–70. For the position that Ezek. 20 aims to set up Ezek. 40–48 as a new law, see Corrine Patton, "'I Myself Gave Them Laws That Were Not Good': Ezekiel 20 and the Exodus Traditions," *Journal for the Study of the Old Testament* 21 (1996): 73–90.

21. See Michael Fishbane, "Sin and Judgement in the Prophecies of Ezekiel," *Interpretation* 38 (1984): 131–50.

22. Blenkinsopp sums up contemporary scholarship on this text: "Ezekiel does not rule out the possibility of resuscitation, of a reversal of the natural life-death sequence. He does not affirm it either, since belief in the postmortem survival of the individual was not part of Israelite faith at that time; even considerably later the author of Job raises it as a possible solution only to dismiss it (Job 7:9–10, 21; 14:7–12). He leaves it up to God—'Lord Yahweh, thou knowest'—who is the living God, the source

of life, he who kills and restores to life (Deut. 32:39). That death was not an insuperable obstacle to the life-bestowing power of God was also illustrated by well-known stories of restoration of the dead to life through the intercession of Elijah and Elisha (I Kings 17:17–24; II Kings 4:18–37). . . . While, therefore, Ezekiel's vision certainly deals with the restoration of Israel—as the explanation in vs. 11–14 makes abundantly clear—it would probably be mistaken to exclude systematically any hint of the postmortem destiny of the individual" (*Ezekiel*, 172–73).

23. Harold W. Attridge observes (in words that also apply to biblical Israel in the Old Testament period): "The summons to 'remember' (ἀναμιμνῄσκεσθε) is a regular feature of early Christian homiletics. Here, however, the memory is not to be of the words of scripture or of Christ, but of the experience of the community itself, its own 'former days'" (*The Epistle to the Hebrews: A Commentary on the Epistle to the Hebrews* [Minneapolis: Fortress, 1989], 298). In Heb. 11:3, it is admittedly unclear to what aspects of faith that Christians share with those who lived prior to Christ the text is referring.

24. Attridge notes that "Hebrews' understanding of faith obviously stands in continuity with Jewish tradition or, more precisely, with a certain type of Jewish tradition. This continuity is underscored by the lack of any explicit christological referent in the notion of faith" (*Hebrews*, 313). Regarding Heb. 11:3, Luke Timothy Johnson comments: "The author clearly alludes to the creation account in Genesis 1, where God creates by a word alone (see also Ps 33:6; Wis 9:1; Sir 42:15; 2 Pet 3:5; Philo, *God's Immutability* 57)" (*Hebrews: A Commentary* [Louisville: Westminster John Knox, 2006], 280). On Heb. 11:6 Attridge explains that the "articles of faith mentioned here, God's existence and providence, were widely presumed, both by pagans and by Jews, to be fundamental conditions sine qua non for a proper understanding of and hence relationship to God" (*Hebrews*, 318).

25. Against the view that Heb. 11 "seeks to denationalize Israel" or "to denationalize biblical history," see Gregory W. Lee, *Today When You Hear His Voice: Scripture, the Covenants, and the People of God* (Grand Rapids: Eerdmans, 2016), 128, 131; Matthew Thiessen, "Hebrews and the End of the Exodus," *Novum Testamentum* 49 (2007): 353–69; Thiessen, "Hebrews 12.5–13, the Wilderness Period, and Israel's Discipline," *New Testament Studies* 55 (2009): 366–79. Lee and Thiessen are responding to Pamela Michelle Eisenbaum, *The Jewish Heroes of Christian Antiquity: Hebrews 11 in Literary Context* (Atlanta: Scholars Press, 1997). Lee concludes: "Hebrews contributes two insights concerning the identity of God's people. First, there is a sharp contrast between the Old Testament heroes of faith and those who presently trust in Christ precisely because the redemptive benefits of his salvific work were not available prior to his establishment as high priest. Second, though, this point of discontinuity does not suggest a radical fissure in God's people between Old Testament Israel and the Gentile church of the New Testament. For the author of this Jewish epistle, Christ's establishment as high priest may be taken as a renewal and not an abrogation of God's covenant with the Israelites, founded now as at the beginning on a common hope for

an eternal inheritance" (*Today*, 132). For the "sharp contrast" due to the establishment of Christ as high priest, see George B. Caird, "The Exegetical Method of the Epistle to the Hebrews," *Canadian Journal of Theology* 5 (1959): 44–51; Susanne Lehne, *The New Covenant in Hebrews* (Sheffield: Sheffield Academic, 1990).

26. Attridge provides context here: "In the Hellenistic Judaism represented by Philo this understanding of the imagery of the alien is used extensively to interpret the biblical motif of the patriarchs as resident aliens" (*Hebrews*, 330).

27. Luke Johnson states with regard to Heb. 11:26, "The phrase *oneidismon tou Christou* ('reproach of the Messiah') is difficult, and almost impossible to translate adequately, but two points can confidently be made. First, in the honor-shame world of the author, *oneidismos* falls emphatically on the side of shame (see Josh 5:8; 1 Sam 17:26; Neh 5:9; Hos 12:8; Joel 2:19; Jer 6:10; 23:40; *T. Reu.* 4.7; *T. Jud.* 23.3). Second, just as the hearers were reminded that in earlier days they had been exposed to afflictions and *oneidismoi* and were partners of people who lived that way (Heb 10:33), so Moses here serves as a model of identifying with the shame of those who are being shamed" (*Hebrews*, 300).

28. As Attridge remarks, "Why these figures should be singled out is not immediately clear. Jephthah, remembered for his tragic vow, seems to be particularly inappropriate. Our author may have relied on a traditional summary of the period of the Judges at this point. Whatever his sources and rationale, the naming of these six figures serves primarily as a transition from the preceding pericope with its attention to individuals of the patriarchal and exodus periods to the generically depicted later history of Israel" (*Hebrews*, 348).

29. Attridge comments: "That some were 'stoned' . . . refers either to Zechariah, son of Jehoida, or to Jeremiah, who, according to legend, met this fate in Egypt. That some were 'sawed asunder' . . . applies primarily to Isaiah, who, again according to legend, met his end in this fashion. Only one case of 'death by the sword' . . . is recorded of an Old Testament prophet, that of the obscure Uriah. The phrase used here is, however, a common biblical expression, and that prophets were regularly persecuted and slain was a commonplace" (*Hebrews*, 350).

30. In this regard Attridge explains that for Hebrews, "perfection, which involves cleansing of conscience, sanctification, and ultimate glorification, is made possible by Christ's sacrifice. Hence the perfection of the Old Testament figures mentioned here cannot take place 'apart from us'" (*Hebrews*, 352).

31. Note that I am not trying here to show a genetic link between Ezek. 20 and Acts 7, although I assume that the author of Acts (Luke) knew Ezek. 20.

32. Thus, commenting on Acts 6:10-15, where Stephen is accused and arrested (and where the members of the Sanhedrin see "that his face was like the face of an angel" [Acts 6:15]), Luke Timothy Johnson draws a parallel to the scenes pertaining to Jesus's passion: "the succession of events leading to Stephen's speech imitates the sequence of Jesus' passion: the open confrontation, the suborning of spies, the agitation of the populace, the arrest, and the delivery to the council (6:10-12). . . . Luke has

shifted to Stephen's 'passion' elements that the other Synoptists made part of Jesus' passion: not Jesus but Stephen has 'false witnesses' stand against him and accuse him; not Jesus but Stephen has the charge of 'blasphemy' laid against him; not Jesus but Stephen is accused of speaking against the temple" (*The Acts of the Apostles* [Collegeville, MN: Liturgical Press, 1992], 112). As Johnson goes on to say, "Stephen is deliberately portrayed by Luke in terms that insistently evoke the passion and death of Jesus. As did Jesus, so does Stephen have grace and power, and works wonders and signs among the people (6:8); he enters into dispute with those who challenge him (6:9; see Luke 20:1–7), including those who are sent as spies (6:11; see Luke 20:20). He is arrested (6:12; see Luke 22:54), and brought to trial before the Sanhedrin (6:12–15; see Luke 22: 66–71). Stephen has false witnesses accuse him (6:13), an element left out of Luke's passion narrative, though found in the Synoptic parallels of Mark 14:56 and Matt 26:59. Stephen is taken out of the city to be executed (7:58) as was Jesus (23:32). At his death, there is the disposition of clothing (7:58), though not of his own as it was for Jesus (Luke 23:34). Stephen prays that his spirit be accepted (7:59) as did Jesus (Luke 23:46). Stephen asks forgiveness for his murderers (7:60) as did Jesus (23:34). Stephen is buried by pious people (8:2) as was Jesus (Luke 23:50–55). The major contrast between the death of Jesus and of his witness Stephen (apart from the mode of execution) is the fact that Jesus was portrayed as keeping silence in the face of his accusers, whereas Stephen's speech is precisely the sort of response to an accusation a sage would be expected to make (7:1–53). But even this is in fulfillment of Jesus' prophecy: 'I will give you speech and wisdom such that all those opposing you will not be able to resist or contradict' (Luke 21:15)" (143). For my purposes, the key point is that Stephen's speech is framed entirely by his dying, even if his speech can be read in other ways as well.

33. In response to scholars who argue against the historicity of Acts's account of Stephen on the grounds that "it portrays Jewish murderous behavior and hence is an example of Luke's rhetorical violence against Jewish people," Keener shows in detail that "an anti-Jewish reading of the Stephen narrative runs counter to Luke's narrative as a whole" (*Acts*, 2:1295). As Keener observes, Stephen's speech should be read within the context of Hellenistic forensic rhetoric and Jewish use of historical retrospectives: "Historical retrospectives and lists of heroes of the faith were a common literary device. . . . Moses recites God's past deliverances (Adam, Noah, Abraham, and Joseph) to encourage Israel (Jos. *Ant.* 3.87); Josephus recounts history to address his own day in a speech as well as in his writings (*War* 5.379–411). . . . Minority groups within Judaism could recount these historical retrospectives in different ways. Most such voices, whether the Qumran sectarians, or Hellenistic Jewish philosophers such as Philo, or authors of apocalypses recounting history with a view to the future, reread the biblical narratives from their own perspectives and with their own agendas" (1334). Keener remarks, with what to me seems like understatement, "Given Stephen's execution immediately after his speech, it might also be relevant that such historical retrospectives could provide exhortation in testaments, a dying father's final instructions to his successors (e.g., 1 Macc 2:51–60)" (1335). I consider it appropriate to read Stephen's speech within the

context of his dying, though admittedly I have taken this approach partly due to my interest in Christian dying.

34. Keener notes that Stephen's (or Luke's) account differs somewhat from Genesis's: "Terah died in Gen 11:32, in Haran (also in Jos. *Ant.* 1.152); then Abram's call to the promised land came explicitly in Gen 12:1–3 (also Jos. *Ant.* 1.154), but Luke approaches the chronology differently. Because the family had already started en route to Canaan when they settled in Haran (Gen 11:31), Luke reports the calling (Acts 7:2–3) not only before the migration to Canaan but also before the migration to Haran" (*Acts*, 2:1357).

35. Certainly, as Luke Johnson says, "for Luke the story of Abraham reaches its true fulfillment only now in the messianic realization of the promise" (*Acts*, 121). Johnson rightly remarks that "Luke seeks to legitimize the messianic appropriation of Torah by showing how Torah itself demanded such an appropriation" (120).

36. For background to the phrase "beautiful before God," see Luke Johnson, *Acts*, 125.

37. On this reference to Jesus, see Luke Johnson, *Acts*, 126.

38. For discussion of the connection here between Moses and Jesus, see Keener, *Acts*, 2:1401–3.

39. For Jewish condemnations of the golden calf from the same broad time period of the book of Acts, see Keener, *Acts*, 2:1407. Keener notes that Jewish sources, in criticizing the people of Israel for the golden calf, "could be quite harsh (e.g., R. Simeon ben Yohai in *Exod. Rab.* 42:7). For the sin of the golden calf, R. Eliezer ben Jacob lamented, God could justly punish Israel until the resurrection of the dead (*'Abot R. Nat.* 34A)" (1407).

40. As Keener points out, "Stephen's speech follows the LXX, which speaks not of 'Sikkuth' or 'Kiyyun' but of 'Moloch' (Μόλοχ) and 'Raiphan' ('Ραιφάν). . . . Rabbis and other ancient interpreters who had access to various readings usually selected the reading, translation, or interpretation that best fit their point. Even had Stephen known the Hebrew *Sikkun*, his use of the LXX interpretation σκηνή (tent; shared in Hebrew by CD VII) plays into his midrashic application. Israel's singular 'tent' in its wilderness wanderings (the quoted context in Amos 5:25; Acts 7:42) could be only the tabernacle, but Amos called this 'tent' (Heb. *Sikkun*) an idolatrous image (Amos 5:26; Acts 7:43). Thus, with this reading, Israel made an idol even of the holy tabernacle!" (*Acts*, 2:1410–11).

41. Keener notes here: "In the context of answering the charge that he denounces the temple (6:11–14), Stephen prepares to respond that his accusers have made an idol of it" (*Acts*, 2:1411).

42. See Keener's discussion in *Acts*, 2:1417–18.

43. Keener provides helpful context: "'Stiff-necked and uncircumcised in heart and ears' was familiar Jewish language, though not, of course, normally directed against one's judges. . . . Israelite prayers of penitence recalled the stubbornness of the ancestors in the wilderness (Neh 9:16–17). . . . Qumran scrolls condemned those walking in the 'stubbornness' of their 'hearts.' Some later rabbis claimed that Jews in the Diaspora

were stiff-necked. . . . Scripture complains about uncircumcised hearts (Lev 26:41), which made Israel's people like spiritual pagans (Jer 9:26; cf. Ezek 44:7, 9). Some later Jewish thinkers continued this emphasis; God would circumcise Israel's heart (*Jub.* 1:23); God's servants must circumcise their desire (or inclination; lit., *yetzer*) and remove what was hard (1QS V, 5); the wicked leader failed to circumcise his heart (1QpHab XI, 12–13, esp. XI, 13). Rabbi Samuel later prayed that God would circumcise the heart of his people to fear him (*b. Ber.* 29a)" (*Acts*, 2:1423–24).

44. With respect to the troubling intensification of Stephen's rhetoric, Keener notes: "Returning charges against one's accusers was standard rhetorical practice in all periods of Greek and Roman forensic rhetoric" (*Acts*, 2:1419). Stephen engages in this turning of the tables: "Had Stephen's accusers charged him with opposition to the law (Acts 6:11–14)? Stephen now returns the charge with interest (7:51–53). It was in fact his accusers who were the law's violators—spiritually uncircumcised (7:51), murderers of the prophets (7:52), and general disobeyers of the law (7:53)" (1419). Keener rightly comments that in saying that his hearers killed the prophets, "Stephen apparently essentially invites them (and certainly at least expects them) to kill him, thereby confirming his message and prophetic status" (1423). Crucially, Keener makes clear that Stephen is not simply blaming the Jewish people as though he were not a Jew. As Keener says, "Some scholars contrast later rabbis' explanation of the temple's destruction with Luke's explanation as the difference between confessing 'our sins' and pointing out 'your sins.' Although this was undoubtedly the historical trajectory that Christian polemic followed (when it moved from intra-Jewish to interreligious polemic), it overlooks the frequency of 'our fathers' in Stephen's speech. This is instead part of the polemical turn in the closing argument. '*Your* fathers' rhetorically emphasizes moral continuity among those in all generations who break God's covenant, but it does not repudiate Stephen's ethnic continuity with Israel or hope for Israel. 'Your fathers' is not negative in Acts 3:25 or 7:32 (though it is equivalent toward Acts' conclusion in 28:25), and 'our fathers' is far more common (3:13; 5:30; 13:17; 15:10; 22:3, 14; 24:14; 26:6; also at the conclusion in 28:17), including in this speech (7:11–12, 15, 19, 38–39, 44–45)" (1425).

45. Luke Johnson identifies the important place of the "glory of God" in this passage: "Three separate connections are established by Stephen's vision of the *doxa tou kyriou*: a) he is connected to the story of the people, which began with the appearance of the 'God of glory' to Abraham (Acts 7:2); Stephen is therefore a legitimate spokesperson for the people; b) *doxa* is associated with Jesus, especially with his resurrection (Luke 9:31–32; 24:26; Acts 3:13); thus, Stephen is a witness (*martys*) to the resurrection, a status explicitly affirmed by Paul in Acts 22:20; c) *doxa* is also associated with the coming of the Son of Man (Luke 9:26; 21:27), which sets up the content of Stephen's vision" (*Acts*, 139). Johnson also notes that the report of a vision during a martyr's death was common at the time, and Johnson also reflects helpfully upon why Stephen sees Jesus "standing" rather than sitting (as in Ps. 110:1 and Luke 22:69).

46. See Costantino Antonio Ziccardi, *The Relationship of Jesus and the Kingdom*

of God according to Luke-Acts (Rome: Gregorian University Press, 2008). Rather surprisingly, Stephen's claim that his hearers had killed the Messiah, just as their (and his) fathers had killed the prophets, did not cause his hearers to attack him violently. Although the charge of killing the Messiah certainly caused his hearers to become "enraged" (Acts 7:54), it was not until Stephen proclaimed that he saw "the Son of Man standing at the right hand of God" that his hearers "covered their ears, and with a loud shout all rushed together against him" (Acts 7:57). This fact suggests that his remembering of Israel's history corresponded well enough to the accepted genre of prophetic condemnation that his hearers were willing to listen to it, even while becoming angry. By contrast, they were not willing to hear his proclamation of the fulfillment of Daniel's prophecy, since they deemed this proclamation to be blasphemous against the Lord rather than simply insulting toward themselves.

47. Note that the parallel text in Luke 23:34 ("Father, forgive them; for they do not know what they are doing") belongs to canonical Scripture but not necessarily to the original text. For discussion of the manuscript evidence, in which Luke 23:34 is "omitted in very early and important mss. from diverse geographical areas," see Joseph A. Fitzmyer, SJ, *The Gospel according to Luke (X–XXIV)* (Garden City, NY: Doubleday, 1985), 1503. On the death of Stephen and the death of Jesus, see also Vogt, *Patience, Compassion, Hope*, 101. Vogt provides an insightful account of Jesus's patience in accepting suffering and of how we should imitate Jesus's patience (103–9). In Vogt's view, Luke 23:39–43 depicts Jesus as offering forgiveness to the good thief "without repentance or conversion" (116), but it seems to me that repentance is sufficiently indicated by the good thief's acceptance of his guilt (the fact that he deserves death).

48. Yves Congar, OP, "The Church: The People of God," in *The Church and Mankind: Dogma*, vol. 1: *Concilium*, ed. Hans Küng and Edward Schillebeeckx (Glen Rock, NJ: Paulist, 1964), 11–37.

49. Catherine of Siena, *The Dialogue*, trans. Suzanne Noffke, OP (New York: Paulist, 1980), 87.

50. Possidius, *The Life of Saint Augustine*, trans. Herbert T. Weiskotten (Merchantville, NJ: Evolution, 2008), 56. For a succinct discussion of Augustine's theology of divine mercy, followed by representative texts by Augustine on the topic, see the Pontifical Council for the Promotion of the New Evangelization, *Mercy in the Fathers of the Church* (Huntington, IN: Our Sunday Visitor, 2015), 31–57.

Notes to Chapter 5

1. Peter J. Leithart, *Gratitude: An Intellectual History* (Waco, TX: Baylor University Press, 2014), 227.

2. Leithart, *Gratitude*, 229. For Leithart, a Reformed theologian and pastor, this means that "the church must restore its ritual of gift and gratitude, the Eucharist, to its historically central place in worship, piety, and communal life" (229). See also Margaret

Visser, *The Gift of Thanks: The Roots and Rituals of Gratitude* (Boston: Houghton Mifflin Harcourt, 2009). Although Visser writes in a more popular style and draws some different conclusions from those of Leithart, I find some of her final statements quite moving: "In the 'anti-economy' that is the realm of the gift, people do not hang on to what they have, nor do they seek profit above all else. . . . Instead, in the gifting scenario the whole is greater than the parts. This is, for example, the original meaning of giving presents at Christmas. The significance of the festival is that the baby Jesus is the first Christmas gift, inspiring everybody else to give to one other out of joyful gratitude. The Christmas story and its celebration demonstrate God's love and express his desire that we should now 'turn around' and give to others, wherever an opportunity for giving arises, and especially where people are most in need" (392).

3. Nina Lesowitz and Mary Beth Sammons, *Living Life as a Thank You: The Transformative Power of Daily Gratitude* (San Francisco: Cleis, 2009), 25.

4. Lesowitz and Sammons, *Living Life*, 27. Lesowitz and Sammons go on to advise as a "Gratitude Practice": "Try this *mudra* (a yogic hand gesture) that is a way to bless yourself and remind yourself that you are protected and loved. Hold your thumb and your first two fingers together and circle your heart while you chant, 'One earth, one people, and one love.' Repeat as many times as you want. It reminds you that you are one with the earth and the people who love you" (211).

5. Lesowitz and Sammons, *Living Life*, 28.

6. Not, however, gratitude for an "escape" of the spirit from the bonds of the flesh, which would in fact be radical ingratitude toward our embodied constitution.

7. Henri J. M. Nouwen, *Our Greatest Gift: A Meditation on Dying and Caring* (New York: HarperCollins, 1994), 61.

8. Nouwen, *Our Greatest Gift*, 67.

9. John Swinton, "Practicing the Presence of God: Earthly Practices in Heavenly Perspective," in *Living Well and Dying Faithfully: Christian Practices for End-of-Life Care*, ed. John Swinton and Richard Payne (Grand Rapids: Eerdmans, 2009), 7. See also John Swinton and Richard Payne, "Introduction: Christian Practices and the Art of Dying Faithfully," in *Living Well and Dying Faithfully*, xv–xxiv. Swinton and Payne argue for the need to reframe "the relationship between theology and medicine" so that dying is seen primarily as a spiritual human experience rather than primarily as a medical event; and they propose that the key question for "Christian approaches to end-of-life care" is *"How can the faithful who are dying (and those who care for them) be enabled to love God and to hold on to the reality that God is love even in the midst of their suffering?"* (xviii). In his foreword to Swinton and Payne's volume, similarly, Stanley Hauerwas emphasizes that Christian dying must be determined by "confidence in the love of God" and therefore marked by a desire for time to prepare for death by reconciling with those whom we have wronged and especially with God: Hauerwas, "Foreword," in *Living Well and Dying Faithfully*, xiii.

10. See Sherwin B. Nuland, *How We Die: Reflections on Life's Final Chapter* (New York: Knopf, 1994). For a critique of Nuland's book (a critique quite similar to my own),

see Vigen Guroian, *Life's Living toward Dying: A Theological and Medical-Ethical Study* (Grand Rapids: Eerdmans, 1996), 14–16.

11. See Gregory of Nyssa, *The Life of Saint Macrina*, trans. Kevin Corrigan (Eugene, OR: Wipf & Stock, 2005). Reflecting on the contemporary practice of conducting a "life review" as part of the dying process, Donald Heinz observes in a manner that (in my view) pertains to Macrina: "Might an artful dying grant us the gift to look back over our life and know the entire story we have been living? . . . We need great storytellers who turn their last chapters into examples for us all" (*The Last Passage: Recovering a Death of Our Own* [Oxford: Oxford University Press, 1999], 106).

12. The "death awareness movement" was/is a response to the medicalization and hiddenness of death due to the post–World War II expectation that people die in hospitals rather than at home. For an early contribution to this movement, see the anthology *The Meaning of Death*, ed. Herman Feifel (New York: McGraw-Hill, 1959). Well-known early works in the "death awareness movement" include Elisabeth Kübler-Ross, *On Death and Dying* (New York: Macmillan, 1969), and Ernest Becker, *The Denial of Death* (New York: Free Press, 1973). For background to this movement, see Allen Verhey, *The Christian Art of Dying: Learning from Jesus* (Grand Rapids: Eerdmans, 2011), 49–59; Lucy Bregman, *Beyond Silence and Denial: Death and Dying Reconsidered* (Louisville: Westminster John Knox, 1994); Karen D. Scheib, "'Make Love Your Aim': Ecclesial Practices of Care at the End of Life," in *Living Well and Dying Faithfully*, ed. Swinton and Payne, 37–41. For a critique of Kübler-Ross's overly positive (dualistic) view of death in her later writings, see George Kuykendall, "Care for the Dying: A Kübler-Ross Critique," *Theology Today* 38 (1981): 37–48, responding especially to her *Death: The Final Stage of Growth* (New York: Simon & Schuster, 1986). William J. O'Malley, SJ, aptly describes the medicalization of death in his *Redemptive Suffering: Understanding Suffering, Living with It, Growing through It* (New York: Crossroad, 1997), 50. See also Eric J. Cassell, "Dying in a Technological Society," in *Death Inside Out*, ed. Peter Steinfels and Robert M. Veatch (New York: Harper & Row, 1975), 43–48.

13. See Verhey, *Christian Art of Dying*, 57–58.

14. Douglas J. Davies notes, "In and through ecology individuals have had held out to them a new way of thinking about themselves, their lives and their world. This perspective avoids both the more speculative elements of religion concerning an afterlife and the numerous and often contradicting doctrinal formulae of churches and religions. It presents something more concrete and apparently 'real.' . . . This trend [toward natural burial rather than cremation] reflects what might be seen as an ecological framing of identity, one that produces its own form of secular eschatology. . . . If I give my body back to the earth I am expressing a hope for the future of the planet: this is no longer only a self-related hope of survival but one that also ponders future generations. . . . The 'earth' that returns to the earth is not the sinful son or daughter of Adam and Eve but the natural human body that had once been formed by earthy, natural processes, and now continues those processes through its death" (*A Brief History of Death* [Oxford: Blackwell, 2005], 79–80, 83).

NOTES TO PAGE 82

15. Heinz, *Last Passage*, 97–98; Joseph Ratzinger, *Faith and the Future* (San Francisco: Ignatius, 2009), 50. In this respect, Ratzinger cites the reflections of Simone de Beauvoir in her *Force of Circumstance*, trans. Richard Howard (London: Weidenfeld & Nicolson, 1965). See also J. I. Packer, *Weakness Is the Way: Life with Christ Our Strength* (Wheaton, IL: Crossway, 2013), 89–90.

16. Peter C. Phan, *Living into Death, Dying into Life: A Christian Theology of Death and Life Eternal* (Hobe Sound, FL: Lectio, 2014), ix. Phan draws a conclusion from his aphorism that strikes me as misguided: he suggests that writing about dying and the afterlife has as its purpose "to arouse and nurture human hope about the future so that driven and energized by that hope, we can work toward a better world for all humanity and even the cosmos itself" (2). In my view, our focus must be first and foremost on deeper union with God in Christ and his Spirit rather than first and foremost on the practical purpose of building a better this-worldly society. Union with God in Christ necessarily involves love of neighbor (see James 2; 1 John 4:20–21), but the "pearl of great price" (Matt. 13:46) is God. It is of course true that, as Phan says, "the hope for heaven has an immense power for social and political transformation" (70). Later in his book, Phan rightly states that "the more united we are with the Triune God, the more united we are with the whole humanity, and vice versa"; and he adds that "the universe itself, in all its material reality, will be transformed in this heaven" (76).

17. Nuland engages the hospice movement only in passing (*How We Die*, 242), and this is a weakness of his book. See Fran Smith and Sheila Himmel, *Changing the Way We Die: Compassionate End-of-Life Care and the Hospice Movement* (Berkeley, CA: Cleis, 2013). Although hospice was formally founded by Dr. Cicely Saunders in England in 1967, Smith and Himmel trace the movement back to work done in 1879 by the Irish Sisters of Charity and in the 1890s by the founding in London of St. Luke's Home for the Dying Poor and St. Joseph's Hospice, as well as (around the same time) by Rose Hawthorne Lathrop in America. As Smith and Himmel report, a large percentage of Americans now die in hospice. Unfortunately, Smith and Himmel give their support to an aged man's decision, despite the fact that he was not in the throes of mortal illness, to starve himself to death. Quite justifiably, of course, "many patients naturally lose their appetite at the very end of life and stop eating without a big announcement," since mortal illness and bodily decay naturally cause a dying person to stop being interested in normal eating and drinking (76–77), but deliberate starving of oneself (assuming proper functioning of one's digestive system) is a different matter.

For a positive testimonial to hospice, see also Ira Byock, *Dying Well: Peace and Possibilities at the End of Life* (New York: Riverhead, 1997). Byock makes the crucial point that "caring and being cared for, are the way in which community is created. . . . Community comes about in the process of caring for those in need among us" (96). As Byock instructs one of his patients who had threatened to stop eating and starve himself to death: "in allowing yourself to be cared for, and being a willing recipient of care, you're contributing in a remarkably valuable way to the community. In a real sense, we need to care for you" (96). Verhey also praises hospice, particularly with respect to its original Christian mission, which he fears has been diluted. See also the valuable advice for hospice volunteers, and the appreciative history of hospice, in Sioned Evans and Andrew Davison, *Care for the Dying: A Practical and Pastoral Guide* (Norwich, Eng.: Canterbury, 2014); and Kathy Kalina, *Midwife for Souls: Spiritual Care for the Dying*, rev. ed. (Boston: Pauline Books & Media, 2007). For further background see Florence S. Wald, "The Emergence of Hospice Care in the United States," in *Facing Death: Where Culture, Religion, and Medicine Meet*, ed. Howard M. Spiro, Mary G. McCrea Curnen, and Lee Palmer Wandel (New Haven: Yale University Press, 1996), 81–89; and Shirley du Boulay and Marianne Rankin, *Cicely Saunders: The Founder of the Modern Hospice Movement* (London: SPCK, 2007).

18. Nuland, *How We Die*, 266.

19. Nuland, *How We Die*, 265. Here Nuland has constantly in view the example of his brother Harvey's death from colon cancer (which occurred shortly before Nuland began writing *How We Die*). Nuland expresses regret for his own role in trying to do the impossible for his dying brother. Nuland's hope is that by describing the deadly processes of the main diseases that kill us, he will be able to help others make a better decision: "The more knowledge we have about the realities of lethal illness, the more sensible we can be about choosing the time to stop or the time to fight on, and the less we expect the kind of death [serene and conscious] most of us will not have. For those who die and those who love them, a realistic expectation is the surest path to tranquillity. When we mourn, it should be the loss of love that makes us grieve, not the guilt that we did something wrong" (267; cf. 268).

20. See Jeanne Fitzpatrick and Eileen M. Fitzpatrick, *A Better Way of Dying: How to Make the Best Choices at the End of Life* (New York: Penguin, 2010). The Fitzpatricks put forward a "Contract for Compassionate Care," which enables the person (in advance of a crisis situation) to specify whether one wants to be resuscitated and whether one wants to receive antibiotics, other medications, and intravenous fluid/feeding tubes (or any food or liquid unless actively requested). The key is the refusal of hydration and nutrition; the "Contract" ensures that, for instance, people who enter into dementia for a certain length of time can specify that they do not want other people to feed them or give them liquid (the Fitzpatricks want to be starved/dehydrated to death if they lose their cognitive powers).

For a critique of this perspective, a critique with which I agree, see John Paul II's Address to the Participants in the International Congress on "Life-Sustaining Treatments and Vegetative State: Scientific Advances and Ethical Dilemmas," March 20, 2004 (available at www.vatican.va). A dying person—such as someone in the final days of stomach cancer—may licitly refuse further nutrition and hydration, due to the added and unnecessary pain caused by the delivery of food and water. But normally, even in the cases of people in a persistent "vegetative state" or long-term dementia, it is immoral to withhold nutrition and hydration, since for modern hospitals such care is not an extraordinary or disproportionate means. Verhey disagrees with my position in this regard, although he nonetheless cautions—inevitably ineffectually, in my view—against

NOTES TO PAGES 83-85

the danger of desiring to "[eliminate] *our* burdens by making certain that biologically tenacious persons die" (Verhey, *Christian Art of Dying*, 372). Certainly dying persons need not (and often should not) avail themselves of invasive medical treatments that promise to extend their lives at the cost of great pain—although neither should governments ration such treatments and refuse them to older persons. See Katy Butler, *Knocking on Heaven's Door: The Path to a Better Way of Death* (New York: Scribner, 2013)—including her distinction between "Slow Medicine" and "Fast Medicine"; as well as Atul Gawande, *Being Mortal: Medicine and What Matters in the End* (New York: Holt, 2014), who explicitly builds upon Nuland's book (which Gawande terms a "classic" [8]).

21. Nuland, *How We Die*, 267. Hereafter in this section, page references from this work will be given in parentheses in the text.

22. For Christian analysis of "dignity" in relation to human dying, see Daniel P. Sulmasy, "Death with Dignity: What Does It Mean?," *Josephinum Journal of Theology* 4 (1997): 13–23; Sulmasy, "More than Sparrows, Less than Angels: The Christian Meaning of Death with Dignity," in *Living Well and Dying Faithfully*, ed. Swinton and Payne, 226–45; Sulmasy, "Death, Dignity, and the Theory of Value," in *Euthanasia and Palliative Care in the Low Countries*, ed. P. Schotsmans and T. Meulenberg (Leuven: Peeters, 2005), 95–119. In addition to opposing euthanasia, Sulmasy argues that dying persons—and, specifically, dying Christians—"need to know the value they have by virtue of being the kinds of things that they are—beings in relationship with God and with God's people. They need to know that while they are finite—morally, intellectually, and physically—they are loved radically and exuberantly by the God who created them and offers them redemption in Christ" (241). Dying people have the opportunity to realize that their true dignity does not depend upon their achievements or even their human relationships. As Sulmasy says, "Christians are called to point out, in word and in deed, the dignity that is already there to be grasped by their dying brothers and sisters. The dying need to be reminded of their dignity at a time of fierce doubt. The dying need to understand that they are not grotesque because of the way disease has altered their appearance; that they are not merely bothersome because they are dependent; that they are not unvalued because they are unproductive; that they are worth the time, attention, and resources of others. In short, they need a demonstration that the community affirms their intrinsic dignity" (241).

23. Dylan Thomas, "Do Not Go Gentle into That Good Night," in *The Top 500 Poems*, ed. William Harmon (New York: Columbia University Press, 1992), 1050–51.

24. For discussion of the position that because we no longer exist "death is nothing to us," as Epicurus puts it (*Principal Doctrines*, trans. Cyril Bailey, in *The Stoic and Epicurean Philosophers*, ed. Whitney J. Oates [New York: Modern Library, 1940], 35), see Bernard N. Schumacher, *Death and Mortality in Contemporary Philosophy*, trans. Michael J. Miller (Cambridge: Cambridge University Press, 2011), 151–212. For critiques of Epicurus's view (from a materialist perspective), see also Thomas Nagel, *The View from Nowhere* (Oxford: Oxford University Press, 1986), 224; Nagel, "Death," in *Mor-*

tal Questions (Cambridge: Cambridge University Press, 1979), 1–10; Fred Feldman, *Confrontations with the Reaper: A Philosophical Study of the Nature and Value of Death* (Oxford: Oxford University Press, 1992), 127–56. Schumacher sums up his own critique of Epicurus's view: "The difference between the state of preconception (or prenatal nonexistence) and the state of death lies, in the final analysis, in the fact that the second constitutes a real privation of the subject, unlike the first; this difference is on the order of the loss and destruction of an already existing human being. Unlike death, in which the subject is no more and the possibility of life belongs definitively to the past, the state of preconception is characterized by a 'possibility' that a subject may come into existence" (*Death and Mortality*, 211–12).

25. Sadly, Nuland approves euthanasia or suicide in certain relatively rare cases, and it is part of his book's purposes, though not the main emphasis. With approval, he speaks of "some whose hope is centered on maintaining the kind of control that will permit them the means to decide the moment of their death, or actually to make their own quietus unhindered" (*How We Die*, 257). He also notes, "Like so many of my colleagues, I have more than once broken the law to ease a patient's going" (242–43). Earlier, he gives his own opinion: "Taking one's own life is almost always the wrong thing to do. There are two circumstances, however, in which that may not be so. Those two are the unendurable infirmities of a crippling old age and the final devastations of terminal disease. The nouns are not important in that last sentence—it is the adjectives that cry out for attention, for they are the very crux of the issue and will tolerate no compromise or 'well, almost': *unendurable, crippling, final*, and *terminal*" (151). By emphasizing these adjectives, he seeks to critique and reject lesser reasons for euthanasia. Thus, criticizing a passage from Seneca in which the Stoic philosopher argued that he would commit suicide if the alternative was to suffer without relief, Nuland remarks: "The flaw in Seneca's proposition is a striking example of the error that permeates virtually every one of the publicized discussions of modern-day attitudes toward suicide—a very large proportion of the elderly men and women who kill themselves do it because they suffer from quite remediable depression. With proper medication and therapy, most of them would be relieved of the cloud of oppressive despair that colors all reason gray, would then realize that the edifice topples not quite so much as thought, and that hope of relief is less hopeless than it seemed. I have more than once seen a suicidal old person emerge from depression, and rediscovered thereby a vibrant friend. When such men or women return to a less despondent vision of reality, their loneliness seems to them less stark and their pain more bearable because life has become interesting again and they realize that there are people who need them" (152). But he nonetheless favors some euthanasia, and he describes the Netherlands' practice of euthanasia in glowing terms because of its supposedly careful and cautious guidelines and because of the involvement of a family doctor with long acquaintance with the patient.

For a theological critique of euthanasia, see Christopher P. Vogt, *Patience, Compassion, Hope, and the Christian Art of Dying Well* (Lanham, MD: Rowman & Littlefield, 2004), 53–96, in which Vogt responds especially to Timothy E. Quill, who advocates euthanasia not least on the grounds (rooted in an ethics of autonomy) that each person should have the right to be in full control of his or her own dying. See Quill, *Death and Dignity: Making Choices and Taking Charge* (New York: Norton, 1993); Quill, *A Midwife through the Dying Process: Stories of Healing and Hard Choices at the End of Life* (Baltimore: Johns Hopkins University Press, 1996). See also Paul Ramsey, *The Patient as Person* (New Haven: Yale University Press, 1971); Ramsey, "The Indignity of 'Death with Dignity,'" in *Death Inside Out*, ed. Steinfels and Veatch, 81–96; David Albert Jones, *Approaching the End: A Theological Exploration of Death and Dying* (Oxford: Oxford University Press, 2007), 205–19; and Alan B. Astrow, "Thoughts on Euthanasia and Physician-Assisted Suicide," in *Facing Death*, 44–51; by contrast with Margaret P. Battin, *Least Worst Death: Essays in Bioethics on the End of Life* (New York: Oxford University Press, 1994); and T. Patrick Hill and David Shirley, *A Good Death: Taking More Control at the End of Your Life* (Reading, MA: Addison-Wesley, 1992), especially 100–106.

26. Cf. 3: "Every life is different from any that has gone before it, and so is every death. The uniqueness of each of us extends even to the way we die."

27. Ratzinger, *Faith and the Future*, 49. Hereafter, page references from this work will be given in parentheses in the text.

28. For a compilation of texts by Gregory about Macrina, and a historical introduction, see Anna M. Silvas, *Macrina the Younger, Philosopher of God* (Turnhout: Brepols, 2008).

29. Gregory of Nyssa, *The Life of Saint Macrina*, trans. Kevin Corrigan (Eugene, OR: Wipf & Stock, 2005), 23. Hereafter in this section, page references from this work will be given in parentheses in the text.

30. Athanasius, "A Letter of Athanasius, Our Holy Father, Archbishop of Alexandria, to Marcellinus on the Interpretation of the Psalms," in *The Life of Antony and the Letter to Marcellinus*, trans. Robert C. Gregg (Mahwah, NJ: Paulist, 1980), 125.

31. Michel René Barnes argues that for Gregory of Nyssa, bodily "decomposition is sexuality on display," since Gregory sees a connection between sex and death ("Snowden's Secret: Gregory of Nyssa on Passion and Death," in *A Man of the Church: Honoring the Theology, Life, and Witness of Ralph del Colle*, ed. Michel René Barnes [Eugene, OR: Pickwick, 2012], 111). Even for virgins such as Macrina, of course, Gregory recognizes the presence of bodily deterioration, although he does not dwell at length upon the symptoms of her disease.

32. See 2 Tim. 4:7–8.

33. Hans Boersma rightly points out that "in his account of her passing away, it is Gregory who is constantly weeping, while the dying Macrina is characterized by 'manliness' (ἀνδρεία). Furthermore, both here and in *De anima et resurrectione*, Macrina takes on the role of the teacher" (*Embodiment and Virtue in Gregory of Nyssa: An Anagogical Approach* [Oxford: Oxford University Press, 2013], 109). As Boersma notes, Elizabeth Clark holds that Macrina simply plays the role of a stand-in for Gregory, just as in Plato's *Symposium* Diotima serves as a stand-in for Socrates. See Clark, "Holy

Women, Holy Words: Early Christian Women, Social History, and the 'Linguistic Turn,'" *Journal of Early Christian Studies* 6 (1998): 413–30. Boersma remarks (and I agree with him), "I am much less convinced than Clark is of Macrina's lack of philosophical and theological knowledge. . . . Such a position requires not only that we read *De anima et resurrectione* as shaped significantly by Platonic rhetorical style (which it is), but it also requires us to seriously question many of the historical references provided by Basil and Gregory about their sister's organizational and philosophical abilities" (*Embodiment and Virtue*, 111n103). Silvas also critiques Clark's position (*Macrina the Younger*, 163–67). See also J. Warren Smith, "Macrina, Tamer of Horses and Healer of Souls: Grief and Hope in Gregory of Nyssa's *De Anima et Resurrectione*," *Journal of Theological Studies* 52 (2001): 37–60; Smith, "'A Just and Reasonable Grief': The Death and Function of a Holy 'Woman' in Gregory of Nyssa's *De Vita Macrinae*," *Journal of Early Christian Studies* 12 (2004): 57–84; Smith, *Passion and Paradise: Human and Divine Emotion in the Thought of Gregory of Nyssa* (New York: Crossroad, 2004), ch. 3 (which takes up his 2001 article).

34. See Rowan Williams, "Macrina's Deathbed Revisited: Gregory of Nyssa on Mind and Passion," in *Christian Faith and Greek Philosophy in Late Antiquity: Essays in Tribute to George Christopher Stead*, ed. Lionel R. Wickham and Caroline P. Bammel with Erica C. D. Hunter (Leiden: Brill, 1993), 227–46. For Williams, Gregory's own freely expressed grief at his sister's dying shows that the passion of grief is positive for Gregory (by contrast to a Platonic dualism between reason and emotions). However, I agree with Boersma that "Gregory is a radically anagogical theologian, for whom embodied existence (and gender in particular) simply does not have the importance that it carries for our contemporaries" (*Embodiment and Virtue*, 11). Boersma shows that Gregory, with 1 Thess. 4:13 and 2 Cor. 7:10 in view, distinguishes carefully between "worldly grief" and "godly grief," with the former displaying "inordinate attachment to bodily and material realities" rather than "an appropriate anagogical orientation" (136). For Boersma, the arguments that some scholars have made "that Gregory deeply appreciates materiality, that he holds marriage in higher regard than virginity, that he regards human beings as closely akin to animals, and that he wants to integrate emotions such as grief in a proper understanding of the human person . . . are ultimately unsuccessful because they fail to recognize the anagogical bent of Nyssen's theology; Gregory . . . wants to move from the material to the spiritual, from this-worldly, earthly existence to otherworldly, heavenly existence" (12). Thus Boersma rightly emphasizes: "In *Vita s. Macrinae*, Gregory depicts his sister, Macrina, as the virgin par excellence. On her deathbed, she no longer appears to Gregory as a woman. Instead, she has embarked on the angelic life, which for Gregory is a life modeled on Christ, in whom there is neither male nor female (Gal 3:28). . . . Gregory regards eschatological life as a restoration of the paradisal or heavenly angelic life," a state in which glorified bodies will be neither male nor female (15, 112). I disagree with Gregory on this point; indeed, Gregory's position here is quite eccentric among the fathers and later Christian theologians.

35. Of course, I accept that, as David Albert Jones observes (indebted to Augus-

tine and Thomas Aquinas), "we should expect some residual fear of death even among those who desire to depart and be with Christ" (*Approaching the End: A Theological Exploration of Death and Dying* [Oxford: Oxford University Press, 2007], 195). Jones provides three reasons: (1) "as death destroys the natural union of body and soul, human nature naturally recoils from it," as Jesus does at Gethsemane; (2) since Christians do fear death, trying to pretend otherwise will result in a rigorist perfectionism; (3) "If there were no fear of death, and no sense of human fragility (both physical and moral), then human beings would not so readily realize their need for God's grace," not least in light of the threat of divine judgment for sin (195–96). Jones points out that to these reasons (adduced by Augustine), Aquinas adds that "not only is a certain fear of death excusable, but . . . the failure to fear death sufficiently could even be a sin (*ST* IIaIIae 126. 1). We fear to lose what we love. Hence a lack of fear can be due to a lack of love" (196). For Augustine's theology of death, by contrast to Ambrose's (a contrast that drives Jones's argument), see also John C. Cavadini, "Ambrose and Augustine—*De Bono Mortis*," in *The Limits of Ancient Christianity*, ed. William E. Klingshirn and Mark Vessey (Ann Arbor: University of Michigan Press, 1999), 232–49.

36. See also Allen Verhey's reflections on the value of "looking heavenward" in his "The Practice of Prayer and Care for the Dying," in *Living Well and Dying Faithfully*, ed. Swinton and Payne, 102–6. Verhey comments, "Looking heavenward, we are reminded that we rely on a grace that we should not be reticent to share. . . . Looking heavenward, we may learn courage and humility. . . . We may learn of turnings and new beginnings in repentance" (104).

37. Nuland, *How We Die*, 143.

38. In his study of John Climacus, Jonathan L. Zecher comments that in Climacus's *Ladder of Divine Ascent*, mourning for sin is central, not surprisingly. As Zecher points out, "Climacus' sixth rung, on the Memory of Death (Μνήμη τοῦ Θανάτου) links the rungs of Repentance (Μετάνοια, which assumes a memory of death and judgment) and Joy-bearing Mourning (Χαροιὸν Πένθος), which . . . is preceded by memory of 'death and faults'" (*The Role of Death in the Ladder of Divine Ascent and the Greek Ascetic Tradition* [Oxford: Oxford University Press, 2015], 213). Although Climacus (whose dates are uncertain) probably wrote more than three centuries after the publication of Gregory of Nyssa's text, nonetheless the same concerns for memory and repentance in light of sin, death, and judgment are present in the *Life of Saint Macrina*. Zecher remarks, "Mourning is one of those activities the monk never abandons as he ascends toward higher virtues. . . . The memory of death (as also of judgment) is central in the activity of those repenting and the begetter of mourning and tears" (214). In a passage that reminds me of Macrina (and Paul), he adds that "repentance is the state of mind in which a monk, through increasing awareness of God's judgment and his own failures, learns to rely at all times on God's mercy and to hope only in God's love" (215).

39. Henry L. Novello argues that "the traditional theological treatment of death," because it focused upon sin, failed to accord significance to the "event of death itself . . . in respect of the person's final salvation" ("New Life as Life out of Death: Sharing

in the 'Exchange of Natures' in the Person of Christ," in *The Role of Death in Life: A Multidisciplinary Examination of the Relationship between Life and Death*, ed. John Behr and Conor Cunningham [Eugene, OR: Cascade, 2015], 98). I think he is quite mistaken here. In addition, the theological tradition avoids the tension that Novello poses (somewhat tentatively) between "death as a personal act of *self*-fulfillment" and death as "a situation of passivity of receptivity, of becoming 'clay in God's hands'" (118). The active fulfillment of self, in the event of dying, consists fundamentally in an act of humble receptivity.

40. Nuland, *How We Die*, 8; cf. 140–42. Hereafter in this section, page references from this work will be given in parentheses in the text.

41. Somewhat similarly, the Methodist ethicist Paul Ramsey states, "There is nobility and dignity in caring for the dying, but not in dying itself. . . . If the dying die with a degree of nobility it will be mostly their doing in doing their own dying" ("Indignity of 'Death with Dignity,'" 82). He insists quite rightly, "We do not begin to keep human community with the dying if we interpose between them and us most of the current notions of 'death with dignity.' Rather do we draw closer to them if and only if our conception of 'dying with dignity' encompasses—nakedly and without dilution—the final indignity of death itself" (82). Later in his essay, he denies that "our 'final end' is 'equally' beautiful as birth, growth and fullness of life. Moreover, if revelation disclosed any such thing it would be contrary to reason and to the human reality and experience of death. The views of our 'pre-death morticians' [who advocate euthanasia] are simply discordant with the experienced reality they attempt to beautify" (85). Ramsey's point is that death is not natural for the human being, and he appropriately insists upon "the contradiction death poses to the unique worth of an individual human life" (81; cf. 92–95).

At the same time, Ramsey affirms that dying can have a certain dignity "as a final act among the actions of life" and "as the finale of the self's relationships in this life to God or to fellowman" (88). In his view, the true dignity of dying consists in dying persons' "awareness of dying and of its indignity to the knowing human spirit" (89). Here Ramsey cites Blaise Pascal's marvelous observation, "Man is only a reed, the weakest in nature, but he is a thinking reed. There is no need for the whole universe to take up arms to crush him: a vapour, a drop of water is enough to kill him. But even if the universe were to crush him, man would still be nobler than his slayer, because he knows that he is dying and the advantage the universe has over him. The universe knows none of this" (Pascal, *Pensées*, trans. A. J. Krailsheimer, rev. ed. [London: Penguin, 1995], §200, p. 66).

By contrast, Leon R. Kass, in an essay responding to Ramsey, argues that "dignity is something that belongs to a human being and is displayed in the way he lives, and hence something not easily taken away from him; therefore, that death is, at the very least, neutral with respect to dignity; that, further, human mortality may even be the necessary condition for the display of at least *some* aspects of a human being's dignity" ("Averting One's Eyes, or Facing the Music?—On Dignity and Death," in *Death*

Inside Out, ed. Steinfels and Veatch, 102–3). With Maimonides—albeit aware (unlike Maimonides) of the possibility of the extinction of the human race—Kass holds that death is a good insofar as it allows for the ongoing course of the human race down the generations. But in my view, Ramsey too holds this ongoing course to be a good, even while recognizing that for the dying person, death is neither good nor in accord with his or her dignity as a person-in-communion. I think that Kass, who rightly points out that some people die "willingly" (110), has missed Ramsey's central point. Kass considers that "to live is to be mortal; death is the necessary price for life" (109). Evolutionarily speaking, this is so, and Ramsey does not deny it; but the human person is made for communion, and the "price" of death (understood as a permanent or seemingly permanent negation of communion) conflicts with the dignity of a person made for communion. Kass also emphasizes that "as many instances of heroism or martyrdom show, death can be for some human beings the occasion for the display of dignity, indeed of the greatest dignity" (108)—a point that Ramsey fully accepts.

42. Ramsey nicely captures the problem with Nuland's appeal to the "evolving process": "Socially and biologically, one generation follows another. So there must be death, else social history would have no room for creative novelty and planet earth would be glutted with humankind. True enough, no doubt, from the point of view of evolution (which—so far—never dies). But the man who is dying happens not to be evolution. He is a part of evolution, no doubt: but not to the whole extent of his being or his dying. A crucial testimony to the individual's transcendence over the species is man's problem and his dis-ease in dying" ("Indignity of 'Death with Dignity,'" 83).

43. Guroian describes the "sting" as "the spiritual poison of sin" (*Life's Living toward Dying*, 51). As Ramsey writes, "The dread of death is the dread of oblivion," insofar as "for the dying, death means the loss of every loved one, total loss of everything that constituted the self in its world, separation from every experience, even from future possible, replacing experiences—nothingness beyond" ("Indignity of 'Death with Dignity,'" 84). Grateful dying requires faith, hope, and love that span such "separation."

44. Gregory of Nyssa, *Life of Saint Macrina*, 42.

45. Gregory of Nyssa, *Life of Saint Macrina*, 41.

46. Nuland, *How We Die*, xii.

47. Elizabeth of the Trinity, *General Introduction; Major Spiritual Writings*, vol. 1 of *I Have Found God: Complete Works*, trans. Aletheia Kane, OCD (Washington, DC: ICS, 1984), 128.

Notes to Chapter 6

1. Jeffry Hendrix describes "redemptive suffering" succinctly: "*with* God's grace in His act of salvation, our suffering and death become part of the action; part of His working out the salvation of the world" (*A Little Guide for Your Last Days* [Plano, TX:

Bridegroom, 2009], 80). See also Louis Dupré, *The Deeper Life: An Introduction to Christian Mysticism* (New York: Crossroad, 1981), 63–66.

2. Christopher P. Vogt, *Patience, Compassion, Hope, and the Christian Art of Dying Well* (Lanham, MD: Rowman & Littlefield, 2004), 74. Vogt states, "Although I can see the value of desiring to join one's own suffering with that of Jesus Christ, I am concerned that it can lead to the distorted view that pain and suffering is in itself a good thing" (74). For Vogt, "the dying patient should not endure physical agony for its own sake by refusing pain medication. Instead, the proper expression of patience by the dying would be to endure *unavoidable* suffering associated with dying in order to pursue other goods that come in the midst of and sometimes as a result of that suffering, such as coming to terms with one's own mortality and dependence, experiencing the compassion of loved ones as expressed in physical care, and to be a role model of hopeful, patient endurance (and thereby a sign of hope for those around the deathbed" (75).

I generally agree with Vogt in this regard, but I wish to leave room for two important points that seem to be missing. First, some Christians, even during periods of suffering, have mortified themselves ascetically (in loving union with Christ) as a rebuke to pride or as a way of embodying their desire for a deeper union with Christ's redemptive cross. Such practices need to be overseen by spiritual directors, but I do not think it right to rule them out a priori, even while I am not recommending such practices for those who are not divinely called to them. Second, and more importantly, one of the goods associated with unavoidable suffering—a good that is not named by Vogt—is that when we embrace such unavoidable suffering freely with love, we can unite our suffering with Christ's redemptive suffering on the cross and participate in the working out of redemption. The value of this "co-crucifixion" with Christ (which does not in any way deny that his suffering on the cross superabundantly accomplished the redemption of the world, but instead participates in the power of his cross and helps to extend the application of that power in the world) will be discussed below. Part of the question is whether Christ's *suffering* and *dying* in love—rather than simply Christ's love—belongs to his work of salvation by restoring the relational order of justice between humans and God (i.e., by paying our penalty). I argue that it does in ch. 7 of *Engaging the Doctrine of Creation: Cosmos, Creatures, and the Wise and Good Creator* (Grand Rapids: Baker Academic, 2017).

3. Bart D. Ehrman, *God's Problem: How the Bible Fails to Answer Our Most Important Question—Why We Suffer* (New York: HarperCollins, 2008), 156. He goes on to give examples: "The eighty-year-old grandmother who is savagely raped and strangled; the eight-week-old grandchild who suddenly turns blue and dies; the eighteen-year-old killed by a drunk driver on the way to the prom—trying to see good in such evils is to deprive evil of its character. It is to ignore the helplessness of those who suffer for no reason and to no end. It robs other people of their dignity and their right to enjoy life every bit as much as we do" (156–57). Ehrman is particularly disturbed by the biblical insistence that God punishes us for sin, but his view of this punishment (as something that God adds, i.e., it is fundamentally extrinsic to the sin) is simplistic, due in part

to the strict literalism of his reading of certain biblical texts (while overlooking others). The intrinsic relationship of sin, innocent suffering, and punishment (and divine mercy) in the fallen world is portrayed by the story of Cain and Abel (Gen. 4). God is the one who overcomes suffering and gives meaning to what would otherwise be absurd and meaningless suffering. In this sense—and only in this sense, because God is utterly innocent—Joseph tells his brothers, "Even though you intended to do harm to me, God intended it for good, in order to preserve a numerous people, as he is doing today" (Gen. 50:20). See also Jürgen Moltmann, *The Coming of God: Christian Eschatology* (London: SCM, 1996), 117–18.

4. See David Bentley Hart, *The Doors of the Sea: Where Was God in the Tsunami?* (Grand Rapids: Eerdmans, 2005).

5. See Katherine Sonderegger, *The Doctrine of God*, vol. 1 of *Systematic Theology* (Minneapolis: Fortress, 2015), 224–28. See also R. E. Clements, *Jeremiah* (Atlanta: John Knox, 1988), 123–24. Clements concludes in a way that can be applied to our dying, since the value of our dying does not depend upon its outward dignity but upon our inward perseverance in faith, hope, and love: "Despairing of the possibility of fulfilling the demands of such an office [that of the prophet], Jeremiah discovered a wholly new understanding of the true nature of that office" (124).

6. From a historical-critical perspective, W. D. Davies and Dale C. Allison Jr. surmise that, whether it represents Jesus's words or those of the evangelist, "10.34 is about the proper interpretation of the present, and the main point is this: the time of Jesus and his church is not, despite the presence of the kingdom of God, the messianic era of peace. As Hahn has written, 'with the coming of Jesus the ultimate age of peace has not yet dawned, but instead the last struggle has broken out. In what way this struggle is to be carried on is not stated, but the fact that now more than ever is the time of confrontation, is decisive'" (*A Critical and Exegetical Commentary on the Gospel according to Saint Matthew*, 3 vols. [London: T. & T. Clark, 1988–97], 2:218–19; citing Ferdinand Hahn, *The Titles of Jesus in Christology: Their History in Early Christianity*, trans. Harold Knight and George Ogg [New York: World, 1969], 153).

7. Craig S. Keener points out, "Like Paul, Luke seems to understand Paul's call in terms of Jeremiah's call narrative" (*Acts: An Exegetical Commentary*, 4 vols. [Grand Rapids: Baker Academic, 2012–15], 2:1656). Keener provides a valuable excursus on "Meritorious Suffering in Judaism" (1658–60). As Keener observes, for many postbiblical rabbinic texts, "The sufferings of the righteous in this life often constituted their share of punishment to free them from greater punishment in the world to come"; and "God's elect at Qumran atoned for sin by their sufferings" (1659–60). With regard to Acts 9:16, he notes that "Luke's view of suffering here is more closely connected with sharing Christ's sufferings (e.g., bearing the cross, Luke 9:23; 14:27)" (1660).

8. Supporting the view that the sufferings endured by Christians are redemptive as a participation in Christ's sufferings, Frank Matera comments: "Although *ta pathēmata tou Christou* could refer to the sufferings that Jesus endured (see 1 Pet 1:11), the immediate context equates 'the sufferings of Christ' with afflictions, suggesting that

afflictions endured on behalf of the gospel are a direct participation in Christ's sufferings. . . . For Paul, then, there is an intimate relation between the sufferings of Christ and the consolation believers experience; for when the former abounds (*perisseuei*), so does the latter. The establishment of this relationship between apostolic affliction and the sufferings of Christ allows Paul to make a bold move. Aware that Christ suffered 'for' (*hyper*) others, and having related his own afflictions to these sufferings, Paul now views his own afflictions as sufferings 'for' (*hyper*) others. Accordingly, he writes that if he is afflicted, it is 'for' their 'consolation and salvation' (v. 6), and if he is consoled, it is 'for' their consolation. For when he is consoled by God through Christ, the Corinthians will also find consolation from the assurance that if they endure the sufferings of Christ, then they will share in the consolation Paul himself has received. But what does Paul mean when he says that his affliction is *for their salvation*? He certainly does not mean that he is the one who saves them. Rather, when they participate in the sufferings of Christ as he does, then they will understand the paradoxical message of the gospel that God is at work in weakness" (*II Corinthians: A Commentary* [Louisville: Westminster John Knox, 2003], 42). Matera directs attention to A. E. Harvey's *Renewal through Suffering: A Study of 2 Corinthians* (Edinburgh: T. & T. Clark, 1996).

9. Brendan Byrne, SJ, notes that the governing theme of Rom. 5–8 is "the hope of glory held out for all believers despite the sufferings of the present time" (*Romans* [Collegeville, MN: Liturgical Press, 1996], 248). As Byrne points out, Paul hinges much upon the outpouring of the Spirit: "What believers have received (v 15b) is a Spirit that enables them to be confident that they enjoy filial status (*huiothesia*) in the household of God" (249). Commenting on Rom. 8:17, Byrne makes the crucial point that "union with Christ, however, is not simply a static attachment to his person but a dynamic insertion into what may be termed his total 'career'—his passage to resurrection and glory via the obedience of the cross (cf. already 6:3–5, 8). It is by sharing his sufferings (*sympaschomen*) that we are to share also the glory (*syndoxasthōmen*) into which he, as prime 'heir of God,' has already entered" (251).

10. Matera explains, "Since the risen Lord is no longer subject to weakness, his power is now perfected in and through the weakness of believers such as Paul. . . . The divine 'favor' (*charis*), which is the manifestation of Christ's power, takes up residence in Paul's weakness" (*II Corinthians*, 285).

11. N. T. Wright argues insightfully with respect to this verse: "Two ideas from Paul's Jewish understanding of God's purposes help us to see what he means. First, there is *corporate Christology*, expressed in the second half of the verse by the concept of the church as Christ's body. That which is true of Christ is true also of his people. Second, there is the concept of the *Messianic woes*, which Paul alludes to also in Romans 8:18–25. This latter idea, developed out of Old Testament hints by some intertestamental and Rabbinic writers, is part of the view (shared by Jesus and Paul) that world history is to be divided into two ages—the present (evil) age (*cf.* Gal. 1:4) and the age to come. . . . Instead of the old and new ages standing as it were back to back, [Paul] understood them as overlapping. Jesus' resurrection had inaugurated the new

age, but the old would continue alongside it until Jesus' second coming. The whole of the time-span between the Lord's resurrection and his return was, then, the period of the turn-around of the eras: and therefore the whole period would be characterized by 'the Messianic woes.' Such suffering, indeed, is actually regarded as evidence that the sufferers really are God's new people" (*The Epistles of Paul to the Colossians and to Philemon: An Introduction and Commentary* [Grand Rapids: Eerdmans, 1986], 87–88). Wright concludes by linking this to corporate Christology: "Just as the Messiah was to be known by the path of suffering he freely chose—and is recognized in his risen body by the mark of the nails (Lk. 24:39; Jn. 20:20, 25, 27)—so his people are to be recognized by the sufferings they endure. . . . They are not merely imitating him. They are incorporated into his life, his paradoxical new way of life" (88).

Like Wright, Marianne Meye Thompson perceives that in Col. 1:24 "Paul seems to envision not simply an imitation of Christ's suffering, but a participation in that very suffering (see also Gal 4:19; 2 Cor 1:5; 4:10–11; Phil 3:10). Paul likely has in mind a participation in the so-called 'Messianic birth-pangs'" (*Colossians and Philemon* [Grand Rapids: Eerdmans, 2005], 45). But in her view, this means that "the afflictions of which Paul speaks are not . . . the sufferings that are the lot of all human beings, including Christians, but rather particularly the afflictions that beset Paul as he bears testimony to Christ and to the gospel" (45). I do not see why this is the case, since Paul requires all Christians to "be imitators of me, as I am of Christ" (1 Cor. 11:1) and since all Christians participate (for Paul) in the "Messianic birth-pangs" until the final consummation (see, for example, Rom. 8).

12. For the validity of lament according to Paul, even while "lament stands under the mark and influence of our experience of the Spirit, the knowledge of God's salvific work in Jesus, and hope in the fulfilment of all time," see Markus Öhler, "To Mourn, Weep, Lament and Groan: On the Heterogeneity of the New Testament's Statements on Lament," in *Evoking Lament: A Theological Discussion*, ed. Eva Harasta and Brian Brock, trans. Martina Sitling et al. (London: T. & T. Clark, 2009), 150–67 (my quotation here is from 167).

13. Michael J. Gorman, *Cruciformity: Paul's Narrative Spirituality of the Cross* (Grand Rapids: Eerdmans, 2001), 350. Gorman goes on to say: "The church for Paul was 'the dawning of the new age,' 'the blueprint and beachhead of the kingdom of God,' 'the interim eschatological community that looks forward to the future of the coming reign of God.' Like Israel from its inception, this community of the new age was called by God to be a distinct, peculiar minority presence in the world, set off from the rest of its culture and age by virtue of its consecration to God, its holiness and internal unity. For Paul, it is cruciformity that manifests all these features; cruciformity constitutes the distinctiveness of the community and its dedication to God, even as it creates the requisite unity within the community" (351; citing J. Christiaan Beker, *Paul the Apostle: The Triumph of God in Life and Thought* [Philadelphia: Fortress, 1980], 303, 326). Gorman directs attention to Raymond Pickett, *The Cross in Corinth: The Social Significance of the Death of Jesus* (Sheffield: Sheffield Academic, 1997).

14. Michael J. Gorman, *Inhabiting the Cruciform God: Kenosis, Justification, and Theosis in Paul's Narrative Soteriology* (Grand Rapids: Eerdmans, 2009), 40. After outlining various positions on Paul's understanding of justification, Gorman explains that in his view "for Paul there is *one* soteriological model: justification is by crucifixion, specifically co-crucifixion, understood as participation in Christ's act of covenant fulfillment. . . . Paul has not *two* soteriological models (juridical and participationist) but *one*, justification by co-crucifixion, meaning restoration to right covenant relations with God and others by participation in Christ's quintessential covenantal act of faith and love on the cross; this one act fulfilled both the 'vertical' and 'horizontal' requirements of the Law, such that those who participate in it experience the same life-giving fulfillment of the Law and therein begin the paradoxical, christologically grounded process of resurrection through death" (43-44). I strongly agree with Gorman here, and I have made a similar argument (inclusive of the Eucharist) in *Sacrifice and Community: Jewish Offering and Christian Eucharist* (Oxford: Blackwell, 2005), ch. 2.

Gorman adds that his view of Paul's position is similar to the view offered by Richard B. Hays, *The Faith of Jesus Christ: The Narrative Substructure of Galatians 3:1-4:11*, 2nd ed. (Grand Rapids: Eerdmans, 2001), xxix-xxxiii, 210-15; and by Robert Tannehill, "Participation in Christ: A Central Theme in Pauline Soteriology," in *The Shape of the Gospel: New Testament Essays* (Eugene, OR: Cascade, 2007), 223-37. His position does not rule out justification by faith, since in his view Paul "understands faith as co-crucifixion, and 'justification by faith' as new life/resurrection via crucifixion with the Messiah Jesus, or 'justification by co-crucifixion,' and therefore as inherently participatory" (*Inhabiting the Cruciform God*, 44).

15. Oscar Romero, *The Violence of Love*, ed. and trans. James R. Brockman (Maryknoll, NY: Orbis, 2004), 88.

16. Henri J. M. Nouwen, *Our Greatest Gift: A Meditation on Dying and Caring* (New York: HarperCollins, 1994), 31. Nouwen wrote the foreword to Romero's *Violence of Love*, ix-xiv. As the activist and theologian William Stringfellow points out with some justice, though without taking into account certain horrific places of violence and oppression in the world: "In the slums and in the suburbs, among both poor and rich, black and white, the elderly and the young, men and women, the literate and the illiterate, the lives of people encompass buying and selling, fighting and forgiving, working and playing, illness and health, hate and love—living for awhile in all these ways and then dying and, after a time, being forgotten. The significant issues of life are essentially the same for every person in every place as they are for you or me" (*Instead of Death*, new and expanded ed. [Eugene, OR: Wipf & Stock, 2004], 17). See also Stringfellow, *A Second Birthday* (Garden City, NY: Doubleday, 1970), written after a brush with death.

17. Gorman, *Inhabiting the Cruciform God*, 106. Thus, as Michael G. Lawler remarks, it is significant that in the sacrament of anointing of the sick "the church clarifies for the sick the in-Christ and for-others dimension of their infirmity, and even of their death. It issues them a ritual invitation, to perceive not just the physical dimensions of their suffering, but also the symbolic, Christian dimension of suffering for others. The

sick are told ritually that in their sickness, their weakness, their condition of apparent uselessness, they are strongest and most valuable for 'carrying in the body the death of Jesus, so that the life of Jesus may also be manifested' (2 Cor. 4:10). They are told that in sickness they are not just people who need to be ministered to, but Christians who can now minister to the church in a way that was not open to them when they were healthy" (*Symbol and Sacrament: A Contemporary Sacramental Theology* [Omaha: Creighton University Press, 1995], 172).

18. As Gorman puts it in the language of contemporary Pauline exegesis, "by participating in Christ's sacrificial (forgiving), apocalyptic (liberative), and covenantal (law-fulfilling) crucifixion, believers are forgiven, freed from Sin, and empowered to fulfill the vertical and horizontal requirements of the covenant instead of continuing in the various transgressions that previously characterized their existence and that manifested, inseparably for Paul, both their slavery to Sin and their covenantal dys-functionality" (*Inhabiting the Cruciform God*, 102).

19. Ruth Ashfield, "The Gift of the Dying Person," *Communio* 39 (2012): 382. Ashfield draws especially upon the writings of the founder of the modern hospice movement, Ciceley Saunders. For important insights into compassion, drawing upon Thomas Aquinas and Henri Nouwen (among others), see Diana Fritz Cates, *Choosing to Feel: Virtue, Friendship, and Compassion for Friends* (Notre Dame: University of Notre Dame Press, 1997). Notably, Cates is concerned with how we can feel compassion for those whom we do not like or whose desires we recognize to be wrong. She explores "the way in which charity can form selves-in-relation to perceive *all* selves as 'other themselves' in whose pain-alleviation they have a personal interest" (236).

20. Pope Benedict XVI, *Spe Salvi* (Vatican City: Libreria Editrice Vaticana, 2007), §38. Along similar lines, Allen Verhey remarks that followers of Christ must learn "to count care for those in need, including the sick and dying, as care rendered to Christ" (*The Christian Art of Dying: Learning from Jesus* [Grand Rapids: Eerdmans, 2011], 70).

21. Jon Sobrino, SJ, *Where Is God? Earthquake, Terrorism, Barbarity, and Hope*, trans. Margaret Wilde (Maryknoll, NY: Orbis, 2004), 148. (Hereafter in this section, page references from this work will be given in parentheses in the text.) See Pope Francis, *Evangelii Gaudium*, Vatican trans. (Boston: Pauline Books & Media, 2013), especially §§186–202. Pope Francis documents the presence of the same concern in the exercise of the papal magisterium over the past fifty years, and he rightly traces this "option for the poor" and "divine preference" (§198) to Scripture and the patristic and medieval theologians. Pope Francis comments, "The word 'solidarity' is a little worn and at times poorly understood, but it refers to something more than a few sporadic acts of generosity. It presumes the creation of a new mindset which thinks in terms of community and the priority of the life of all over the appropriation of goods by a few" (§188). See also Miguel J. Romero, "The Call to Mercy: *Veritatis Splendor* and the Preferential Option for the Poor," *Nova et Vetera* 11 (2013): 1205–27. Romero shows that in Pope John Paul II's encyclical *Veritatis Splendor*, "The *splendor of the truth* that

Christians proclaim is the perfection of *love in truth* called *mercy*. For Pope John Paul and Aquinas, mercy is the historical revelation and morally perfect actualization of charity vis-à-vis the reality of evil" (1207).

22. See also Sobrino, *Jesus the Liberator: A Historical-Theological Reading of Jesus of Nazareth*, trans. Paul Burns and Francis McDonagh (Maryknoll, NY: Orbis, 1993), 217. For a fully appreciative study of Sobrino's theology, see Sturla J. Stålsett, *The Crucified and the Crucified: A Study in the Liberation Christology of Jon Sobrino* (New York: Lang, 2003). Sobrino's Christology bears significant debts to Leonardo Boff, SJ, *Jesus Christ Liberator: A Critical Christology for Our Time*, trans. Patrick Hughes (Maryknoll, NY: Orbis, 1978).

23. On Romero and Ellacuría, see also Jon Sobrino, SJ, *No Salvation outside the Poor: Prophetic-Utopian Essays* (Maryknoll, NY: Orbis, 2008), especially the prologue and chs. 1 and 6. Romero was murdered at the altar while saying Mass on March 24, 1980; Ellacuría, along with five other Jesuits and two devout women, was murdered on Nov. 16, 1989. For an early biography of Romero, see James R. Brockman, SJ, *Romero: A Life*, 2nd ed. (Maryknoll, NY: Orbis, 1989). The following statement by Romero (on June 19, 1977) makes clear his guiding perspective, which is the church's faith in Christ: "As Christians formed in the gospel you have the right to organize and, inspired by the gospel, to make concrete decisions. But be careful not to betray those evangelical, Christian, supernatural convictions in the company of those who seek other liberations that can be merely economic, temporal, political. Even though working for liberation along with those who hold other ideologies, Christians must cling to their original liberation" (*Violence of Love*, 2). See also Christoph Schönborn, OP, "The Church between Hope in Life after Death and Responsibility for Life Here on Earth," in his *From Death to Life: The Christian Journey*, trans. Brian McNeil, CRV (San Francisco: Ignatius, 1995), 99-124.

24. For this phrase, he cites Ellacuría, "El Pueblo crucificado. Ensayo de soteriología historia," *Revista Latinoamericana de Teología* 18 (1989): 305-33. On "the crucified people," see also ch. 10 of Sobrino's *Jesus the Liberator* and ch. 1 of Sobrino's *No Salvation outside the Poor*. In *Jesus the Liberator*, comparing "the crucified people" to the Suffering Servant of Isa. 53, Sobrino asks: "Is there really a court to defend the cause of the poor, or at least to hear them? Is there a court that will take any notice of them and give them justice? During their lives they are not seriously listened to and when they are murdered their deaths are not investigated. . . . And truly, what crimes were committed by the Guatemalan Indians who were burned alive inside the church of San Francisco, in Huehuetenango, or by the peasants murdered at the River Sumpul or the children dying of hunger in Ethiopia, Somalia or Sudan? What guilt do they have for the greed of those who rob their lands or the geopolitical interests of the great powers? This is the crucified people's reality. It is the reality of 'peoples,' not just individuals. They are suffering peoples and they suffer in a way that is like the horrors we are told are inflicted on the Servant. In their poverty and death they are like the Servant and at least in this—but this least is a maximum—they are also like Jesus crucified. In the way

they die, there can be no doubt that these people are the ones who go on filling up in their flesh what is lacking in Christ's passion" (*Jesus the Liberator*, 257–58). Since Sobrino's account of the saving power of the cross does not give a place to Jesus's shedding of his blood, but instead focuses solely on love and solidarity, it is unclear here what it means for the people to "[fill] up in their flesh what is lacking in Christ's passion," since Sobrino does not seem to have redemptive suffering in view (except for in the sense that he considers the poor, in these cases at least, to be martyrs for love of justice).

25. Cf. *Jesus the Liberator*, 228–31; Romero, *Violence of Love*, 152; Romero, *Voice of the Voiceless: The Four Pastoral Letters and Other Statements*, trans. Michael J. Walsh (Maryknoll, NY: Orbis, 1985), 105–10. I note that although Jesus's love is primary (as Sobrino says), it is important also to recognize that Jesus's shedding of his blood saves us by lovingly paying the penalty of sin (namely, death) that belongs to the order of justice between humans and God. For concerns about Sobrino's Christology, see the Congregation for the Doctrine of the Faith's 2006 "Notification on the Works of Father Jon Sobrino, SJ," http://www.vatican.va/roman_curia/congregations/cfaith/documents/rc_con_cfaith_doc_20061126_notification-sobrino_en.html. This document addresses parts of Sobrino's *Jesus the Liberator* and his *Christ the Liberator: A View from the Victims*, trans. Paul Burns (Maryknoll, NY: Orbis, 2001). In particular, the CDF corrects Sobrino's formulation of the incarnation. Paragraph 5 of the notification quotes p. 242 of *Jesus the Liberator*: "From a dogmatic point of view, we have to say, without any reservation, that the Son (the second person of the Trinity) took on the whole reality of Jesus and, although the dogmatic formula never explains the manner of this being affected by the human dimension, the thesis is radical. The Son experienced Jesus' humanity, existence in history, life, destiny and death." Sobrino is here discussing how "suffering affects God" (*Jesus the Liberator*, 242), but his formulation—the Son "took on the whole reality of Jesus"—makes it sound as though there were a "whole reality of Jesus" prior to the incarnation, which undermines the dogmatic claims that the Son *is* Jesus and that the Son *is* the Redeemer. A similarly problematic passage appears in *Christ the Liberator*, 223: "the limited human is predicated of God, but the unlimited divine is not predicated of Jesus." See also Aaron Riches, *Ecce Homo: On the Divine Unity of Christ* (Grand Rapids: Eerdmans, 2016), including his critique of Sobrino on 219–22.

For Sobrino on Nicaea and Chalcedon, see *Christ the Liberator*, chs. 16–19. On the one hand, he affirms the "ultimateness Chalcedon gives to the basic unity—despite being dual—of Jesus Christ" and he holds (less clearly) that God's "initiative is what makes him *be*, what calls his human nature into being, what 'personalizes' him" (300–301). But on the other hand, Sobrino states that the "hypostatic union took place between *this* God and *this* human being" (303) and that "Jesus is constituted as person precisely in this self-giving to this 'other' who is God. In this self-giving Jesus rescues and actualizes his generic personality. The way he keeps it up to the end, absolutely radically, demonstrates his special and essential relationship to this 'other' who is God" (309). Arguing that "adoptionism is not a current theoretical problem" (306), Sobrino defends himself against the charge of adoptionist Christology by suggesting (unpersuasively in my view) that the real issue is the historical unfolding of Jesus's revelatory humanity: "not even Jesus can make 'the whole of divinity' present at a stroke; he can do so only through a process" (307).

26. Behind this point, I think, is Sobrino's ecclesiology of the "church of the poor" (*Jesus the Liberator*, 28–31). This ecclesiology receives correction in the notification, because Sobrino seems to ground the church in a primary sense not on the apostles (bearers of the revelation of Jesus Christ) but upon the poor. Sobrino contrasts "*primary ecclesiality*: the community's act of faith in Christ and the presentation of Christ in history in his dimension as head of a body that is the church" with "*secondary ecclesiality*, that is . . . the church defined as an institution, in this case as guardian of the deposit of faith and ultimate guarantor of truth" (29). Having placed the institutional and apostolic dimensions of the church in a secondary position, Sobrino fills out the content of what is ecclesiologically primary: "By 'primary ecclesiality' I mean that the ecclesial substance is embodied in the church, that in it real faith, hope and charity are put into practice; in christological terms, discipleship is enacted" (29). Enacted discipleship means the "church of the poor": "This real community faith and this embodiment of Christ are the primary ecclesial realities, and in Latin American christology they are brought into relation with the poor. When church and poor are brought into an essential relationship, then we get the church of the poor, and this church becomes the ecclesial setting for Latin American christology" (30). Thus the "ecclesial setting" for Christology is not the "secondary ecclesiality" of the institutional apostolic church but rather the "primary ecclesiality" of the enacted discipleship of the poor, who are our primary teachers about the reality of Christ. According to Sobrino, they teach us as following three things: (1) "the faith of the church of the poor takes the form first and foremost of liberating activity, discipleship of Jesus, which resembles Jesus in his options for the poor, in his condemnations and in his historical destiny" (30); (2) "the church of the poor attaches importance to the communal nature of faith. . . . Just because they are poor, the poor make a difference to the faith of those who are not poor, so that in the church there cannot be mere addition of individual faiths, but complementarity— put more precisely, solidarity—a mutual carrying of one another in faith, allowing oneself to be given faith by the poor and offering them one's own faith. Then, and at the level of content, since the poor are those to whom Jesus' mission was primarily directed, they ask the fundamental questions of faith and do so with power to move and activate the whole community in the process of 'learning to learn' what Christ is. Because they are God's preferred, and because of the difference between their faith and the faith of the non-poor, the poor, within the faith community, question christological faith and give it its fundamental direction" (30); (3) "In the church of the poor, finally, Christ becomes present, and this church is his body in history. It is not his body automatically, but insofar as it offers Christ the liberating hope and action that can make him present as risen and as crucified" (30). A number of concerns arise

at this juncture, primarily having to do with Sabrino's mishandling of the relationship of Christ and the church and the relationship of faith and action.

27. Se also Pope Francis, *Evangelii Gaudium*, §§190–92.

28. In the words of Pope John Paul II's 1980 encyclical *Dives in Misericordia*, words that accord with Sobrino's urgency, there is a "*gigantic remorse* caused by the fact that, side by side with wealthy and surfeited people and societies, living in plenty and ruled by consumerism and pleasure, the same human family contains individuals and groups *that are suffering from hunger*" (§11, in *The Encyclicals of John Paul II*, ed. J. Michael Miller, CSB [Huntington, IN: Our Sunday Visitor, 2001], 126). During the past century, however, numerous politicians in many countries have worked with activists in implementing plans for alleviating poverty that have in fact greatly exacerbated poverty. A relatively wealthy and privileged scholar or scientist, researching property laws, tax systems, or crop production (for example), may contribute a great deal to alleviating poverty without entering into the kind of solidarity that Sobrino envisions— which suggests to me that Sobrino's approach needs to be expanded to include a fuller range of ways of serving the poor.

29. On this point, see Donald Haggerty, *Conversion: Spiritual Insights into an Essential Encounter with God* (San Francisco: Ignatius, forthcoming).

30. In his foreword to Paul Farmer's *Pathologies of Power: Health, Human Rights, and the New War on the Poor* (Berkeley: University of California Press, 2005), Amartya Sen remarks: "'Every man who lives is born to die,' wrote John Dryden, some three hundred years ago. That recognition is tragic enough, but the reality is sadder still. We try to pack in a few worthwhile things between birth and death, and quite often succeed. It is, however, hard to achieve anything significant if, as in sub-Saharan Africa, the median age at death is less than five years" (xi). I agree with Sen about the need to increase dramatically the median age of death in sub-Saharan Africa, yet I note that infants can be baptized—an achievement in relation to God. In poorer areas of the world, the lack of medicine and of pain control for the dying is a disaster that Christians must fight strenuously; see Sioned Evans and Andrew Davison, *Care for the Dying: A Practical and Pastoral Guide* (London: Canterbury, 2014), 149.

31. For reflections in this vein, see Vogt, *Patience, Compassion, Hope*, 136–38.

32. Pope Francis points out that the poor "not only share in the *sensus fidei*, but in their difficulties they know the suffering Christ. We need to let ourselves be evangelized by them" (*Evangelii Gaudium*, §198). He adds, much like Sobrino, "The new evangelization is an invitation to acknowledge the saving power at work in their [the poor's] lives and to put them at the center of the church's pilgrim way. We are called to find Christ in them, to lend our voice to their causes, but also to be their friends, to listen to them, to speak for them, and to embrace the mysterious wisdom which God wishes to share with us through them" (§198). Similarly, Archbishop Romero states, "If Christ, the God of majesty, became a lowly human and lived with the poor and even died on a cross like a slave, our Christian faith should also be lived in the same way. The Christian who does not want to live this commitment of solidarity with the poor

is not worthy to be called Christian" (*Violence of Love*, 191). For the church's presence to the poor across the centuries, see Brandon Vogt, *Saints and Social Justice: A Guide to Changing the World* (Huntington, IN: Our Sunday Visitor, 2014).

33. I hold that the just punishment of original sin is death, because original sin dissolves the grace of "original justice," disorders human nature through its rebellion, and leaves humans fully vulnerable to the material corruption that is natural to humans absent original justice. For discussion see ch. 6 of my *Engaging the Doctrine of Creation*; and see also Paul O'Callaghan, *Christ Our Hope: An Introduction to Eschatology* (Washington, DC: Catholic University of America Press, 2011), 260–65. For an all-too-commonplace caricature of the view that human death is rooted in original sin, see William J. O'Malley, SJ, *Redemptive Suffering: Understanding Suffering, Living with It, Growing through It* (New York: Crossroad, 1997), 17–19.

34. Pope Francis, *Evangelii Gaudium*, §200. Pope Francis goes on to say, "The great majority of the poor have a special openness to the faith; they need God and we must not fail to offer them his friendship, his blessing, his word, the celebration of the sacraments, and a journey of growth and maturity in the faith. Our preferential option for the poor must mainly translate into a privileged and preferential religious care" (§200).

35. As the Orthodox theologian Jean-Claude Larchet states, "God cannot be considered to be the author of illness, suffering and death. The Fathers affirm this unanimously" (*The Theology of Illness*, trans. John and Michael Breck [Crestwood, NY: St. Vladimir's Seminary Press, 2002], 17). Well aware that material bodies naturally corrupt, Larchet holds that "the incorruptibility and immortality of the first man were due solely to divine grace. . . . According to the Fathers, then, we need to seek the source of illness, infirmities, sufferings, corruption, and death, together with all other evils that presently afflict human nature, in the personal will of man, in the bad use to which he has put his free will. . . . By choosing to follow the Devil's suggestion to become 'like gods' (Gen 3:5)—that is, to become gods apart from God—Adam and Eve deprived themselves of grace, and from that time on they lost the qualities that would have bestowed on them in some manner a supernatural condition" (21, 26–27). Larchet is concerned not solely with "protology" or origins, but also with the present, in which suffering and dying are often treated as though humans were mere animals. He observes, "The person does not merely *have* a body, it *is* a body, even though the person as such infinitely transcends bodily limits. This is why everything that involves the body involves the person as a whole. By refusing to consider the spiritual dimension of human persons when we seek to alleviate their physical ailments we do them immeasurable harm" (14).

36. Mother Teresa puts the main point more accurately: "Our poor people are great people, a very lovable people. They don't need our pity and sympathy. They need our understanding love and they need our respect. We need to tell the poor that they are somebody to us, that they, too, have been created, by the same loving hand of God, to love and be loved" (*Come Be My Light: The Private Writings of the "Saint of*

Calcutta," ed. and with commentary by Brian Kolodiejchuk, MC [New York: Double-day, 2007], 296).

37. As Romero states, "The existence of poverty as a lack of what is necessary is an indictment. Those who say the bishop, the church, and the priests have caused the bad state of our country want to paper over the reality. Those who have created the evil are those who have made possible the hideous social injustice our people live in. Thus, the poor have shown the church the true way to go. A church that does not join the poor, in order to speak out from the side of the poor against the injustices committed against them, is not the true church of Jesus Christ" (*Violence of Love*, 188–89).

38. In "Theology: An Ecclesial Function," in Gustavo Gutiérrez and Gerhard Ludwig Müller, *On the Side of the Poor: The Theology of Liberation*, trans. Robert A. Krieg and James B. Nickoloff (Maryknoll, NY: Orbis, 2015), 1–10—this book was orig-inally published in 2004, but Gutiérrez's essay was originally published ten years ear-lier—Gustavo Gutiérrez insightfully comments: "Social and political liberation should not in any way hide the final and radical significance of liberation from sin which can only be a work of forgiveness and of God's grace. It is important then to refine our means of expression in order to avoid confusion in this matter. We must pay attention to these dangers and reaffirm the proper and direct level of the gospel; its content is the reign [the kingdom of God], but the reign must be accepted by people who live in his-tory and consequently the proclamation of a reign of love, peace, and justice impinges on life together in society. Nevertheless, the demands of the gospel go beyond the po-litical project of building a different society" (5). Gutiérrez cautions against falling "into the 'verticalism of a disembodied spiritual union with God or into a simple existential personalism . . . nor, even less, into socioeconomic-political horizontalism' (Puebla, 329). Both deviations, each in its own way, distort at the same time the transcendence and the immanence of the reign of God" (8).

39. Romero poetically remarks in this regard, "There can be no true liberation / until people are freed from sin. / All the liberationist groups that spring up in our land / should bear this in mind. / This first liberation to be proposed by a political group / that truly wants the people's liberation / must be to free oneself from sin. / While one is a slave of sin— / of selfishness, violence, cruelty, and hatred— / one is not fitted for the people's liberation" (*Violence of Love*, 198). See also Romero, *Voice of the Voiceless*, 74: "The church, like Jesus, has to go on denouncing sin in our own day. It has to denounce the selfishness that is hidden is everyone's heart, the sin that dehumanizes persons, destroys families, and turns money, possessions, profit, and power into the ultimate ends for which persons strive. And, like anyone who has the smallest degree of foresight, the slightest capacity for analysis, the church has also to denounce what has rightly been called 'structural sin': those social, economic, cultural, and political structures that effectively drive the majority of our people onto the margins of society."

40. Thus William Stringfellow argues in a book originally published in 1973, "Biblically, all men and all principalities are guiltily implicated in the violence which pervades all relationships in the Fall. Though this neither dilutes nor exonerates spe-

cific commissions, particular acts of some do not release everyone else of their social guilt, either. We may consider Governor Nelson Rockefeller culpable, in a concrete and immediate sense, for the slaughter of Attica inmates and hostages. But if we do, we must remember that he is, at the same time, joined in that position by all the rest of us. His guilt does not absolve others; corporate guilt does not relieve him" (*An Ethic for Christians and Other Aliens in a Strange Land* [repr., Eugene, OR: Wipf & Stock, 2004], 130–31). This reminder that we are all fallen and all in need of repentance and forgiveness helps avoid self-righteousness or postulating a privileged class devoid of sin (and so not in need of Christ), without denying the gravity of the personal sins committed by oppressors.

41. See also Matthew L. Lamb, *Solidarity with Victims: Toward a Theology of Social Transformation* (New York: Crossroad, 1982). Lamb points out that "religion lost its innocence long ago. Its crusades, wars, and bigotry occasioned modernity's quest for the purity of reason. Now that pure reason has brought us even more victims than the old impure religion, we can no longer responsibly practice reason or religion without self-critical solidarity with the victims of both" (x). In proclaiming Christ, we must indeed be in "self-critical solidarity with the victims" and must embrace the universal call to holiness. Lamb cites as an ally to his perspective Alasdair MacIntyre, *After Virtue* (Notre Dame: University of Notre Dame Press, 1981).

42. Thus in contemporary Christian churches, as Sioned Evans and Andrew Davison say, "care of the elderly, sick and dying can be given second place to projects that are directed to the young" (*Care for the Dying*, 148).

43. In failing to discuss "redemptive suffering," Sobrino misses an important opportunity. I agree with Hans Urs von Balthasar when he writes, "All who suffer in this world, the sick and incurable and dying, those in prison and tortured, the oppressed and those who are hopelessly poor, must know that, in their situation, they are not condemned to total powerlessness; if they unite their hopelessness with that of the crucified Son of God [the supreme victim], they will do more to build the real kingdom of God than many an architect of earthly happiness" ("Hosanna—For Which Liberation Theology?," in *"You Crown the Year with Your Goodness": Radio Sermons*, trans. Graham Harrison [San Francisco: Ignatius, 1989], 74). At the same time, Balthasar insists that "people, and Christians in particular, should do all they can to minimize mankind's present and future misery" (74). Balthasar adds that "the Christian paradox" is that "the man who fashions his inner attitude and orients himself toward the eternal kingdom according to the instructions of Jesus, that is, who is gentle, merciful, peacemaking, pure of heart, thirsting for God's righteousness, inwardly poor and humble—such a man can have a deeper and more lasting effect on world history than the magnates to whom nothing is more important than the exercise of power. It is precisely what *cannot* be manufactured on earth by political, economic and social programs, in other words, what comes from the kingdom of God and its righteousness" (73–74).

44. M. Romero, "Call to Mercy," 1207.

45. See Jon Sobrino, SJ, *The Principle of Mercy: Taking the Crucified People from*

the Cross (Maryknoll, NY: Orbis, 1994). In the preface of this well-integrated collection of essays, Sobrino states that its goal is "to demonstrate the imperative need that the crucified peoples be shown mercy" (vii). In working out this goal, he devotes chapters to "the essential character of mercy and . . . the importance of shaping the mission of the church and the task of theology in function of that mercy," and he describes priesthood and "solidarity" as "manifestations of mercy" (vii). He observes that "in the primary reaction of mercy, for which there is no ulterior argumentation or motivation but the sheer fact of the crucifixion of peoples, both the human and the Christian are at stake. Mercy is not sufficient, but it is absolutely necessary—in a world that does all that is possible to conceal suffering and avoid a definition of the human—in terms of a reaction to that suffering" (viii). I agree with Sobrino that we must respond to the sufferings of our neighbor with mercy and that without such a response we are not yet Christian. For Sobrino, as he explains in the first chapter of *Principle of Mercy*, this means awakening to our need to help liberate the poor from economic and political oppression (i.e., death-dealing structures of sin), and it also means recognizing that the poor are the true teachers of the gospel. Sobrino suggests that the problem with the wealthy is their neo-Pelagianism, their assumption that they do not need God's merciful grace in order to achieve what is necessary (see 7). While rejecting his Marxism as a false path for the liberation of the poor, I deeply value Sobrino's emphasis on co-suffering (which is his definition of mercy): "making someone else's pain our very own and allowing that pain to move us to respond" (10).

46. Pope John Paul II, *Salvifici Doloris*, Vatican translation (Boston: St. Paul Books and Media, 1984), §19, pp. 30–31. For discussion of redemptive suffering according to *Salvifici Doloris*, see especially Eduardo J. Echeverria, "The Gospel of Redemptive Suffering: Reflections on John Paul II's *Salvifici Doloris*," in *Christian Faith and the Problem of Evil*, ed. Peter van Inwagen (Grand Rapids: Eerdmans, 2004), 125, 134–47; Dawn Eden Goldstein, "The Mystical Body and Its Loving Wounds: Redemptive Suffering in Magisterial Teaching, Pre-Papal Writings, and Popes' Teachings as Private Theologians, 1939–2015" (STD diss., University of Saint Mary of the Lake, 2016), ch. 3. On redemptive suffering see also, for example, Hubert van Zeller, OSB, *Suffering: The Catholic Answer: The Cross of Christ and Its Meaning for You* (Manchester, NH: Sophia Institute, 2002), 9, 18; Russell Shaw, *Does Suffering Make Sense?* (Huntington, IN: Our Sunday Visitor, 1987), 105–7.

47. Maria Faustina Kowalska, *Diary: Divine Mercy in My Soul*, trans. Adam and Danuta Pasicki et al., ed. George Kosicki, CSB, et al., 3rd ed. (Stockbridge, MA: Marian, 2007), 9. Hereafter in this section, page references from this work will be given in parentheses in the text.

48. See also the spiritual darkness experienced by Mother Teresa, as conveyed in *Come Be My Light*, 168–234. Kolodiejchuk comments, "She too felt unclaimed—not by the poor who found a mother in her, but by God, the child of whose love she claimed to be. Her interior darkness gave Mother Teresa the capacity to comprehend the feelings of the poor. . . . Without her interior darkness, without knowing such a longing for love and

the pain of being unloved, and without this radical identification with the poor, Mother Teresa would not have won over their trust and their hearts to the extent that she did" (233–34). Citing 1 Tim. 2:11–15 as a biblical example, Arnfríður Guðmundsdóttir notes with concern, however, that "women's sufferings have been justified by appealing to the salvific significance of their suffering. . . . For centuries, women's suffering has been justified, based on the idea of its salvific meaning" (*Meeting God on the Cross: Christ, the Cross, and the Feminist Critique* [Oxford: Oxford University Press, 2010], 115–16). Guðmundsdóttir also expresses concern about "the exclusion of women's experience from the formulation of theological doctrines within the Christian tradition" (10), although in her view the experience of suffering is "basic to all human experience" and therefore "despite different social and cultural situations, there are not only differences but also similarities in women's universal experiences of suffering" (14). She affirms Elisabeth Schüssler Fiorenza's "feminist model of critical interpretation, beginning with *a hermeneutic of suspicion*, which takes as its starting point the assumption that biblical texts and their interpretations are androcentric and serve patriarchal functions" (16). For Guðmundsdóttir, as for Elizabeth Johnson (and *pace* such thinkers as Daphne Hampson and Carter Heyward), the cross of Jesus remains a fundamentally positive reality for women, because it demonstrates Jesus's solidarity with women who are suffering. She states: "Despite the abuse of theological arguments in order to justify women's suffering, women have been able to experience Jesus' solidarity with them not only in their suffering but also in their fight against unjust causes of their suffering. . . . The cross itself launches the harshest criticism of any abuse of power represented in abusive theology of the cross" (116). Guðmundsdóttir approvingly cites Elizabeth Johnson's viewpoint that Christ is crucified "in solidarity with violated women" (*She Who Is: The Mystery of God in Feminist Theological Discourse* [New York: Crossroad, 1992], 271, cited in Guðmundsdóttir, *Meeting God on the Cross*, 117). For Guðmundsdóttir, "It is important to highlight *passive* and *active* aspects of the symbol of the cross: the passive aspect demonstrated in Jesus' solidarity with women in their suffering and the active aspect as it is found in his empowering of women in their struggle for liberation" (*Meeting God on the Cross*, 118). As an example of abusive use of the cross, she describes a priest who advised a woman to tolerate physical abuse from her husband on the grounds that in this way the woman would imitate Christ. (For this example and for related concerns about the consequences for women of Christianity's exaltation of the cross and of self-sacrifice, see Rita Nakashima Brock and Rebecca Ann Parker, *Proverbs of Ashes: Violence, Redemptive Suffering, and the Search for What Saves Us* [Boston: Beacon, 2001].)

I agree with Guðmundsdóttir that such an interpretation of the cross is radically opposed to its reality. True co-suffering with Christ in love does not mean bearing abuse that can be avoided, just as it does not mean enduring illness that can be cured, since Christ does not want us to suffer, even though the fallenness of the world means that inevitably we do suffer, not least from mortal illness. As Guðmundsdóttir observes, "While I agree with Brock and Parker about the abuse, I think it is radically different to talk about something being abused and to argue that something is abusive in itself"

(*Meeting God on the Cross*, 124). She emphasizes that suffering can indeed be a force for good if it is suffering endured in the struggle for liberation, such as the freely accepted suffering of Martin Luther King Jr. and Oscar Romero. As Virginia M. M. Fabella rightly remarks, "Only that suffering endured for the sake of one's neighbor, for the sake of the kingdom, for the sake of greater life, can be redeeming and rooted in the Paschal mystery" ("Christology from an Asian Woman's Perspective," in *We Dare to Dream: Doing Theology as Asian Women*, ed. Virginia M. M. Fabella and Sun Ai Lee Park [Maryknoll, NY: Orbis, 1990], 7–8, cited in *Meeting God on the Cross*, 127). This is the kind of suffering (as described by Fabella) that God called Faustina to undertake. See also Marie M. Fortune, "The Transformation of Suffering: A Biblical and Theological Perspective," in *Violence against Women and Children: A Christian Theological Sourcebook*, ed. Carol J. Adams and Marie M. Fortune (New York: Continuum, 1995), 85–91.

49. C. Vogt discusses patience as a virtue of dying in *Patience, Compassion, Hope*, 74–77.

50. As Pope John Paul II observes in *Dives in Misericordia*, "Christ undergoes the Passion and Cross because of the sins of humanity. This constitutes even a 'superabundance' of justice, for the sins of man are 'compensated for' by the sacrifice of the Man-God. Nevertheless, this justice, which is properly justice 'to God's measure,' springs completely from love" (§7, p. 119).

51. See Donald Haggerty, *The Contemplative Hunger* (San Francisco: Ignatius, 2016), 75, 77–78: "The reluctance to being a servant may explain why many people who have a genuine sympathy for the poor keep their physical distance from them. Getting physically close to a destitute person makes a claim on us, which at the time we ordinarily do not realize. If a person is helpless in his poverty and we draw close enough, we cannot backtrack and walk away without suffering our own callousness. And if we do take some action, it is never an isolated assistance that is soon finished and done with. . . . Charitable love admired in thought cannot be compared to bending down to a poor and dirty man in the street. Noble aspirations and fine words have value, but they are not equivalent to sacrificial deeds. Every religious person must take care in this regard. Spiritual reflection in quiet hours is a necessary sustenance, but it must lead outward to hard, concrete demands on our life, or else it may be an escape from reality. The religious ideal is chimerical and even deceptive without the steady labor of sacrificial generosity to others, and especially to the poor. It is love for the poor, in all disguises of their misery, that draws us to a deeper love for prayer."

52. Megory Anderson makes the point that staying "through to the end" brings profound graces upon the co-sufferers: "The journey into death is such an important one that I believe each person deserves as much support as possible. The loved ones who decide to stay and vigil with the dying person receive, I believe, as much grace and blessing as the dying. It is truly a remarkable experience" (*Sacred Dying: Creating Rituals for Embracing the End of Life*, rev. ed. [New York: Marlowe, 2004], 46). See also Anderson, *Attending the Dying: A Handbook of Practical Guidelines* (New York: Morehouse, 2005), 55–63.

53. B., *Vita s. Dunstani*, in *The Early Lives of St Dunstan*, ed. and trans. Michael Winterbottom and Michael Lapidge (Oxford: Oxford University Press, 2012), 105.

54. B., *Vita s. Dunstani*, 79.

55. See B., *Vita s. Dunstani*, 71.

56. Pope Benedict XVI, *Spe Salvi*, §38.

57. Pontifical Council for the Promotion of the New Evangelization, *The Corporal and Spiritual Works of Mercy* (Huntington, IN: Our Sunday Visitor, 2015), 67.

58. Pope Francis, *Evangelii Gaudium*, §193.

59. Nouwen, *Our Greatest Gift*, 39, 43. James F. Keenan, SJ, describes the origins of hospitals in the Christian commission to care personally for the sick: "The deacons' care for pilgrims and the sick was a particularly onerous duty in pilgrimage centers. These centers of hospitality would eventually appropriately be called 'hospitals.' Deacons became progressively associated with providing spiritual and physical support to the weak stranger. As their ministry developed, the church constructed appropriate institutions. The emperor Constantine, for instance, authorized every city to build and maintain facilities for the pilgrim, the sick, and the poor. As early as the fourth century, we have reports of hospitals. From the writings of St. Jerome we learn of a hospital in Rome; from St. Basil we hear about one he erected. . . . Monasteries, too, began to construct medical facilities for infirmed pilgrims. . . . The Hospitallers of St. Lazarus of Jerusalem, founded in 1120, was a military religious order. Sensitive to the fact that persons with contagious diseases were regularly excluded from hospitals, the Hospitallers operated hospitals for lepers, spread the faith, and protected pilgrims in the Holy Land. They also founded as many as three thousand *leprosaria* throughout Europe. The motto of another group, the lay Order of the Holy Spirit founded by Guy de Montpellier, was 'The sick person is the head of the household; those who assist are the servants in the household.' At its height, the order had founded and staffed in Europe some eight hundred hospitals. One of them, the Hospital of the Holy Spirit, still stands in Rome, a few hundred yards from St. Peter's Basilica" (*The Works of Mercy: The Heart of Catholicism*, 2nd ed. [Lanham, MD: Rowman & Littlefield, 2008], 46–47).

60. As Kathleen Anne McManus puts it, with reference to Edward Schillebeeckx's theology (with respect to which I admittedly have some serious concerns): "The mysticism of the cross experienced in each personal 'turning' or *metanoia* is at the core of the human solidarity in grace that becomes manifest in ethical, political praxis. . . . At the place where human effort or understanding reaches its limit, at the place where God seems absent, there is evoked a praxis of solidarity. . . . In situations of the most extreme suffering, it appears as faithful waiting: attentive love in a 'now' that belies the very promise that sustains us. The praxis of solidarity is a contemplative, relational praxis rooted in Jesus' intimacy with God, an intimacy that sustained the cross and issued in resurrection. It is manifest in the most hopeless situations by the courageous, ministering human presence that alone witnesses to God's final word over suffering, sin, and death" (*Unbroken Communion: The Place and Meaning of Suffering in the Theology of Edward Schillebeeckx* [Lanham, MD: Rowman & Littlefield, 2003],

5). Like Schillebeeckx, McManus speaks of "solidarity" and "redemptive memory" but not of "redemptive suffering." McManus affirms that "experiences of negative contrast mysteriously bring us to the heart of God's purposes for us. It is in the face of the world's negativity that we see and experience the power of Jesus' unbroken trust in God" (96–97). This could be translated into a doctrine of redemptive suffering, especially if Jesus's own suffering (and not simply his trust) were accorded soteriological value.

61. Nouwen, *Our Greatest Gift*, 29–30.

62. Nouwen, *Our Greatest Gift*, 30.

63. Nouwen, *Our Greatest Gift*, 30.

64. Nouwen, *Our Greatest Gift*, 29.

65. Pope Benedict XVI, *Spe Salvi*, §39, p. 83; §43, p. 91.

66. Nouwen, *Our Greatest Gift*, 46.

67. Pope Benedict XVI, *Spe Salvi*, §40, p. 84. Pope Benedict goes on to emphasize that, for Christians, "our hope is always essentially also hope for others; only thus is it truly hope for me too. As Christians we should never limit ourselves to asking: how can I save myself? We should also ask: what can I do in order that others may be saved and that for them too the star of hope may rise?" (§48, pp. 101–2).

68. Kristine M. Rankka, *Women and the Value of Suffering: An Aw(e)ful Rowing toward God* (Collegeville, MN: Liturgical Press, 1998), 192. Rankka adds that "what radical suffering and a tragic vision of reality can also bring us to is the realization of our need for something transcendent" (203). For the importance of co-suffering with someone who is suffering (the importance of a friend's simple presence in giving the sufferer hope), see 216–17. Rankka draws in helpful ways upon Constance FitzGerald's reflections on the spirituality of John of the Cross: "Impasse and Dark Night," in *Women's Spirituality: Resources for Christian Development*, ed. Joann Wolski Conn (Mahwah, NJ: Paulist, 1986), 287–311.

69. Gorman, *Inhabiting the Cruciform God*, 164, 173.

70. John Behr, "Life and Death in the Age of Martyrdom," in *The Role of Death in Life: A Multidisciplinary Examination of the Relationship between Life and Death*, ed. John Behr and Conor Cunningham (Eugene, OR: Cascade, 2015), 86. Behr goes on to explain, "By freely 'dying' to oneself (to 'the old man,' to 'Adam,' to our involuntary created existence) and beginning to live ecstatically, beyond ourselves, for others and for God, the life that is begun is, even now, a life that has been entered into through death and, therefore, a life that can no longer be touched by death. . . . In and through Christ, we now have the possibility of freely using the givenness of our creaturely mortality to enter, freely and willing, through birth, *gennesis*, into existence as a human being with a life without end, 'born from above . . . from the water and the Spirit' (John 3:3, 5)" (89). At the same time, the actual act of dying obviously differs from dying to self—though the latter should characterize the former. As David Albert Jones remarks with Rahner's theology in view, "if an individual act of spiritual submission can constitute the 'act of dying' (and this is supported by taking the act of dying to be any act informed by faith, hope, and love) then why claim that there is something unique or transcendent about

physical dying?" (*Approaching the End: A Theological Exploration of Death and Dying* [Oxford: Oxford University Press, 2007], 178). Jones warns "about the enthusiasm that some Christians have shown for martyrdom. This is in part because wishing for martyrdom involves wishing that someone else commit a great injustice, but it is also because the courage of martyrdom is a gift from God which should not be presumed" (203). Yet martyrs exemplify Christian dying because, as Jones says, "a martyr is not someone who seeks death but someone who remains faithful to the truth even in the face of death" (203). Like myself, Jones cites Acts 7:59 as an exemplification of the good death, and Jones confirms Rahner's fundamental insight: "Either death is accepted from God or God is rejected in death. . . . Rahner is at his most profound in describing how the need to surrender oneself to God in death (the need to die like a martyr) is anticipated throughout life" (220).

Notes to Chapter 7

1. Servais Pinckaers, OP, "The Sources of the Ethics of St. Thomas Aquinas," trans. Mary Thomas Noble, OP, with Michael Sherwin, OP, in *The Pinckaers Reader: Renewing Thomistic Moral Theology*, ed. John Berkman and Craig Steven Titus (Washington, DC: Catholic University of America Press, 2005), 13. Pinckaers goes on rightly to remark that in order to appreciate the place that humility has in the *Summa theologica*, one must group the question on humility (II-II, q. 161) "with the two following questions on pride and Adam's sin, in which . . . the fundamental importance of humility appears to better advantage" (14). For the concern that Aquinas underestimates humility in his *Summa theologiae*—due to his reliance upon Cicero's pagan philosophical way of organizing virtues (Cicero places humility under modesty)—see Sheryl Overmyer, "Exalting the Meek Virtue of Humility in Aquinas," *Heythrop Journal* 56 (2015): 650–62.

In the *Nicomachean Ethics*, Aristotle rejects humility, as does David Hume in his *Enquiries Concerning Human Understanding and Concerning the Principles of Morals* (repr., Oxford: Clarendon, 1975), 270. On feminist grounds, Mary Wollstonecraft rejects humility as well in *A Vindication of the Rights of Woman: With Strictures on Political and Moral Subjects* (Cambridge: Cambridge University Press, 2010). For these critics, see also Jeanine Grenberg, *Kant and the Ethics of Humility: A Story of Dependence, Corruption and Virtue* (Cambridge: Cambridge University Press, 2005), although Grenberg herself values humility as a way of virtuously correcting our desire to overthrow or ignore "morally relevant human limits" (6). The key concern of humility's detractors is that the powerful promote the virtue of humility as part of their oppression of the weak, a concern that reflects an abuse of the virtue, not a negation of the virtue's value when properly understood.

2. Thomas Aquinas, *Summa theologica*, trans. Fathers of the English Dominican Province (Westminster, MD: Christian Classics, 1981), II-II, q. 160, a. 2. Hereafter in this section, references from this work will be given in parentheses in the text.

3. As Stephen T. Pardue points out, "Any Christian account of humility must . . . depend on a deep understanding of pride, over against which it is formed" (*The Mind of Christ: Humility and the Intellect in Early Christian Theology* [London: Bloomsbury, 2013], 29).

4. Aquinas cites Gregory the Great, *Moralia* 31.45.

5. John Milton's *Paradise Lost*, with its portrait of Satan, provides a marvelous depiction of such pride. From a Christian medical perspective, Daniel B. Hinshaw comments (in a manner that links "humility" with "poverty") that "the role of palliative care is to limit the burden of distressing symptoms so that dying persons can fully engage in an active remembrance of their death. The process of kenosis beginning with the physical decline of aging and more dramatically manifested for some in the phenomenon of cachexia [a metabolic syndrome connected with cancer] extends to all aspects of the person, stripping away any remaining illusions and pretense. This is the beginning of the blessed poverty mentioned in the Gospel according to Luke; not only are the dying invited to experience poverty of spirit but theirs is a poverty that if they can accept it, is complete, encompassing their whole being. With this poverty as a solid foundation, the dying person can now fully engage and reconcile with the other, first with one's neighbor and then with the ultimate Other" ("The Kenosis of the Dying: An Invitation to Healing," in *The Role of Death in Life: A Multidisciplinary Examination of the Relationship between Life and Death*, ed. John Behr and Conor Cunningham [Eugene, OR: Cascade, 2015], 163).

6. For a political reading (shaped partly by the work of Stanley Hauerwas) of Aquinas's theology of humility in the context of Cicero and Augustine, on the one hand, and modern philosophers and theologians, on the other, see Joseph Lawrence Tadie, "Between Humilities: A Retrieval of Saint Thomas Aquinas on the Virtue of Humility" (PhD diss., Boston College, 2006). Humility is not an individualistic virtue, but belongs to our struggle to attain a community of love. See also J. I. Packer, *Finishing Our Course with Joy: Guidance from God for Engaging with Our Aging* (Wheaton, IL: Crossway, 2014), 94–95.

7. W. D. Davies and Dale C. Allison Jr. observe that Matt. 10:37 "is all but universally credited to Jesus," but they are less clear about the other verses of Matt. 10 (*A Critical and Exegetical Commentary on the Gospel according to Saint Matthew*, 3 vols. [London: T. & T. Clark, 1988–97], 2:221). They note that "10.34 is about the proper interpretation of the present, and the main point is this: the time of Jesus and his church is not, despite the presence of the kingdom of God, the messianic era of peace" (218). Even if 10:38–39 could be demonstrated to have come from the lips of Jesus (and I think that attempts to achieve such demonstrations are theologically unnecessary for those who believe in the Spirit's inspiration of Scripture), the question would remain as to why God would choose to save his people by means of an ongoing path of terrible suffering.

8. Christopher P. Vogt, *Patience, Compassion, Hope, and the Christian Art of Dying Well* (Lanham, MD: Rowman & Littlefield, 2004), 97.

NOTES TO PAGE 120

9. For the absolute agony that we experience when a child (even an adult child) dies, see Nicholas Wolterstorff, *Lament for a Son* (Grand Rapids: Eerdmans, 1987). See also C. S. Lewis, *A Grief Observed* (repr., New York: HarperCollins, 2001) on the death of his wife, Joy. Since God does not take pleasure in human death, no one's dying can be understood without reference to original sin and the loss of the grace of original justice. As Wolterstorff says, "We cannot live at peace with death. . . . God is appalled by death" (*Lament for a Son*, 63, 66). I add that this does not mean that God lacks the ability to forestall death or that God lacked love for Wolterstorff's son; in his providence, God permits our mortal susceptibility to material corruption and dissolution. Wolterstorff puts it well: "I cannot fit it all together by saying, 'He did it,' but neither can I do so by saying, 'There was nothing he could do about it.' . . . I have no explanation [for his son's death]. I can do nothing else than endure in the face of this deepest and most painful of mysteries" (67–68). For further discussion see my *Engaging the Doctrine of Creation: Cosmos, Creatures, and the Wise and Good Creator* (Grand Rapids: Baker Academic, 2017), chs. 6–7.

10. As Wolterstorff asks, "Why isn't Love-*without*-suffering the meaning of things? Why does God endure his suffering? Why does he not at once relieve his agony by relieving ours?" (*Lament for a Son*, 90). Somewhat similarly, Douglas J. Davies expresses the concern that Christianity "establishes death as the central moral pivot around which God works with the cross as its symbol" (*The Theology of Death* [London: T. & T. Clark, 2008], 8). For Davies, however, what we need to overcome is not so much death as "a certain Christian romantic commitment to death as evil" (8). Davies considers that the notion that death is evil conflicts with Christianity's commitment to the goodness of creation, since science has made clear how much death and destruction are embedded naturally in the whole of creation. His solution of declaring human death to be natural (and good) rather than the result of the fall is in my view an impossible one, since the destruction of the human body-soul unity—the destruction of a person with his or her unique consciousness—cannot rightly be conceived as a mere good of nature (though, in Christ, dying can be conceived of as a good, insofar as it is a participation in Christ's dying). On God and suffering, see also the insights of Thomas G. Weinandy, OFM, Cap., *Does God Suffer?* (Notre Dame: University of Notre Dame Press, 2000).

11. Brant Pitre shows that Second Temple Jewish authors outside the New Testament attribute to the eschatological tribulation the following characteristics: it is linked to the end of exile and the corresponding restoration of Israel (either as a return to the promised land or as an exaltation into a heavenly realm); it involves the coming of the Messiah, and the possible suffering and/or death of the Messiah; it involves the suffering and/or death of a righteous remnant that opposes an anti-Messiah; it is the climax of Israel's exilic sufferings and has two stages, ending in a great tribulation; it atones for sins; it produces the ingathering or conversion of the Gentiles; it involves the destruction of the temple; and it precedes the final judgment, the resurrection of the dead, and the arrival of the eschatological kingdom or new creation. See Pitre,

Jesus, the Tribulation, and the End of Exile: Restoration Eschatology and the Origin of the Atonement (Grand Rapids: Baker Academic, 2005), 128–29. (Hereafter in this section, page references from this work will be given in parentheses in the text.) See also N. T. Wright, *Jesus and the Victory of God* (Minneapolis: Fortress, 1996), 570, 577–78, 584. Like Pitre, Wright draws upon an insight advanced by Albert Schweitzer in his seminal 1906 book, *The Quest of the Historical Jesus: A Critical Study of Its Progress from Reimarus to Wrede* (repr., London: Black, 1954), 384–90; see also Wright, *The New Testament and the People of God* (Minneapolis: Fortress, 1992), 277–78, where he observes: "Some [Second Temple] writers spoke of a coming period of intense suffering in terms of the birth-pangs of the new age, the so-called 'messianic woes'. . . . Israel will pass through intense and climactic suffering; after this she will be forgiven, and then and thus the world will be healed."

12. Behr, "Life and Death in the Age of Martyrdom," in *Role of Death in Life*, ed. Behr and Cunningham, 92. Behr goes on to specify: "Life, as *zoe*, lives when life, as *bios*, no longer lives for itself, but rather lays itself down for others, in the manner initiated by Christ and exemplified in the martyrs" (92–93).

13. Pitre, *Jesus, the Tribulation*, 131. Hereafter in this section, page references from this work will be given in parentheses in the text.

14. As Benjamin D. Sommer—who fully embraces the results of historical-critical research into the biblical texts—observes regarding the relationship of this narrative to history: "Contrary to what one sometimes reads in the popular press or hears from less learned pulpits, there are no archaeological or historical reasons to doubt the core elements of the Bible's presentation of Israel's history: namely, that the ancestors of the Israelites included an important group who came from Mesopotamia; that at least some Israelites were enslaved to Egyptians and were surprisingly rescued from Egyptian bondage; that they experienced a revelation that played a crucial role in the formation of their national, religious, and ethnic identity; that they settled down in the hill country of the land of Canaan at the beginning of the Iron Age, around 1300 or 1200 BCE; that they formed kingdoms there a few centuries later, around 1000 BCE; and that these kingdoms were eventually destroyed by Assyrian and Babylonian armies. To be sure, the fact that there are no reasons to doubt these basic elements of the biblical story line does not prove that one *should* believe them, either; my point here is simply to alert my readers to the specious nature of claims that any of these elements is contradicted or even undermined by what archaeologists have or have not found" (*Revelation and Authority: Sinai in Jewish Scripture and Tradition* [New Haven: Yale University Press, 2015], 17). See also my *Engaging the Doctrine of Revelation: The Mediation of the Gospel through Church and Scripture* (Grand Rapids: Baker Academic, 2014), ch. 7.

To my mind, the significance of the first five books of the Bible does not stand or fall upon a determination of whether God providentially arranged the historical events, or formed his people Israel in some other way that included the typologically and morally instructive narratives that we find in the first five books of the Bible. Either way, God chose his people Israel and formed them over many centuries to be the bearers of the promise of God's salvation. Like Sommer, however, I do not think that skepticism about the historicity of (for example) the figure of Moses is appropriate given the available evidence, which is insufficient to compel either certitude or skepticism, but which bears witness to a widespread remembrance of a decisive figure in the founding of Israel as a people. For the view that "Exodus does not qualify as history," although "the tradition of salvation as liberation from Egyptian rule is formative in the religious practice of Israel during the monarchical period," and that in the thirteenth century BCE "Israel appears to be an indigenous group within Canaan who were the object of Egyptian conquest," see Thomas B. Dozeman, *Commentary on Exodus* (Grand Rapids: Eerdmans, 2009), 28–30.

15. Thomas Joseph White, OP, seeks to balance two main points in this regard. First, "the Old Testament contains certain ways of denoting the mystery of divine justice that are quite grave. These denotations are inspired by the Holy Spirit and are instructive as saving truth, but they are also portrayed through the idioms of a culture that was archaic and (at least in some respects) politically brutal" (*Exodus* [Grand Rapids: Brazos, 2016], 90). Second, in light of original sin, "God has the prerogative for wise reasons to withdraw the privilege of being and life from his creatures. . . . By taking the lives of the firstborn (and in doing so, taking these personal, innocent creatures 'back' into God's own eternal mystery), God reveals to pagan humanity that he is the author of life and that his providence alone can safeguard their future. The project of life without God is a project that is futureless. The chastisement of the Pharaoh and the Egyptians is thus meant to open them up to the reality of their dependence upon the transcendent mystery not only of God's sovereign justice but also God's sovereign goodness and mercy. The hidden, inner side of this mystery is that the Lord God of Israel also intends eventually to 'make use' of human death to save the human race" (93). I agree with White's emphasis on the "archaic" idioms and on the theological lesson.

For my part, I think that there are good theological reasons to question whether in response to Pharaoh's hardness of heart, God withdrew the privilege of life from all the Egyptian firstborn males. The implementation of the plague of the firstborn may belong to divine revelation in a manner that does not have literal reference (at least insofar as it pertains to divine action). Although God certainly permits human death, and this permission is just, I do not think that God slaughters children in order to punish their political leaders. See Trent Horn, *Hard Sayings: A Catholic Approach to Answering Bible Difficulties* (El Cajon, CA: Catholic Answers, 2016), 290–91; see also the book to which he responds, Steve Wells, *Drunk with Blood: God's Killings in the Bible* (New York: SAB, 2013).

Although Augustine accepts the slaughter of the Egyptian firstborn as God's action, Augustine's exegetical principle in *On Christian Doctrine* may be instructive here: "Those things which seem almost shameful to the inexperienced, whether simply spoken or actually performed either by the person of God or by men whose sanctity is commended to us, are all figurative, and their secrets are to be removed as kernels from the husk as nourishment for charity" (*On Christian Doctrine*, trans. D. W. Robertson Jr.

[New York: Macmillan, 1958], 3.12.18, p. 90). See also Mark Sheridan, OSB, *Language for God in Patristic Tradition: Wrestling with Biblical Anthropomorphism* (Downers Grove, IL: IVP Academic, 2015). On the other hand, if we assume the historicity of the account of the tenth plague, Jonathan Sacks offers a helpful explanation: "Whereas the first two plagues were symbolic representations of the Egyptian murder of Israelite children, the tenth plague was the enactment of retributive justice, as if heaven was saying to the Egyptians: You committed, or supported, or passively accepted the murder of innocent children. There is only one way you will ever realize the wrong you did, namely, if you suffer what you did to others" (*Covenant and Conversation: A Weekly Reading of the Jewish Bible. Exodus: The Book of Redemption* [New Milford, CT: Maggid, 2010], 74).

16. On the view that many Second Temple Israelites understood themselves to be in ongoing exile, a view advocated strongly by N. T. Wright, see also Craig A. Evans's response to Wright's critics on this point: "Jesus and the Continuing Exile," in *Jesus and the Restoration of Israel: A Critical Assessment of N. T. Wright's* Jesus and the Victory of God, ed. Carey C. Newman (Downers Grove, IL: InterVarsity Press, 1999), 77-100. James D. G. Dunn summarizes the point, even while taking a critical stance: "Based on Deut. 30.1-10, there was a widespread belief [Dunn had previously footnoted a large range of biblical and extrabiblical texts] that after a period of dispersion among the nations, the outcasts/scattered of Israel would be gathered again and brought back to the promised land, the unity of the twelve tribes reestablished, and the relation of Israel as God's people, and Yahweh as Israel's God, restored. Wright summarises it as the hope of *return from exile*" (*Jesus Remembered* [Grand Rapids: Eerdmans, 2003], 393). After listing fourteen "clearly attested and most relevant motifs which suggest the sort of expectations that were cherished and may have been evoked by Jesus' kingdom talk among Jews living in the land of Israel in the first century CE," including the motif of the end of exile, Dunn emphasizes that it remains important to allow for diverse and competing versions of Judaism in the Second Temple period (393; cf. 397). This concern leads Dunn to conclude that "Wright exaggerates the importance of the theme of return from exile in Palestinian Judaism. The return of the scattered outcasts of Israel to the homeland in accordance with the original schema of Deuteronomy 30 was certainly a feature of Jewish eschatological hope. But there is no real evidence that *those who actually were living in the land* thought of themselves as still in exile" (473). To my mind, however, many Israelites did still think of the people of Israel as in a state of sin—as not yet fully being the holy people they were called to be—and they looked forward to the end of this alienated condition as part of the other elements of the end of exile. This is so even if, as Dunn insists, "there was no single comprehensive grand narrative shaping the thought of Jesus' contemporaries" (475). Others who criticize or nuance Wright's position include Luke Timothy Johnson, "A Historiographical Response to Wright's Jesus," in *Jesus and the Restoration*, ed. Newman, 210-12; Steven M. Bryan, *Jesus and Israel's Traditions of Judgment and Restoration* (Cambridge: Cambridge University Press, 2002), 16.

17. Focusing on the Last Supper, Scot McKnight similarly proposes that "Jesus' last

supper is a fundamental reorientation of the temple order. The scholars, wide-ranging as they are, who connect these three dots (entry, temple incident, and last supper) have offered a potent hypothesis that helps explain how Jesus understood his death. The temple, standing for the nation, is about to be destroyed; God has appointed Jesus' death as a means of escape; those who eat his body and drink his blood will be passed over" (*Jesus and His Death: Historiography, the Historical Jesus, and Atonement Theory* [Waco, TX: Baylor University Press, 2005], 326). For McKnight, "Jesus saw his death as the *beginning of the eschatological ordeal*. . . . He, as representative, is about to cross the threshold into the last hour. . . . Not only did Jesus see his death as the onset of the eschatological tribulation, he knew (as a Jew) that the tribulation was to lead into the kingdom. Thus, Jesus must have seen his death as the onset of the kingdom of God" (337). In McKnight's view, Jesus understood himself not in light of Isa. 53 but in light of Dan. 7.

18. See also the extended argument found in Pitre, *Jesus and the Last Supper*, as well as his comments on pp. 28–52 in which he refines his understanding of the criteria of authenticity (essentially, he turns to three criteria proposed by E. P. Sanders). Along generally similar lines, McKnight concludes that Jesus "sees his death as representative, but it appears also that he sees his death as somehow *vicarious and protecting*. In stating that the bread was his body and the wine his blood, Jesus suggested that he was the Passover victim whose blood would protect his followers from the imminent judgment of God against Jerusalem and its corrupt leadership (embodied in the temple especially). We have here the first genuine glimpse of a death that somehow atones. Jesus' theory of the atonement then is that his own death, and his followers' participation in that death by ingestion, protects his followers from the Day of YHWH, which in the prophets especially is often described as the wrath of YHWH. As the avenging angel of the Passover in Egypt 'passed over' the firstborn children whose fathers had smeared blood on the door, so the Father of Jesus would 'pass over' those followers who ingested Jesus' body and blood" (*Jesus and His Death*, 339).

19. For a detailed discussion see Brant Pitre, *Jesus and the Last Supper* (Grand Rapids: Eerdmans, 2015), ch. 5.

20. Pitre notes that his overall reconstruction of Jesus's aims in many ways was already anticipated by Schweitzer: "To put it bluntly: with regard to the link between the tribulation and the atonement, Schweitzer was right. While his lack of emphasis on the restoration of Israel and the resurrection of the dead is surely a weakness in his reconstruction of Jesus' eschatology, nevertheless, his basic insight into the Great Tribulation and the atonement stands" (*Jesus, the Tribulation*, 506). Pitre especially draws upon Schweitzer, *The Mystery of the Kingdom of God: The Secret of Jesus' Messiahship and Passion*, trans. Walter Lowrie (repr., Amherst, NY: Prometheus, 1985), the German original of which is titled *Das Messianitäts- und Leidensgeheimnis: Eine Skizze des Lebens Jesu* (Tübingen: Mohr, 1901).

21. The Dead Sea Scrolls, for instance, have proven to be a goldmine for eschatological texts that indicate a worldview broadly similar to that of Jesus. For example, the Damascus Document[b] (CD[b] 20:13–16) teaches that the Teacher of Righteousness,

in dying, will usher in a forty-year period of tribulation, culminating in the coming of the Messiah, who will make atonement for sins.

22. On Paul's understanding of the "messianic woes" and our participation in Christ, see C. Marvin Pate and Douglas W. Kennard, *Deliverance Now and Not Yet: The New Testament and the Great Tribulation* (New York: Lang, 2003).

23. Aquinas, *Summa theologica*, III, q. 46, a. 6, obj. 1. (Hereafter, references from this work will be given in parentheses in the text.) For an excellent, succinct discussion, see Aaron Riches, *Ecce Homo: On the Divine Unity of Christ* (Grand Rapids: Eerdmans, 2016), 192–96. Riches points out that by contrast to Aquinas's position in the *Summa theologica*, "the young Thomas held that the bodily pain suffered by Christ did not exceed his body, that the sufferings of the Cross affected Christ physically but not psychologically" (197).

24. See also Emmanuel Falque, *Le passeur de Gethsémani: Angoisse, souffrance et mort: Lecture existentielle et phénoménologique* (Paris: Cerf, 1999), though Aquinas's position differs (as does my own) from Falque on some important points. Falque and Aquinas can agree on the fact that Christ, in dying, "inhabit[s] our own darkness" (Falque, "Suffering Death," in *Role of Death in Life*, ed. Behr and Cunningham, 50). Falque's insistence that Christ experiences not only "abandonment" (which he certainly does) but also "a feeling of transience, indeed of futility, of all of existence" (51), goes too far in my view. Falque's perspective, in certain respects quite like that of Hans Urs von Balthasar, is shaped too much by Heidegger's critique of Christian understandings of death. Thus, according to Falque, "Christ plunges into this 'nothing' of the meaning of life in order to allow us metaphysically to remain a 'being in question,' and hence properly human, at the hour of dying, or better, of living in full consciousness of death" (53). For Falque, too, solely the Father (not the divine Son) "is capable of transforming or even of metamorphosing" our finitude (52). Yet, though I do not think that Christ experiences our feeling of meaninglessness, I agree with Falque—and I think Aquinas would too—that Christ concentrates fully upon his suffering in a manner that brackets meaning (though without renouncing his beatific communion with God: at least, Falque affirms "the Son's unceasing addressing of the Father in the greatest abandonment, sure that the link could never be broken" [53]). Insightfully, Falque proposes that Christ's existential stance here is "not that life has no meaning, but that we cannot and should not *ourselves* give it meaning" (53). The key idea is that the Son endures and redeems our real anxiety in the face of death, and I fully agree with this point—though in the way that Aquinas construes it.

25. Gisbert Greshake speculates that not only did Jesus die "the death of a sinner" (which he certainly did), but also that "the possibility cannot be excluded that he died in bitter despair" ("Towards a Theology of Dying," trans. Robert Nowell, in *The Experience of Dying*, ed. Norbert Greinacher and Alois Müller [New York: Herder & Herder, 1974], 89). I think that this possibility can and must be excluded, since despair is a condition of hopeless separation from God. Greshake goes on to construe "despair" as entailing a movement toward God, but it is hope that entails such a movement.

26. Thomas Joseph White, OP, notes that "Aquinas does not think the suffering of Christ and his knowledge of God simply coexist on separate but unrelated 'levels' of his soul. Rather, he distinguishes between the objects and subject of the various faculties of Christ's soul so as to make clear in what way the suffering and spiritual consolation of Christ occur simultaneously in the same human experience. On the one hand, he notes that the faculties of the human soul of Jesus experience irreducibly diverse objects during the crucifixion as either consolations or pains. Just as Christ could suffer terrible pain in his physical body or sorrow in his sensible feelings (stemming from the 'objects' of his bodily sensation and inner emotional life, respectively), so he could also enjoy the immediate knowledge of God stemming from the object of his intellectual activity" (White, *The Incarnate Lord: A Thomistic Study in Christology* [Washington, DC: Catholic University of America Press, 2015], 329–30). The chapter from which I draw this quotation—chapter 7 of White's book, on "Did God Abandon Jesus? The Dereliction on the Cross"—is a magnificent exposition of Christ's suffering. White points out that Christ took upon himself "some of the *consequences* of sin in our fallen humanity (including the fear of mortality, deep sadness, and a loss of the sense of the consoling presence of God) without an experience of that sin itself" (331; cf. 334–37). See also Guy Mansini, OSB, "Christology in Context: Review Essay of Thomas Joseph White, O.P., *The Incarnate Lord*," *Nova et Vetera* 14 (2016): 1271–91.

27. As Greshake observes, therefore, "dying with Christ is not anything negative but rather a liberation from a life that only seeks itself" ("Towards a Theology of Dying," 90).

28. For further discussion, see the section titled "Suffering with and for Christ (1 Peter)," in Daniel Harrington, SJ, *Why Do We Suffer? A Scriptural Approach to the Human Condition* (Franklin, WI: Sheed & Ward, 2000), 132–36. Harrington grants in this section that suffering "is participation in the paschal mystery," a participation that he rightly distinguishes (earlier in his book) from the "belief that we can add to the sacrifice of Christ" (68, 136).

29. See Joseph J. McInerney, *The Greatness of Humility: St. Augustine on Moral Excellence* (Eugene, OR: Pickwick, 2016); Brian E. Daley, SJ, "A Humble Mediator: The Distinctive Elements of St. Augustine's Christology," *Word and Spirit* 9 (1987): 100–117.

30. Thomas Aquinas, *Commentary on the Letter of Saint Paul to the Philippians*, trans. Fabian R. Larcher, OP, ed. J. Mortensen and E. Alarcón, in *Commentary on the Letters of Saint Paul to the Philippians, Colossians, Thessalonians, Timothy, Titus, and Philemon* (Lander, WY: Aquinas Institute for the Study of Sacred Doctrine, 2012), §65, p. 28.

31. *Commentary on Philippians*, §66, p. 28.

32. Unlike ourselves, Jesus gave up life and honor with full freedom, since he did not owe the penalty of death and he could have miraculously preserved his life.

33. Adrian J. Walker, "*Singulariter in spe constituisti me*: On the Christian Attitude Towards Death," *Communio* 39 (2012): 355.

34. Thomas Aquinas, *Commentary on the Gospel of St. Matthew*, trans. Paul M.

Kimball (Camillus, NY: Dolorosa, 2012), 419. Overmyer also treats humility in Aquinas's *Commentary on Matthew*, focusing on Matt. 3 and Matt. 18 ("Exalting the Meek," 658). She also discusses Aquinas's commentary on John 13.

35. Aquinas, *Commentary on Matthew*, 419.

36. Aquinas, *Commentary on Matthew*, 419.

37. See also the succinct account of Aquinas's sacramental ecclesiology offered by Frederick Christian Bauerschmidt, "'That the Faithful Become the Temple of God': The Church Militant in Aquinas's *Commentary on John*," in *Reading John with St. Thomas Aquinas: Theological Exegesis and Speculative Theology*, ed. Michael Dauphinais and Matthew Levering (Washington, DC: Catholic University of America Press, 2005), 293–311.

38. Joseph Ratzinger, *Dogma and Preaching: Applying Christian Doctrine to Daily Life*, trans. Michael J. Miller and Matthew J. O'Connell (San Francisco: Ignatius, 2011), 251; see also 253.

39. Pardue, *Mind of Christ*, 156. Pardue devotes a good bit of his book, which is focused on epistemology, to showing how Gregory of Nyssa conceives of humility as involving "suffering as part of the process of spiritual growth" (157). Pardue also rightly emphasizes (in ch. 4 of his book) that "Augustine takes humility to be a chief characteristic of the Godhead in God's self-revelation to us, and that the characteristic shape of divine humility—as an embracing of human limitation which results eventually in the outstripping of those very limitations—is basically identical to the shape of human humility, in which humans recognize, confess, and exceed their own limitations by divine grace" (157–58).

40. White, *The Incarnate Lord*, 338.

41. I do not mean, of course, to suggest that pride is the cause of every sin that humans commit (although, like Aquinas, I hold that pride was the sin of the first humans). As Aquinas says, citing the Vulgate version of Sir. 10:13, "Pride is said to be *the beginning of all sin*, not as though every sin originated from pride, but because any kind of sin is naturally liable to arise from pride" (II-II, q. 162, a. 7, ad 1). See also Jesse Couenhoven, "Not Every Wrong Is Done with Pride?," *Scottish Journal of Theology* 61 (2008): 32–50.

42. Edward Sri, *Love Unveiled: The Catholic Faith Explained* (San Francisco: Ignatius, 2015), 264.

43. Ratzinger, *Dogma and Preaching*, 250. Ratzinger is indebted to Dietrich von Hildebrand's *Transformation in Christ* (Manchester, NH: Sophia Institute, 1990), 3–29, 481–500. Ratzinger adds, "Thus Christianity, unlike idealism, does not simply deny the terror and frightfulness of death. Instead, that continues to exist, but it becomes, precisely as such, the instrument of grace and of salvation, in a reversal that could never be imagined from an earthly perspective but can only be decreed by God" (*Dogma and Preaching*, 252).

44. As Thomas Joseph White says, "Christ's passion can affect all of human history as an efficient cause of salvation, and this by virtue of his deity. . . . God has united

NOTES TO PAGES 134–35

himself to us amidst death so that we might be united to God in life" (*The Incarnate Lord*, 362–63).

45. I should note that I agree with Phillip Cary that historically speaking, "Christians are in no position to be chauvinistic, as if we (rather than the Jews!) were in possession of a religion of love" in the sense of being historically "better and more loving than others" (Phillip Cary and Jean-François Phelizon, *Does God Have a Strategy? A Dialogue*, trans. Anne François [Eugene, OR: Cascade, 2015], 153). Jesus does indeed enact the salvation of the whole human race by his self-sacrificial love, and he pours out his Holy Spirit so as to enable his followers to follow him in Christlike humility. The saints, and indeed all who truly follow him, possess this humility (including all who have been united in charity to Christ through the Spirit by *implicit* faith: see Aquinas, *Summa theologica* II-II, q. 2, a. 7, ad 3; I-II, q. 106, a. 1, ad 3 and a. 3, ad 2). Historically speaking, however, the claim to being God's truly humble people, over against other people, can only fuel a false and deadly pride. For evidence of the depth and breadth of Christian sinfulness, see Ephraim Radner, *A Brutal Unity: The Spiritual Politics of the Christian Church* (Waco, TX: Baylor University Press, 2012).

Notes to Chapter 8

1. Richard John Neuhaus, *As I Lay Dying: Meditations upon Returning* (New York: Basic Books, 2002), 102. See also ch. 2 above. Neuhaus's perspective on the act of dying is similar to that which we found in Josef Pieper, *Death and Immortality*, trans. Richard and Clara Winston (South Bend, IN: St. Augustine's Press, 2000).

2. Neuhaus, *As I Lay Dying*, 102.

3. Richard John Neuhaus, "While We're at It," *First Things* 190 (2009): 71–72. Neuhaus's insight here accords, I think, with that of Esther E. Acolatse: "It is because death is both friend and foe that it stands as a means of both grace and condemnation by God. It is a means of grace because it is that by which sinful humanity is rescued from perduring in a sinful state. It is a state of condemnation because it is at the same time the awful reminder of sin's effect" (Acolatse, "Embracing and Resisting Death: A Theology of Justice and Hope for Care at the End of Life," in *Living Well and Dying Faithfully: Christian Practices for End-of-Life Care*, ed. John Swinton and Richard Payne [Grand Rapids: Eerdmans, 2009], 250). Acolatse emphasizes the importance of the virtue of patience, as well as the importance of boldly praying for the sick and the dying. She concludes that "the Scriptures are right when they point to dying daily as the way to find life. Jesus tells the disciples that they would lose their lives if they cling to them but find their lives if they lose them. It is the self-transformational experience that comes to many through conversion experiences, and to the Christian through the working of the Holy Spirit in sanctifying the believer" (269).

4. Neuhaus, "While We're at It," 72. For further background, especially with regard to Neuhaus's first bout with cancer, see Randy Boyagoda, *Richard John Neuhaus: A*

Life in the Public Square (New York: Doubleday, 2015). It was a great privilege for me to know Fr. Neuhaus through my involvement with Evangelicals and Catholics Together. Neuhaus's last few days were difficult ones because his cancer affected his brain and thus also his mental and emotional states. Let me emphasize that in the present book, although I describe the "virtues of dying," I am not suggesting that we are in a competition for the best outwardly holy dying. Indeed, I am arguing for the very contrary, namely that dying is a trial and that we must rely utterly on God's mercy in Christ. At the same time, I recognize that some people receive the gift of beautiful deaths, as described for instance in Kathy Kalina, *Midwife for Souls: Spiritual Care for the Dying*, rev. ed. (Boston: Pauline Books & Media, 2007), 23–26. Kalina also describes a "bad death" or at least a "near bad death": "Suddenly her eyes flew open and she said in a guttural voice, 'I don't want to die.' I will never forget those eyes. They were brimming with hate. I prayed out loud for her, and every time I mentioned the name of Jesus, her eyes flashed hatred" (41). Kalina recognizes, however, that "we never know what happens between a soul and God at the moment of death" (43).

5. Henri J. M. Nouwen, *Our Greatest Gift: A Meditation on Dying and Caring* (New York: HarperCollins, 1994), 59.

6. Colman E. O'Neill, OP, *Sacramental Realism: A General Theory of the Sacraments* (Chicago: Midwest Theological Forum, 1998), 202. See also ch. 6 above.

7. O'Neill, *Sacramental Realism*, 203. O'Neill explains the development of the church's understanding of this sacrament in terms of a gradual realization of the "sacramentality of grave illness" in light of the fact that "death permits appeal to no one but to the risen Christ" (203). He adds: "It is in conformity with the facts to treat the sacraments as a system, having a structure that culminates in the Eucharist, with each of the others either being directly intelligible in terms of the Eucharist or so shaping human life in Christ as to endow it with meaning that calls out for that union with Christ that only the Eucharist can give. The Eucharist then will shed its light on the others, for they are either intrinsic to the eucharistic mystery or participate in its fullness by making explicit, where the life of the church requires it, what Christ's sacramental union with the church implies" (207).

8. Vigen Guroian, *Life's Living toward Dying: A Theological and Medical-Ethical Study* (Grand Rapids: Eerdmans, 1996), 58–59; cf. 85–87. Guroian makes this point in the context of a brilliant analysis of Leo Tolstoy's novella *The Death of Ivan Ilych*, in *Great Short Works of Leo Tolstoy*, trans. Louis Maude and Aylmer Maude, ed. John Bayley (New York: Harper & Row, 1967), 245–302. As Guroian notes, "There are among the clergy and laity of every church contemporary counterparts of Job's so-called friends who are motivated by an inflexible orthodoxy or other reasons to assume the divine prerogative of judgment and who add to the suffering of countless afflicted by reminding them incessantly of their sins and failures. But these abuses of a penitential theology do not discredit the profound and practical wisdom of the church when it places repentance and forgiveness at the center of its ministry to the sick and dying. This emphasis makes perfect sense in light of the Gospels and indeed of the whole of

Scripture. The Orthodox rites wisely take account of the burden of personal guilt that frequently weighs heavily on the mind of a sick or dying person. In such circumstances, the mistakes that a person has made or the wrongs and injustices he has committed over a lifetime can suddenly return to haunt him in devastating ways. . . . The Byzantine rite of Holy Unction contains several psalms and prayers that invite sick persons to review their lives penitently. . . . The Armenian Rite of Communion of the Sick is an occasion for just this sort of reconciliation and forgiveness" (85, 87). Guroian cites a conversation with Sr. Sharon M. Burns, then director of Stella Maris Hospice in Towson, Maryland, in which she tells him that "reconciliation is the most crucial thing for the dying irrespective of whether or not the person is religious or secular" (87).

9. Johann Christoph Arnold, *Be Not Afraid: Overcoming the Fear of Death* (Farmington, PA: Plough, 2002), 68.

10. Arnold, *Be Not Afraid*, 69.

11. Arnold, *Be Not Afraid*, 69.

12. Amy Plantinga Pauw, "Dying Well," in *Practicing Our Faith: A Way of Life for a Searching People*, ed. Dorothy C. Bass (San Francisco: Jossey-Bass, 1997), 174. For a Lutheran position, agreeing with Luther's view that James 5:14–15 describes a "sacramental" rather than a sacrament, and calling for a return in contemporary Lutheran churches to regular intercessory prayer for the sick and to an active ministry of visitation of the sick, see Peter Meinhold, "Healing and Sanctification in Luther's Theology," in *Temple of the Holy Spirit: Sickness and Death of the Christian in the Liturgy. The Twenty-First Liturgical Conference Saint-Serge*, ed. Achille M. Triacca, SDB, trans. Matthew J. O'Connell (New York: Pueblo, 1983), 107–25. Andrew Davison, an Anglican, affirms the sacramental status of anointing the sick, while noting that the sacrament "was completely eclipsed in the church of England following the Reformation" (Davison, *Why Sacraments?* [Eugene, OR: Cascade, 2013], 120). Davison's view that anointing of the sick is a sacrament is not shared by all (or even most) Anglicans or Episcopalians. See also Charles W. Gusmer, *The Ministry of Healing in the Church of England: An Ecumenical-Liturgical Study* (Great Wakering, Eng.: Mayhew-McCrimmon, 1974). In his *Doxology: The Praise of God in Worship, Doctrine and Life: A Systematic Theology* (New York: Oxford University Press, 1980), the Methodist theologian Geoffrey Wainwright states: "The Orthodox and Catholic churches practise a sacramental unction of the sick; Pentecostals and others pray for sick persons with the laying on of hands; all churches include the sick in their intercessions" (76).

13. Guroian points out the significance of the social dimension of the sacrament of anointing of the sick, a dimension that must not be neglected: "the Orthodox rites of holy unction place personal sin firmly within the social matrix of evil and suffering. . . . The Byzantine Rite of Holy Unction draws attention not only to the sins of the sick person but also to the sins of the family and friends who gather at the bedside or in the church. This attention to corporate sin is important for a Christian ethic of care for the dying, because it helps to take some of the weight of failure off the sick and preclude their alienation from the healthy. Even more important, the prayer reconstitutes the

church as a community of penitent sinners aware of their common frailty and mortality" (*Life's Living toward Dying*, 89–90). He adds that the Byzantine Rite of Holy Unction, by recalling numerous biblical and saintly exemplars, joins "the natural healing symbolism of oil with the biblical and sacramental meaning of anointment as the mark of salvation and a person's full incorporation into the communion of saints" (96).

14. John C. Kasza, *Understanding Sacramental Healing: Anointing and Viaticum* (Chicago: Hillenbrand, 2007), ix. Hereafter in this section, page references from this work will be given in parentheses in the text.

15. See also the similar perspective of Paul Meyendorff, *The Anointing of the Sick* (Crestwood, NY: St. Vladimir's Seminary Press, 2009). He observes: "The form in which the anointing of the sick takes place . . . varies greatly from parish to parish. At times, the priest alone comes to the hospital or to the home of an ill parishioner and performs an abbreviated form of the rite. Occasionally, the sick person is brought to the church for the celebration, and a few other parishioners may be in attendance. Particularly in churches following Slavic traditions, the rite is rarely performed, because it is understood to be a rite for the dying, the 'last rites.' Consequently, both patients and their families misunderstand its purpose and see it rather as a last resort, a capitulation to imminent death. The priest who comes is perceived more as a 'grim reaper' than as a 'physician of souls and bodies'" (92). I note that the fact that the sacrament scares dying persons shows how much courage is needed not to cling to earthly life to the bitter end.

It is worth mentioning that among Greek Orthodox, the sacrament is also celebrated in church on Holy Wednesday (during Holy Week). Meyendorff states, "When performed in this way, the rite is understood to be a preparation for the reception of communion on Holy Thursday and Pascha, and often a substitute for the sacrament of confession" (92). Meyendorff finds this to be an inadequate understanding of the sacrament of anointing of the sick, and he suggests that parishes that currently celebrate the sacrament on Holy Wednesday should "shift the celebration to a time before Holy Week, perhaps to a day during the sixth week of Lent" (100). Slavic parishes that do not currently celebrate the sacrament on Holy Wednesday should avoid doing so, since the result of doing so is that "instead of specifically addressing persons facing the challenge of serious illness, it [the sacrament] is now used for a different purpose altogether" (101). Meyendorff adds that some Orthodox churches also have a rule that the celebration of the sacrament requires that seven priests be present—since "the number seven is a symbol of fullness and completeness" (101) and makes the sacrament a truly communal event, as it should be. The unfortunate result of the rule, however, is to make celebration of the sacrament quite rare due to lack of priests.

Meyendorff holds that only one priest need be present to administer the sacrament, and like Kasza he emphasizes the need for the involvement of the whole community: "pastors ought to bring back into practice the service of anointing of the sick as a properly liturgical celebration, normally performed in church, and with as many of the faithful in attendance as possible. Where possible, ill parishioners should be brought to the church, and the rite can be celebrated over several people at a time. In this way, the sick can be reintegrated into the life of the church, surrounded by family, friends, and the members of Christ's body. All will pray for and with the sick as the priest or priests in attendance repeatedly lay their hands on them and anoint them. . . . If the rite must be celebrated elsewhere than in the church, the priest should strive to bring parishioners with him" (96, 98).

16. For emphasis on the sacrament as offering to sick persons the community's compassionate and liberative solidarity, see Megan McKenna, *Rites of Justice: The Sacraments and Liturgy as Ethical Imperatives* (Maryknoll, NY: Orbis, 1997); James L. Empereur, SJ, *Prophetic Anointing: God's Call to the Sick, the Elderly, and the Dying* (Wilmington, DE: Glazier, 1982); Juan Luis Segundo, *The Sacraments Today* (Maryknoll, NY: Orbis, 1974); Thomas Talley, "Healing: Sacrament or Charism," *Worship* 46 (1972): 518–27.

17. Citing Miguel Angel Monge, "Integral Care of the Sick: The Role of Spiritual Help," *Dolentium Hominum* 11 (1989): 15. Daniel Berrigan, SJ, describes trying to change the popular mind by altering "the expectation of the dying as to the function of a priest. I appear at bedside to greet them, hold their hands. I am dressed in old clothes, ready for whatever service seems required or helpful. They can take me or leave, as can the nuns, orderlies, families. I do not bring the holy oils, or pray the sacrament of the sick, or give communion, except on special occasions. Others are available to do those things" (*We Die before We Live: Talking with the Very Ill* [New York: Seabury, 1980], 137). I think that Berrigan made a mistake in this regard, underestimating the value of his particular priestly ministries.

For the view that one need not be a priest in order to administer the sacrament of anointing of the sick, see John J. Ziegler, *Let Them Anoint the Sick* (Collegeville, MN: Liturgical Press, 1987). Ziegler strives to show that the Council of Trent's teaching that only priests can administer this sacrament is not a definitive teaching. I disagree with Ziegler, and indeed the Congregation of the Doctrine of the Faith has clarified (on Feb. 11, 2005) that the church's unchangeable teaching is that only priests can administer the sacrament. From a Methodist perspective, Ben Witherington III notes that James 5:14 makes clear that the anointing is the task of the church leaders, as distinct from other members of the church ("James," in *Letters and Homilies for Jewish Christians: A Socio-Rhetorical Commentary on Hebrews, James and Jude* [Downers Grove, IL: IVP Academic, 2007], 543).

18. In my view, the church's promotion of the Commendation of the Dying as the "last rite" (when viaticum is impossible) should not displace the sacrament of anointing of the sick for those who are imminently dying, including those who cannot receive viaticum. Nonetheless, I agree with the formulation of Michael G. Lawler (with whom, I expect, Kasza would be sympathetic): "In the case of the sick who are not just in danger of death but are also on the point of death, the new ritual prescribes a further rite in addition to anointing, namely, Viaticum. In fact, for such sick it prescribes a continuous rite, comprised of reconciliation, anointing and Viaticum. That order marks a change from the order of the previous ritual, and is not without symbolic import. The prior

sequence was reconciliation, Viaticum and anointing, a sequence which emphasized ritually the dogmatic position that anointing was the sacrament of the dying, a true extreme unction. Now that it is established, again, that it is not a sacrament of the dying, but of the sick, the ritual order is made to manifest that fact" (*Symbol and Sacrament: A Contemporary Sacramental Theology* [Omaha: Creighton University Press, 1995], 173). I concur with this description of "a continuous rite," and it is correct to emphasize that the sacrament of anointing of the sick is for all who are seriously ill, and not only persons who are on the verge of dying. Lawler goes on to say: "First, there is effected reconciliation and peace with the church; then, united or reunited with the church as the case may be, the church ministers to the sick person in the ritual of anointing; finally it ministers to the dying person in the ritual of Viaticum" (173). I hold that the dying person is the prime instance of a seriously sick person, and so the sacrament of anointing of the sick is primarily (but not exclusively) for persons suffering from a mortal illness, including for those who happen to be imminently dying.

In his "Anointing of the Sick," in *The Oxford Handbook of Sacramental Theology*, ed. Hans Boersma and Matthew Levering (Oxford: Oxford University Press, 2015), 558–71, Kasza states: "There are several effects of the sacrament. For the first eight centuries, the primary effect was healing. In the following twelve centuries, the effect was preparation for death. At the beginning of the third millennium, all of the effects of the sacrament must be explored. Moreover, these effects must be seen in balance with one another" (565). I agree that spiritual and bodily healing must be held in balance (without excluding either one), even though normally the sacrament does not produce bodily healing, and even though its *primary* effect is spiritual. As Lawler remarks: "This view of anointing, broadened beyond either purely physical or purely spiritual health to the raising up of the whole human person, is the view endorsed by the Council of Trent" (*Symbol and Sacrament*, 168).

19. See also Randy Stice, *Understanding the Sacraments of Healing: A Rite-Based Approach* (Chicago: Liturgy Training, 2015), 142.

20. Kasza, "Anointing of the Sick," 568.

21. *Sacrosanctum Concilium*, §73, in *Decrees of the Ecumenical Councils*, ed. Norman P. Tanner, SJ, 2 vols. (Washington, DC: Georgetown University Press, 1990), 2:834.

22. Lizette Larson-Miller, *The Sacrament of the Anointing of the Sick* (Collegeville, MN: Liturgical Press, 2005), 120. (Hereafter in this section, page references from this work will be given in parentheses in the text.) It seems to me that in moving from one extreme to the other, those who sought to "remove any association with the last rites" provide an instance of what Uwe Michael Lang calls the need for "the acknowledgment that infelicitous decisions have been made in the implementation of the Council's principles for a renewal of divine worship" (*Signs of the Holy One: Liturgy, Ritual, and Expression of the Sacred* [San Francisco: Ignatius, 2015], 154).

Here we should listen to Susan K. Wood, SCL (without suggesting that her view and my own are in full accord): "It is time for the pendulum to find center. Certainly viaticum is for the dying, and anointing is for the sick. It was necessary to retrieve an emphasis on anointing for the sick in order both to return to the original meaning of anointing as healing the sick and to correct the abuses and malformations that had occurred through the emphasis on the dying. However, we cannot drive a wedge too firmly between sickness and death, for they are inevitably a continuum revealing the mortality of the body" ("The Paschal Mystery: The Intersection of Ecclesiology and Sacramental Theology in the Care of the Sick," in *Recovering the Riches of Anointing: A Study of the Sacrament of the Sick*, ed. Genevieve Glen [Collegeville, MN: Liturgical Press, 1989], 9). Wood seeks to connect the sacrament of anointing of the sick with baptism and the Eucharist rather than with the sacrament of reconciliation, partly in order to open up theological room for nonpriests to administer the anointing of the sick (Wood was writing prior to the Congregation of the Doctrine of the Faith's decree on this topic). I agree that anointing of the sick is and must be profoundly connected with the sacrament of baptism and the Eucharist, but I think that the connection with reconciliation is more illuminating with respect to anointing's role in perfecting our baptism (by removing the remnants of sin) and opening us to the self-surrender needed for the journey of dying.

23. In a footnote to this sentence, she refers to Kristiaan Depoortere's observation that in the rite for anointing of the sick, the word *death* occurs only with reference to Christ. See Depoortere, "You Have Striven with God (Genesis 32:28): A Pastoral-Theological Reflection on the Image of God and Suffering," in *God and Human Suffering*, ed. Jan Lambrecht and Raymond F. Collins (Louvain: Peeters, 1990), 211–34. Davison comments insightfully: "For those who are *not* in perilous danger of death, but seriously sick, there is a question of balance over when and whether to receive anointing. That balance has helpfully shifted in the last 50 years towards a less cautious use of anointing, but today it can swing too far and make the sacrament somewhat frivolous" (*Why Sacraments?*, 123).

24. Lawler offers a helpful discussion of viaticum: "Every eucharist in the church, we have already seen, proclaims by recalling, making explicit and celebrating not only the Lord's death but also his resurrection. It recalls for her that her passage will be not only into the liminal state of death, but also into the totally new state of eternal life with the Father and Christ and their Spirit" (*Symbol and Sacrament*, 174). Lawler points out that, with the goal of emphasizing the communal and eschatological meanings of viaticum, "The new ritual prescribes . . . that Viaticum should be received during Mass when possible, so that the sick person may receive communion under both species" (174). On viaticum, see also Stice, *Understanding the Sacraments of Healing*, 128–29, 142–44.

25. Depoortere, "Recent Developments in the Anointing of the Sick," in *Illness and Healing*, ed. Louis-Marie Chaubet and Miklós Tomka (London: SCM, 1998), 93. In "The Development of Sacramental Doctrine in the Church: Theory and Practice," in *Recovering the Riches of Anointing*, ed. Glen, 59–81, Kevin W. Irwin warns that "a Catholic fundamentalism that is restorationist in its preference for the celebration of liturgy and sacraments according to a former age's rites and rubrics does severe

harm to the very *communio* that is Catholicism" (60). I note that reflections such as Depoortere's can be tarred with a "restorationist" brush by those who exaggerate the authority and absoluteness of the postconciliar rubrics (as distinct from *Sacrosanctum Concilium* itself).

26. Depoortere, "Recent Developments," 96, cited in Larson-Miller, *Sacrament of the Anointing*, 121.

27. Depoortere, "Recent Developments," 96. For Irwin, "The church reinvents its sacramental teachings in light of the needs of the times" ("Development of Sacramental Doctrine," 64). Although I think that the term *reinvent* has inappropriate connotations—at least if one adheres to anything like John Henry Newman's way of understanding development in the church—it is clear that Irwin's principle requires attention to Depoortere's findings.

28. See her summary, *Sacrament of the Anointing*, 124. See also the church's *Pastoral Care of the Sick: Rites of Anointing and Viaticum* (New York: Catholic Book Publishing, 1983). For further discussion, see Bruce T. Morrill, SJ, *Divine Worship and Human Healing: Liturgical Theology at the Margins of Life and Death* (Collegeville, MN: Liturgical Press, 2009). For Morrill, only in "less than ideal circumstances when serious illness is acknowledged only when active dying is already underway" does the church employ the "Continuous Rite of Penance, Anointing, and Viaticum"; yet he grants that "pastoral care experts consistently observe the desire of Catholics of all ages that the dying person be sacramentally anointed" (197), and he accepts that their desire should not be thwarted, even if "in principle this surely is not ideal" (198).

29. *Catechism of the Catholic Church*, 2nd ed. (Vatican City: Libreria Editrice Vaticana, 1997), §1514. (Hereafter in this section, references to paragraphs of this work will be given in parentheses in the text.) Lawler, like Kasza, argues that the statement in *Sacrosanctum Concilium* §73 that Christians should have recourse to the sacrament of anointing of the sick when they begin "to be in danger of death, either through illness or old age," should be taken in a very broad sense. He argues that even though the text insists upon the "danger of death," it is likely that not only the "periodically infirm [or sick]" but also the "chronically infirm . . . have need of the strengthening envisioned by the sacrament of anointing, precisely to raise them up and insert them explicitly into the mystery of Christ who gives himself that the church might be built up" (*Symbol and Sacrament*, 167). I think that anything that risks severing the connection with real "danger of death" would be a mistake. Whereas Lawler considers that James 5:14–15 "does not envision danger of death, only sickness" (167), it seems to me that James has in mind persons who are too weak to attend church and who are therefore in danger of death (and thus in need of being saved and raised up). See also Kasza, "Anointing of the Sick," 568: "Clearly, the recipient of sacramental anointing is one who is seriously ill owing to age or condition. The definition has broadened over time to include those who suffer from mental illness, which may include addictive behavior as well." Kasza notes that "since the promulgation of the *Pastoral Care of the Sick* in 1972, one sees that the definition of sickness has become broader. Rather than localizing the illness to a specific

part of the body, we now have a more holistic approach, recognizing that sickness as well as health affects the mind, body, and spirit of the patient. . . . A serious illness or disorder represents a severe dysfunction of the balance in one's psycho-physiological make-up" ("Anointing of the Sick," 563–64).

30. The Lutheran scholar Donald Heinz argues that the "Christian tradition must demonstrate far more effectively than it recently has its adequacy to the human condition—this amidst the massive collapse of many Christian systems of meaning in a secular age. . . . It is *the ritualizing human community* coming together to face death, binding living and dead, offering renewed connection for all the living, that is *the most hopeful resource we have in recovering a death of our own*" (*The Last Passage: Recovering a Death of Our Own* [Oxford: Oxford University Press, 1999], 210).

Against such a view, David Power, OMI, argues, "One cannot relate the seven sacraments to moments of the life-cycle. This only distorts their meaning, as appears from the history of baptism, confirmation or the anointing of the sick" ("The Odyssey of Man in Christ," in *Liturgy and Human Passage*, ed. David Power and Luis Maldonado [New York: Seabury, 1979], 101). In an endnote, Power adds that "Aquinas's synthesis . . . is based on an analogy with the natural life-cycle, but does not relate the sacraments to moments of the life-cycle" (111n3). Yet Power grants that the life-cycle has a certain relation to the sacraments, a relation that is found "in the *call* to personal conversion experienced at moments of the life-cycle and expressed in terms of christian belief in these rites" (109). Power makes some odd claims on this basis, for instance by asserting, "If the Church were to maintain a marriage sacrament (i.e., rite) truly signifying the personal choice to be married in Christ, this would have to be dissociated from the beginning of marriage and allowed for at a moment chosen in faith by the partners, within the compass of their experience of marriage" (110). In my view, Power underestimates the power of the sacraments to mark persons at crucial stages of life. The exigencies of Christ, not the exigencies of the stages of life, take priority precisely by defining the crucial stages of life.

31. See Thomas Aquinas, *Summa theologica*, trans. the Fathers of the English Dominican Province, 5 vols. (repr., Westminster, MD: Christian Classics, 1981), 5:2653–66. (Hereafter in this section, references from this work will be given in parentheses in the text.) After his death, Aquinas's students completed his unfinished *Summa* by means of material drawn from his earliest work, his *Commentary on the Sentences of Peter Lombard*; and it is this material that forms the supplement. John F. Boyle has pointed out a deficiency of the supplement by comparison with Aquinas's *Summa contra gentiles*: the latter text ably employs "the frame of the analogy from corporeal life" ("Saint Thomas Aquinas on the Anointing of the Sick (Extreme Unction)," in *Rediscovering Aquinas and the Sacraments: Studies in Sacramental Theology*, ed. Matthew Levering and Michael Dauphinais [Chicago: Hillenbrand, 2009], 81). For my purposes here, bearing Boyle's corrective in mind, the supplement serves well. For more extensive reflection on Aquinas's theology of anointing of the sick, see Colman E. O'Neill, OP, *Meeting Christ in the Sacraments*, ed. Romanus Cessario, OP (Staten Island, NY: Alba

House, 1991), 283–92; Jean-Hervé Nicolas, OP, *Synthèse dogmatique de la Trinité à la Trinité* (Paris: Beauchesne, 1985), 1063–72; Jean-Philippe Revel, OP, *L'onction des maladies: Rédemption de la chair et par la chair*, vol. 6 of *Traité des sacrements* (Paris: Cerf, 2009), 95–102.

32. From a Protestant perspective, see William F. Brosend II, *James and Jude* (Cambridge: Cambridge University Press, 2004), 153–55, 159–61, for the way in which James addresses "sickness, sin, health, and forgiveness together" (161). In favor of the view that James 5:14–15 describes a "sacrament," see the reflections of the Orthodox scholar Elie Mélia, "The Sacrament of the Anointing of the Sick: Its Historical Development and Current Practice," in *Temple of the Holy Spirit*, ed. Triacca, 131–32. Mélia goes on to observe, "We find no trace of the euchelaion before the third century. This silence during a period of bloody persecution is really not surprising. It is easy to imagine an interruption in the celebration of the sacrament mentioned in the letter of James, if for no other reason than this may have been a practice peculiar to the Jewish-Christian milieu and would have disappeared at the end of the first century. But Christians never ceased to read the scriptures, and the formal statement in the letter of James could not have remained simply a dead letter" (134).

33. Regarding "the prayer of faith will save the sick, and the Lord will raise them up," Witherington argues: "*Sōsei* does not likely refer to a person's spiritual salvation, but to curing the sick person. James 5:15b is simply another way of saying James 5:15a: if the person is cured, he or she has been raised up from the sick bed. This is not a reference to resurrection at the last day as a consolation prize" (*James*, 545). Pace Witherington, James knows well that the laying on of hands often does not produce a miracle cure. The words "saved" and "raised up" are deliberately ambiguous, leaving room not for a "consolation prize," but for the great reward of resurrected life with Christ. For this ambiguity, see, for example, Nicolas, *Synthèse dogmatique*, 1065; Ambroise Verheul, "The Paschal Character of the Sacrament of the Sick: Exegesis of James 5:14–15 and the New Rite for the Sacrament of the Sick," in *Temple of the Holy Spirit*, ed. Triacca, 251–53; and Edouard Cothenet, "Healing as a Sign of the Kingdom, and the Anointing of the Sick," in *Temple of the Holy Spirit*, ed. Triacca, 44. See also Empereur, *Prophetic Anointing*, 125: "the major meaning of raising up in the New Testament is the resurrection of the dead. . . . In the broad sense, then, raising up must be seen in terms of God's saving action: raising up prophets, raising up Jesus, raising up the dead." At the same time, Empereur observes that James 5:14–15 has "total healing" in view, which involves both physical and spiritual healing (125).

34. Geoffrey Wainwright remarks, "Oil, and particularly olive oil, is less universal [than water] in its use and associations with healing, health, beauty, blessing, and appointment to office and honour. Could it be that the 'protestant' abandonment of its use in initiation, ordination and the sacrament of the sick was due at least in part to a Northern failure to appreciate the Mediterranean commodity? Nevertheless its scriptural resonance remains great: Genesis 8:11; Deuteronomy 6:11; 1 Samuel 10:1; 1 Kings 17:14; Psalms 23:5; 104:15; 133:2; Hosea 14:6; Luke 10:34; Romans 11:17–24;

James 5:14; Revelation 11:4. It is as close to Christianity as the title given to Jesus, the Spirit-anointed Christ" (*Doxology*, 364).

35. See also Davison, *Why Sacraments?*, 8–9.

36. Thomas Joseph White, OP, specifies, "The medium by which the past events of the passion now act upon us is *the deity of God* working both then and now, through and in light of the passion. By the power of the Godhead, the Paschal mystery is the source of our grace, such that our supernatural faith, hope, and charity, our sacramental graces and so on, come to us by virtue of what Christ did and underwent for us in and through his crucifixion and resurrection" (White, *The Incarnate Lord: A Thomistic Study in Christology* [Washington, DC: Catholic University of America, 2015], 363). For the saving significance of the entire Paschal mystery in the sacraments, see Dominic M. Langevin, OP, *From Passion to Paschal Mystery: A Recent Magisterial Development concerning the Christological Foundation of the Sacraments* (Fribourg: Academic Press Fribourg, 2015).

37. For Joseph Martos, by contrast, the sacraments are such only if they are meaningful to the people who receive them, and so "any words, symbols or gestures that are culturally appropriate can be used to express spiritual realities" (*Deconstructing Sacramental Theology and Reconstructing Catholic Ritual* [Eugene, OR: Resource, 2015], 301).

38. I note that O'Neill specifies that the sacrament of anointing of the sick "is directed against those defects which weaken the patient's Christian life and impede his adopting a Christian attitude to suffering," and he further explains that these defects are "the after-effects of sin which sap the vigor of the Christian; foremost among them is the disinclination to confront the burdens of suffering as a means of conformation to Christ" (*Meeting Christ in the Sacraments*, 288). In my treatment of Aquinas's position, I emphasize the "aftereffects" of pride, namely the disinclination to surrender our lives to God.

39. Lawler rightly remarks that the sacrament of anointing of the sick "connotes life, specifically life as both from and with God, not only present life but also, and more importantly, future and eternal life. . . . It is revealed to them [the recipients of the sacrament] also in symbolic reality that if, and when, they pass from this life, they do not pass back into the nothingness from which they came, but rather to the new and eternal life with God which they began symbolically in baptism" (*Symbol and Sacrament*, 171).

40. Aquinas's comparison of the sacrament of anointing to baptism reflects such biblical texts as Rom. 6:3–4, "Do you not know that all of us who have been baptized into Christ Jesus were baptized into his death? Therefore we have been buried with him by baptism into death, so that, just as Christ was raised from the dead by the glory of the Father, so we too might walk in newness of life." Persons who are enduring serious illness have a proximity to death that gives existential concreteness to the meaning of the baptismal anointing. Lawler helpfully shows that "the intimate link between anointing and baptism is insinuated from the outset of the ritual" (*Symbol and Sacrament*, 171).

41. Davison, *Why Sacraments?*, 121.

42. See the chapter on "Tears" in Catherine of Siena, *The Dialogue*, trans. Suzanne Noffke, OP (New York: Paulist, 1980), 161–83. Catherine describes various kinds of tears, from worldly to holy. When a "soul begins to practice virtue," Catherine says (or, more accurately, the Lord says to Catherine), "her tears well up from the fountain of her heart. But these tears are often sensual because she is not yet very perfect. If you ask me why, I answer: because of the root of selfish love" (162). Warning against trite comments in the face of tragedy, Arnold captures the incredible pain caused by death: "How is a mother supposed to respond when, after having lost a baby, someone helpfully assures her that God 'must have needed another angel'? The first thing most grieving people need is an arm around their shoulders, and permission to cry" (*Be Not Afraid*, 182). Similarly, describing a mother's dealing with the death of her adult son Matt, Arnold indicates that sometimes silence is best: "The day before Matt died, Linda spent a long time in her living room, sitting quietly on the couch with a friend. A few days later, the same friend came back with another woman, and the three of them held hands as the tears trickled down their cheeks. . . . In short, there is no 'answer' to the riddle of grief. But there is such a thing as community, and the knowledge of those who have experienced its blessings that even if one person, alone, cannot hold up under the crushing weight of loss, the heaviest burden *can* be lifted, or at least lightened when it is shared" (184, 186).

43. Boyle, "Saint Thomas Aquinas on Anointing," 82 (emphasis added).

44. Boyle, "Saint Thomas Aquinas on Anointing," 82. Boyle nicely sums up Aquinas's contribution to the development of the theology of the sacrament of anointing of the sick: "The emergence of the analogical frame for the sacraments of spiritual life conformed to corporeal life recasts the sacrament and simultaneously gives a new unity to the treatment. From then on an increasingly clear and precise analysis of the primary analog of corporeal health makes for an increasingly clear distinction between Penance and Reconciliation and the Anointing of the Sick" (83).

45. Bede, *Life of Cuthbert*, in *The Age of Bede*, ed. D. H. Farmer, trans. J. F. Webb, rev. ed. (New York: Penguin, 1998), 92.

46. Eddius Stephanus, *Life of Wilfrid*, in *Age of Bede*, ed. Farmer, 180. Philippe Ariès argues that with respect to dying, "The medieval saint was borrowed by monastic scholars from a secular and chivalric tradition that was itself of folkloric origin" (*The Hour of Our Death*, trans. Helen Weaver [New York: Knopf, 1981], 5). Although I admire Ariès's wide erudition, I think his reading of Christianity's impact upon the experience of dying should be challenged at points, as when he holds that the general resurrection "was accepted as a dogma but never really assimilated at the popular level" (606). I do not think that most Christians over the course of the centuries have anticipated forever being bodiless spirits.

47. See Marilyn Chandler McEntyre, *A Faithful Farewell: Living Your Last Chapter with Love* (Grand Rapids: Eerdmans, 2015), 49–50.

48. Ariès holds that when, "after Vatican II, the church changed the traditional name of Extreme Unction to the 'anointing of the sick,'" the church was in fact "implic-

itly admitting its own absence at the moment of death, the lack of necessity for 'calling the priest'" (*Hour of Our Death*, 563). I think that, on the contrary, the church must be and is present at the deathbed.

49. *Catechism of the Catholic Church*, §1523.

50. Davison, *Why Sacraments?*, 120.

51. Davison, *Why Sacraments?*, 75. The sociologist Allan Kellehear warns, "Across our entire human history we have provided . . . support to our dying through the social offerings of recognition, presence, giving and receiving, and ritual. Sadly, those deep-seated responses towards our dying now increasingly seem endangered" (*A Social History of Dying* [Cambridge: Cambridge University Press, 2007], 256).

52. Megory Anderson, *Sacred Dying: Creating Rituals for Embracing the End of Life*, rev. ed. (New York: Marlowe, 2004), 139–40. She notes, "Many Christian chaplains who make pastoral calls will anoint with small amounts of oil on the head and sometimes the hands" (139). In her view, "There is something about the intimacy of touch that opens an area of trust and confidence. It helps people relax so they can begin to let go. Many times when people are very close to death, in that in-between state, I have found that they often have visions or other profound experiences. By relaxing the body, the mind and soul are free to go through the natural process of dying" (138–39).

53. Michael Drumm, "The Practice of Anointing and the Development of Doctrine," in *Recovering the Riches of Anointing*, ed. Glen, 48. Drumm observes, "When Christians hear of anointing, they should think immediately of baptism, whereas the reality is that it reminds them more of serious illness and death" (38)—but I would point out here that baptism, properly understood, should also remind Christians of death (Christ's and our own). See also Empereur's remark, with which I agree, that in a certain sense "there is a special vocation in the church of the sick and the aged. Anointing is the ritualization of that vocation. . . . It is an articulation of the truth that by dying to oneself, by being the kind of marginal human being a sick and old person is, one opens oneself to far greater wholeness" (*Prophetic Anointing*, 141). The sacrament of anointing of the sick opens the seriously ill person in this way, so that self-surrender becomes fully possible. Empereur rightly makes the connection to co-suffering with Christ (150), drawing upon Leonard Bowman, *The Importance of Being Sick* (Wilmington, DE: Consortium, 1976).

54. Drumm, "Practice of Anointing," 49.

55. Drumm, "Practice of Anointing," 49. Drumm states, "The most significant sacrament of all seven is the Eucharist; participation in it is the fullest expression of Catholic faith, and it draws believers into the heart of the mystery of the death and resurrection of Christ. The most important journey that any human being ever makes is that across the threshold of life into the mystery of death, and it is only right . . . to associate this passage with the Eucharist by partaking of the body of Christ. . . . The best way of understanding the pastoral relationship between the anointing of the sick and viaticum might be to celebrate the former at the beginning of, and in the midst of, serious illness and old age, while the latter should be the sacrament for the end of life" (50–51).

I fully agree that the Eucharist is the central sacrament (paired with baptism) and that the Eucharist, as viaticum, should be received at the very end of life if possible. But it is a mistake to try to remove the sacrament of anointing from the deathbed, because the sacrament of anointing plays a crucial role in enabling the complete surrender (freed from the remnants of rebellion) that dying persons need. Drumm points out that the sacrament of anointing of the sick, when received in a hospital, can be misinterpreted as "something akin to a medical intervention" and is sometimes received without the presence of a Christian community, risking "an all too privatized piety" (42, 51). I agree that ideally the Christian community (priest, family, and friends) should be present and that the sacrament is not a "medical intervention," but these possible imperfections should not prevent a dying person from receiving anointing's power to refresh the dying person, body and soul, with the Christic self-surrender that marks Christ's body. Notably, Empereur—even though he holds that "anointing is not the sacrament of the dying" and urges that the sacrament not be given to those who are imminently dying—asserts that the sacrament assists "the anointed to deal with the mystery which confronts all; namely, the significance of one's life in terms of human limits, the greatest being death" (*Prophetic Anointing*, 149). The connection with actual dying cannot be denied even by those who wish to exclude anointing from the deathbed.

56. *Pastoral Care of the Sick*, no. 261.

57. Paul Keller, OP, points out that the Second Vatican Council "urged the use of the sacrament [of anointing of the sick] for those who are seriously sick, as well as those who are in danger of death. . . . In an emergency, when there is insufficient time for this order [the normal order of penance, anointing of the sick, and viaticum], penance with absolution is first given, then the apostolic pardon, followed by viaticum and finally anointing" (*101 Questions and Answers on the Sacraments of Healing: Penance and Anointing of the Sick* [Mahwah, NJ: Paulist, 2010], 105). In cases where the dying person can no longer swallow, viaticum would logically be excluded, but penance and anointing remain highly appropriate; and anointing is appropriate even for unconscious persons (see *101 Questions and Answers*, 119). Persons who are in a state of objective mortal sin and who refuse the sacrament of penance cannot receive either viaticum or the anointing of the sick. See also Pope Paul VI's 1972 Apostolic Constitution *Sacram Unctionem Infirmorum*, which promulgated the new postconciliar rite for the sacrament of anointing of the sick, as well as Verheul, "Paschal Character."

58. Ernest Becker, *The Denial of Death* (New York: Free Press, 1973), 285. For contextualization of Becker's work within the culture of psychoanalysis from the 1950s through the 1970s, see Kellehear, *A Social History of Dying*, 54–62. He notes that Becker and his colleagues had to ignore that "social institutions in all early societies seem geared towards another world" (55) and also to ignore that ethnographic evidence indicates that most humans who have ever existed have not expected to be annihilated by death but rather have worked to prepare themselves and their loved ones for a life after death. For arguments in favor of Becker's perspective, see Sheldon Solomon, Jeff Greenberg, and Tom Psyzczynski, *The Worm at the Core: On the*

Role of Death in Life (New York: Random House, 2015). After confirming Becker's case for the terrible social and personal costs of our efforts to repress or deny death, they propose (rather lamely in my view) a "terror management theory" according to which we can rely upon human culture to provide us with sufficient order and purpose. For a Christian appreciation of Becker's work, suggesting that Becker, rightly rejecting hedonistic views of life, was reaching for a transcendence that his atheism did not permit him to affirm, see Richard Beck, *The Slavery of Death* (Eugene, OR: Cascade Books, 2013).

59. M. Therese Lysaught, "Suffering in Communion with Christ: Sacraments, Dying Faithfully, and End-of-Life Care," in *Living Well and Dying Faithfully*, ed. Swinton and Payne, 68. I disagree, however, with Lysaught's contrast between "instrumental sacramentality" and "ecclesial sacramentality," insofar as she argues that concern to articulate the sacrament's "effect" upon the recipient is instrumentalist, "individualistic," "mechanistic," and "dualistic" (64–65). Exhibiting the communal or ecclesial character of the sacrament of anointing does not require rejecting inquiry into the sacrament's effect upon the individual; indeed, it is precisely this effect—which draws the sick or dying person into a deeper union with Christ and so also with his body the church—that highlights the way in which the individual recipient belongs to Christ's body. Lysaught notes that she has "no wish to deny that individuals benefit from sacraments" (66).

60. Hans Urs von Balthasar, *You Have Words of Eternal Life: Scripture Meditations*, trans. Dennis Martin (San Francisco: Ignatius, 1991), 253.

Notes to Chapter 9

1. For historical-critical reflection, see Christopher B. Hays, *A Covenant with Death: Death in the Iron Age II and Its Rhetorical Uses in Proto-Isaiah* (Grand Rapids: Eerdmans, 2015). Too restrictively in my view, Hays holds that "the image of swallowing up Death was *not eschatological* in its original composition, however much it may have invited such a reading in later periods. It is very much in line with the images of YHWH overcoming the covenant with Death in Isa 28:15, 18 (and the swallowing of the elites in Isa 5:14); as such, its primary reference is to historical/geopolitical events" (323).

2. As Hays notes with "Trito-Isaiah" in view, "the list of texts in Isaiah that relate to the theme of death and life grows to a point that it becomes arguably *the* dominant theme of the book" (*Covenant with Death*, 361).

3. Henri J. M. Nouwen, *Our Greatest Gift: A Meditation on Dying and Caring* (New York: HarperCollins, 1994), 4. As he goes on to say: "Am I willing to make that journey? Am I willing to let go of whatever power I have left, to unclench my fists and trust in the grace hidden in complete powerlessness? I don't know. I really don't know. It seems impossible, since everything alive in me protests against this journey into nothingness" (4). From the perspective of "psomatic psychology," Stanley Keleman

urges us to consider that "the *feeling* of dying" may be different from society's images of dying (*Living Your Dying* [Berkeley: Center, 1974], 3). Contrasting "big dying" and "little dying," he states, "We are always losing and finding things, always breaking with the old and establishing the new. That's little dying. My experience, my myth, is that big dying is similar to little dying, at least in terms of process and of feeling. Our little dyings are meant to teach us what our big dying may be like" (5). He argues, "Dying can be exciting if you value moving toward the unknown" (140).

4. Carol Zaleski, *The Life of the World to Come: Near-Death Experience and Christian Hope* (New York: Oxford University Press, 1996), 38. With respect to the "price" of dying, I note that Ernest Becker suggests that hope for eternal life is rooted in cowardice and (inevitably violent) denial of death: "Man is a trembling animal who pulls the world down around his shoulders as he clutches for protection and support and tries to affirm in a cowardly way his feeble powers" (*The Denial of Death* [New York: Free Press, 1973], 139). Becker is right about our sinful tendency to try to establish through our own powers a kind of immortality, but his atheism blocks him from affirming the possibility of fruitful self-surrender to God.

5. Zaleski, *Life*, 39. Zaleski rightly observes that given such banal portraits of eternal life, "we can appreciate Thoreau's remark that he would gladly trade his immortality for a glass of cold beer" (39). The same instructive complaint regarding banal portraits of eternal life is found in Hillel Halkin, *After One-Hundred-and-Twenty: Reflecting on Death, Mourning, and the Afterlife in the Jewish Tradition* (Princeton: Princeton University Press, 2016), 207–9.

6. Miguel de Unamuno, *The Tragic Sense of Life in Men and Nations*, trans. Anthony Kerrigan (Princeton: Princeton University Press, 1972), 252.

7. Raymond Tallis, *The Black Mirror: Looking at Life through Death* (New Haven: Yale University Press, 2015), 337.

8. Tallis, *Black Mirror*, 339.

9. According to Patrick M. Clark, "courage is the virtue that coordinates one's experiences of suffering and mortality with one's larger view of the human good" (*Perfection in Death: The Christological Dimension of Courage in Aquinas* [Washington, DC: Catholic University of America Press, 2015], xix).

10. As Marjorie Casebier McCoy says, "We can say 'yes' to belief in a God who created this life and will create a different one for us when this one ends, and still feel the dread of losing the self as we know it in earthly form" (*To Die with Style!* [Nashville: Abingdon, 1974], 25).

11. Plato, *Gorgias* 523a–b, trans. W. D. Woodhead, in *The Collected Dialogues of Plato*, ed. Edith Hamilton and Huntington Cairns (Princeton: Princeton University Press, 1961), 303.

12. Plato, *Phaedo* 109c, trans. Hugh Tredennick, in *Collected Dialogues of Plato*, ed. Hamilton and Cairns, 90. Hereafter in this section, paragraph and page references from this work will be given in parentheses in the text.

13. Note that Muslim theologians generally hold that paradise has "eight basic

NOTES TO PAGE 151

levels" (which go beyond our imagining) and that "once a week the faithful are taken for the Day of Visitation, in which they are given the highest blessing of the Garden, the vision of God" (William C. Chittick, "'Your Sight Today Is Piercing': The Muslim Understanding of Death and Afterlife," in *Death and Afterlife: Perspectives of World Religions*, ed. Hiroshi Obayashi [New York: Praeger, 1992], 138). See also Christian Lange, "The 'Eight Gates of Paradise' Tradition in Islam: A Genealogical and Structural Study," in *Foundations and the Formation of a Tradition: Reflections on the Hereafter in the Quran and Islamic Religious Thought*, ed. Sebastian Günther and Todd Lawson, 341–70, vol. 1 of *Roads to Paradise: Eschatology and Concepts of the Hereafter* (Leiden: Brill, 2017); Chittick, "Eschatology," in *Islamic Spirituality: Foundations*, ed. S. H. Nasr (New York: Crossroad, 1987), 378–409; J. I. Smith and Y. Y. Haddad, *The Islamic Understanding of Death and Resurrection* (Albany: State University of New York Press, 1981). Ira M. Lapidus sums up: "The blessed enter into heaven for an eternal existence of bliss and pleasure. For the blessed, body and soul are comforted by green lands, trees, and rivers; rich furnishings of tents and beds; abundant heavenly food; the company of one's loved ones; the companionship of the virgin houris; and, above all, the vision and contemplation of God. . . . The traditional view continues to be the vision of Muslims the world over. Contemporary writings on the subject affirm the resurrection of the body and the physical rewards and punishments, often with the proviso that the physical life of the world to come is not like our own and cannot be known or imagined" ("The Meaning of Death in Islam," in *Facing Death: Where Culture, Religion, and Medicine Meet*, ed. Howard M. Spiro, Mary G. McCrea Curnen, and Lee Palmer Wandel [New Haven: Yale University Press, 1996], 152–53). For Muslim doctrines of becoming like God and union with God, see Josephine Lombardi, "The Dialogue of Salvation: Salvation in this Life and the Next in Islamic and Catholic Thought," *Science et Esprit* 68 (2016): 287–308. For Muslim catechetical literature that differentiates between paradise and hell, but that does not highlight bodily pleasures, see, for example, Maulana Wahiduddin Khan, *The Qur'an for All Humanity*, trans. Farida Khanam (New Delhi: Goodword, 2000); Abul A'la Maududi, *Towards Understanding Islam*, ed. Yahiya Emerick (New Delhi: Saeed International, 2013). For Muslim eschatology in relation to the fate of members of other religions, see Yasir Qadhi, "The Path of Allah or the Paths of Allah? Revisiting Classical and Medieval Sunni Approaches to the Salvation of Others," in *Between Heaven and Hell: Islam, Salvation, and the Fate of Others*, ed. Mohammad Hassan Khalil (Oxford: Oxford University Press, 2013), 109–21.

14. *The Koran*, trans. J. M. Rodwell (London: Dent, 1994), 298. Hereafter in this section, page references from this work will be given in parentheses in the text. See Ailin Qian, "Delights in Paradise: A Comparative Survey of Heavenly Food and Drink in the Quran," in *Foundations and Formation*, ed. Günther and Lawson, 251–70.

15. See the details in Maher Jarrar, "The Martyrdom of Passionate Lovers: Holy War as a Sacred Wedding," in *Ḥadīth: Origins and Developments*, ed. Harald Motzki (Aldershot: Ashgate, 2004), 317–37.

16. Angelika Neuwirth, however, has offered noteworthy historical-critical anal-

ysis that complicates this apparent similarity: "What was already looming in the earlier paradise descriptions becomes evident in the elaborate portrayal of Q55: the Quranic paradisal abode presents itself as surprisingly distinct from both the Jewish and Christian eschatological paradise. Though it is meant as a reward granted to the virtuous in general, the space is obviously a gendered space. Those invited to enter the garden are male persons, who are honored according to the decorum of contemporary courtly hospitality. Part of their reward is the enjoyment of the erotic company of beautiful maidens, whom they find present at the site. . . . They are—indirectly—assigned to be their sexual partners; this thought seems to underlie the assertion that they are 'untouched before them by any man or jinn,' Q 55:56, 74. There should be no surprise that this gendered social image of paradise later called for an adjustment: later Suras and even secondary additions to early Suras (Q 52:21) contain promises securing the participation of the families (Q 13:23, 36:56: wives) of the inhabitants of paradise, as well, in the eschatological bliss. Yet, the image of the eschatological paradise first arises in the shape described above: as a space promising courtly enjoyments to a privileged male elect" ("Paradise as a Quranic Discourse: Late Antique Foundations and Early Quranic Developments," in *Foundations and Formation*, ed. Günther and Lawson, 83). For further historical-critical background see Angelika Neuwirth, Nicolai Sinai, and Michael Marx, eds., *The Qur'ān in Context: Historical and Literary Investigations into the Qur'ānic Milieu* (Leiden: Brill, 2009); Neuwirth, *Scripture, Poetry, and the Making of a Community: Reading the Qur'an as a Literary Text* (Oxford: Oxford University Press, 2015).

 17. Mona Siddiqui notes that "sensual images of rivers of milk and honey, pure, non-intoxicating wines, silken couches, jewel-encrusted thrones, black-eyed houris, and youths described as 'pearls well guarded' dominate the popular imagination of heavenly delights (47:15; 52:17–20, 24). Whether such images are to be understood literally or allegorically, Islamic thought is not apologetic about the heavenly fulfillment of physical human desires. This has been the case even when Christian polemicists have accused Muslims of being obsessed with the flesh and of not understanding that in the next life such physical pleasures do not matter for the children of God" ("Death, Resurrection, and Human Destiny: Qur'ānic and Islamic Perspectives," in *Death, Resurrection, and Human Destiny: Christian and Muslim Perspectives*, ed. David Marshall and Lucinda Mosher [Washington, DC: Georgetown University Press, 2014], 32). Asma Afsaruddin similarly observes that, although "according to a number of accounts, the ultimate reward for the pious is the beatific vision of God," and although Muslim thinkers argue that "the nature of the bounties awaiting the righteous in the next world defies worldly categories and description," it remains the case that "traditional theologians generally accept at face value the descriptions of heavenly pleasures contained in ḥadīths found in the authoritative collections while emphasizing their otherworldly nature" ("Death, Resurrection, and Human Destiny in the Islamic Tradition," in *Death, Resurrection, and Human Destiny*, ed. Marshall and Mosher, 48). By contrast, Marcia Hermansen thoroughly downplays the presence of physical plea-

sures in heaven, though she correctly remarks that "the nature of heaven and hell has been subjected to a range of interpretations stretching from the purely literal to the utterly allegorical" ("Eschatology," in *The Cambridge Companion to Classical Islamic Theology*, ed. Tim Winter [Cambridge: Cambridge University Press, 2008], 319). For a similar perspective, commenting that in the Qur'an there are no "sexual situations or even sleeping" and that "Muslims usually express great surprise that many Westerners seem to criticize the physical pleasures in the Quranic paradise," see Muhammad Abdel Haleem, "Quranic Paradise: How to Get to Paradise and What to Expect There," in *Foundations and Formation*, ed. Günther and Lawson, 61. See also the texts from the Hadith in Muhammad Yusuf Kandhlawi and Muhammad Saad Kandhlawi, comps., *Muntakhab Ahadith: A Selection of Ahadith Relating to the Six Qualities of Da'wa* (Damascus: Malek, 2013), 66–97, with their appreciation for the pleasures of paradise.

18. Abu Hamid Muhammad ibn Muhammad al-Ghazali, *The Remembrance of Death and the Afterlife*, trans. T. J. Winter (Cambridge: Islamic Texts Society, 1989), 250.

19. Al-Ghazali, *Remembrance of Death*, 251.

20. See al-Ghazali, *Remembrance of Death*, 245. Aisha Geissinger remarks, "As is well known, the Quran presents the inhabitants of paradise enjoying physical pleasures such as eating, drinking, and sex. . . . While the Quran maintains that paradise and what it contains is superior to this world, it is not presented as a wholly otherworldly realm; on the contrary, the inhabitants of paradise will declare, 'We have been given this before' (Q 2:25)" (Geissinger, "'Are Men the Majority in Paradise, or Women?' Constructing Gender and Communal Boundaries in Muslim b. al-Ḥajjāj's (d. 261/875) *Kitāb al-Janna*," in *Foundations and Formation*, ed. Günther and Lawson, 312). Geissinger notes that "the *Kitāb al-Janna* is not intended to relativize or undermine gendered hierarchies, whether in this world or the next. The collapse of such hierarchies (and the chaos that it was assumed would inevitably follow) would vitiate the perfection of paradise. This denouement is avoided in this text by clearly delineating the categories of 'masculinity' and 'femininity' in paradise through sexual roles. While the Quran contains a few evocative portrayals of earthly women entering paradise, and depicts polymorphous 'snapshots' of paradisal eroticism in which the (male) inhabitants of paradise enjoy the company of cup-bearing youths as well as *ḥūrīs*, the picture outlined in the *Kitāb al-Janna* is more starkly hierarchical. In the latter, paradisal 'masculine' sexuality is depicted as unambiguously active and assertive, and moreover, as requiring multiple female partners for its satisfaction. By contrast, paradisal 'feminine' sexuality is presented as passive and receptive. The question of whether these paradisal females are human or *ḥūrī* is . . . left unclear. This distinction is important, as earthly women would potentially have some opinions or desires of their own, but *ḥūrīs* are believed to have been expressly created for the sexual enjoyment of paradise's male inhabitants— and to be perfectly content in that role" (322–23). See also Niall Christie, "Paradise and Hell in the *Kitāb al-Jihād* of 'Alī b. Ṭāhir al-Sulamī (d. 500/1106)," in *Foundations and Formation*, ed. Günther and Lawson, 407–21; Nerina Rustomji, *The Garden and the Fire: Heaven and Hell in Islamic Culture* (New York: Columbia University Press, 2009).

21. The medieval Muslim philosophers downplayed the paradisal physical pleasures: on al-Kindī, al-Fārābī, Ibn Sīnā, and Ibn Bājja, see Michael E. Marmura, "Paradise in Islamic Philosophy," in *Foundations and Formation*, ed. Günther and Lawson, 445–67. Marmura concludes, "In the eschatology of these four philosophers there is a tension between their concept of 'an intellectual paradise,' consisting in the eternal proximity of the immaterial rational souls to God, and the Quranic description of a physical paradise. This tension remains for the most part implicit in much of what they say. The one philosopher who explicitly recognizes it and poses a theory that would ease it is Avicenna. He suggests that in the hereafter, the immaterial souls of the non-philosophical masses, who in their mundane existence have obeyed the commands of the revealed law and have lived virtuous lives, experience eternally the Quranic joys of a physical paradise by means of their imaginative faculties. For Avicenna, however, this paradise remains on a lower level than the philosophers' 'intellectual paradise'" (466). See also Elizabeth Alexandrin, "Paradise as the Abode of Pure Knowledge: Reconsidering al-Mu'ayyad's 'Ismaʻili Neoplatonism,'" in *Foundations and Formation*, ed. Günther and Lawson, 649–61.

22. N. T. Wright, *Surprised by Hope* (New York: HarperCollins, 2008), 161. Hereafter in this section, page references from this work will be given in parentheses in the text.

23. For a broadly similar perspective, see Scot McKnight, *The Heaven Promise: Engaging the Bible's Truth about Life to Come* (Colorado Springs: WaterBrook, 2015). As McKnight says with regard to his wife Kris and his favorite dogs (excluding a dog who bit him frequently), "Kris and I will be watching out the window with Webster [his bichon frise] and the other two (not three) dogs as we all frolic in Heaven's home for us" (186). On the other hand, McKnight states earlier, "The perfected pleasure of Heaven will be to gaze on the face of God, to enjoy the beauty of our Father, and to dwell in the Spirit alongside our brother, the Lord Jesus, as we find our desires consumed by love of God and love of one another" (80).

24. For contemporary Christian theologians who suggest that there will be eating in eternal life, see Norman Wirzba, *Food and Faith: A Theology of Eating* (Cambridge: Cambridge University Press, 2011); Stephen H. Webb, *Good Eating* (Grand Rapids: Brazos, 2001), 173–75. Augustine considered that eating will be possible, though not necessary, for the blessed in eternal life. For the suggestion that there will be sex in heaven, see Margaret D. Kamitsuka, "Sex in Heaven? Eschatological Eros and the Resurrection of the Body," in *The Embrace of Eros: Bodies, Desires, and Sexuality in Christianity*, ed. Margaret D. Kamitsuka (Minneapolis: Fortress, 2010), 261–75; Corey L. Barnes, "Thomas Aquinas on the Body and Bodily Passions," in *Embrace of Eros*, ed. Kamitsuka, 94–95.

25. Wright's position may be subject to the concerns raised by Bernard Williams and others that immortality, understood as endless duration, would eventually become unbearably boring. See Bernard Williams, "The Makropulos Case: Reflections on the Tedium of Immortality," in *Problems of the Self* (Cambridge: Cambridge University Press, 1973), 82–100. For his part, Samuel Scheffler argues that "eternal life would, in

a sense, be no life at all," since "our lives are so pervasively shaped by the understanding of them as temporally limited that to suspend that understanding would call into question the conditions under which we value our lives and long for their extension" (*Death and the Afterlife*, ed. Niko Kolodny [Oxford: Oxford University Press, 2013], 95–96). Scheffler assumes that we could not live without goals, stages of life, loss, risk, danger, and so forth—and he also holds that life without "all the constraints imposed by our biology" would not be human life at all (98). But I think that this is because Scheffler conceives of an immortal life entirely without the triune God, and therefore does not recognize either our potential for deification (in the Christian sense) or the real adventure contained in eternal life. Having left God out of the picture, he assumes that "our ability to lead value-laden lives is not only compatible with the fact that we will die but actually depends on it" (108). For engagement with issues such as these, see also Bernard N. Schumacher, "Le désir d'immortalité à l'aube du troisième millénaire: Enjeux anthropologiques," *Nova et Vetera* 90 (2015): 207–25.

26. Jeffrey Burton Russell makes clear that Wright's emphasis on a fundamentally this-worldly afterlife is not a new phenomenon among Christian thinkers. Focusing on the nineteenth century, Russell remarks that "Novalis, Goethe, Charles Kingsley, and Emily Dickinson all believed that heaven was less a matter of saints than of lovers, and heaven would include intense experience of sexual love. Others emphasized happy families who would re-unite in family gatherings among 'homes, schools, pets, and suburbs' with good food, cookies, games, pianos, machines, and whatever else one finds useful or pleasing. . . . A very large number of books were published on heaven in the mid-nineteenth century. A frequent theme of nineteenth-century views was marital and domestic bliss, a view promoted by Queen Victoria's personal chaplain, the well-known writer Charles Kingsley, and by the famous evangelists Dwight Moody and David Sankey. Presbyterian sermons announced that heaven is where we meet our friends and family and enjoy their company together" (Russell, *Paradise Mislaid: How We Lost Heaven—and How We Can Regain It* [Oxford: Oxford University Press, 2006], 80–81). With regard to Colleen McDannell and Bernhard Lang's *Heaven: A History* (New Haven: Yale University Press, 1988), Russell adds: "McDannell and Lang are right that the idea of working hard in heaven seems to be a creation of the famous 'Protestant Ethic' of the [nineteenth] century. It was thought that leisure corrupts, that adoration of God is indolence, and that we cannot be happy in heaven unless we continue to do good works in the service of others, even of those already in heaven. By striving, we move ahead in heaven, just as for secular Progressives we strive to move ahead in this life" (81–82).

27. N. T. Wright, "Response to Reza Shah-Kazemi," in *Death, Resurrection, and Human Destiny*, ed. Marshall and Mosher, 23. Indebted to al-Ghazali, Reza Shah-Kazemi offers a much more spiritual vision of eternal life (and of spiritual life in the here and now) than does Wright. Shah-Kazemi advances an argument for "a dazzling vision of the hierarchical states of being unfolding within the center or heart of human consciousness" and for the view that "the chronological flow of outward time is arrested

and transformed into the ontological space of the kingdom within" ("Response to N. T. Wright," in *Death, Resurrection, and Human Destiny*, ed. Marshall and Mosher, 21).

28. J. Richard Middleton, *A New Heaven and a New Earth: Reclaiming Biblical Eschatology* (Grand Rapids: Baker Academic, 2014), 12. Hereafter in this section, page references from this work will be given in parentheses in the text.

29. See especially George Eldon Ladd, *The Presence of the Future: The Eschatology of Biblical Realism* (Grand Rapids: Eerdmans, 1974).

30. Middleton observes that after Augustine (indeed well before) "there is a shift of expectation from earth to heaven, accompanying a shift from the resurrection of the body to the immortality of the soul. [Caroline] Walker Bynum explains the shift this way: 'Early Christians expected the body to rise in a restored earthly paradise, whose arrival was imminent. Most late medieval Christians thought resurrection and the coming of the kingdom waited afar off in another space and time'—a euphemistic way to refer to an immaterial realm. This is true even for Thomas Aquinas, whose commitment to an Aristotelian view of the soul as the form or unity of the body inclined him to emphasize the importance of bodily resurrection as central to the Christian hope. Aquinas even argues for the eschatological renewal of the world rather than its destruction. Yet before we celebrate this bold move, we should note that Aquinas understands this renewed world, in which the resurrected saints will spend eternity, as an atemporal realm (time will cease) and a world without animals or plants (indeed humans, though bodily, will have transcended their animal nature)" (294; citing Caroline Walker Bynum, *The Resurrection of the Body in Western Christianity, 200–1336* [New York: Columbia University Press, 1995], 14). Both Augustine and Aquinas, of course, provide extensive discussion and defense of the resurrection of the body and the new creation.

31. For the phrase "cosmic temple," see also Joseph Blenkinsopp, *Creation, Un-Creation, Re-Creation: A Discursive Commentary on Genesis 1–11* (London: T. & T. Clark, 2011), 22. For a popular discussion informed by contemporary historical-critical scholarship, see John H. Walton, *The Lost World of Genesis One: Ancient Cosmology and the Origins Debate* (Downers Grove, IL: IVP Academic, 2009).

32. See also J. Richard Middleton, *The Liberating Image: The Imago Dei in Genesis 1* (Grand Rapids: Brazos, 2005). The Orthodox theologian John Behr has argued insightfully that Jesus's words in John 19:30, "It is finished," signify the completion of God's project to "make man in our image, after our likeness" (Gen. 1:26); thus Pilate can say truly, "Here is the man!" (John 19:5). As Behr points out, "That Christ is the first true human being in history is a position maintained right through the first millennium and more" ("Life and Death in the Age of Martyrdom," in *The Role of Death in Life: A Multidisciplinary Examination of the Relationship between Life and Death*, ed. John Behr and Conor Cunningham [Eugene, OR: Cascade, 2015], 85). See also Joseph Ratzinger, *Dogma and Preaching: Applying Christian Doctrine to Daily Life*, trans. Michael J. Miller and Matthew J. O'Connell (San Francisco: Ignatius, 2011), 159.

33. For relevant biblical texts see also Christopher J. H. Wright, *The Mission of*

God: Unlocking the Bible's Grand Narrative (Downers Grove, IL: IVP Academic, 2006). Regarding Gen. 12:1–3, however, see R. W. L. Moberly's view that "the supposition that those who invoke Abraham in blessing actually receive the blessing invoked is a non sequitur that goes well beyond the meaning of the Genesis text. The textual concern is to assure Abraham that he really will be a great nation, and the measure of that greatness is that he will be invoked on the lips of others as a model of desirability. The condition of other nations in their own right is not in view, beyond their having reason not to be hostile to Abraham" (*The Theology of the Book of Genesis* [Cambridge: Cambridge University Press, 2009], 155). Yet, as Moberly goes on to show, "A construal of Abraham as mediator of divine blessing to the nations is in fact also attested in Jewish interpretation down the ages" (159–60).

34. See also Richard Bauckham, *Living with Other Creatures: Green Exegesis and Theology* (Waco, TX: Baylor University Press, 2011).

35. For further discussion see Jon D. Levenson, *Resurrection and the Restoration of Israel: The Ultimate Victory of the God of Life* (New Haven: Yale University Press, 2006).

36. See also Richard Bauckham, *The Fate of the Dead: Studies on the Jewish and Christian Apocalypses* (Leiden: Brill, 1998).

37. Discussing Isa. 40–55 and 65–66, which influence the New Testament texts on the new heavens and new earth, Moyer V. Hubbard states that "the Isaianic motif of new creation is both anthropological and cosmological in scope. It includes God's people and God's world. Addressing the needs of a community in exile, it speaks of a transformed people (40–55) in a transformed universe (65–66)" (*New Creation in Paul's Letters and Thought* [Cambridge: Cambridge University Press, 2002], 17).

38. For further discussion, emphasizing the cosmic aspect, see G. K. Beale, *The Temple and the Church's Mission: A Biblical Theology of the Dwelling Place of God* (Downers Grove, IL: InterVarsity Press, 2004), 365–73.

39. Isaac Augustine Morales, OP, points out that Middleton consistently undervalues the element of worship that is central to Scripture's portraits of the mission of the *imago Dei*: "While it is true that the cultural mandate plays an important part in Genesis, I am unconvinced that the resumption of work and cultural creativity is the primary feature of the human destiny. Middleton gives insufficient attention to the role of the Sabbath, which forms the culmination of the first creation account in Genesis (Gen. 2:1–3). Human activity is not an end in itself; rather, like God's own work of creation, it is ordered to Sabbath rest. The author of Hebrews picks up and develops this theme (via Ps. 95) in Hebrews 3–4, a text Middleton does not discuss. Throughout the passage the author warns his audience of the danger of failing to enter into God's rest.... It is significant that a large part of Hebrews is taken up with Christ's work as priest in the heavenly temple, a temple the writer contrasts with the earthly tabernacle. One implication of this comparison would seem to be that Christ definitively brings about the rest toward which the Exodus was ordered. This notion of rest is implied in the very structure of the book of Exodus.... Israel's liberation from slavery to Egypt

is ordered not to a 'cultural mandate,' but rather to liturgical service of the Lord. To be sure, Exodus does contain an element of the royal rule that plays such an important part in Middleton's account. At Sinai, God tells the people of Israel through Moses, 'But you shall be for me a priestly kingdom and a holy nation' (Exod. 19:6). Nevertheless, the structure of the book places the accent far more on worship than on royal rule. The same can be said for the book of Revelation. Whereas Middleton highlights the promise that the redeemed will reign together with God, Revelation, reflecting this element of the Exodus story, likewise places the emphasis on worship" ("'With My Body I Thee Worship': New Creation, Beatific Vision, and the Liturgical Consummation of All Things," *Pro Ecclesia* 25 [2016]: 340–41).

40. For N. T. Wright's view of the intermediate state prior to the general resurrection, see *Surprised by Hope*, 162, 172.

41. I discuss the relationship of the kingdom and the church at length in *Engaging the Doctrine of the Holy Spirit: Love and Gift in the Trinity and the Church* (Grand Rapids: Baker Academic, 2016), ch. 5.

42. See Paul J. Griffiths, *Decreation: The Last Things of All Creatures* (Waco, TX: Baylor University Press, 2014). (Hereafter in this section, page references from this work will be given in parentheses in the text.) See also the understanding of Christian eschatology that I present in *Jesus and the Demise of Death: Resurrection, Afterlife, and the Fate of the Christian* (Waco, TX: Baylor University Press, 2012). Let me note here that Griffiths uses "heaven" in a manner that, because it combines the intermediate state and the state after the general resurrection, can be misleading. Griffiths's understanding of the vision of God and of the everlasting relationship of the blessed to God could be enriched; see Daniel A. Keating, *Deification and Grace* (Naples, FL: Sapientia, 2007), 91–113.

43. See, for example, Griffiths, *Decreation*, 4. As Matthew L. Lamb observes, "Only with the strength of the Spirit can the extended passion narratives of all of human history narrated in the new covenant be accepted as Gospel, as good news of salvation in the glory of the resurrection. Incorporated within the Paschal Victim are all the victims of history. . . . If the depth of human suffering is to birth understanding, it is because of the kenosis of the Divine Wisdom who alone can bring good out of evil, grace out of sin, life out of death. Only in the eternal kingdom of God will the empires of history be fully transformed into the justice and agapic love of the Triune God" ("Nature, History, and Redemption," in *Eternity, Time, and the Life of Wisdom* [Naples, FL: Sapientia, 2007], 28).

44. See also Anthony C. Thiselton, *Life after Death: A New Approach to the Last Things* (Grand Rapids: Eerdmans, 2012), 185–215, including his remark that "Christians will see, after the resurrection, the relative worthlessness of the created order in comparison with God himself" (190)—a remark that does not denigrate creation. Thiselton notes that "even the most exalted experiences of singing God's praises on earth are marred by distractions and other attractions, concerns about time, repetitious imperfections, and, above all, remains of self-concern, self-love, or sin. These things will not

detract [in the state of glory] from the sheer joy of praising God 'for his own sake' and of beholding his beauty 'face-to-face'" (205). He sums up his position, which adds certain elements to Griffiths's but is largely in accord with it: "The glorification of God *after* the resurrection of the dead will involve at least three key factors. (1) First, *Christ's* own sufferings, death, and resurrection will permeate everything. They will provide the lens through which everything else is seen, including even our fellow humans. (2) Secondly, the 'spiritual body,' or mode of existence after resurrection, as marked by the character and action of the Holy Spirit, will *embrace* our experience of God to a degree hitherto unimaginable. (3) Third, just as prayer on earth was *by* the Holy Spirit, *through* Jesus Christ the Son, *to* God the Father (Rom. 8:26–27), this *Trinitarian* process will move from faith to sight, and we shall participate in it with heightened awareness" (205–6).

45. See also the portrait of eternal life offered by Paul O'Callaghan, *Christ Our Hope: An Introduction to Eschatology* (Washington, DC: Catholic University of America Press, 2011), ch. 6. The distinction between God and humans fully remains in eternal life, and so Peter C. Phan's remark, "In heaven we live a life *no less divine* than God the Father, God the Son, and God the Spirit do," needs to be qualified in order to make clear that the distinction between God and creatures perdures even in deification (*Living into Death, Dying into Life: A Christian Theology of Death and Life Eternal* [Hobe Sound, FL: Lectio, 2014], 73–74 [emphasis added]).

46. Unamuno questions how "beatific vision" can come to be "without annihilation of the consciousness of self" (*Tragic Sense of Life*, 252). Griffiths appears to think that Unamuno is basically right about this, but that the loss does not matter. I agree with Unamuno, however, that "to think without knowing we think is the same as not sensing ourselves and the same as not being ourselves" (252). In my view, Unamuno is right when he proposes that "eternal life" involves not solely "seeing God, but seeing that we see Him, seeing ourselves at the same time that we see ourselves as beings distinct from Him" (252–53). Unamuno insists, however, that "what we long for is a prolongation of this life, of this life and no other, this life of flesh and suffering, this life which we abominate at times precisely because it comes to an end" (254). I agree that we love this life and desire not only a spiritual but also a "corporal felicity" (255), but I disagree that we therefore must retain the feeling of "the innermost tragedy of the soul" (279) that Unamuno treasures. Unamuno also offers a helpful defense of the vision of God, even while at the same time challenging the Thomistic understanding of it (without fully appreciating the full dimensions of Aquinas's position): "A beatific vision, a loving contemplation in which the soul is absorbed in God and, as it were, lost in Him, appears, to our inherent sensibilities, either as an annihilation of self or as a prolonged tedium. . . . It is clear enough that people who feel in such wise have failed to realize that man's highest pleasure consists in achieving and intensifying consciousness" (249). Rightly insisting that the beatific vision cannot be a frozen stasis, Unamuno reasons that "perhaps the joy of the beatific vision may be, not precisely the contemplation of the supreme Truth, whole and entire, for no soul could endure so much, but rather the continuous discovery of it all, the ceaseless learning through an effort which maintains

the sense of personal consciousness forever active. It is difficult to imagine a beatific vision of mental quietude, of full knowledge rather than of gradual perception, as in any way different from a kind of Nirvana, a kind of spiritual diffusion, a kind of dissipation of energy in the essence of God, a return to the unconscious through lack of tension, lack of differentiation, in short, of a lack of activity" (250).

47. Phan notes that "heaven may be imagined as a reunion with one's loved ones," but he rightly points out that "the loved ones include not only those people who are close and known to us, such as spouses, family members, and friends, but all the angels and the saints, and indeed all humans who have been saved (the blessed)" (*Living into Death*, 74). Citing the authority of *Lumen Gentium* §16, Phan also comments that the blessed will include many persons who in the present life were not Christian, since God has ways of uniting people to Christ other than by explicit faith. For further reflection on the topic of a heavenly reunion with loved ones, citing a wide range of sources and perspectives and (as is his wont) leaving the question open, see Dale C. Allison Jr., *Night Comes* (Grand Rapids: Eerdmans, 2016), 134–39.

48. Aquinas notes that it can be true to say that "out of charity, we love more those who are more nearly connected with us, since we love them in more ways" (*Summa theologica*, II-II, q. 26, a. 7). For example, we will always love our parents not only for the goods of grace that God has given them, but also because they are the "principles of our natural origin" (II-II, q. 26, a. 10).

49. See Suppl., q. 91, especially a. 5. Aquinas assumes simply that "animals and plants were made for the upkeep of human life," and he draws the conclusion that "when man's animal life ceases [i.e., eating and clothing are no longer necessary], animals and plants should cease" (a. 5, *sed contra*).

50. In light of the resurrection of Christ, as Joseph Ratzinger says, we now know that "death does not belong fundamentally and irrevocably to the structure of creation, to matter" (*The God of Jesus Christ: Meditations on the Triune God*, trans. Brian McNeil [San Francisco: Ignatius, 2008], 100).

51. Aquinas notes that "since their form comes to nothing, they cannot resume the same identical form" (Suppl., q. 91, a. 5, *sed contra*).

52. W. Norris Clarke, SJ, has put the matter well when critiquing the position of nonreductive physicalists such as Nancey C. Murphy: "They admit that when we die, we die totally; there is nothing left of my original uniqueness, nothing but aggregates of more elementary material particles. What then about the Resurrection at the Last Day—an essential ingredient of any authentic Christian belief? Their answer is that God 'recreates' the original *me* again at an appropriate later time. But this is a metaphysical impossibility. The recreated entity might be a clone, *like* me in many ways, but not the *same* unique personal *me*, because the new unity, the self—the 'I'—organizing the similar body is not the same as me, for the simple reason that it never experienced the same personal life, the same *story* with all its challenges, successes and failures, that became an inseparable part of my identity before my death. That self is simply gone, and not even the omnipotence of God can do what is a metaphysical impossibility:

recreate the identical being that existed before, with no bond of continuity on the personal level between the before and the after" ("The Immediate Creation of the Human Soul by God and Some Contemporary Challenges," in *The Creative Retrieval of Saint Thomas Aquinas: Essays in Thomistic Philosophy, New and Old* [New York: Fordham University Press, 2009], 188).

53. For investigation of animal pain, see C. S. Lewis, *The Problem of Pain* (New York: Macmillan, 1962). For an analytic philosophical approach that offers reasons why it may be that a cosmos in which animals suffer was the best alternative open to the Creator God, Michael J. Murray, *Nature Red in Tooth and Claw: Theism and the Problem of Animal Suffering* (Oxford: Oxford University Press, 2008). It seems to me that in a material cosmos that unfolds in time (i.e., rather than being glorified from the outset), animal pain is unavoidable and is an acceptable part of a good creation, and so I deny that God owes eschatological reconstitution to all animals who have suffered.

54. For discussion of this worship see Morales, "With My Body," 338. Morales insightfully concludes: "The drive by scholars like Middleton and Wright to recover the biblical vision of a new heaven and a new earth stems in part from a concern that a widespread piety regarding 'heaven' devalues the present world and human activity. In their desire to preserve the worth and importance of the present life, they paint a picture of the next life nearly identical to this one, with the exception that sin will have been eradicated. Ironically, such a reading of the biblical view of the end itself obscures the importance of the present life. If in the next life, the redeemed are constantly busy with new projects as Wright suggests, then it would seem that there will be no opportunity to rest in the beauty and glory of the great works of human history, to say nothing of the God who makes all those works possible. Augustine offers a vision of the new heavens and the new earth that retains the significance of the present life by redeeming all aspects of human history. In the new heavens and the new earth, the memory of past ills will be transformed. In recalling the earthly sorrows of the present life the saints will not re-experience those sufferings, but rather will intellectually recall them in order to praise the God whose mercy endures forever. The point could easily be extended to the glories of human history, which also find their origin in God. . . . Far from detracting from the significance of the present life, an Augustinian conception of a beatific vision in a new heavens and a new earth holds forth the promise of a full understanding of human history that will burst forth into embodied and communal praise, thus fulfilling the deepest human desires" (355–56). For a similar view, enriched by a profound sense for "sapiential eschatology" and for the suffering of the innumerable victims of history, see Matthew Lamb, "The Eschatology of St. Thomas Aquinas," in *Eternity, Time*, 55–72.

55. Christian Wiman, *My Bright Abyss: Meditation of a Modern Believer* (New York: Farrar, Straus and Giroux, 2013), 105. Admittedly, I think Wiman's conception of God is "not strange enough," as for instance when he describes God as "ever-perfecting process" (104).

56. Middleton, *New Heaven*, 174.

57. With regard to the marital imagery (specifically in the book of Revelation),

Morales notes that "Middleton's account of these chapters . . . appears remarkably tone deaf to the marital imagery that pervades them. Again, while it is true that Revelation promises the saints a share in God's royal rule, this is hardly the heart of the matter. Rather, the last two chapters of Revelation portray the fulfillment of an earlier beatitude in the book: 'And [the angel] said to me, "Write this: Blessed are those who are called to the marriage supper of the Lamb"' (Rev. 19:9). The elaborate description of the Bride of the Lamb, combined with the invitation, 'The Spirit and the Bride say, "Come!"' (Rev. 22:17), suggests that the consummation of all things should be seen not primarily as human participation in a glorious reign, but rather as the love story of God and his people. A common biblical image for this love story is the notion of face-to-face encounter with God (Rev. 22:4), a notion that played a crucial role in traditional theological reflection on the end of human beings" ("With My Body," 342; see also 342–44 for further important biblical texts in this regard). See also Brant Pitre, *Jesus the Bridegroom: The Greatest Love Story Ever Told* (New York: Random House, 2014).

58. Allison, *Night Comes*, 39. Allison points out, for instance, that "it's mighty hard to fathom that bodies designed for earthly life are, with only modest revision, equally designed for life eternal" (39).

59. Donald Heinz, *The Last Passage: Recovering a Death of Our Own* (Oxford: Oxford University Press, 1999), 218.

60. Madeleine L'Engle, "Foreword," in Johann Christoph Arnold, *Be Not Afraid: Overcoming the Fear of Death* (Farmington, PA: Plough, 2002), xi.

61. Craig Steven Titus, *Resilience and the Virtue of Fortitude: Aquinas in Dialogue with the Psychosocial Sciences* (Washington, DC: Catholic University of America Press, 2006), 367.

Notes to Conclusion

1. Bartholomew J. Collopy, SJ, "Theology and the Darkness of Death," *Theological Studies* 39 (1978): 52.

2. Philippe Rouillard, "The Liturgy of the Dead as a Rite of Passage," trans. John Griffiths, in *Liturgy and Human Passage*, ed. David Power and Luis Maldonado (New York: Seabury, 1979), 81.

3. Christopher P. Vogt, *Patience, Compassion, Hope, and the Christian Art of Dying Well* (Lanham, MD: Rowman & Littlefield, 2004), 117. Vogt adds that even "for many Christians today, when the time comes for them to die or for their loved ones to die, their belief in Providence or divine planning is eclipsed by something more powerful. Few seem willing to embrace the sense that God may have called them to their dying—to live out the last of their days vulnerable and in the care of family" (118). I agree with Vogt's constructive proposal: "Alongside the traditional image of a Christian making the ultimate sacrifice of self (which has such rich support in the stories of the Christian martyrs as well) there should be an additional model of patience—that

of one who is willing to be 'handed over' in a very different sense, one who is willing to be cared for by loved ones" (119). For early Christian stories and homilies about martyrs, see J. Warren Smith, "Martyrdom: Self-Denial or Self-Exaltation? Motives for Self-Sacrifice from Homer to Polycarp: A Theological Reflection," *Modern Theology* 22 (2006): 169–96; Bryan M. Litfin, *Early Christian Martyr Stories: An Evangelical Introduction with New Translations* (Grand Rapids: Baker Academic, 2014); Johan Leemans, Wendy Mayer, Pauline Allen, and Boudewijn Dehandschutter, eds. and trans., *"Let Us Die That We May Live": Greek Homilies on Christian Martyrs from Asia Minor, Palestine and Syria (c. AD 350–AD 450)* (London: Routledge, 2003). See also the rich reflections on Christian martyrdom found in Miroslav Volf, "Death and the Love of Life: A Response to Sajjad Rizvi," in *Death, Resurrection, and Human Destiny: Christian and Muslim Perspectives,* ed. David Marshall and Lucinda Mosher (Washington, DC: Georgetown University Press, 2014), 111–16.

4. Ephraim Radner, *A Time to Keep: Theology, Mortality, and the Shape of a Human Life* (Waco, TX: Baylor University Press, 2016), x.

5. See Radner, *A Brutal Unity: The Spiritual Politics of the Christian Church* (Waco, TX: Baylor University Press, 2012).

6. *Catechism of the Catholic Church,* 2nd ed. (Vatican City: Libreria Editrice Vaticana, 1997), §§208, 1697.

7. Karl Rahner, SJ, *On the Theology of Death,* trans. Charles H. Henkey (Freiburg: Herder, 1961), 82; see also Rahner, "Ideas for a Theology of Death," in *Theology, Anthropology, Christology,* trans. David Bourke, vol. 13 of *Theological Investigations* (New York: Seabury, 1975), 169–86. For a theology of dying that is deeply indebted to Rahner, see Peter C. Phan, *Living into Death, Dying into Life: A Christian Theology of Death and Life Eternal* (Hobe Sound, FL: Lectio, 2014), ch. 1. See also David Albert Jones's critical summary of Rahner's perspective in *Approaching the End: A Theological Exploration of Death and Dying* (Oxford: Oxford University Press, 2007), ch. 6. Jones criticizes Rahner's "belief that death necessarily brings the soul nearer to God" since in a certain sense (for Rahner, according to Jones) "without the body the soul is free, opened up to the cosmos as a whole, fulfilled" (174; cf. 175). As Jones points out, "Rahner is strongly resistant to the view that death is, in itself, a bad thing"; and Rahner instead prefers to consider death, in itself, as neutral since death can be either good or bad (174). Jones rightly concludes, "Rahner generally seems to hold that the true and inner meaning of death is positive but that, due to the fall, it now has a negative aspect and has the possibility of a negative outcome" (175). In my view, human death as the separation of body and soul is always negative and not what God willed for humans at the beginning, although God could have used something like death, understood more as a kind of sleep, as part of transitioning the first humans (had they not fallen) to the glorious new creation. For a critique of Rahner's theology of death (along the same lines as Jones's), see Cornelius Ernst, OP, "The Theology of Death," *Clergy Review* 44 (1959): 588–602; as well as Edward Schillebeeckx, OP, "The Death of a Christian I: The Objective Fact," and "The Death of a Christian II: Our Personal Approach," *Life in the Spirit* 16 (1962):

270–79 and 335–45. In addition to his criticisms, Jones has positive things to say about Rahner's theology of death, especially Rahner's later writings in which "Rahner came to acknowledge more openly the negative aspects of death from a naturalistic point of view, and the dialectic of activity and passivity involved in the 'act of dying'" (*Approaching the End*, 178). I appreciate that for Rahner, "the 'continuance of life' after death is not to be thought of as the self-prolongation of time, or as a further extension in time of acts and experiences following one upon another in a series arising from some neutral substantial entity which impels itself forward through ever fresh epochs," and I agree with Rahner that Christian hope recognizes "to the full the powerlessness of man either in thinking or willing when confronted with the absurd arch-contradiction of existence" ("Ideas," 174, 182).

8. Amy Plantinga Pauw, "Dying Well," in *Practicing Our Faith: A Way of Life for a Searching People*, ed. Dorothy C. Bass (San Francisco: Jossey-Bass, 1997), 175. Pauw is referring to the physical side of dying, but she could equally be referring to the spiritual side.

9. Eberhard Jüngel, *Death: The Riddle and the Mystery*, trans. Iain and Ute Nicol (Philadelphia: Westminster, 1975), vii.

10. J. Todd Billings, *Rejoicing in Lament: Wrestling with Incurable Cancer and Life in Christ* (Grand Rapids: Brazos, 2015), 91.

11. David Bentley Hart, *The Experience of God: Being, Consciousness, Bliss* (New Haven: Yale University Press, 2013), 331; cf. 298, 321. Hart is deeply influenced here by the English poet Thomas Traherne, but also by Plato, Gregory of Nyssa, the Sufi poet Mahmud Shabestari, and others.

12. For death as an annihilating return to the wondrous (though brutal) cosmic life force, see Michael Fishbane, *Sacred Attunement: A Jewish Theology* (Chicago: University of Chicago Press, 2008); and my review of this book in *Nova et Vetera* 8 (2010): 711–16. Fishbane is influenced by Martin Heidegger, as is Paul Tillich, who advocates a focus upon the "now" of being as the way to experience the eternal, in *The Courage to Be* (New Haven: Yale University Press, 1952) and *The Eternal Now* (New York: Scribner's Sons, 1963); cf. the excerpt from the latter book published as "The Eternal Now," in *The Modern Vision of Death*, ed. Nathan A. Scott Jr. (Richmond, VA: John Knox, 1967), 97–106. Anthony C. Thiselton rightly comments, "Only from a retrospective viewpoint acquired *after* resurrection can the 'meaning' of our lives become definitive. Disbelief in life after death makes life meaningless; belief in life after death invites a working and provisional meaning, which is grounded in God's promise and human trust" (*Life after Death: A New Approach to the Last Things* [Grand Rapids: Eerdmans, 2012], 15).

13. David Bentley Hart, "Death, Final Judgment, and the Meaning of Life," in Hart, *The Hidden and the Manifest: Essays in Theology and Metaphysics* (Grand Rapids: Eerdmans, 2017), 253, 255. Hart comments that "death can never be wholly and unequivocally 'natural' for us, precisely because we are conscious of it; hence—quite unnaturally—it has a meaning for us, even if we think that meaning to be no more than the end of all meaning. As organisms, we are subject—like all animals—to the

NOTES TO PAGES 166–67

inescapable circularity of natural existence: 'birth and copulation and death,' to use T. S. Eliot's phrase; the pitiless regularity with which one generation succeeds another; the survival of some, the defeat of others, the ultimate extinction of all. But, as rational beings, blessed and burdened with reflective consciousness, our existence is not simply 'circular' or organic, but prospective and creative. The horizon of human awareness is one of indeterminate futurity, an openness that aims *naturally* beyond nature; we have projects, plans, expectations, ambitions, ideas that cannot be contained within the close confines of the present, designs that can be only incrementally embodied, desires that can be only progressively pursued; we are capable of novelty, we understand time as a realm of possibilities, and we know that there will be an end to all our striving. To be human is to possess—consciously, that is—a future, and to be able to turn one's will and imagination toward it" (254–55).

14. Hart, "Death, Final Judgment, and the Meaning of Life," 255.

15. Arthur E. Imhof, "An *Ars Moriendi* for Our Time: To Live a Fulfilled Life; to Die a Peaceful Death," in *Facing Death: Where Culture, Religion, and Medicine Meet*, ed. Howard M. Spiro, Mary G. McCrea Curnen, and Lee Palmer Wandel (New Haven: Yale University Press, 1996), 118. Imhof adds, "Even for those who still die early [rather than in old age], as victims of accidents or incurable diseases, the realization of a life plan makes sense, I think, even if it is cut short. Everything happened for them, too, at the right time. Dying young or old, nobody should berate him- or herself on the deathbed for having missed something. There should be no last-minute, panicky attempt to catch up on what cannot be recouped" (119). But why should we suppose that "everything" happened for such persons "at the right time," and indeed how can we dare to say such a thing, absent the power of divine providence that can draw good from evil?

16. Abul A'la Maududi, *Towards Understanding Islam*, ed. Yahiya Emerick (New Delhi: Saeed International, 2013), 119. Rationally speaking—although people are capable of doing self-sacrificial acts despite what their reason tells them—"a person who thinks only of the success or failure of this world will be concerned with the benefits and drawbacks that come to him in this life only. He will not be prepared to undertake any good act if he has no hope of making a profit of some sort, nor will he be eager to avoid any wrong act if that is not particularly harmful to his interests in this world" (119). For further reflection on this topic, and a response to Nicholas Lash's concern that eschatology gets in the way of care for this world, see Dale C. Allison Jr., *Night Comes: Death, Imagination, and the Last Things* (Grand Rapids: Eerdmans, 2016), 71–77, 86–92, citing Lash's "Eternal Life: Life 'after Death'?," *Heythrop Journal* 19 (1978): 282. Allison points out, "If death is the end, then we're all snow: we arrive, we melt, we are no more. Eschatology is a way of saying that we're more. It's a way of resisting the diminishing value of the dead. It's a way of making all our stories longer-lasting and so more meaningful. It's the claim that human beings matter greatly because they matter persistently. That claim, even if one doubts it, shouldn't be dismissed as a recipe for escapism, moral complacency, or some other social sin" (*Night Comes*, 88).

17. Against individualistic accounts, Allison observes: "If resurrection effectually

communicates the hope that life in the world to come is full rather than attenuated, it also effectually conveys that the fate of the one is bound up with the fate of the many. Bodily resurrection isn't about the lone individual. It's rather a public and communal event at one point in time. . . . Resurrection isn't about you or about me but about us, and about a kingdom" (*Night Comes*, 41).

18. Vogt, *Patience, Compassion, Hope*, 130–31. Vogt's emphasis on patience makes sense and fits with my attention to such virtues as gratitude and self-surrender. He states, "I have singled out patience as the key virtue to be practiced over a lifetime because it is the inability to be patient that makes dying a horror for so many Americans today" (131). He has the euthanasia movement particularly in view here, with its focus on preserving control. To learn patience, Vogt points out, we must practice keeping our equanimity in the midst of small trials and learn to be obedient to God's will. For contrasting perspectives on euthanasia (with many of the pro-euthanasia essays grounding their arguments in deficiencies in palliative care), see the essays in Ronald P. Hamel and Edwin R. DuBose, eds., *Must We Suffer Our Way to Death? Cultural and Theological Perspectives on Death by Choice* (Dallas: Southern Methodist University Press, 1996). Patricia Beattie ("Dying Well Isn't Easy: Thoughts of a Roman Catholic Theologian on Assisted Death," in *Must We Suffer?*, ed. Hamel and DuBose, 174–97) opposes euthanasia, while supporting the provision of palliative care and the withdrawal of overzealous efforts to preserve the life of mortally ill people. See also the profound reflections on Christian opposition to any form of suicide in Radner, *Time to Keep*, ch. 2.

19. Vigen Guroian, *Life's Living toward Dying: A Theological and Medical-Ethical Study* (Grand Rapids: Eerdmans, 1996), 97, 104. Guroian nicely highlights "the synergy of human and divine activity through which redemptive death is accomplished" (98).

20. Guroian, *Life's Living toward Dying*, 97.

21. Guroian, *Life's Living toward Dying*, 103. Thus, as Gisbert Greshake remarks, "the Christian is fundamentally liberated from the kind of dying that . . . is merely meaningless and absurd" ("Towards a Theology of Dying," trans. Robert Nowell, in *The Experience of Dying*, ed. Norbert Greinacher and Alois Müller [New York: Herder & Herder, 1974], 91). Greshake grants, as I also do, that even for the Christian "dying is experienced not simply as the natural consummation of his life but is always also experienced as the pressing in of non-existence, as the depths of misery and alarm" (96). The sense of death (and life) as absurd is articulated and rejected by Allison, who notes that, if dying annihilates us, then "the cosmos is finally apathetic, and death can separate us from the love of God; and if that's so, then love doesn't endure all things but finally fails. Which cannot be" (*Night Comes*, 18).

22. See for example Neil deGrasse Tyson, Michael A. Strauss, and J. Richard Gott, *Welcome to the Universe: An Astrophysical Tour* (Princeton: Princeton University Press, 2016).

23. Christoph Schönborn, OP, *From Death to Life: The Christian Journey*, trans. Brian McNeil, CRV (San Francisco: Ignatius, 1995), 181. Schönborn is well aware that this "gateway" requires Christ (and thus requires living and dying in Christ): "The dead

person stands in all the nakedness of his misery on the threshold to the life beyond death. What can he present in his favor; how can he authenticate himself? The transition is judgment, for in the stripping of death it is the entire life that is laid bare" (184).

24. Joseph Ratzinger, *Dogma and Preaching: Applying Christian Doctrine to Daily Life*, trans. Michael J. Miller and Matthew J. O'Connell (San Francisco: Ignatius, 2011), 249.

25. See Ratzinger, *Dogma and Preaching*, 250. With Rabbi Jonathan Sacks, I affirm that "what is revolutionary in Judaism is not simply the concept of monotheism—that the universe is not a blind clash of conflicting powers but the result of a single creative will. It is that God is *involved* in His creation"—and thus in our dying (*Covenant and Conversation: A Weekly Reading of the Jewish Bible. Exodus: The Book of Redemption* [New Milford, CT: Maggid, 2010], 64).

26. Silence opens us to God, in a way that cannot happen if we seek instead to rely upon our "own conceptualizing" (Collopy, "Theology and the Darkness," 52).

Bibliography

Abdel Haleem, Muhammad. "Quranic Paradise: How to Get to Paradise and What to Expect There." In *Foundations and the Formation of a Tradition: Reflections on the Hereafter in the Quran and Islamic Religious Thought*, edited by Sebastian Günther and Todd Lawson, 49–66. Vol. 1 of *Roads to Paradise: Eschatology and Concepts of the Hereafter in Islam*. Leiden: Brill, 2017.

Acolatse, Esther E. "Embracing and Resisting Death: A Theology of Justice and Hope for Care at the End of Life." In *Living Well and Dying Faithfully: Christian Practices for End-of-Life Care*, edited by John Swinton and Richard Payne, 246–71. Grand Rapids: Eerdmans, 2009.

Adams, Marilyn McCord. *Horrendous Evils and the Goodness of God*. Ithaca, NY: Cornell University Press, 1999.

Afsaruddin, Asma. "Death, Resurrection, and Human Destiny in the Islamic Tradition." In *Death, Resurrection, and Human Destiny: Christian and Muslim Perspectives*, edited by David Marshall and Lucinda Mosher, 43–56. Washington, DC: Georgetown University Press, 2014.

Alexandrin, Elizabeth. "Paradise as the Abode of Pure Knowledge: Reconsidering al-Mu'ayyad's 'Isma'ili Neoplatonism.'" In *Foundations and the Formation of a Tradition: Reflections on the Hereafter in the Quran and Islamic Religious Thought*, edited by Sebastian Günther and Todd Lawson, 649–61. Vol. 1 of *Roads to Paradise: Eschatology and Concepts of the Hereafter in Islam*. Leiden: Brill, 2017.

Allison, Dale C., Jr. *Night Comes: Death, Imagination, and the Last Things*. Grand Rapids: Eerdmans, 2016.

Anderson, Gary A. *Charity: The Place of the Poor in the Biblical Tradition*. New Haven: Yale University Press, 2013.

———. *Sin: A History*. New Haven: Yale University Press, 2009.

Anderson, Megory. *Attending the Dying: A Handbook of Practical Guidelines*. New York: Morehouse, 2005.

————. *Sacred Dying: Creating Rituals for Embracing the End of Life*. New York: Marlowe, 2004.

Ariès, Philippe. *The Hour of Our Death*. Translated by Helen Weaver. New York: Knopf, 1981.

Arnold, Johann Christoph. *Be Not Afraid: Overcoming the Fear of Death*. Farmington, PA: Plough, 2002.

Ashfield, Ruth. "The Gift of the Dying Person." *Communio* 39 (2012): 381–97.

Astrow, Alan B. "Thoughts on Euthanasia and Physician-Assisted Suicide." In *Facing Death: Where Culture, Religion, and Medicine Meet*, edited by Howard M. Spiro, Mary G. McCrea Curnen, and Lee Palmer Wandel, 44–51. New Haven: Yale University Press, 1996.

Athanasius. "A Letter of Athanasius, Our Holy Father, Archbishop of Alexandria, to Marcellinus on the Interpretation of the Psalms." In Athanasius, *The Life of Antony and the Letter to Marcellinus*, translated by Robert C. Gregg, 101–29. Mahwah, NJ: Paulist, 1980.

————. *On the Incarnation*. Translated and edited by a Religious of CSMV. Crestwood, NY: St. Vladimir's Orthodox Seminary Press, 1993.

Atkinson, David William, ed. *The English Ars Moriendi*. New York: Lang, 1992.

Atkinson, Joseph C. *Biblical and Theological Foundations of the Family: The Domestic Church*. Washington, DC: Catholic University of America Press, 2014.

Attridge, Harold W. *The Epistle to the Hebrews: A Commentary on the Epistle to the Hebrews*. Minneapolis: Fortress, 1989.

Augustine. *On Christian Doctrine*. Translated by D. W. Robertson Jr. New York: Macmillan, 1958.

————. *On Free Choice of the Will*. Translated by Thomas Williams. Indianapolis: Hackett, 1993.

B. *Vita s. Dunstani*. In *The Early Lives of St Dunstan*, edited and translated by Michael Winterbottom and Michael Lapidge, 3–109. Oxford: Oxford University Press, 2012.

Balthasar, Hans Urs von. *Dare We Hope "That All Men Be Saved"? with a Short Discourse on Hell*. Translated by David Kipp and Lothar Krauth. San Francisco: Ignatius, 1988.

————. "Hosanna—For Which Liberation Theology?" In *"You Crown the Year with Your Goodness": Radio Sermons*, translated by Graham Harrison, 69–75. San Francisco: Ignatius, 1989.

————. *The Last Act*. Vol. 5 of *Theo-Drama: Theological Dramatic Theory*. Translated by Graham Harrison. San Francisco: Ignatius, 1998.

————. *Life out of Death: Meditations on the Paschal Mystery*. Translated by Martina Stöckl. San Francisco: Ignatius, 2012.

————. *Love Alone Is Credible*, translated by D. C. Schindler. San Francisco: Ignatius, 2004.

————. *The Moment of Christian Witness*. Translated by Richard Beckley. San Francisco: Ignatius, 1994.

————. *Prolegomena*. Vol. 1 of *Theo-Drama: Theological Dramatic Theory*. Translated by Graham Harrison. San Francisco: Ignatius, 1988.

————. *Two Sisters in the Spirit: Thérèse of Lisieux and Elizabeth of the Trinity*. San Francisco: Ignatius, 1992.

————. *Unless You Become like This Child*. Translated by Erasmo Leiva-Merikakis. San Francisco: Ignatius, 1991.

————. *You Have Words of Eternal Life: Scripture Meditations*. Translated by Dennis Martin. San Francisco: Ignatius, 1991.

Barnes, Corey L. "Thomas Aquinas on the Body and Bodily Passions." In *The Embrace of Eros: Bodies, Desires, and Sexuality in Christianity*, edited by Margaret D. Kamitsuka, 83–97. Minneapolis: Fortress, 2010.

Barnes, Michel René. "Snowden's Secret: Gregory of Nyssa on Passion and Death." In *A Man of the Church: Honoring the Theology, Life, and Witness of Ralph del Colle*, edited by Michel René Barnes, 107–22. Eugene, OR: Pickwick, 2012.

Battin, Margaret P. *Least Worst Death: Essays in Bioethics on the End of Life*. New York: Oxford University Press, 1994.

Bauckham, Richard. *The Fate of the Dead: Studies on the Jewish and Christian Apocalypses*. Leiden: Brill, 1998.

————. *Living with Other Creatures: Green Exegesis and Theology*. Waco, TX: Baylor University Press, 2011.

Bauerschmidt, Frederick Christian. "'That the Faithful Become the Temple of God': The Church Militant in Aquinas's *Commentary on John*." In *Reading John with St. Thomas Aquinas: Theological Exegesis and Speculative Theology*, edited by Michael Dauphinais and Matthew Levering, 293–311. Washington, DC: Catholic University of America Press, 2005.

Beale, G. K. *The Temple and the Church's Mission: A Biblical Theology of the Dwelling Place of God*. Downers Grove, IL: InterVarsity Press, 2004.

Beattie, Patricia. "Dying Well Isn't Easy: Thoughts of a Roman Catholic Theologian on Assisted Death." In *Must We Suffer Our Way to Death? Cultural and Theological Perspectives on Death by Choice*, edited by Ronald P. Hamel, and Edwin R. DuBose. 174–97. Dallas: Southern Methodist University Press, 1996.

Beauvoir, Simone de. *The Force of Circumstance*. Translated by Richard Howard. London: Weidenfeld & Nicolson, 1965.

Beck, Richard. *The Slavery of Death*. Eugene, OR: Cascade Books, 2013.

Becker, Ernest. *The Denial of Death*. New York: Free Press, 1973.

Bede. *Life of Cuthbert*. In *The Age of Bede*, edited by D. H. Farmer, 43–104. Translated by J. F. Webb. Rev. ed. New York: Penguin, 1998.

Behr, John. "Life and Death in the Age of Martyrdom." In *The Role of Death in Life: A Multidisciplinary Examination of the Relationship between Life and Death*, edited by John Behr and Conor Cunningham, 79–95. Eugene, OR: Cascade, 2015.

Behr, John, and Conor Cunningham, eds. *The Role of Death in Life: A Multidisciplinary Examination of the Relationship between Life and Death*. Eugene, OR: Cascade, 2015.

Bellarmine, Robert, SJ. *The Art of Dying Well*. In *Spiritual Writings*. Translated and edited by John Patrick Donnelly, SJ, and Roland Teske, SJ, 233–386. New York: Paulist, 1989.

Benard, Elisabeth. "The Tibetan Tantric View of Death and Afterlife." In *Death and*

Afterlife: Perspectives of World Religions, edited by Hiroshi Obayashi, 169–80. New York: Praeger, 1992.

Benedict XVI, Pope. *Spe Salvi*. Vatican City: Libreria Editrice Vaticana, 2007.

Berdyaev, Nicholas. *The Destiny of Man*. New York: Harper & Row, 1960.

Berrigan, Daniel, SJ. *Job: And Death No Dominion*. Franklin, WI: Sheed & Ward, 2000.

———. *We Die before We Live: Talking with the Very Ill*. New York: Seabury, 1980.

Billings, J. Todd. *Rejoicing in Lament: Wrestling with Incurable Cancer and Life in Christ*. Grand Rapids: Brazos, 2015.

———. *Union with Christ: Reframing Theology and Ministry for the Church*. Grand Rapids: Baker Academic, 2011.

Blenkinsopp, Joseph. *Creation, Un-Creation, Re-Creation: A Discursive Commentary on Genesis 1–11*. London: T. & T. Clark, 2011.

———. *Ezekiel*. Louisville: John Knox, 1990.

Boersma, Hans. *Embodiment and Virtue in Gregory of Nyssa: An Anagogical Approach*. Oxford: Oxford University Press, 2013.

Boff, Leonardo, SJ. *Jesus Christ Liberator: A Critical Christology for Our Time*. Translated by Patrick Hughes. Maryknoll, NY: Orbis, 1978.

Boros, Ladislaus, SJ. *The Mystery of Death*. New York: Seabury, 1973.

Bowker, John. *The Meanings of Death*. Cambridge: Cambridge University Press, 1991.

Boyagoda, Randy. *Richard John Neuhaus: A Life in the Public Square*. New York: Doubleday, 2015.

Boyle, John F. "Saint Thomas Aquinas on the Anointing of the Sick (Extreme Unction)." In *Rediscovering Aquinas and the Sacraments: Studies in Sacramental Theology*, edited by Matthew Levering and Michael Dauphinais, 76–84. Chicago: Hillenbrand, 2009.

Braine, David. *The Human Person: Animal and Spirit*. Notre Dame: University of Notre Dame Press, 1992.

———. *Language and Human Understanding: The Roots of Creativity in Speech and Thought*. Washington, DC: Catholic University of America Press, 2014.

Bregman, Lucy. *Beyond Silence and Denial: Death and Dying Reconsidered*. Louisville: Westminster John Knox, 1994.

Brock, Rita Nakashima, and Rebecca Ann Parker. *Proverbs of Ashes: Violence, Redemptive Suffering, and the Search for What Saves Us*. Boston: Beacon, 2001.

Brockman, James R., SJ. *Romero: A Life*. 2nd ed. Maryknoll, NY: Orbis, 1989.

Brosend, William F., II. *James and Jude*. Cambridge: Cambridge University Press, 2004.

Brown, Ian. *Sixty*. New York: Experiment, 2016.

Brown, Sally A., and Patrick D. Miller, eds. *Lament: Reclaiming Practices in Pulpit, Pew, and Public Square*. Louisville: Westminster John Knox, 2007.

Bryan, Steven M. *Jesus and Israel's Traditions of Judgment and Restoration*. Cambridge: Cambridge University Press, 2002.

Buber, Martin. "Job." In *On the Bible: Eighteen Studies*, edited by Nahum N. Glatzer, 188–98. New York: Schocken, 1982.

Burrell, David B., CSC. *Deconstructing Theodicy: Why Job Has Nothing to Say to the Puzzled Suffering*. Grand Rapids: Brazos, 2008.

Butler, Katy. *Knocking on Heaven's Door: The Path to a Better Way of Death*. New York: Scribner, 2013.

Butler, Robert. "The Life Review: An Interpretation of Reminiscence in the Aged." *Psychiatry* 26 (1963): 65–76.

Bynum, Caroline Walker. *The Resurrection of the Body in Western Christianity, 200–1336*. New York: Columbia University Press, 1995.

Byock, Ira. *Dying Well: Peace and Possibilities at the End of Life*. New York: Riverhead, 1997.

Byrne, Brendan, SJ. *Romans*. Collegeville, MN: Liturgical Press, 1996.

Caird, George B. "The Exegetical Method of the Epistle to the Hebrews." *Canadian Journal of Theology* 5 (1959): 44–51.

Callanan, Maggie, and Patricia Kelley. *Final Gifts: Understanding the Special Awareness, Needs, and Communications of the Dying*. New York: Bantam, 1993.

Cary, Phillip, and Jean-François Phelizon. *Does God Have a Strategy? A Dialogue*. Translated by Anne François. Eugene, OR: Cascade, 2015.

Cassell, Eric J. "Dying in a Technological Society." In *Death Inside Out*, edited by Peter Steinfels and Robert M. Veatch, 43–48. New York: Harper & Row, 1975.

Catechism of the Catholic Church. 2nd ed. Vatican City: Libreria Editrice Vaticana, 1997.

Cates, Diana Fritz. *Choosing to Feel: Virtue, Friendship, and Compassion for Friends*. Notre Dame: University of Notre Dame Press, 1997.

Catherine of Siena. *The Dialogue*. Translated by Suzanne Noffke, OP. New York: Paulist, 1980.

Caussade, Jean-Pierre de, SJ. *Abandonment to Divine Providence*. Translated by John Beevers. New York: Doubleday, 1975.

Cavadini, John C. "Ambrose and Augustine—*De Bono Mortis*." In *The Limits of Ancient Christianity*, edited by William E. Klingshirn and Mark Vessey, 232–49. Ann Arbor: University of Michigan Press, 1999.

Cessario, Romanus, OP. *Christian Faith and the Theological Life*. Washington, DC: Catholic University of America Press, 1996.

————. *The Virtues, or the Examined Life*. London: Continuum, 2002.

Chittick, William C. "Eschatology." In *Islamic Spirituality: Foundations*, edited by S. H. Nasr, 378–409. New York: Crossroad, 1987.

————. "'Your Sight Today Is Piercing': The Muslim Understanding of Death and Afterlife." In *Death and Afterlife: Perspectives of World Religions*, edited by Hiroshi Obayashi, 125–39. New York: Praeger, 1992.

Choron, Jacques. *Death and Western Thought*. New York: Collier, 1963.

Christie, Niall. "Paradise and Hell in the *Kitāb al-Jihād* of 'Alī b. Ṭāhir al-Sulamī (d. 500/1106)." In *Foundations and the Formation of a Tradition: Reflections on the Hereafter in the Quran and Islamic Religious Thought*, edited by Sebastian Günther and Todd Lawson, 407–21. Vol. 1 of *Roads to Paradise: Eschatology and Concepts of the Hereafter in Islam*. Leiden: Brill, 2017.

Clark, Elizabeth. "Holy Women, Holy Words: Early Christian Women, Social History, and the 'Linguistic Turn.'" *Journal of Early Christian Studies* 6 (1998): 413–30.

Clark, Patrick M. *Perfection in Death: The Christological Dimension of Courage in Aquinas*. Washington, DC: Catholic University of America Press, 2015.

Clarke, W. Norris, SJ. "The Immediate Creation of the Human Soul by God and Some Contemporary Challenges." In *The Creative Retrieval of Saint Thomas Aquinas: Essays in Thomistic Philosophy, New and Old*, 173–90. New York: Fordham University Press, 2009.

Clines, David J. A. *Job 1–20*. Dallas: Word, 1989.

———. *Job 38–42*. Nashville: Nelson, 2011.

Collopy, Bartholomew J., SJ. "Theology and the Darkness of Death." *Theological Studies* 39 (1978): 22–54.

Congar, Yves, OP. "The Church: The People of God." In *The Church and Mankind: Dogma*, edited by Hans Küng and Edward Schillebeeckx, 11–37. Glen Rock, NJ: Paulist, 1964.

Congregation for the Doctrine of the Faith. "Notification on the Works of Father Jon Sobrino, SJ." (2006) http://www.vatican.va/roman_curia/congregations/cfaith/documents/rc_con_cfaith_doc_20061126_notification-sobrino_en.html.

Cothenet, Edouard. "Healing as a Sign of the Kingdom, and the Anointing of the Sick." In *Temple of the Holy Spirit: Sickness and Death of the Christian in the Liturgy: The Twenty-First Liturgical Conference Saint-Serge*, edited by Achille M. Triacca, SDB, translated by Matthew J. O'Connell, 33–51. New York: Pueblo, 1983.

Couenhoven, Jesse. "Not Every Wrong Is Done with Pride?" *Scottish Journal of Theology* 61 (2008): 32–50.

Crawford, David S. "The Gospel of Life and the Integrity of Death." *Communio* 39 (2012): 364–80.

Cross, Frank Moore. *Canaanite Myth and Hebrew Epic*. Cambridge: Harvard University Press, 1973.

Cullmann, Oscar. *Immortality of the Soul: or, Resurrection of the Dead? The Witness of the New Testament*. New York: Macmillan, 1958.

Cunningham, Conor. "Is There Life before Death?" In *The Role of Death in Life: A Multidisciplinary Examination of the Relationship between Life and Death*, edited by John Behr and Conor Cunningham, 120–51. Eugene, OR: Cascade, 2015.

Daley, Brian E., SJ. *The Hope of the Early Church: A Handbook of Patristic Eschatology*. Cambridge: Cambridge University Press, 1991.

———. "A Humble Mediator: The Distinctive Elements of St. Augustine's Christology." *Word and Spirit* 9 (1987): 100–117.

Daniélou, Jean. "Job: The Mystery of Man and God." In *The Dimensions of Job: A Study and Selected Readings*, edited by Nahum N. Glatzer, 100–111. Reprint, Eugene, OR: Wipf & Stock, 2002.

Davies, Douglas J. *A Brief History of Death*. Oxford: Blackwell, 2005.

———. *The Theology of Death*. London: T. & T. Clark, 2008.

Davies, W. D., and Dale C. Allison Jr. *A Critical and Exegetical Commentary on the Gospel according to Saint Matthew*. 3 vols. London: T. & T. Clark, 1988–97.

Davison, Andrew. *Why Sacraments?* Eugene, OR: Cascade, 2013.

Deathbed Wisdom of the Hasidic Masters: The Book of Departure and Caring for People at the End of Life. Translated and annotated by Joel H. Baron and Sara Paasche-Orlow. Woodstock, VT: Jewish Lights, 2016.

Depoortere, Kristiaan. "Recent Developments in the Anointing of the Sick." In *Illness and Healing*, edited by Louis-Marie Chaubet and Miklós Tomka, 89–100. London: SCM, 1998.

―――. "You Have Striven with God (Genesis 32:28): A Pastoral-Theological Reflection on the Image of God and Suffering." In *God and Human Suffering*, edited by Jan Lambrecht and Raymond F. Collins, 211–34. Louvain: Peeters, 1990.

Derrida, Jacques. *The Gift of Death*. 2nd ed. In *The Gift of Death and Literature in Secret*, translated by David Wills, 3–116. Chicago: University of Chicago Press, 2008.

Dozeman, Thomas B. *Commentary on Exodus*. Grand Rapids: Eerdmans, 2009.

Drumm, Michael. "The Practice of Anointing and the Development of Doctrine." In *Recovering the Riches of Anointing: A Study of the Sacrament of the Sick*, edited by Genevieve Glen, OSB, 37–58. Collegeville, MN: Liturgical Press, 2002.

D'Souza, Dinesh. *Life after Death: The Evidence*. Washington, DC: Regnery, 2009.

Du Boulay, Shirley, and Marianne Rankin. *Cicely Saunders: The Founder of the Modern Hospice Movement*. London: SPCK, 2007.

Dunn, James D. G. *Jesus Remembered*. Grand Rapids: Eerdmans, 2003.

Dupré, Louis. *The Deeper Life: An Introduction to Christian Mysticism*. New York: Crossroad, 1981.

Echeverria, Eduardo J. "The Gospel of Redemptive Suffering: Reflections on John Paul II's *Salvifici Doloris*." In *Christian Faith and the Problem of Evil*, edited by Peter van Inwagen, 111–47. Grand Rapids: Eerdmans, 2004.

Eddius Stephanus. *Life of Wilfrid*. In *The Age of Bede*, edited by D. H. Farmer, 107–84. Translated by J. F. Webb. Rev. ed. New York: Penguin, 1998.

Ehrman, Bart D. *God's Problem: How the Bible Fails to Answer Our Most Important Question—Why We Suffer*. New York: HarperCollins, 2008.

Eire, Carlos. *A Very Brief History of Eternity*. Princeton: Princeton University Press, 2010.

Eisenbaum, Pamela Michelle. *The Jewish Heroes of Christian Antiquity: Hebrews 11 in Literary Context*. Atlanta: Scholars Press, 1997.

―――. "Locating Hebrews within the Literary Landscape of Christian Origins." In *Hebrews: Contemporary Methods—New Insights*, edited by Gabriella Gelardini, 213–37. Leiden: Brill, 2005.

Elizabeth of the Trinity. *General Introduction; Major Spiritual Writings*. Vol. 1 of *I Have Found God: Complete Works*. Translated by Aletheia Kane, OCD. Washington, DC: ICS, 1984.

Empereur, James L., SJ. *Prophetic Anointing: God's Call to the Sick, the Elderly, and the Dying*. Wilmington, DE: Glazier, 1982.

Epicurus. *Principal Doctrines*. Translated by Cyril Bailey. In *The Stoic and Epicurean Philosophers*, edited by Whitney J. Oates, 35–39. New York: Modern Library, 1940.

Erasmus. *Preparing for Death (De praeparatione ad mortem)*. Translated by John M. Grant. In *Spiritualia and Pastoralia*, edited by John W. O'Malley, SJ, 389–450. Vol. 70 of *Collected Works of Erasmus*. Toronto: University of Toronto Press, 1998.

Ernst, Cornelius, OP. "The Theology of Death." *Clergy Review* 44 (1959): 588–602.

Eslinger, Lyle. "Ezekiel 20 and the Metaphor of Historical Teleology: Concepts of Biblical History." *Journal for the Study of the Old Testament* 23 (1998): 93–125.

Evans, Craig A. "Jesus and the Continuing Exile." In *Jesus and the Restoration of Israel: A Critical Assessment of N. T. Wright's* Jesus and the Victory of God, edited by Carey C. Newman, 77–100. Downers Grove, IL: InterVarsity Press, 1999.

Evans, Sioned, and Andrew Davison. *Care for the Dying: A Practical and Pastoral Guide.* Norwich, Eng.: Canterbury, 2014.

Fabella, M. M. "Christology from an Asian Woman's Perspective." In *We Dare to Dream: Doing Theology as Asian Women*, edited by Virginia M. M. Fabella and Sun Ai Lee Park, 3–14. Maryknoll, NY: Orbis, 1990.

Falque, Emmanuel. *Le passeur de Gethsémani: Angoisse, souffrance et mort. Lecture existentielle et phénoménologique.* Paris: Cerf, 1999.

———. "Suffering Death." In *The Role of Death in Life: A Multidisciplinary Examination of the Relationship between Life and Death*, edited by John Behr and Conor Cunningham, 45–55. Eugene, OR: Cascade, 2015.

Farmer, D. H., ed. *The Age of Bede.* Translated by J. F. Webb. Rev. ed. New York: Penguin, 1998.

Farmer, Paul. *Pathologies of Power: Health, Human Rights, and the New War on the Poor.* Foreword by Amartya Sen. Berkeley: University of California Press, 2005.

Feifel, Herman, ed. *The Meaning of Death.* New York: McGraw-Hill, 1959.

Feldman, Fred. *Confrontations with the Reaper: A Philosophical Study of the Nature and Value of Death.* Oxford: Oxford University Press, 1992.

Feser, Edward. *Aquinas.* Oxford: Oneworld, 2009.

———. *Philosophy of Mind: A Beginner's Guide.* Oxford: Oneworld, 2006.

Fishbane, Michael. *Sacred Attunement: A Jewish Theology.* Chicago: University of Chicago Press, 2008.

———. "Sin and Judgment in the Prophecies of Ezekiel." *Interpretation* 38 (1984): 131–50.

FitzGerald, Constance. "Impasse and Dark Night." In *Women's Spirituality: Resources for Christian Development*, edited by Joann Wolski Conn, 287–311. Mahwah, NJ: Paulist, 1986.

Fitzmyer, Joseph A., SJ. *The Gospel according to Luke (X–XXIV).* Garden City, NY: Doubleday, 1985.

Fitzpatrick, Jeanne, and Eileen M. Fitzpatrick. *A Better Way of Dying: How to Make the Best Choices at the End of Life.* New York: Penguin, 2010.

Flanagan, Owen. *The Problem of the Soul.* New York: Basic Books, 2002.

Flannery, Austin, OP, ed. *The Conciliar and Post Conciliar Documents.* Vol. 1 of *Vatican Council II.* Rev. ed. Northport, NY: Costello, 1996.

Florovsky, Georges. *Creation and Redemption.* Collected Works of Georges Florovsky 3. Belmont, MA: Nordland, 1976.

Fortune, Marie M. "The Transformation of Suffering: A Biblical and Theological Perspective." In *Violence against Women and Children: A Christian Theological Source-*

book, edited by Carol J. Adams and Marie M. Fortune, 85–91. New York: Continuum, 1995.

Foucauld, Charles de. *Charles de Foucauld: Writings*. Edited by Robert Ellsberg. Maryknoll, NY: Orbis, 1999.

Francis, Pope. *Evangelii Gaudium*. Vatican trans. Boston: Pauline Books & Media, 2013.

Frankfurt, Harry G. "How the Afterlife Matters." In Samuel Scheffler, *Death and the Afterlife*, edited by Niko Kolodny, 131–41. Oxford: Oxford University Press, 2013.

Freedman, David Noel, with Jeffrey C. Geoghegan and Michael M. Homan. *The Nine Commandments: Uncovering the Hidden Pattern of Crime and Punishment in the Hebrew Bible*, edited by Astrid B. Beck. New York: Doubleday, 2000.

Garrett, Greg. *Entertaining Judgment: The Afterlife in Popular Imagination*. Oxford: Oxford University Press, 2015.

Garrigues, Jean-Migule, OP. *Dieu sans idée du mal: Méditations sur la miséricorde*. 3rd ed. Geneva: Ad Solem, 2016.

Gawande, Atul. *Being Mortal: Medicine and What Matters in the End*. New York: Holt, 2014.

Geissinger, Aisha. "'Are Men the Majority in Paradise, or Women?' Constructing Gender and Communal Boundaries in Muslim b. al-Ḥajjāj's (d. 261/875) *Kitāb al-Janna*." In *Foundations and the Formation of a Tradition: Reflections on the Hereafter in the Quran and Islamic Religious Thought*, edited by Sebastian Günther and Todd Lawson, 311–40. Vol. 1 of *Roads to Paradise: Eschatology and Concepts of the Hereafter in Islam*. Leiden: Brill, 2017.

Gerson, Johannes. *Opusculum Tripertitum*. In *Opera Omnia*, edited by Louis Ellier Du Pin, 1:425–50. Hildesheim: Olms, 1987.

Ghazali, Abu Hamid Muhammad ibn Muhammad al-. *The Remembrance of Death and the Afterlife*. Translated by T. J. Winter. Cambridge: Islamic Texts Society, 1989.

Gilbert, Maurice. "Immortalité? Résurrection? Faut-il choisir? Témoignage du judaïsme ancient." In *Le judaïsme à l'aube de l'ère chrétienne*, edited by Philippe Abadie and Jean-Pierre Lemonon, 271–97. Paris: Cerf, 2001.

Glatzer, Nahum N., ed. *The Dimensions of Job: A Study and Selected Readings*. Reprint, Eugene, OR: Wipf & Stock, 2002.

Gleason, R. W. "Toward a Theology of Death." *Thought* 23 (1957): 39–68.

Goldstein, Dawn Eden. "The Mystical Body and Its Loving Wounds: Redemptive Suffering in Magisterial Teaching, Pre-Papal Writings, and Popes' Teachings as Private Theologians, 1939–2015." STD diss., Mundelein, IL: University of Saint Mary of the Lake, 2016.

Gorman, Michael J. *Cruciformity: Paul's Narrative Spirituality of the Cross*. Grand Rapids: Eerdmans, 2001.

———. *Inhabiting the Cruciform God: Kenosis, Justification, and Theosis in Paul's Narrative Soteriology*. Grand Rapids: Eerdmans, 2009.

Grabbe, Lester L. *Wisdom of Solomon*. New York: T. & T. Clark, 2003.

Greenberg, Moshe. *Ezekiel 1–20*. New Haven: Yale University Press, 1983.

Greenway, William. *For the Love of All Creatures: The Story of Grace in Genesis*. Grand Rapids: Eerdmans, 2015.

Gregory of Nyssa. *The Life of Saint Macrina*. Translated by Kevin Corrigan. Eugene, OR: Wipf & Stock, 2005.

Greinacher, Norbert, and Alois Müller, eds. *The Experience of Dying*. New York: Herder & Herder, 1974.

Grenberg, Jeanine. *Kant and the Ethics of Humility: A Story of Dependence, Corruption and Virtue*. Cambridge: Cambridge University Press, 2005.

Greshake, Gisbert. "Towards a Theology of Dying." Translated by Robert Nowell. In *The Experience of Dying*, edited by Norbert Greinacher and Alois Müller, 80–98. New York: Herder & Herder, 1974.

Griffiths, Paul J. *Decreation: The Last Things of All Creatures*. Waco, TX: Baylor University Press, 2014.

Guardini, Romano. *The Death of Socrates: An Interpretation of the Platonic Dialogues: Euthyphro, Apology, Crito and Phaedo*. Translated by Basil Wrighton. Cleveland: Meridian, 1962.

———. *The Last Things: Concerning Death, Purification after Death, Resurrection, Judgment, and Eternity*. Translated by Charlotte E. Forsyth and Grace B. Branham. New York: Pantheon, 1954.

———. *Rilke's Duino Elegies: An Interpretation*. Translated by K. G. Knight. Chicago: Regnery, 1961.

Gudmundsdóttir, Arnfríður. *Meeting God on the Cross: Christ, the Cross, and the Feminist Critique*. Oxford: Oxford University Press, 2010.

Guroian, Vigen. *Life's Living toward Dying: A Theological and Medical-Ethical Study*. Grand Rapids: Eerdmans, 1996.

Gusmer, Charles W. *The Ministry of Healing in the Church of England: An Ecumenical-Liturgical Study*. Great Wakering, Eng.: Mayhew-McCrimmon, 1974.

Guthrie, George H. "Hebrews' Use of the Old Testament: Recent Trends in Research." *Currents in Biblical Research* 1 (2003): 271–94.

Gutiérrez, Gustavo. *On Job: God-Talk and the Suffering of the Innocent*. Translated by Matthew J. O'Connell. Maryknoll, NY: Orbis, 1987.

———. "Theology: An Ecclesial Function." In Gustavo Gutiérrez and Gerhard Ludwig Müller, *On the Side of the Poor: The Theology of Liberation*, translated by Robert A. Krieg and James B. Nickoloff, 1–10. Maryknoll, NY: Orbis, 2015.

Haggerty, Donald. *The Contemplative Hunger*. San Francisco: Ignatius, 2016.

———. *Conversion: Spiritual Insights into an Essential Encounter with God*. San Francisco: Ignatius, forthcoming.

Hahn, Scott. *The Creed: Professing the Faith through the Ages*. Steubenville, OH: Emmaus Road, 2016.

Hain, Raymond. "Aquinas and Aristotelian Hylomorphism." In *Aristotle in Aquinas's Theology*, edited by Gilles Emery, OP, and Matthew Levering, 48–69. Oxford: Oxford University Press, 2015.

Haldane, J. B. S. *Possible Worlds and Other Essays*. London: Chatto & Windus, 1932.

Halkin, Hillel. *After One-Hundred-and-Twenty: Reflecting on Death, Mourning, and the Afterlife in the Jewish Tradition*. Princeton: Princeton University Press, 2016.

Hamel, Ronald P., and Edwin R. DuBose, eds. *Must We Suffer Our Way to Death? Cul-*

tural and Theological Perspectives on Death by Choice. Dallas: Southern Methodist University Press, 1996.

Harasta, Eva, and Brian Brock, eds. *Evoking Lament: A Theological Discussion*. Translated by Martina Sitling, Stephen Lakkis, Daniel Schultz, and Anna Schneider. London: T. & T. Clark, 2009.

Haroutunian, Joseph. "Life and Death among Fellowmen." In *The Modern Vision of Death*, edited by Nathan A. Scott, Jr., 79–96. Richmond, VA: John Knox, 1967.

Harrington, Daniel, SJ. *Why Do We Suffer? A Scriptural Approach to the Human Condition*. Franklin, WI: Sheed & Ward, 2000.

Hart, David Bentley. *The Beauty of the Infinite: The Aesthetics of Christian Truth*. Grand Rapids: Eerdmans, 2003.

———. "Death, Final Judgment, and the Meaning of Life." In *The Hidden and the Manifest: Essays in Theology and Metaphysics*, 253–68. Grand Rapids: Eerdmans, 2017.

———. *The Doors of the Sea: Where Was God in the Tsunami?* Grand Rapids: Eerdmans, 2005.

———. *The Experience of God: Being, Consciousness, Bliss*. New Haven: Yale University Press, 2013.

Hauerwas, Stanley. "Foreword." In *Living Well and Dying Faithfully: Christian Practices for End-of-Life Care*, edited by John Swinton and Richard Payne, xii–xiv. Grand Rapids: Eerdmans, 2009.

Hays, Christopher B. *A Covenant with Death: Death in the Iron Age II and Its Rhetorical Uses in Proto-Isaiah*. Grand Rapids: Eerdmans, 2015.

Hays, Richard B. *The Faith of Jesus Christ: The Narrative Substructure of Galatians 3:1–4:11*. 2nd ed. Grand Rapids: Eerdmans, 2001.

———. "'Here We Have No Lasting City': New Covenantalism in Hebrews." In *The Epistle to the Hebrews and Christian Theology*, edited by Richard Bauckham, Daniel R. Driver, Trevor A. Hart, and Nathan MacDonald, 151–73. Grand Rapids: Eerdmans, 2009.

Heidegger, Martin. *Being and Time*. Translated by Joan Stambaugh, revised by Dennis J. Schmidt. Albany: State University of New York Press, 2010.

Heinz, Donald. *The Last Passage: Recovering a Death of Our Own*. Oxford: Oxford University Press, 1999.

Hendrix, Jeffry. *A Little Guide for Your Last Days*. Plano, TX: Bridegroom, 2009.

Hengstenberg, H. E. *Einsamkeit und Tod*. Regensburg: Pustet, 1938.

Hermansen, Marcia. "Eschatology." In *The Cambridge Companion to Classical Islamic Theology*, edited by Tim Winter, 308–24. Cambridge: Cambridge University Press, 2008.

Hess, Jonathan M. *Germans, Jews and the Claims of Modernity*. New Haven: Yale University Press, 2002.

Hibbs, Thomas S. *Virtue's Splendor: Wisdom, Prudence, and the Human Good*. New York: Fordham University Press, 2001.

Hildebrand, Dietrich von. *Transformation in Christ*. Manchester, NH: Sophia Institute, 1990.

Hill, T. Patrick, and David Shirley. *A Good Death: Taking More Control at the End of Your Life*. Reading, MA: Addison-Wesley, 1992.

Hinshaw, David. "The Kenosis of the Dying: An Invitation to Healing." In *The Role of Death in Life: A Multidisciplinary Examination of the Relationship between Life and Death*, edited by John Behr and Conor Cunningham, 155–63. Eugene, OR: Cascade, 2015.

Hitchens, Christopher. *Mortality*. New York: Twelve, 2012.

Horn, Trent. *Hard Sayings: A Catholic Approach to Answering Bible Difficulties*. El Cajon, CA: Catholic Answers, 2016.

Hubbard, Moyer V. *New Creation in Paul's Letters and Thought*. Cambridge: Cambridge University Press, 2002.

Hughes, Aaron W. *The Art of Dialogue in Jewish Philosophy*. Bloomington, IN: Indiana University Press, 2008.

Hughes, Richard A. *Lament, Death and Destiny*. New York: Lang, 2004.

Hume, David. *Enquiries Concerning Human Understanding and Concerning the Principles of Morals*. Oxford: Clarendon, 1975.

Hummel, Horace D. *Ezekiel 1–20*. Saint Louis: Concordia, 2005.

Hütter, Reinhard. *Dust Bound for Heaven: Explorations in the Theology of Thomas Aquinas*. Grand Rapids: Eerdmans, 2012.

Ignatius of Loyola. *The Spiritual Exercises and Selected Works*. Edited by George E. Ganss, SJ. New York: Paulist, 1991.

Imhof, Arthur E. "An *Ars Moriendi* for Our Time: To Live a Fulfilled Life; to Die a Peaceful Death." In *Facing Death: Where Culture, Religion, and Medicine Meet*, edited by Howard M. Spiro, Mary G. McCrea Curnen, and Lee Palmer Wandel, 114–20. New Haven: Yale University Press, 1996.

Irwin, Kevin W. "The Development of Sacramental Doctrine in the Church: Theory and Practice." In *Recovering the Riches of Anointing: A Study of the Sacrament of the Sick*, edited by Genevieve Glen, 59–81. Collegeville, MN: Liturgical Press, 1989.

Jackon, Timothy P. *Love Disconsoled: Meditations on Christian Charity*. Cambridge: Cambridge University Press, 1999.

———. "Must Job Live Forever? A Reply to Aquinas on Providence." *The Thomist* 62 (1998): 1–39.

Janzen, J. Gerald. *Job*. Atlanta: John Knox, 1985.

Jarrar, Maher. "The Martyrdom of Passionate Lovers: Holy War as a Sacred Wedding." In *Ḥadīth: Origins and Developments*, edited by Harald Motzki, 317–37. Aldershot: Ashgate, 2004.

John Paul II, Pope. Address to the Participants in the International Congress on "Life-Sustaining Treatments and Vegetative State: Scientific Advances and Ethical Dilemmas," 20 March 2004. www.vatican.va.

———. *Dives in Misericordia*. In *The Encyclicals of John Paul II*, edited by J. Michael Miller, CSB, 104–37. Huntington, IN: Our Sunday Visitor, 2001.

———. *Salvifici Doloris*. Vatican translation. Boston: St. Paul Books and Media, 1984.

———. *To the Elderly*. Vatican translation. Boston: Pauline Books & Media, 2000.

———. *Ut Unum Sint*. In *The Encyclicals of John Paul II*, edited by J. Michael Miller, CSB, 782–831. Huntington, IN: Our Sunday Visitor, 2001.

Johnson, Elizabeth. *She Who Is: The Mystery of God in Feminist Theological Discourse*. New York: Crossroad, 1992.

Johnson, Luke Timothy. *The Acts of the Apostles*. Collegeville, MN: Liturgical Press, 1992.

———. *Hebrews: A Commentary*. Louisville: Westminster John Knox, 2006.

———. "A Historiographical Response to Wright's Jesus." In *Jesus and the Restoration of Israel*, edited by Carey C. Newman, 206–24. Downers Grove, IL: InterVarsity Press, 1999.

Johnson, Samuel. *Rasselas*. New York: Penguin, 1976.

Jones, David Albert. *Approaching the End: A Theological Exploration of Death and Dying*. Oxford: Oxford University Press, 2007.

Jüngel, Eberhard. *Death: The Riddle and the Mystery*. Translated by Iain and Ute Nicol. Philadelphia: Westminster, 1975.

Kalina, Kathy. *Midwife for Souls: Spiritual Care for the Dying*. Rev. ed. Boston: Pauline Books & Media, 2007.

Kamitsuka, Margaret D. "Sex in Heaven? Eschatological Eros and the Resurrection of the Body." In *The Embrace of Eros: Bodies, Desires, and Sexuality in Christianity*, edited by Margaret D. Kamitsuka, 261–75. Minneapolis: Fortress, 2010.

Kandhlawi, Muhammad Yusuf, and Muhammad Saad Kandhlawi, comps. *Muntakhab Ahadith: A Selection of Ahadith Relating to the Six Qualities of Da'wa*. Damascus: Malek, 2013.

Kass, Leon R. "Averting One's Eyes, or Facing the Music?—On Dignity and Death." In *Death Inside Out: The Hastings Center Report*, edited by Peter Steinfels and Robert M. Veatch, 101–14. New York: Harper & Row, 1975.

Kasza, John C. "Anointing of the Sick." In *The Oxford Handbook of Sacramental Theology*, edited by Hans Boersma and Matthew Levering, 558–71. Oxford: Oxford University Press, 2015.

———. *Understanding Sacramental Healing: Anointing and Viaticum*. Chicago: Hillenbrand, 2007.

Keating, Daniel A. *Deification and Grace*. Naples, FL: Sapientia, 2007.

Keenan, James F., SJ. *The Works of Mercy: The Heart of Catholicism*. 2nd ed. Lanham, MD: Rowman & Littlefield, 2008.

Keener, Craig S. *Acts: An Exegetical Commentary*. 4 vols. Grand Rapids: Baker Academic, 2012–2015.

Keleman, Stanley. *Living Your Dying*. Berkeley: Center, 1974.

Kellehear, Allan. *A Social History of Dying*. Cambridge: Cambridge University Press, 2007.

Keller, Paul, OSB. *101 Questions and Answers on the Sacraments of Healing: Penance and Anointing of the Sick*. Mahwah, NJ: Paulist, 2010.

Kerry, Walter. *The Art of Dying and Living: Lessons from Saints of Our Time*. Maryknoll, NY: Orbis, 2011.

Kessler, David. *The Needs of the Dying*. New York: HarperCollins, 2000.

Khan, Maulana Wahiduddin. *The Qur'an for All Humanity*. Translated by Farida Khanam. New Delhi: Goodword, 2000.

Kinast, Robert L. *When a Person Dies: Pastoral Theology in Death Experiences*. New York: Crossroad, 1984.

Knasas, John F. X. *Aquinas and the Cry of Rachel: Thomistic Reflections on the Problem of Evil*. Washington, DC: Catholic University of America Press, 2013.

The Koran. Translated by J. M. Rodwell. London: Dent, 1994.

Kowalska, Maria Faustina. *Diary: Divine Mercy in My Soul*. Edited by George Kosicki, CSB, et al. Translated by Adam and Danuta Pasicki et al. 3rd ed. Stockbridge, MA: Marian, 2007.

Kramer, Kenneth. *The Sacred Art of Dying: How World Religions Understand Death*. Mahwah, NJ: Paulist, 1988.

Kübler-Ross, Elisabeth. *Death: The Final Stage of Growth*. New York: Simon & Schuster, 1986.

———. *On Death and Dying*. New York: Macmillan, 1969.

Kuhl, David. *What Dying People Want: Practical Wisdom for the End of Life*. New York: PublicAffairs, 2002.

Küng, Hans. *Eternal Life? Life after Death as a Medical, Philosophical, and Theological Problem*. Translated by Edward Quinn. New York: Doubleday, 1984.

Kunzler, Michael. "Die kosmische Dimension der Eucharistiefeier: Zu Fragen ihrer liturgischen Gestalt bei Joseph Ratzinger." In *Der Logos-gemäße Gottesdienst: Theologie der Liturgie bei Joseph Ratzinger*, edited by Rudolf Voderholzer, 172–204. Regensburg: Pustet, 2009.

Kuykendall, George. "Care for the Dying: A Kübler-Ross Critique." *Theology Today* 38 (1981): 37–48.

Ladd, George Eldon. *The Presence of the Future: The Eschatology of Biblical Realism*. Grand Rapids: Eerdmans, 1974.

Lamb, Matthew L. "The Eschatology of St. Thomas Aquinas." In *Eternity, Time, and the Life of Wisdom*, 55–72. Naples, FL: Sapientia Press, 2007.

———. *Eternity, Time, and the Life of Wisdom*. Naples, FL: Sapientia Press, 2007.

———. "Nature, History, and Redemption." In *Eternity, Time, and the Life of Wisdom*, 13–28. Naples, FL: Sapientia Press, 2007.

———. *Solidarity with Victims: Toward a Theology of Social Transformation*. New York: Crossroad, 1982.

Lambert, David A. *How Repentance Became Biblical: Judaism, Christianity, and the Interpretation of Scripture*. Oxford: Oxford University Press, 2016.

Lang, Uwe Michael. *Signs of the Holy One: Liturgy, Ritual, and Expression of the Sacred*. San Francisco: Ignatius, 2015.

Lange, Christian. "The 'Eight Gates of Paradise' Tradition in Islam: A Genealogical and Structural Study." In *Foundations and the Formation of a Tradition: Reflections on the Hereafter in the Quran and Islamic Religious Thought*, edited by Sebastian Günther and Todd Lawson, 341–70. Vol. 1 of *Roads to Paradise: Eschatology and Concepts of the Hereafter in Islam*. Leiden: Brill, 2017.

Langevin, Dominic M., OP. *From Passion to Paschal Mystery: A Recent Magisterial*

Development concerning the Christological Foundation of the Sacraments. Fribourg: Academic Press Fribourg, 2015.

Lapidus, Ira M. "The Meaning of Death in Islam." In *Facing Death: Where Culture, Religion, and Medicine Meet*, edited by Howard M. Spiro, Mary G. McCrea Curnen, and Lee Palmer Wandel, 148–59. New Haven: Yale University Press, 1996.

Larchet, Jean-Claude. *The Theology of Illness*. Translated by John and Michael Breck. Crestwood, NY: St. Vladimir's Seminary Press, 2002.

Larson-Miller, Lizette. *The Sacrament of the Anointing of the Sick*. Collegeville, MN: Liturgical Press, 2005.

Lawler, Michael G. *Symbol and Sacrament: A Contemporary Sacramental Theology*. Omaha: Creighton University Press, 1995.

Lee, Gregory W. *Today When You Hear His Voice: Scripture, the Covenants, and the People of God*. Grand Rapids: Eerdmans, 2016.

Leemans, Johan, Wendy Mayer, Pauline Allen, and Boudewijn Dehandschutter, eds. and trans. *"Let Us Die That We May Live": Greek Homilies on Christian Martyrs from Asia Minor, Palestine and Syria (c. AD 350–AD 450)*. London: Routledge, 2003.

Lehne, Susanne. *The New Covenant in Hebrews*. Sheffield: Sheffield Academic Press, 1990.

Leithart, Peter J. *Gratitude: An Intellectual History*. Waco, TX: Baylor University Press, 2014.

Lepp, Ignace. *Death and Its Mysteries*. Translated by Bernard Murchland. New York: Macmillan, 1968.

Lesowitz, Nina, and Mary Beth Sammons. *Living Life as a Thank You: The Transformative Power of Daily Gratitude*. San Francisco: Cleis, 2009.

Levenson, Jon D. *The Death and Resurrection of the Beloved Son: The Transformation of Child Sacrifice in Judaism and Christianity*. New Haven: Yale University Press, 1993.

———. *Resurrection and the Restoration of Israel: The Ultimate Victory of the God of Life*. New Haven: Yale University Press, 2006.

Levering, Matthew. *The Betrayal of Charity: The Sins That Sabotage Divine Love*. Waco, TX: Baylor University Press, 2011.

———. *Christ's Fulfillment of Torah and Temple: Salvation according to Thomas Aquinas*. Notre Dame: University of Notre Dame Press, 2002.

———. "The Dying of Macrina and Death with Dignity." *Trinity Journal* 38 (2017): 29–52.

———. *Engaging the Doctrine of Creation: Cosmos, Creatures, and the Wise and Good Creator*. Grand Rapids: Baker Academic, 2017.

———. *Engaging the Doctrine of Revelation: The Mediation of the Gospel through Church and Scripture*. Grand Rapids: Baker Academic, 2014.

———. *Engaging the Doctrine of the Holy Spirit: Love and Gift in the Trinity and the Church*. Grand Rapids: Baker Academic, 2016.

———. *Jesus and the Demise of Death: Resurrection, Afterlife, and the Fate of the Christian*. Waco, TX: Baylor University Press, 2012.

———. *Predestination: Biblical and Theological Paths*. Oxford: Oxford University Press, 2011.

————. *Proofs of God: Classical Arguments from Tertullian to Karl Barth.* Grand Rapids: Baker Academic, 2016.

————. *Sacrifice and Community: Jewish Offering and Christian Eucharist.* Oxford: Blackwell, 2005.

Lewis, C. S. *A Grief Observed.* Reprint, New York: HarperCollins, 2001.

————. *The Problem of Pain.* New York: Macmillan, 1962.

Lifton, Robert Jay. *The Broken Connection: On Death and the Continuity in Life.* New York: Simon & Schuster, 1979.

Litfin, Bryan M. *Early Christian Martyr Stories: An Evangelical Introduction with New Translations.* Grand Rapids: Baker Academic, 2014.

Lombardi, Josephine. "The Dialogue of Salvation: Salvation in This Life and the Next in Islamic and Catholic Thought." *Science et Esprit* 68 (2016): 287–308.

López, Antonio. *Gift and the Unity of Being.* Eugene, OR: Cascade, 2014.

Louis of Granada, OP. *The Sinner's Guide.* Translated by a Dominican Father. Rockford, IL: TAN, 1985.

Luper, Steven. *The Philosophy of Death.* Cambridge: Cambridge University Press, 2009.

Lysaught, M. Therese. "Suffering in Communion with Christ: Sacraments, Dying Faithfully, and End-of-Life Care." In *Living Well and Dying Faithfully: Christian Practices for End-of-Life Care,* edited by John Swinton and Richard Payne, 59–85. Grand Rapids: Eerdmans, 2009.

MacIntyre, Alasdair. *After Virtue.* Notre Dame: University of Notre Dame Press, 1981.

————. *Dependent Rational Animals: Why Human Beings Need the Virtues.* Chicago: Open Court, 1999.

Mansini, Guy, OSB. "Christology in Context: Review Essay of Thomas Joseph White, O.P., *The Incarnate Lord.*" *Nova et Vetera* 14 (2016): 1271–91.

Marmura, Michael E. "Paradise in Islamic Philosophy." In *Foundations and the Formation of a Tradition: Reflections on the Hereafter in the Quran and Islamic Religious Thought,* edited by Sebastian Günther and Todd Lawson, 445–67. Vol. 1 of *Roads to Paradise: Eschatology and Concepts of the Hereafter in Islam.* Leiden: Brill, 2017.

Marschler, Thomas. "Perspektiven der Eschatologie bei Joseph Ratzinger." In *Joseph Ratzinger: Ein theologisches Profil,* edited by Peter Hoffmann, 161–88. Paderborn: Schöningh, 2008.

Martos, Joseph. *Deconstructing Sacramental Theology and Reconstructing Catholic Ritual.* Eugene, OR: Resource, 2015.

Matera, Frank J. *II Corinthians: A Commentary.* Louisville: Westminster John Knox, 2003.

Maududi, Abul A'la. *Towards Understanding Islam.* Edited by Yahiya Emerick. New Delhi, India: Saeed International, 2013.

May, William F. "The Metaphysical Plight of the Family." In *Death Inside Out,* edited by Peter Steinfels and Robert M. Veatch, 49–60. New York: Harper & Row, 1975.

McCabe, Herbert, OP. *God, Christ and Us.* Edited by Brian Davies, OP. London: Continuum, 2003.

McCoy, Marjorie Casebier. *To Die with Style!* Nashville: Abingdon, 1974.

McEntyre, Marilyn Chandler. *A Faithful Farewell: Living Your Last Chapter with Love.* Grand Rapids: Eerdmans, 2015.

McInerney, Joseph J. *The Greatness of Humility: St. Augustine on Moral Excellence.* Eugene, OR: Pickwick, 2016.

McKenna, Megan. *Rites of Justice: The Sacraments and Liturgy as Ethical Imperatives.* Maryknoll, NY: Orbis, 1997.

McKnight, Scot. *The Heaven Promise: Engaging the Bible's Truth about Life to Come.* Colorado Springs, CO: WaterBrook, 2015.

———. *Jesus and His Death: Historiography, the Historical Jesus, and Atonement Theory.* Waco, TX: Baylor University Press, 2005.

———. *The King Jesus Gospel: The Original Good News Revisited.* Grand Rapids: Zondervan, 2011.

———. "What Is the Gospel?" In *Theological Theology: Essays in Honour of John B. Webster,* edited by R. David Nelson, Darren Sarisky, and Justin Stratis, 149–66. London: Bloomsbury, 2015.

McManus, Kathleen Anne. *Unbroken Communion: The Place and Meaning of Suffering in the Theology of Edward Schillebeeckx.* Lanham, MD: Rowman & Littlefield, 2003.

Meinhold, Peter. "Healing and Sanctification in Luther's Theology." In *Temple of the Holy Spirit: Sickness and Death of the Christian in the Liturgy: The Twenty-First Liturgical Conference Saint-Serge,* edited by Achille M. Triacca, SDB, translated by Matthew J. O'Connell, 107–25. New York: Pueblo, 1983.

Mélia, Elie. "The Sacrament of the Anointing of the Sick: Its Historical Development and Current Practice." In *Temple of the Holy Spirit: Sickness and Death of the Christian in the Liturgy: The Twenty-First Liturgical Conference Saint-Serge,* edited by Achille M. Triacca, SDB, translated by Matthew J. O'Connell, 127–60. New York: Pueblo, 1983.

Mendelssohn, Moses. *Phädon, or On the Immortality of the Soul.* Translated by Patricia Noble. New York: Lang, 2006.

Meyendorff, Paul. *The Anointing of the Sick.* Crestwood, NY: St. Vladimir's Seminary Press, 2009.

Middleton, J. Richard. *The Liberating Image: The Imago Dei in Genesis 1.* Grand Rapids: Brazos, 2005.

———. *A New Heaven and a New Earth: Reclaiming Biblical Eschatology.* Grand Rapids: Baker Academic, 2014.

Miller, Lisa. *Heaven: Our Enduring Fascination with the Afterlife.* New York: HarperCollins, 2010.

———. *The Visions of Heaven: A Journey through the Afterlife.* New York: TIME, 2014.

Mitchell, Stephen. "Introduction." In *The Book of Job,* translated by Stephen Mitchell, vii–xxxii. New York: HarperCollins, 1992.

Moberly, R. W. L. *The Theology of the Book of Genesis.* Cambridge: Cambridge University Press, 2009.

Moltmann, Jürgen. *The Coming of God: Christian Eschatology.* London: SCM, 1996.

———. *Is There Life after Death?* Milwaukee: Marquette University Press, 1998.

Montaigne, Michel de. "Apology for Raymond Sebond." In *Michel de Montaigne, The*

Complete Works: Essays, Travel Journal, Letters, translated by Donald M. Frame, 387–556. New York: Knopf, 2003.

Moore, Charles E., and Timothy Keiderling, eds. *Bearing Witness: Stories of Martyrdom and Costly Discipleship*. Walden, NY: Plough, 2016.

Morales, Isaac Augustine, OP. "'With My Body I Thee Worship': New Creation, Beatific Vision, and the Liturgical Consummation of All Things." *Pro Ecclesia* 25 (2016): 337–56.

Morrill, Bruce T., SJ. *Divine Worship and Human Healing: Liturgical Theology at the Margins of Life and Death*. Collegeville, MN: Liturgical Press, 2009.

Morrow, Maria C. "Reconnecting Sacrament and Virtue: Penance in Thomas's *Summa theologiae*." *New Blackfriars* 91 (2010): 304–20.

Mother Teresa. *Come Be My Light: The Private Writings of the "Saint of Calcutta."* Edited and with commentary by Brian Kolodiejchuk, MC. New York: Doubleday, 2007.

———. *Total Surrender*. Edited by Br. Angelo Devananda. Ann Arbor: Servant, 1985.

Murnane, William J. "Taking It with You: The Problem of Death and Afterlife." In *Death and Afterlife: Perspectives of World Religions*, edited by Hiroshi Obayashi, 35–48. New York: Praeger, 1992.

Murphy, Francesca Aran. *God Is Not a Story: Realism Revisited*. Oxford: Oxford University Press, 2007.

Murray, Michael J. *Nature Red in Tooth and Claw: Theism and the Problem of Animal Suffering*. Oxford: Oxford University Press, 2008.

Murray, Paul. *Scars: Essays, Poems and Meditations on Affliction*. London: Bloomsbury, 2014.

Nagel, Thomas. *Mortal Questions*. Cambridge: Cambridge University Press, 1979.

———. *The View from Nowhere*. Oxford: Oxford University Press, 1986.

Neale, Robert E. *The Art of Dying*. Reprint, New York: Harper & Row, 1977.

Neuhaus, Richard John. *As I Lay Dying: Meditations upon Returning*. New York: Basic Books, 2002.

———. *Death on a Friday Afternoon: Meditations on the Last Words of Jesus from the Cross*. New York: Basic Books, 2000.

———. "While We're at It." *First Things* 190 (2009): 71–72.

Neuwirth, Angelika. "Paradise as a Quranic Discourse: Late Antique Foundations and Early Quranic Developments." In *Foundations and the Formation of a Tradition: Reflections on the Hereafter in the Quran and Islamic Religious Thought*, edited by Sebastian Günther and Todd Lawson, 67–92. Vol. 1 of *Roads to Paradise: Eschatology and Concepts of the Hereafter*. Leiden: Brill, 2017.

———. *Scripture, Poetry, and the Making of a Community: Reading the Qur'an as a Literary Text*. Oxford: Oxford University Press, 2015.

Neuwirth, Angelika, Nicolai Sinai, and Michael Marx, eds. *The Qur'ān in Context: Historical and Literary Investigations into the Qur'ānic Milieu*. Leiden: Brill, 2009.

Newman, John Henry. *An Essay in Aid of a Grammar of Assent*. Westminster, MD: Christian Classics, 1973.

Nichols, Aidan, OP. *The Thought of Pope Benedict XVI: An Introduction to the Theology of Joseph Ratzinger*. 2nd ed. London: Continuum, 2007.

Nichols, Terence. *Death and Afterlife: A Theological Introduction.* Grand Rapids: Brazos, 2010.

Nicolas, Jean-Hervé, OP. *Synthèse dogmatique de la Trinité à la Trinité.* Paris: Beauchesne, 1985.

Njus, Jeffrey O. "From a Mother's Smile to Our Father's Embrace: Filiation and Mission at the Heart of Hans Urs von Balthasar's Theology." STD diss., Mundelein, IL: University of Saint Mary of the Lake, 2016.

Nouwen, Henri J. M. *Our Greatest Gift: A Meditation on Dying and Caring.* New York: HarperCollins, 1994.

Novello, Henry L. "New Life as Life out of Death: Sharing in the 'Exchange of Natures' in the Person of Christ." In *The Role of Death in Life: A Multidisciplinary Examination of the Relationship between Life and Death,* edited by John Behr and Conor Cunningham, 96–119. Eugene, OR: Cascade, 2015.

Nuland, Sherwin B. *How We Die: Reflections on Life's Final Chapter.* New York: Knopf, 1994.

Obayashi, Hiroshi, ed. *Death and Afterlife: Perspectives of World Religions.* New York: Praeger, 1992.

O'Callaghan, Paul. *Christ Our Hope: An Introduction to Eschatology.* Washington, DC: Catholic University of America Press, 2011.

Ochs, Robert, SJ. *The Death in Every Now.* New York: Sheed & Ward, 1969.

O'Connor, Mary Catherine. *The Art of Dying Well: The Development of the Ars Moriendi.* New York: Columbia University Press, 1942.

Öhler, Markus. "To Mourn, Weep, Lament and Groan: On the Heterogeneity of the New Testament's Statements on Lament." In *Evoking Lament: A Theological Discussion,* edited by Eva Harasta and Brian Brock, translated by Martina Sitling et al., 150–56. London: T. & T. Clark, 2009.

O'Malley, William J., SJ. *Redemptive Suffering: Understanding Suffering, Living with It, Growing through It.* New York: Crossroad, 1997.

O'Neill, Colman E., OP. *Meeting Christ in the Sacraments.* Edited by Romanus Cessario, OP. Staten Island, NY: Alba House, 1991.

———. *Sacramental Realism: A General Theory of the Sacraments.* Chicago: Midwest Theological Forum, 1998.

Overmyer, Sheryl. "Exalting the Meek Virtue of Humility in Aquinas." *Heythrop Journal* 56 (2015): 650–62.

Packer, J. I. *Finishing Our Course with Joy: Guidance from God for Engaging with Our Aging.* Wheaton, IL: Crossway, 2014.

———. *Weakness Is the Way: Life with Christ Our Strength.* Wheaton, IL: Crossway, 2013.

Pannenberg, Wolfhart. *What Is Man? Contemporary Anthropology in Theological Perspective.* Translated by Duane A. Priebe. Philadelphia: Fortress, 1970.

Pardue, Stephen T. *The Mind of Christ: Humility and the Intellect in Early Christian Theology.* London: Bloomsbury, 2013.

Pascal, Blaise. *Pensées.* Translated by A. J. Krailsheimer. Rev. ed. London: Penguin, 1995.

Pastoral Care of the Sick: Rites of Anointing and Viaticum. New York: Catholic Book Publishing, 1983.

Pate, C. Marvin, and Douglas W. Kennard. *Deliverance Now and Not Yet: The New Testament and the Great Tribulation*. New York: Lang, 2003.

Patton, Corrine. "'I Myself Gave Them Laws That Were Not Good': Ezekiel 20 and the Exodus Traditions." *Journal for the Study of the Old Testament* 21 (1996): 73–90.

Paul VI, Pope. *Sacram Unctionem Infirmorum*. www.vatican.va.

Pauw, Amy Plantinga. "Dying Well." In *Practicing Our Faith: A Way of Life for a Searching People*, edited by Dorothy C. Bass, 163–77. San Francisco: Jossey-Bass, 1997.

Payne, Richard. "Hope in the Face of Terminal Illness." In *Living Well and Dying Faithfully: Christian Practices for End-of-Life Care*, edited by John Swinton and Richard Payne, 205–25. Grand Rapids: Eerdmans, 2009.

Pelikan, Jaroslav. *The Shape of Death: Life, Death, and Immortality in the Early Fathers*. Nashville: Abingdon, 1961.

Pellegrino, Edmund D. "Euthanasia and Assisted Suicide." In *Dignity and Dying: A Christian Appraisal*, edited by John F. Kilner, Arlene B. Miller, and Edmund D. Pellegrino, 105–19. Grand Rapids: Eerdmans, 1996.

Perkins, William. *A Salve for a Sicke Man*. In *The English Ars Moriendi*, edited by David William Atkinson, 127–63. New York: Lang, 1992.

Phan, Peter C. *Living into Death, Dying into Life: A Christian Theology of Death and Life Eternal*. Hobe Sound, FL: Lectio, 2014.

Phillips, D. Z. *Death and Immortality*. London: Macmillan, 1970.

Pieper, Josef. *Abuse of Language, Abuse of Power*. Translated by Lothar Krauth. San Francisco: Ignatius, 1992.

———. *Death and Immortality*. Translated by Richard and Clara Winston. South Bend, IN: St. Augustine's Press, 2000.

———. *Hope and History: Five Salzburg Lectures*. Translated by David Kipp. San Francisco: Ignatius, 1994.

———. *In Defense of Philosophy: Classical Wisdom Stands Up to Modern Challenges*. Translated by Lothar Krauth. San Francisco: Ignatius, 1992.

———. *In Tune with the World: A Theory of Festivity*. Translated by Richard and Clara Winston. South Bend, IN: St. Augustine's Press, 1999.

———. *The Philosophical Act*. In *Leisure, the Basis of Culture*, translated by Gerald Malsbary, 61–134. South Bend, IN: St. Augustine's Press, 1998.

Pinckaers, Servais, OP. "The Sources of the Ethics of St. Thomas Aquinas." Translated by Mary Thomas Noble, OP, with Michael Sherwin, OP. In *The Pinckaers Reader: Renewing Thomistic Moral Theology*, edited by John Berkman and Craig Steven Titus, 3–25. Washington, DC: Catholic University of America Press, 2005.

Pitre, Brant. *Jesus and the Last Supper*. Grand Rapids: Eerdmans, 2015.

———. *Jesus the Bridegroom: The Greatest Love Story Ever Told*. New York: Random House, 2014.

———. *Jesus, the Tribulation, and the End of Exile: Restoration Eschatology and the Origin of the Atonement*. Grand Rapids: Baker Academic, 2005.

Plato. *The Collected Dialogues of Plato*. Edited by Edith Hamilton and Huntington Cairns. Princeton: Princeton University Press, 1961.

Pohier, Jacques-Marie. "Death, Nature and Contingency: Anthropological Reflections about the Postponement of Death." Translated by David Smith. In *The Experience of Dying*, edited by Norbert Greinacher and Alois Müller, 64–79. New York: Herder & Herder, 1974.

Pontifical Council for the Promotion of the New Evangelization. *The Corporal and Spiritual Works of Mercy*. Huntington, IN: Our Sunday Visitor, 2015.

———. *Mercy in the Fathers of the Church*. Huntington, IN: Our Sunday Visitor, 2015.

Pope, Marvin H. *Job*. 3rd ed. Garden City, NY: Doubleday, 1973.

Popkin, Richard H. *The History of Scepticism from Savonarola to Bayle*. Oxford: Oxford University Press, 2003.

Possidius. *The Life of Saint Augustine*. Translated by Herbert T. Weiskotten. Merchantville, NJ: Evolution, 2008.

Power, David. "The Odyssey of Man in Christ." In *Liturgy and Human Passage*, edited by David Power and Luis Maldonado, 100–111. New York: Seabury, 1979.

Qadhi, Yasir. "The Path of Allah or the Paths of Allah? Revisiting Classical and Medieval Sunni Approaches to the Salvation of Others." In *Between Heaven and Hell: Islam, Salvation, and the Fate of Others*, edited by Mohammad Hassan Khalil, 109–21. Oxford: Oxford University Press, 2013.

Qian, Ailin. "Delights in Paradise: A Comparative Survey of Heavenly Food and Drink in the Quran." In *Foundations and the Formation of a Tradition: Reflections on the Hereafter in the Quran and Islamic Religious Thought*, edited by Sebastian Günther and Todd Lawson, 251–70. Vol. 1 of *Roads to Paradise: Eschatology and Concepts of the Hereafter in Islam*. Leiden: Brill, 2017.

Quill, Timothy E. *Death and Dignity: Making Choices and Taking Charge*. New York: Norton, 1993.

———. *A Midwife through the Dying Process: Stories of Healing and Hard Choices at the End of Life*. Baltimore: Johns Hopkins University Press, 1996.

Radner, Ephraim. *A Brutal Unity: The Spiritual Politics of the Christian Church*. Waco, TX: Baylor University Press, 2012.

———. *A Time to Keep: Theology, Mortality, and the Shape of a Human Life*. Waco, TX: Baylor University Press, 2016.

Rahner, Karl, SJ. "Ideas for a Theology of Death." In *Theology, Anthropology, Christology*, translated by David Bourke, 169–86. Vol. 13 of *Theological Investigations*. New York: Seabury, 1975.

———. *On the Theology of Death*. Translated by Charles H. Henkey. Freiburg: Herder, 1961.

Raith, Charles, II. "Aquinas and Calvin on Merit, Part II: Condignity and Participation." *Pro Ecclesia* 21 (2012): 195–210.

———. "Calvin's Critique of Merit, and Why Aquinas (Mostly) Agrees." *Pro Ecclesia* 20 (2011): 135–53.

Ramage, Matthew J. *Dark Passages of the Bible: Engaging Scripture with Benedict XVI and Thomas Aquinas*. Washington, DC: Catholic University of America Press, 2013.

Ramsey, Paul. "The Indignity of 'Death with Dignity.'" In *Death Inside Out*, edited by Peter Steinfels and Robert M. Veatch, 81–96. New York: Harper & Row, 1975.

———. *The Patient as Person*. New Haven: Yale University Press, 1971.

Rankka, Kristine M. *Women and the Value of Suffering: An Aw(e)ful Rowing toward God*. Collegeville, MN: Liturgical Press, 1998.

Ratzinger, Joseph. *Dogma and Preaching: Applying Christian Doctrine to Daily Life*. Translated by Michael J. Miller and Matthew J. O'Connell. San Francisco: Ignatius, 2011.

———. *Eschatology: Death and Eternal Life*. Translated by Michael Waldstein with Aidan Nichols, OP. 2nd ed. Washington, DC: Catholic University of America Press, 2007.

———. *Faith and the Future*. San Francisco: Ignatius, 2009.

———. *The God of Jesus Christ: Meditations on the Triune God*. Translated by Brian McNeil. San Francisco: Ignatius, 2008.

Reinis, Austra. *Reforming the Art of Dying: The Ars Moriendi in the German Reformation (1519–1528)*. Aldershot: Ashgate, 2007.

Renan, Ernest. "The Cry of the Soul." In *The Dimensions of Job: A Study and Selected Readings*, edited by Nahum N. Glatzer, 111–23. Reprint, Eugene, OR: Wipf & Stock, 2002.

Revel, Jean-Philippe, OP. *L'onction des maladies: Rédemption de la chair et par la chair*. Vol. 6 of *Traité des sacrements*. Paris: Cerf, 2009.

Riches, Aaron. *Ecce Homo: On the Divine Unity of Christ*. Grand Rapids: Eerdmans, 2016.

Rieff, David. *Swimming in a Sea of Death: A Son's Memoir*. New York: Simon & Schuster, 2008.

Roiphe, Katie. *The Violet Hour: Great Writers at the End*. New York: Random House, 2016.

Romero, Miguel J. "The Call to Mercy: *Veritatis Splendor* and the Preferential Option for the Poor." *Nova et Vetera* 11 (2013): 1205–27.

Romero, Oscar. *The Violence of Love*. Edited and translated by James R. Brockman. Maryknoll, NY: Orbis, 2004.

———. *Voice of the Voiceless: The Four Pastoral Letters and Other Statements*. Translated by Michael J. Walsh. Maryknoll, NY: Orbis, 1985.

Rosenberg, Jay F. *Thinking Clearly about Death*. 2nd ed. Indianapolis: Hackett, 1998.

Rosenberg, Randall S. "Being-toward-a-Death-Transformed: Aquinas on the Naturalness and Unnaturalness of Human Death." *Angelicum* 83 (2006): 747–66.

Rouillard, Philippe. "The Liturgy of the Dead as a Rite of Passage." Translated by John Griffiths. In *Liturgy and Human Passage*, edited by David Power and Luis Maldonado, 73–82. New York: Seabury, 1979.

Rowley, H. H. "The Intellectual versus the Spiritual Solution." In *The Dimensions of Job: A Study and Selected Readings*, edited by Nahum N. Glatzer, 123–31. Reprint, Eugene, OR: Wipf & Stock, 2002.

Roy, Louis, OP. *Self-Actualization and the Radical Gospel*. Collegeville, MN: Liturgical Press, 2002.

Royal, Robert. *The Catholic Martyrs of the Twentieth Century: A Comprehensive World History*. New York: Crossroad, 2000.

Russell, Jeffrey Burton. *A History of Heaven: The Singing Silence*. Princeton: Princeton University Press, 1997.

———. *Paradise Mislaid: How We Lost Heaven—and How We Can Regain It*. Oxford: Oxford University Press, 2006.

Rustomji, Nerina. *The Garden and the Fire: Heaven and Hell in Islamic Culture*. New York: Columbia University Press, 2009.

Sacks, Jonathan. *Covenant and Conversation: A Weekly Reading of the Jewish Bible. Exodus: The Book of Redemption*. New Milford, CT: Maggid, 2010.

Sacks, Oliver. *Gratitude*. New York: Knopf, 2015.

Sales, Francis de. *Introduction to the Devout Life*. New York: Vintage, 2002.

Scheffler, Samuel. *Death and the Afterlife*. Edited by Niko Kolodny. Oxford: Oxford University Press, 2013.

Scheib, Karen D. "'Make Love Your Aim': Ecclesial Practices of Care at the End of Life." In *Living Well and Dying Faithfully: Christian Practices for End-of-Life Care*, edited by John Swinton and Richard Payne, 30–56. Grand Rapids: Eerdmans, 2009.

Schillebeeckx, Edward, OP. "The Death of a Christian I: The Objective Fact." *Life in the Spirit* 16 (1962): 270–79.

———. "The Death of a Christian II: Our Personal Approach." *Life in the Spirit* 16 (1962): 335–45.

Schmemann, Alexander. *O Death, Where Is Thy Sting?* Translated by Alexis Vinogradov. Crestwood, NY: St. Vladimir's Seminary Press, 2003.

Schönborn, Christoph, OP. *From Death to Life: The Christian Journey*. Translated by Brian McNeil, CRV. San Francisco: Ignatius, 1995.

Schumacher, Bernard N. *Death and Mortality in Contemporary Philosophy*. Translated by Michael J. Miller. Cambridge: Cambridge University Press, 2011.

———. "Le désir d'immortalité à l'aube du troisième millénaire: Enjeux anthropologiques." *Nova et Vetera* 90 (2015): 207–25.

Schweitzer, Albert. *The Mystery of the Kingdom of God: The Secret of Jesus's Messiahship and Passion*. Translated by Walter Lowrie. Amherst, NY: Prometheus, 1985.

———. *The Quest of the Historical Jesus: A Critical Study of Its Progress from Reimarus to Wrede*. Translated by W. Montgomery. London: Black, 1954.

Segundo, Juan Luis. *The Sacraments Today*. Maryknoll, NY: Orbis, 1974.

Shah-Kazemi, Reza. "Response to N. T. Wright." In *Death, Resurrection, and Human Destiny: Christian and Muslim Perspectives*, edited by David Marshall and Lucinda Mosher, 19–22. Washington, DC: Georgetown University Press, 2014.

Shaw, Russell. *Does Suffering Make Sense?* Huntington, IN: Our Sunday Visitor, 1987.

Sheridan, Mark, OSB. *Language for God in Patristic Tradition: Wrestling with Biblical Anthropomorphism*. Downers Grove, IL: IVP Academic, 2015.

Siddiqui, Mona. "Death, Resurrection, and Human Destiny: Qur'ānic and Islamic Perspectives." In *Death, Resurrection, and Human Destiny: Christian and Muslim Perspectives*, edited by David Marshall and Lucinda Mosher, 25–37. Washington, DC: Georgetown University Press, 2014.

Silvas, Anna M. *Macrina the Younger, Philosopher of God*. Turnhout: Brepols, 2008.

Singh, Kathleen Dowling. *The Grace in Dying: How We Are Transformed Spiritually as We Die*. New York: HarperCollins, 1998.

Smith, Fran, and Sheila Himmel. *Changing the Way We Die: Compassionate End-of-Life Care and the Hospice Movement.* Berkeley: Cleis, 2013.

Smith, J. I., and Y. Y. Haddad. *The Islamic Understanding of Death and Resurrection.* Albany: State University of New York Press, 1981.

Smith, J. Warren. "'A Just and Reasonable Grief': The Death and Function of a Holy 'Woman' in Gregory of Nyssa's *De Vita Macrinae.*" *Journal of Early Christian Studies* 12 (2004): 57–84.

———. "Macrina, Tamer of Horses and Healer of Souls: Grief and Hope in Gregory of Nyssa's *De Anima et Resurrectione.*" *Journal of Theological Studies* 52 (2001): 37–60.

———. "Martyrdom: Self-Denial or Self-Exaltation? Motives for Self-Sacrifice from Homer to Polycarp: A Theological Reflection." *Modern Theology* 22 (2006): 169–96.

———. *Passion and Paradise: Human and Divine Emotion in the Thought of Gregory of Nyssa.* New York: Crossroad, 2004.

Sobrino, Jon, SJ. *Christ the Liberator: A View from the Victims.* Translated by Paul Burns. Maryknoll, NY: Orbis, 2001.

———. *Jesus the Liberator: A Historical-Theological Reading of Jesus of Nazareth.* Translated by Paul Burns and Francis McDonagh. Maryknoll, NY: Orbis, 1993.

———. *No Salvation outside the Poor: Prophetic-Utopian Essays.* Maryknoll, NY: Orbis, 2008.

———. *The Principle of Mercy: Taking the Crucified People from the Cross.* Maryknoll, NY: Orbis, 1994.

———. *Where Is God? Earthquake, Terrorism, Barbarity, and Hope.* Translated by Margaret Wilde. Maryknoll, NY: Orbis, 2004.

Solomon, Sheldon, Jeff Greenberg, and Tom Psyzczynski, *The Worm at the Core: On the Role of Death in Life.* New York: Random House, 2015.

Sommer, Benjamin D. *Revelation and Authority: Sinai in Jewish Scripture and Tradition.* New Haven: Yale University Press, 2015.

Sonderegger, Katherine. *The Doctrine of God.* Vol. 1 of *Systematic Theology.* Minneapolis: Fortress, 2015.

Spiegelman, Willard. *Senior Moments.* New York: Farrar, Straus and Giroux, 2016.

Sprinkle, Preston, ed. *Four Views on Hell.* Grand Rapids: Zondervan, 2016.

Sri, Edward. *Love Unveiled: The Catholic Faith Explained.* San Francisco: Ignatius, 2015.

Stålsett, Sturla J. *The Crucified and the Crucified: A Study in the Liberation Christology of Jon Sobrino.* New York: Lang, 2003.

Staniloae, Dumitru. *The World: Creation and Deification.* Translated and edited by Ioan Ionita and Robert Barringer. Vol. 2 of *The Experience of God.* Brookline, MA: Holy Cross Orthodox Press, 2000.

Stice, Randy. *Understanding the Sacraments of Healing: A Rite-Based Approach.* Chicago: Liturgy Training, 2015.

Stringfellow, William. *An Ethic for Christians and Other Aliens in a Strange Land.* Reprint, Eugene, OR: Wipf & Stock, 2004.

———. *Instead of Death.* New and expanded ed. Eugene, OR: Wipf & Stock, 2004.

———. *A Second Birthday.* Garden City, NY: Doubleday, 1970.

Stump, Eleonore. *Wandering in Darkness: Narrative and the Problem of Suffering.* Oxford: Oxford University Press, 2010.

Sulmasy, Daniel P. "Death, Dignity, and the Theory of Value." In *Euthanasia and Palliative Care in the Low Countries*, edited by P. Schotsmans and T. Meulenberg, 95–119. Leuven: Peeters, 2005.

———. "Death with Dignity: What Does It Mean?" *Josephinum Journal of Theology* 4 (1997): 13–23.

———. "More than Sparrows, Less than Angels: The Christian Meaning of Death with Dignity." In *Living Well and Dying Faithfully: Christian Practices for End-of-Life Care*, edited by John Swinton and Richard Payne, 226–45. Grand Rapids: Eerdmans, 2009.

Swinton, John. "Practicing the Presence of God: Earthly Practices in Heavenly Perspective." In *Living Well and Dying Faithfully: Christian Practices for End-of-Life Care*, edited by John Swinton and Richard Payne, 3–16. Grand Rapids: Eerdmans, 2009.

Swinton, John, and Richard Payne. "Attending to God in Suffering: Re-Imagining End-of-Life Care." In *Living Well and Dying Faithfully: Christian Practices for End-of-Life Care*, edited by John Swinton and Richard Payne, 272–76. Grand Rapids: Eerdmans, 2009.

———. "Introduction: Christian Practices and the Art of Dying Faithfully." In *Living Well and Dying Faithfully: Christian Practices for End-of-Life Care*, edited by John Swinton and Richard Payne, xv–xxiv. Grand Rapids: Eerdmans, 2009.

Swinton, John, and Richard Payne, eds. *Living Well and Dying Faithfully: Christian Practices for End-of-Life Care.* Grand Rapids: Eerdmans, 2009.

Tadie, Joseph Lawrence. "Between Humilities: A Retrieval of Saint Thomas Aquinas on the Virtue of Humility." PhD diss., Boston College, 2006.

Talley, Thomas. "Healing: Sacrament or Charism." *Worship* 46 (1972): 518–27.

Tallis, Raymond. *Aping Mankind: Neuromania, Darwinitis and the Misrepresentation of Humanity.* Durham, Eng.: Acumen, 2011.

———. *The Black Mirror: Looking at Life through Death.* New Haven: Yale University Press, 2015.

Tannehill, Robert. "Participation in Christ: A Central Theme in Pauline Soteriology." In *The Shape of the Gospel: New Testament Essays*, 223–37. Eugene, OR: Cascade, 2007.

Tanner, Norman P., SJ, ed. *Decrees of the Ecumenical Councils.* 2 vols. Washington, DC: Georgetown University Press, 1990.

Taylor, Jeremy. *Holy Living and Holy Dying.* Edited by P. G. Stanwood. Oxford: Clarendon, 1989.

Thérèse of Lisieux. *Her Last Conversations.* Translated by John Clarke, OCD. Washington, DC: ICS, 1977.

Thielicke, Helmut. *Death and Life.* Translated by Edward H. Schroeder. Philadelphia: Fortress, 1970.

Thiessen, Matthew. "Hebrews 12.5–13, the Wilderness Period, and Israel's Discipline." *New Testament Studies* 55 (2009): 366–79.

———. "Hebrews and the End of the Exodus." *Novum Testamentum* 49 (2007): 353–69.

Thiselton, Anthony C. *Life after Death: A New Approach to the Last Things.* Grand Rapids: Eerdmans, 2012.

Thomas Aquinas. *Commentary on the Gospel of St. Matthew*. Translated by Paul M. Kimball. Camillus, NY: Dolorosa, 2012.

———. *Commentary on the Letter of Saint Paul to the Philippians*. Edited by J. Mortensen and E. Alarcón. Translated by Fabian R. Larcher, OP. In *Commentary on the Letters of Saint Paul to the Philippians, Colossians, Thessalonians, Timothy, Titus, and Philemon*. Lander, WY: Aquinas Institute for the Study of Sacred Doctrine, 2012.

———. *The Literal Exposition on Job: A Scriptural Commentary Concerning Providence*. Translated by Anthony Damico. Atlanta: Scholars Press, 1989.

———. *Summa theologica*. Translated by the Fathers of the English Dominican Province. 5 vols. Reprint, Westminster, MD: Christian Classics, 1981.

Thomas, Dylan. "Do Not Go Gentle into That Good Night." In *The Top 500 Poems*, edited by William Harmon, 1050–51. New York: Columbia University Press, 1992.

Thompson, Marianne Meye. *Colossians and Philemon*. Grand Rapids: Eerdmans, 2005.

The Tibetan Book of the Dead. Translated by Gyurme Dorje. Edited by Graham Coleman with Thupten Jinpa. London: Penguin, 2005.

Tillich, Paul. *The Courage to Be*. New Haven: Yale University Press, 1952.

———. *The Eternal Now*. New York: Scribner's Sons, 1963.

———. "The Eternal Now." In *The Modern Vision of Death*, edited by Nathan A. Scott Jr., 97–106. Richmond, VA: John Knox, 1967.

Titus, Craig Steven. *Resilience and the Virtue of Fortitude: Aquinas in Dialogue with the Psychosocial Sciences*. Washington, DC: Catholic University of America Press, 2006.

Tobin, Daniel R. *Peaceful Dying*. Reading, MA: Perseus, 1999.

Toner, Patrick. "St. Thomas Aquinas on Death and the Separated Soul." *Pacific Philosophical Quarterly* 91 (2010): 587–99.

Triacca, Achille M., SDB, ed. *Temple of the Holy Spirit: Sickness and Death of the Christian in the Liturgy: The Twenty-First Liturgical Conference Saint-Serge*. Translated by Matthew J. O'Connell. New York: Pueblo, 1983.

Troisfontaines, Roger, SJ. *I Do Not Die*. Translated by Francis E. Albert. New York: Desclée, 1963.

Tugwell, Simon, OP. *Human Immortality and the Redemption of Death*. Springfield, IL: Templegate, 1991.

Tyson, Neil deGrasse, Michael A. Strauss, and J. Richard Gott. *Welcome to the Universe: An Astrophysical Tour*. Princeton: Princeton University Press, 2016.

Unamuno, Miguel de. *The Tragic Sense of Life in Men and Nations*. Translated by Anthony Kerrigan. Edited by Martin Nozick and Anthony Kerrigan. Princeton: Princeton University Press, 1972.

Van Zeller, Hubert, OSB. *Suffering: The Catholic Answer: The Cross of Christ and Its Meaning for You*. Manchester, NH: Sophia Institute, 2002.

Verheul, Ambroise. "The Paschal Character of the Sacrament of the Sick: Exegesis of James 5:14–15 and the New Rite for the Sacrament of the Sick." In *Temple of the Holy Spirit: Sickness and Death of the Christian in the Liturgy: The Twenty-First Liturgical Conference Saint-Serge*, edited by Achille M. Triacca, SDB, translated by Matthew J. O'Connell, 247–57. New York: Pueblo, 1983.

Verhey, Allen. *The Christian Art of Dying: Learning from Jesus.* Grand Rapids: Eerdmans, 2011.

———. "The Practice of Prayer and Care for the Dying." In *Living Well and Dying Faithfully: Christian Practices for End-of-Life Care,* edited by John Swinton and Richard Payne, 86–106. Grand Rapids: Eerdmans, 2009.

Vijgen, Jörgen. "St. Thomas Aquinas and the Virtuousness of Penance: On the Importance of Aristotle for Catholic Theology." *Nova et Vetera* 13 (2015): 601–16.

Visser, Margaret. *The Gift of Thanks: The Roots and Rituals of Gratitude.* Boston: Houghton Mifflin Harcourt, 2009.

Vogt, Brandon. *Saints and Social Justice: A Guide to Changing the World.* Huntington, IN: Our Sunday Visitor, 2014.

Vogt, Christian P. *Patience, Compassion, Hope, and the Christian Art of Dying Well.* Lanham, MD: Rowman & Littlefield, 2004.

Volf, Miroslav. "Death and the Love of Life: A Response to Sajjad Rizvi." In *Death, Resurrection, and Human Destiny: Christian and Muslim Perspectives,* edited by David Marshall and Lucinda Mosher, 111–16. Washington, DC: Georgetown University Press, 2014.

Wainwright, Geoffrey. *Doxology: The Praise of God in Worship, Doctrine and Life: A Systematic Theology.* New York: Oxford University Press, 1980.

Wald, Berthold. "Martin Heidegger, Josef Pieper und die neue Thanatologie." In *Tod und Unsterblichkeit: Erkundungen mit C. S. Lewis und Josef Pieper,* edited by Thomas Möllenbeck and Berthold Wald, 81–95. Paderborn: Schöningh, 2015.

Wald, Florence S. "The Emergence of Hospice Care in the United States." In *Facing Death: Where Culture, Religion, and Medicine Meet,* edited by Howard M. Spiro, Mary G. McCrea Curnen, and Lee Palmer Wandel, 81–89. New Haven: Yale University Press, 1996.

Walker, Adrian J. "*Singulariter in spe constituisti me*: On the Christian Attitude towards Death." *Communio* 39 (2012): 351–63.

Walton, John H. *The Lost World of Genesis One: Ancient Cosmology and the Origins Debate.* Downers Grove, IL: IVP Academic, 2009.

Webb, Stephen H. *Good Eating.* Grand Rapids: Brazos, 2001.

Weinandy, Thomas G., OFM, Cap. *Does God Suffer?* Notre Dame: University of Notre Dame Press, 2000.

Wells, Steve. *Drunk with Blood: God's Killings in the Bible.* New York: SAB, 2013.

White, Thomas Joseph, OP. *Exodus.* Grand Rapids: Brazos, 2016.

———. *The Incarnate Lord: A Thomistic Study in Christology.* Washington, DC: Catholic University of America Press, 2015.

Wicks, Jared, SJ. "Applied Theology at the Deathbed: Luther and the Late-Medieval Tradition of the *Ars Moriendi*." *Gregorianum* 79 (1998): 345–68.

Williams, Bernard. "The Makropulos Case: Reflections on the Tedium of Immortality." In *Problems of the Self,* 82–100. Cambridge: Cambridge University Press, 1973.

Williams, Rowan. "Macrina's Deathbed Revisited: Gregory of Nyssa on Mind and Passion." In *Christian Faith and Greek Philosophy in Late Antiquity: Essays in Tribute to*

George Christopher Stead, edited by Lionel R. Wickham and Caroline P. Bammel with Erica C. D. Hunter, 227–46. Leiden: Brill, 1993.

Wiman, Christian. *My Bright Abyss: Meditation of a Modern Believer*. New York: Farrar, Straus and Giroux, 2013.

Winston, David. *The Wisdom of Solomon*. New Haven: Yale University Press, 1979.

Wirzba, Norman. *Food and Faith: A Theology of Eating*. Cambridge: Cambridge University Press, 2011.

Witherington, Ben, III. "James." In *Letters and Homilies for Jewish Christians: A Socio-Rhetorical Commentary on Hebrews, James and Jude*, 385–555. Downers Grove, IL: IVP Academic, 2007.

Wolf, Susan. "The Significance of Doomsday." In Samuel Scheffler, *Death and the Afterlife*, edited by Niko Kolodny, 113–29. Oxford: Oxford University Press, 2013.

Wollstonecraft, Mary. *A Vindication of the Rights of Woman: With Strictures on Political and Moral Subjects*. Cambridge: Cambridge University Press, 2010.

Wolterstorff, Nicholas. *Lament for a Son*. Grand Rapids: Eerdmans, 1987.

Wood, Susan K., SCL. "The Paschal Mystery: The Intersection of Ecclesiology and Sacramental Theology in the Care of the Sick." In *Recovering the Riches of Anointing: A Study of the Sacrament of the Sick*, edited by Genevieve Glen, 1–19. Collegeville, MN: Liturgical Press, 1989.

Wright, Christopher J. H. *The Mission of God: Unlocking the Bible's Grand Narrative*. Downers Grove, IL: IVP Academic, 2006.

Wright, N. T. *The Epistles of Paul to the Colossians and to Philemon: An Introduction and Commentary*. Grand Rapids: Eerdmans, 1986.

———. *Jesus and the Victory of God*. Minneapolis: Fortress, 1996.

———. *The New Testament and the People of God*. Minneapolis: Fortress, 1992.

———. *Paul and the Faithfulness of God*. Book 2, parts 3 and 4. Minneapolis: Fortress, 2013.

———. "Response to Reza Shah-Kazemi." In *Death, Resurrection, and Human Destiny*, edited by David Marshall and Lucinda Mosher, 23–24. Washington, DC: Georgetown University Press, 2014.

———. *The Resurrection of the Son of God*. Minneapolis: Fortress, 2003.

———. *Small Faith, Great God: Biblical Faith for Today's Christians*. 2nd ed. Downers Grove, IL: IVP Books, 2010.

———. *Surprised by Hope: Rethinking Heaven, the Resurrection, and the Mission of the Church*. New York: HarperCollins, 2008.

———. *Surprised by Scripture: Engaging Contemporary Issues*. New York: HarperCollins, 2014.

Zaleski, Carol. *The Life of the World to Come: Near-Death Experience and Christian Hope*. New York: Oxford University Press, 1996.

Zecher, Jonathan L. *The Role of Death in the Ladder of Divine Ascent and the Greek Ascetic Tradition*. Oxford: Oxford University Press, 2015.

Ziccardi, Costantino Antonio. *The Relationship of Jesus and the Kingdom of God according to Luke-Acts*. Rome: Gregorian University Press, 2008.

Ziegler, John J. *Let Them Anoint the Sick*. Collegeville, MN: Liturgical Press, 1987.

Index of Authors

Index of Subjects

Abel: as model of faith, 70
Abraham: as model of faith, 70–71
Adoptionism, 252n25
Afterlife: question not broached in Torah, 15
Almsgiving, 50–51
Animals: do not have souls, 160; pain of, 299n53
Anointing of the sick, 6, 8, 135–47, 249n17, 275n12, 275n13, 276n15, 277n17, 277n18, 279n22, 279n23, 280n29, 281n30, 281n31, 282n32, 282n33, 283n38, 283n39, 284n44, 284n48, 285n53, 285n55, 285n57; as extreme unction, 137–39, 141–42, 278n18; given to dying persons, 139–42, 145–46, 277n18, 278n22, 278n23, 280n28, 280n29, 285n55, 285n57; proper celebrant of, 277n17; as sacrament of the sick, 137–39, 277n17, 282n34; for the seriously ill, 136, 138–39, 146, 277n18, 278n22, 278n23, 280n29, 286n57
Anointing with oil, 136, 142–44, 146, 276n13, 282n34, 285n52
Anthropology: dualistic, 197n21
Aquinas, Thomas: on the anointing of the sick, 137–38, 141–46; on Christ's suffering, 127–33, 270n23; classifi-
cation of virtues, 119; sacramental ecclesiology of, 272n37
Ars moriendi, 6, 46, 206n51, 210n65, 219n19
Augustine: eschatology of, 154, 157, 292n24, 294n30, 299n54; theology of death, 242n35

Baptism, 3, 97, 129, 132–33, 141, 144–45, 279n22, 281n30, 283n40, 283n41, 285n53, 285n55; of infants, 176n24
Beatific vision. *See* Vision of God

Charity. *See* Love
Christ. *See* Jesus Christ
Courage, 5, 9, 43, 100, 148–49, 153, 161, 163, 168, 175n23, 242n36, 263n70, 276n15, 298n9
Creation: *ex nihilo*, 42; goodness of, 33–34, 181n2, 265n10
Cross of Christ, 4, 60–62, 73, 105–6, 109, 112–13, 117, 120, 133–34, 142, 168, 172n9, 174n18, 177n32, 181n2, 209n63, 245n2, 246n7, 247n9, 249n14, 252n24, 254n32, 259n48, 260n50, 261n60, 270n23

Death: as annihilation, 1, 7–8, 14–16, 20–28, 30–32, 34, 44, 47, 53–55, 59,

Index of Scripture References